AF876685

Microsoft®

Access 97

Illustrated Standard Edition, A First Course

Importing
open Excel

File
Get External data
→ Import
OR
link

Files of types (Looking for) - Excel files

Choose Spread Sheet
choose work sheet

Check heading
New table or existing table

Primary key -
Substance - primary key -

Microsoft®

Access 97

Illustrated Standard Edition, A First Course

Elizabeth Eisner Reding
Lisa Friedrichsen

COURSE TECHNOLOGY

ONE MAIN STREET, CAMBRIDGE, MA 02142

an International Thomson Publishing company I(T)P®

Cambridge • Albany • Bonn • Boston • Cincinnati • London • Madrid • Melbourne • Mexico City
New York • Paris • San Francisco • Singapore • Tokyo • Toronto • Washington

Microsoft Access 97—Illustrated Standard Edition, A First Course

is published by Course Technology

Managing Editor: Nicole Jones Pinard
Product Manager: Jeanne Herring
Production Editor: Nancy Ray
Developmental Editor: Rachel Bunin
Composition House: GEX, Inc.
QA Manuscript Reviewers: Chris Hall, John McCarthy, Brian McCooey, Jeff Goding
Text Designer: Joseph Lee
Cover Designer: Joseph Lee

© 1997 by Course Technology — I(T)P®

For more information contact:

Course Technology
One Main Street
Cambridge, MA 02142

ITP Europe
Berkshire House 168-173
High Holborn
London WC1V 7AA
England

Nelson ITP, Australia
102 Dodds Street
South Melbourne, 3205
Victoria, Australia

ITP Nelson Canada
1120 Birchmount Road
Scarborough, Ontario
Canada M1K 5G4

International Thomson Editores
Seneca, 53
Colonia Polanco
11560 Mexico D.F. Mexico

ITP GmbH
Königswinterer Strasse 418
53277 Bonn
Germany

ITP Asia
60 Albert Street, #15-01
Albert Complex
Singapore 189969

ITP Japan
Hirakawacho Kyowa Building, 3F
2-2-1 Hirakawacho
Chiyoda-ku, Tokyo 102
Japan

All rights reserved. This publication is protected by federal copyright law. No part of this publication may be reproduced, stored in a retrieval system, or transmitted in any form or by any means, electronic, mechanical, photocopying, recording, or otherwise, or be used to make a derivative work (such as translation or adaptation), without prior permission in writing from Course Technology.

Trademarks

Course Technology and the open book logo are registered trademarks of Course Technology. Illustrated Projects and the Illustrated Series are trademarks of Course Technology.

I(T)P® The ITP logo is a registered trademark of International Thomson Publishing.

Microsoft and the Office logo are either registered trademarks or trademarkes of Microsoft Corporation in the United States and/or other countries. Course Technology is an independent entity from Microsoft Corporation, and not affiliated with Microsoft Corporation in any manner. This text may be used in assisting students to prepare for a Microsoft Office User Specialist Program Exam. Neither Microsoft Corporation, its designated review company, nor Course Technology warrants that use of this text will ensure passing the relevant Microsoft Office User Specialist Exam.

Some of the product names and company names used in this book have been used for identification purposes only and may be trademarks or registered trademarks of their respective manufacturers and sellers.

Disclaimer

Course Technology reserves the right to revise this publication and make changes from time to time in its content without notice.

ISBN 0-7600-4697-2

Printed in the United States of America

8 9 BM 01 00

From the

Illustrated Series™ Team

At Course Technology we believe that technology will transform the way that people teach and learn. We are very excited about bringing you, instructors and students, the most practical and affordable technology-related products available.

The Development Process

Our development process is unparalleled in the educational publishing industry. Every product we create goes through an exacting process of design, development, review, and testing.

Reviewers give us direction and insight that shape our manuscripts and bring them up to the latest standards. Every manuscript is quality tested. Students whose backgrounds match the intended audience work through every keystroke, carefully checking for clarity and pointing out errors in logic and sequence. Together with our own technical reviewers, these testers help us ensure that everything that carries our name is as error-free and easy to use as possible.

The Products

We show both how and why technology is critical to solving problems in the classroom and in whatever field you choose to teach or pursue. Our time-tested, step-by-step instructions provide unparalleled clarity. Examples and applications are chosen and crafted to motivate students.

The Illustrated Series™ Team

The Illustrated Series™ Team is committed to providing you with the most visual introduction to microcomputer applications. No other series of books will get you up to speed faster in today's changing software environment. This book will suit your needs because it was delivered quickly, efficiently, and affordably. In every aspect of business, we rely on a commitment to quality and the use of technology. Each member of the Illustrated Series™ Team contributes to this process. The names of all our team members are listed below.

The Team

Cynthia Anderson	Mary-Terese Cozzola	Jeanne Herring	Elizabeth Eisner Reding
Chia-Ling Barker	Carol Cram	Meta Chaya Hirschl	Art Rotberg
Donald Barker	Kim T. M. Crowley	Jane Hosie-Bounar	Neil Salkind
Ann Barron	Catherine DiMassa	Steven Johnson	Gregory Schultz
David Beskeen	Stan Dobrawa	Bill Lisowski	Ann Shaffer
Ann Marie Buconjic	Shelley Dyer	Chet Lyskawa	Dan Swanson
Rachel Bunin	Linda Eriksen	Kristine O'Brien	Marie Swanson
Joan Carey	Jessica Evans	Tara O'Keefe	Jennifer Thompson
Patrick Carey	Lisa Friedrichsen	Harry Phillips	Sasha Vodnik
Sheralyn Carroll	Jeff Goding	Nicole Jones Pinard	Jan Weingarten
Brad Conlin	Michael Halvorson	Katherine T. Pinard	Christie Williams
Pam Conrad	Jamie Harper	Kevin Proot	Janet Wilson

Preface

Welcome to *Microsoft Access 97 – Illustrated Standard Edition, A First Course*! This book in our highly visual new design offers new users a hands-on introduction to Microsoft Access 97 and also serves as an excellent reference for future use.

▶ Organization and Coverage

This text contains eight units that cover basic Access skills. In these units students learn how to design, create, edit, and analyze Access databases. The units also cover creating relationships between tables, defining field properties, creating queries, developing forms, and creating reports.

▶ Microsoft Office User Specialist Program Approved Courseware

This book, when used as part of a two-course sequence with the companion textbook *Microsoft Access 97-Illustrated Standard Edition, A Second Course*, has been approved by Microsoft as courseware for the Microsoft Office User Specialist program. After completing the lessons and exercises in these two books, the student will be prepared to take the Proficient level Microsoft Office User Specialist examination for Access 97. By passing the certification exam for a Microsoft software program, students demonstrate their proficiency in that program to employers. Microsoft Office User Specialist exams are offered at participating test centers, participating corporations, and participating employment agencies. For more information about certification, please visit the Microsoft Office User Specialist program World Wide Web site at http://www.microsoft.com/office/train_cert/.

▶ About this Approach

What makes the Illustrated approach so effective at teaching software skills? It's quite simple. Each skill is presented on two facing pages, with the step-by-step instructions on the left page, and large screen illustrations on the right. Students can focus on a single skill without having to turn the page. This unique design makes information extremely accessible and easy to absorb, and provides a great reference for students after the course is over. This hands-on approach also makes it ideal for both self-paced or instructor-led classes. The modular structure of the book also allows for great flexibility; you can cover the units in any order you choose.

Each lesson, or "information display," contains the following elements:

This icon indicates a CourseHelp 97 slide show is available for this lesson. See the Instructor's Resource Kit page for more information.

Each 2-page spread focuses on a single skill.

Concise text that introduces the basic principles in the lesson and integrates the brief case study.

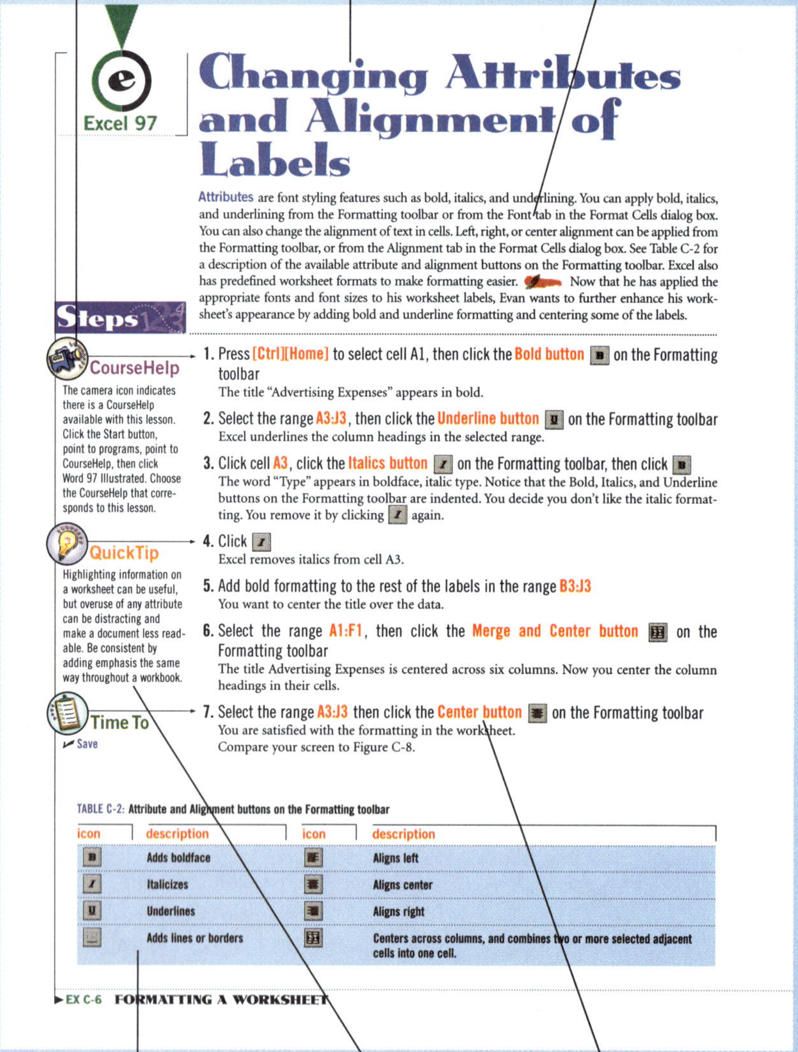

Excel 97

Changing Attributes and Alignment of Labels

Attributes are font styling features such as bold, italics, and underlining. You can apply bold, italics, and underlining from the Formatting toolbar or from the Font tab in the Format Cells dialog box. You can also change the alignment of text in cells. Left, right, or center alignment can be applied from the Formatting toolbar, or from the Alignment tab in the Format Cells dialog box. See Table C-2 for a description of the available attribute and alignment buttons on the Formatting toolbar. Excel also has predefined worksheet formats to make formatting easier. Now that he has applied the appropriate fonts and font sizes to his worksheet labels, Evan wants to further enhance his worksheet's appearance by adding bold and underline formatting and centering some of the labels.

Steps

CourseHelp
The camera icon indicates there is a CourseHelp available with this lesson. Click the Start button, point to programs, point to CourseHelp, then click Word 97 Illustrated. Choose the CourseHelp that corresponds to this lesson.

QuickTip
Highlighting information on a worksheet can be useful, but overuse of any attribute can be distracting and make a document less readable. Be consistent by adding emphasis the same way throughout a workbook.

Time To
Save

1. Press [Ctrl][Home] to select cell A1, then click the Bold button on the Formatting toolbar
The title "Advertising Expenses" appears in bold.
2. Select the range A3:J3, then click the Underline button on the Formatting toolbar
Excel underlines the column headings in the selected range.
3. Click cell A3, click the Italics button on the Formatting toolbar, then click
The word "Type" appears in boldface, italic type. Notice that the Bold, Italics, and Underline buttons on the Formatting toolbar are indented. You decide you don't like the italic formatting. You remove it by clicking again.
4. Click
Excel removes italics from cell A3.
5. Add bold formatting to the rest of the labels in the range B3:J3
You want to center the title over the data.
6. Select the range A1:F1, then click the Merge and Center button on the Formatting toolbar
The title Advertising Expenses is centered across six columns. Now you center the column headings in their cells.
7. Select the range A3:J3 then click the Center button on the Formatting toolbar
You are satisfied with the formatting in the worksheet.
Compare your screen to Figure C-8.

TABLE C-2: Attribute and Alignment buttons on the Formatting toolbar

icon	description	icon	description
B	Adds boldface		Aligns left
I	Italicizes		Aligns center
U	Underlines		Aligns right
	Adds lines or borders		Centers across columns, and combines two or more selected adjacent cells into one cell.

EX C-6 FORMATTING A WORKSHEET

Quickly accessible summaries of key terms, toolbar buttons, or keyboard alternatives connected with the lesson material. Students can refer easily to this information when working on their own projects at a later time.

Hints as well as trouble-shooting advice right where you need it – next to the step itself.

Clear step-by-step directions, with what students are to type in red, explain how to complete the specific task.

Other Features

The two-page lesson format featured in this book provides the new user with a powerful learning experience. Additionally, this book contains the following features:

► Real-World Case

The case study used throughout the textbook, a fictitious company called Nomad Ltd, is designed to be "real-world" in nature and introduces the kinds of activities that students will encounter when working with Microsoft Access 97. With a real-world case, the process of solving problems will be more meaningful to students.

► End of Unit Material

Each unit concludes with a Concepts Review that tests students' understanding of what they learned in the unit. A Skills Review follows the Concepts Review and provides students with additional hands-on practice of the skills they learned in the unit. The Skills Review is followed by Independent Challenges, which pose case problems for students to solve. At least one Independent Challenge in each unit asks students to use the World Wide Web to solve the problem as indicated by a Web Work icon. The Visual Workshops that follow the Independent Challenges help students to develop critical thinking skills. Students are shown completed documents and are asked to recreate them from scratch.

Every lesson features large, full-color representations of what the screen should look like as students complete the numbered steps.

The innovative design draws the students' eyes to important areas of the screens.

Brightly colored tabs above the program name indicate which section of the book you are in. Useful for finding your place within the book and for referencing information from the index.

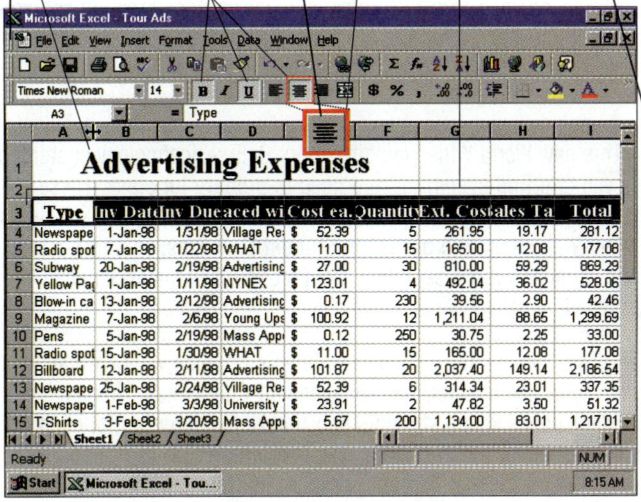

FIGURE C-8: Worksheet with formatting attributes applied

Type	Inv Date	Inv Due	aced wi	Cost ea.	Quantity	Ext. Cost	Sales Ta	Total
Newspape	1-Jan-98	1/31/98	Village Re	$ 52.39	5	261.95	19.17	281.12
Radio spot	7-Jan-98	1/22/98	WHAT	$ 11.00	15	165.00	12.08	177.08
Subway	20-Jan-98	2/19/98	Advertising	$ 27.00	30	810.00	59.29	869.29
Yellow Pag	1-Jan-98	1/11/98	NYNEX	$ 123.01	4	492.04	36.02	528.06
Blow-in ca	13-Jan-98	2/12/98	Advertising	$ 0.17	230	39.56	2.90	42.46
Magazine	7-Jan-98	2/6/98	Young Ups	$ 100.92	12	1,211.04	88.65	1,299.69
Pens	5-Jan-98	2/19/98	Mass Appe	$ 0.12	250	30.75	2.25	33.00
Radio spot	15-Jan-98	1/30/98	WHAT	$ 11.00	15	165.00	12.08	177.08
Billboard	12-Jan-98	2/11/98	Advertising	$ 101.87	20	2,037.40	149.14	2,186.54
Newspape	25-Jan-98	2/24/98	Village Re	$ 52.39	6	314.34	23.01	337.35
Newspape	1-Feb-98	3/3/98	University	$ 23.91	2	47.82	3.50	51.32
T-Shirts	3-Feb-98	3/20/98	Mass Appe	$ 5.67	200	1,134.00	83.01	1,217.01

CLUES TO USE

Using AutoFormat

Excel provides 16 preset formats called AutoFormats, which allow instant formatting of large amounts of data. AutoFormats are designed for worksheets with labels in the left column and top rows and totals in the bottom row or right column. To use AutoFormatting, select the data to be formatted—or place your mouse pointer anywhere within the range to be selected—click Format on the menu bar, click AutoFormat, then select a format from the Table Format list box, as shown in Figure C-9.

FIGURE C-9: AutoFormat dialog box

FORMATTING A WORKSHEET EX C-7

Clues to Use Boxes provide concise information that either expands on of the major lesson skill or describes an independent task that in some way relates to the major lesson skill.

The page numbers are designed like a road map. EX indicates the Excel section, C indicates Excel Unit C, and 7 indicates the page within the unit. This map allows for the greatest flexibility in content – each unit stands completely on its own.

Instructor's Resource Kit

The Instructor's Resource Kit is Course Technology's way of putting the resources and information needed to teach and learn effectively into your hands. With an integrated array of teaching and learning tools that offer you and your students a broad range of instructional options, we believe this kit represents the highest quality and most cutting edge resources available to instructors today. Many of these resources are available online at www.course.com. The resources available with this book are:

CourseHelp 97 CourseHelp 97 is a student reinforcement tool offering online annotated tutorials that are accessible directly from the Start menu in Windows 95. These on-screen "slide shows" help students understand the most difficult concepts in a specific program. Students are encouraged to view a CourseHelp 97 slide show before completing that lesson. This text includes the following CourseHelp 97slide shows:

- Planning a Database
- Sorting Records
- Filtering Records

Adopters of this text are granted the right to post the CourseHelp 97 files on any standalone computer or network.

Course Test Manager Designed by Course Technology, this cutting edge Windows-based testing software helps instructors design and administer tests and pre-tests. This full-featured program also has an online testing component that allows students to take tests at the computer and have their exams automatically graded.

Course Faculty Online Companion This new World Wide Web site offers Course Technology customers a password-protected Faculty Lounge where you can find everything you need to prepare for class. These periodically updated items include lesson plans, graphic files for the figures in the text, additional problems, updates and revisions to the text, links to other Web sites, and access to Student Disk files. This new site is an ongoing project and will continue to evolve throughout the semester. Contact your Customer Service Representative for the site address and password.

Course Student Online Companion This book features its own Online Companion where students can go to access Web sites that will help them complete the WebWork Independent Challenges. This page also contains links to other Course Technology student pages where students can find task references for each of the Microsoft Office 97 programs, a graphical glossary of terms found in the text, an archive of meaningful templates, software, hot tips, and Web links to other sites that contain pertinent information. These new sites are also ongoing projects and will continue to evolve throughout the semester.

Student Files To use this book students must have the Student Files. See the inside front or inside back cover for more information on the Student Files. Adopters of this text are granted the right to post the Student Files on any stand-alone computer or network.

Instructor's Manual This is quality assurance tested and includes:

- Solutions to all lessons and end-of-unit material
- Unit notes with teaching tips from the author
- Extra Independent Challenges
- Transparency Masters of key concepts
- Student Files
- CourseHelp 97

CLUES TO USE

The Illustrated Family of Products

This book that you are holding fits in the Illustrated Series – one series of three in the Illustrated family of products. The other two series are the Illustrated Projects Series and the Illustrated Interactive Series. The Illustrated Projects Series is a supplemental series designed to reinforce the skills learned in any skills-based book through the creation of meaningful and engaging projects. The Illustrated Interactive Series is a line of computer-based training multimedia products that offer the novice user a quick and interactive learning experience. All three series are committed to providing you with the most visual and enriching instructional materials.

Brief Contents

From the Illustrated Series™ Team V

Preface VI

Access 97

Getting Started with Access 97 .... AC A-1

Creating and Managing Data .... AC B-1

Creating a Form .... AC C-1

Creating a Report .... AC D-1

Modifying a Database Structure .... AC E-1

Creating Multiple Table Queries .... AC F-1

Developing Forms with Subforms .... AC G-1

Creating Complex Reports .... AC H-1

Glossary 1

Index 5

Contents

From the Illustrated Series™ Team V
Preface VI

Access

Getting Started with Access 97 AC A-1

Defining Database Software .... AC A-2
Starting Access 97 .... AC A-4
Viewing the Access Window .... AC A-6
Finding Out About Buttons and Menu Commands .... AC A-6
Opening a Database Table .... AC A-8
Entering and Editing Records .... AC A-10
Moving Table Columns .... AC A-10
Previewing and Printing a Datasheet .... AC A-12
Getting Help .... AC A-14
Changing the Office Assistant .... AC A-14
Closing a Database and Exiting Access .... AC A-16
Concepts Review .... AC A-18
Skills Review .... AC A-20
Independent Challenges .... AC A-21
Visual Workshop .... AC A-24

Creating and Managing Data AC B-1

Planning a Database .... AC B-2
Creating a Backup .... AC B-3
Creating a Table .... AC B-4
Creating a Table Manually .... AC B-5
Modifying a Table .... AC B-6

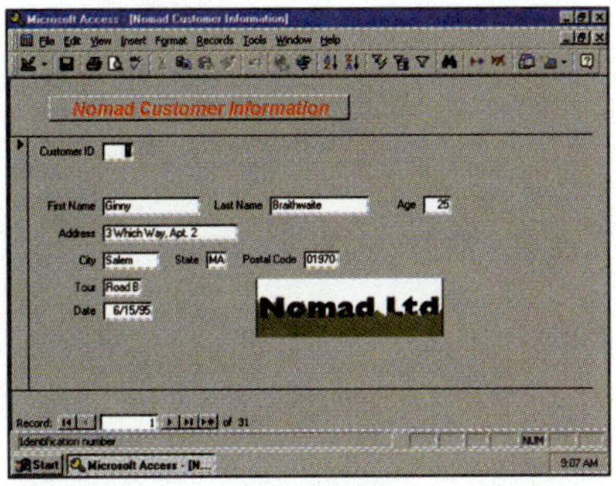

Contents

Finding Records ....AC B-8

Using Wildcards in Find ....AC B-9

Sorting a Table ....AC B-10

Using the Menu Bar to Sort ....AC B-11

Filtering a Table...AC B-12

When to Use a Filter ....AC B-12

Creating a Simple Query ....AC B-14

Creating a Complex Query ....AC B-16

Using And and Or to Affect Query Results ....AC B-17

Concepts Review...AC B-18

Skills Review ....AC B-19

Independent Challenges..AC B-22

Visual Workshop..AC B-24

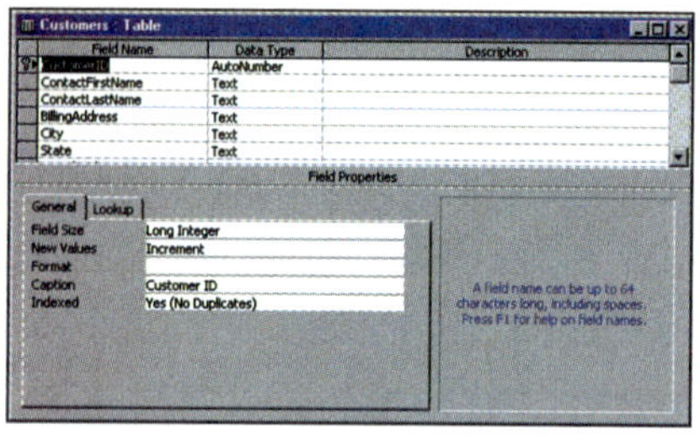

Creating a Form

Creating a Form AC C-1

Creating a Form ....AC C-2

Using AutoForm...AC C-3

Modifying a Form Layout ....AC C-4

Changing the Tab Order..AC C-6

Using the Expression Builder AC-C-8

Formatting Controls..AC C-10

Adding a Field to a Form ....AC C-12

Adding a Graphic Image to a Form.......................................AC C-14

Using a Form to Add a Rrecord ....AC C-16

Concepts Review...AC C-18

Skills Review ....AC C-19

Independent Challenges..AC C-24

Visual Workshop..AC C-24

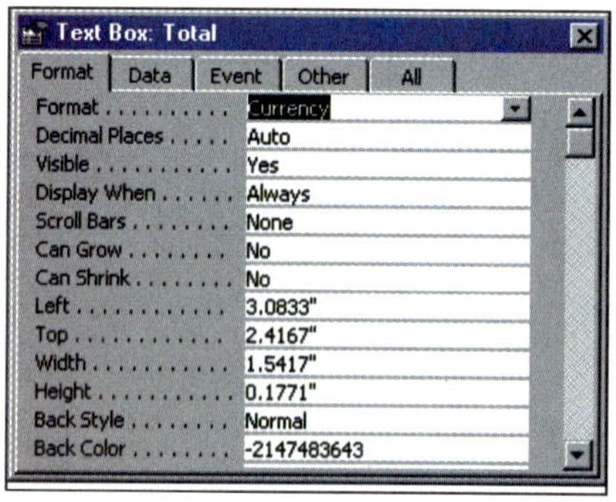

Creating a Report

Creating a Report AC D-1

Creating a Report .... AC D-2

Using Auto Report .... AC D-3

Grouping Records in a Report .... AC D-4

Aligning Fields .... AC D-6

Resizing a Control .... AC D-8

Adding an Expression to a Report .... AC D-10

Adding a Field to a Report .... AC D-10

Creating a Report From a Query .... AC D-12

Saving a Form as a Report .... AC D-14

Creating Labels .... AC D-16

Concepts Review .... AC D-18

Skills Review .... AC D-20

Independent Challenges .... AC D-22

Visual Workshop .... AC D-24

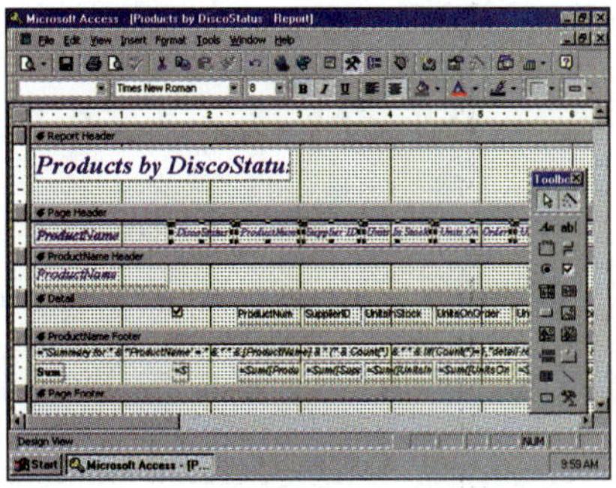

Modifying a Database Structure

Modifying a Database Structure AC E-1

Examining Relational Database Requirements .... AC E-2

Planning a Table .... AC E-4

Key field combinations .... AC E-5

Creating New Tables .... AC E-6

Linked tables .... AC E-7

Creating One-to-Many Relationships .... AC E-8

Why enforcing referential integrity is important .... AC E-9

Deleting Fields .... AC E-10

Defining Field Properties .... AC E-12

Defining Date/Time Field Properties .... AC E-14

Planning for the 21st Century .... AC E-14

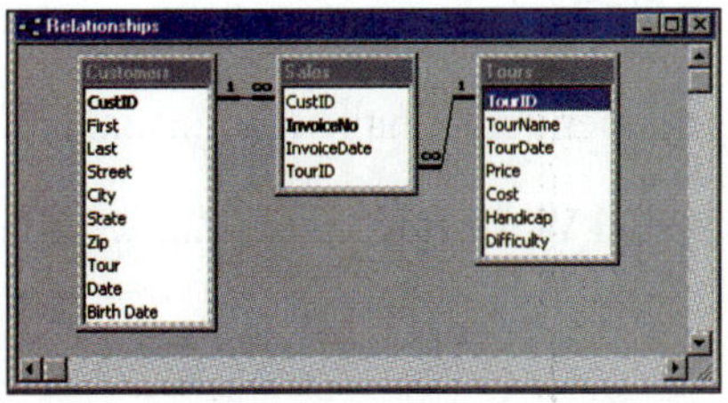

Contents

Defining Field Validation Properties ....AC E-16

Validation property rules ....AC E-17

Concepts Review ....AC E-18

Skills Review ....AC E-19

Independent Challenges ....AC E-21

Visual Workshop ....AC E-24

Creating Multiple Table Queries AC F-1

Creating Select Queries ....AC F-2

The difference between queries and filters ....AC F-3

Sorting a Query on Multiple Fields ....AC F-4

Developing AND Queries ....AC F-6

Developing OR Queries ....AC F-8

Using wildcard characters in query criteria ....AC F-9

Developing Calculated Fields ....AC F-10

Functions in calculated expressions ....AC F-10

Adding Calculations on Groups of Records ....AC F-12

Developing Crosstab Queries ....AC F-14

Types of Query Wizards ....AC F-14

Creating Update Queries ....AC F-16

Concepts Review ....AC F-18

Skills Review ....AC F-20

Independent Challenges ....AC F-21

Visual Workshop ....AC F-24

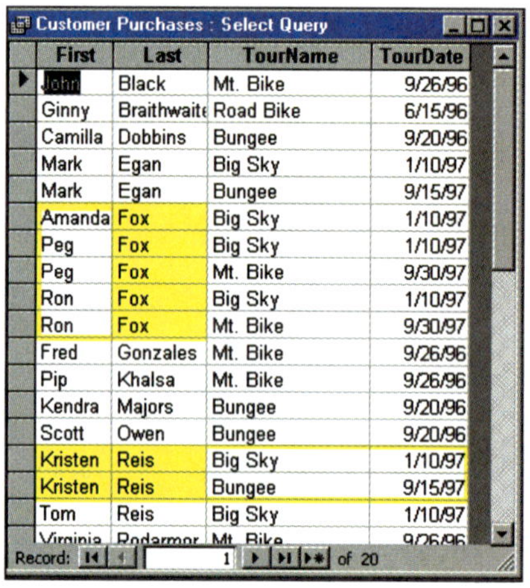

First	Last	TourName	TourDate
John	Black	Mt. Bike	9/26/96
Ginny	Braithwaite	Road Bike	6/15/96
Camilla	Dobbins	Bungee	9/20/96
Mark	Egan	Big Sky	1/10/97
Mark	Egan	Bungee	9/15/97
Amanda	Fox	Big Sky	1/10/97
Peg	Fox	Big Sky	1/10/97
Peg	Fox	Mt. Bike	9/30/97
Ron	Fox	Big Sky	1/10/97
Ron	Fox	Mt. Bike	9/30/97
Fred	Gonzales	Mt. Bike	9/26/96
Pip	Khalsa	Mt. Bike	9/26/96
Kendra	Majors	Bungee	9/20/96
Scott	Owen	Bungee	9/20/96
Kristen	Reis	Big Sky	1/10/97
Kristen	Reis	Bungee	9/15/97
Tom	Reis	Big Sky	1/10/97
Virginia	Rodarmor	Mt. Bike	9/26/96

Developing Forms with Subforms AC G-1

Creating a Form from Multiple Tables .... AC G-2

Using AutoForm .... AC G-3

Moving and Resizing Controls .... AC G-4

Adding Labels and Formatting Controls .... AC G-6

Sorting Records within a Form .... AC G-8

Finding Records within a Form .... AC G-10

Filtering Records within a Form .... AC G-12

Filtering with complex criteria expressions .... AC G-13

Changing the Default Value of a Form Control .... AC G-14

Inherited properties .... AC G-14

Adding List Boxes .... AC G-16

Concepts Review .... AC G-18

Skills Review .... AC G-20

Independent Challenges .... AC G-22

Visual Workshop .... AC G-24

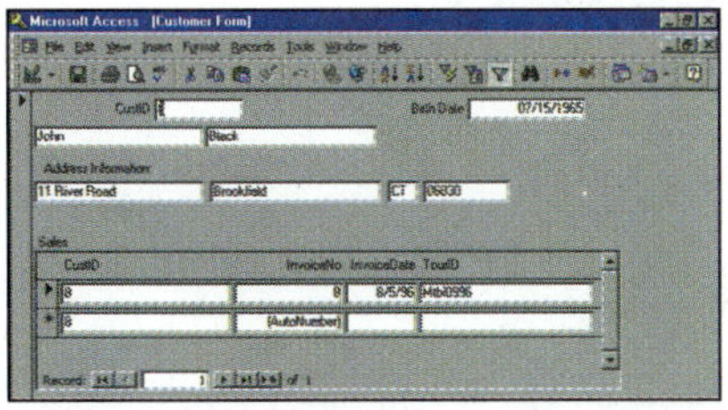

Creating Complex Reports AC H-1

Creating a Report from a Query .... AC H-2

Using Report Sections .... AC H-4

Using Group Headers .... AC H-6

Hide Duplicates property .... AC H-7

Adding Calculations to Group Footers .... AC H-8

Modifying Control Alignment .... AC H-10

Adding Graphics to Reports .... AC H-12

Graphic image files supported by Access .... AC H-13

Using Color .... AC H-14

How to create custom colors .... AC H-15

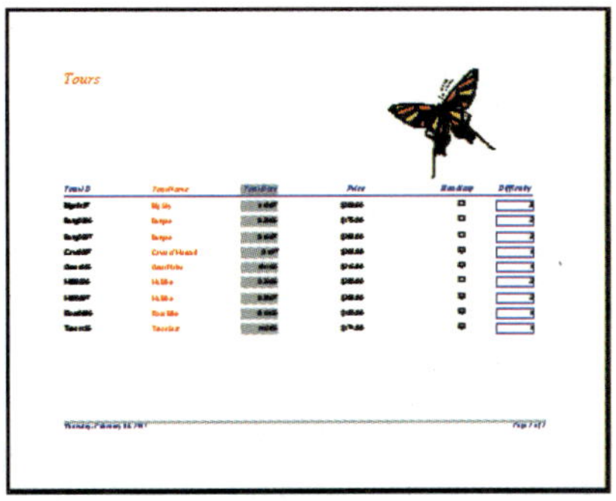

Contents

Adding Special Effects .... AC H-16
Concepts Review .... AC H-18
Skills Review .... AC H-20
Independent Challenges .... AC H-22
Visual Workshop .... AC H-24

Glossary 1
Index 5

Getting Started with Access 97

Objectives

- Define database software
- Start Access 97
- View the Access window
- Open a database table
- Enter and edit records
- Preview and print a datasheet
- Get Help
- Close a database and exit Access

In this unit, you will learn the basic features of Access, a popular database program, and the various components of a database. You will also learn how to use different elements of the Access window, and how to enter and edit records in a table. Finally, you will learn to use the extensive on-line Help system available in Access. Michael Belmont is the Travel Division manager at Nomad Ltd, an outdoor gear and adventure travel company. Recently, Nomad switched to Access from a paper-based system for storing and maintaining customer records. Michael will use Access to maintain customer information for Nomad.

Access 97

Defining Database Software

Access is a database program that runs in the Windows environment. A **database** is a collection of data related to a particular topic or purpose (for example, customer data). Information in a database is organized into **fields**, or categories, such as customer name. A group of related fields, such as all the information on a particular customer, is called a **record**. A collection of related records is called a **table**. A database, specifically a **relational database**, is a collection of one or more related tables that can share information. Figure A-1 shows the structure of a database. Traditionally, businesses kept track of customer information using index cards, as illustrated in Figure A-2. However, with an electronic database, like Access, businesses can store, retrieve, and manipulate data more quickly and easily.

Details

With database software Michael Belmont can:

Enter data quickly and easily
With Access, Michael can enter information on Nomad's customers faster and more accurately than he could using the paper-based method. He can enter data using screen **forms**, which contain **controls** such as check boxes, list boxes, and option buttons, to facilitate data entry. Figure A-3 shows customer information in an Access form.

Organize records in different ways
Michael can review his data sorted by any field, and see records that meet specific criteria by filtering the data. After Michael specifies a sort order, Access automatically keeps records organized, regardless of the order in which they are entered.

Locate specific records quickly
By creating a **query**, a definition of the records he wants to find, Michael can instruct Access to locate the record or records that meet certain conditions. A query can be saved for future use.

Eliminate duplicate data
Access ensures that each record is unique by assigning a **primary key** field to each table. It is not possible for two records in a table to have the same data in their primary key field. Using the paper system, Michael could have duplicate customer records if he forgot that an index card already existed for a particular customer.

Create relationships among tables in a database
Access is a relational database, which allows information within its tables to be shared. This means that Michael needs to enter a customer name only once and it will be referenced in other tables in Nomad's database.

Create reports
Generating professional reports is easy with Access. Michael can produce reports to illustrate different relationships among the data and share these reports with other Nomad employees.

Change the appearance of information
Access provides powerful features for enhancing table data and creating charts so that information is visually appealing and easy to understand.

FIGURE A-1: Structure of a database

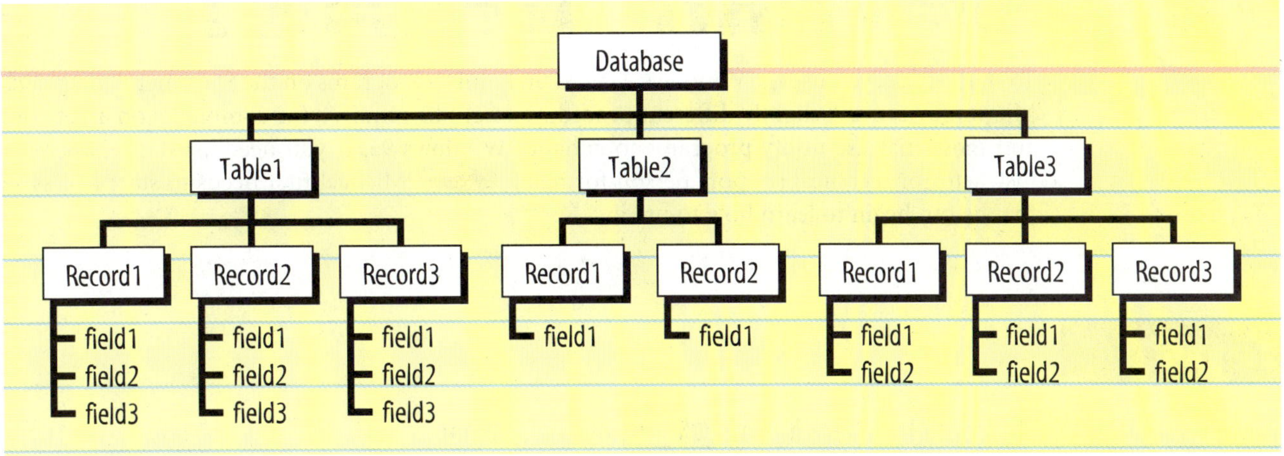

FIGURE A-2: Customer information on an index card

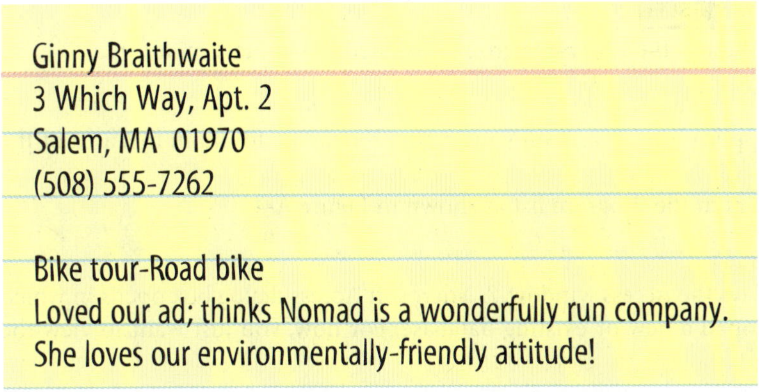
Ginny Braithwaite
3 Which Way, Apt. 2
Salem, MA 01970
(508) 555-7262

Bike tour-Road bike
Loved our ad; thinks Nomad is a wonderfully run company.
She loves our environmentally-friendly attitude!

FIGURE A-3: Customer information in an Access form

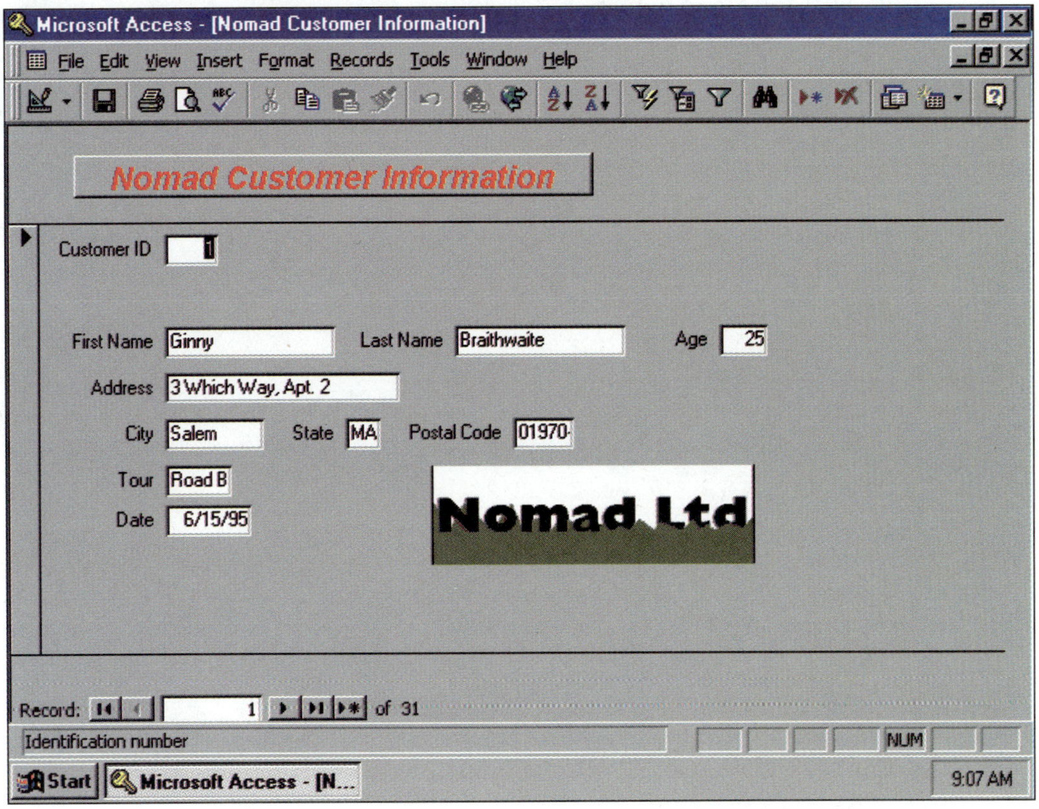

Access 97

Access 97

Starting Access 97

To start Access, you use the Windows 95 taskbar. Point to Programs on the Start menu, then click Microsoft Access. A slightly different procedure might be required for computers on a network and those that use utility programs to enhance Windows 95. If you need assistance, ask your instructor or technical support person for help. Michael first needs to start Access so that he can begin to learn how to use it.

Steps

1. Locate the **Start button** on the taskbar
   The Start button is on the left side of the taskbar and is used to start, or **launch**, programs on your computer.
2. Click the **Start button**
   Microsoft Access is located in the Programs group—located in the Start menu.
3. Point to **Programs**
   All the programs, or applications, found on your computer can be found in this area of the Start menu.
   Microsoft Access appears in the Program list as shown in Figure A-4.
4. Click **Microsoft Access**
   Access opens and displays the Access window. A Microsoft Access dialog box opens in which you select whether to open a new or existing database. For now, you just want to view the Access window.
5. Click **Cancel**
   The dialog box closes and a blank Access window appears. In the next lesson, you will familiarize yourself with the elements of the Access window.

Trouble?

If you can't locate Microsoft Access in the Programs list, point to Microsoft Office, then click Microsoft Access to start Access.

FIGURE A-4: Microsoft Access program selected

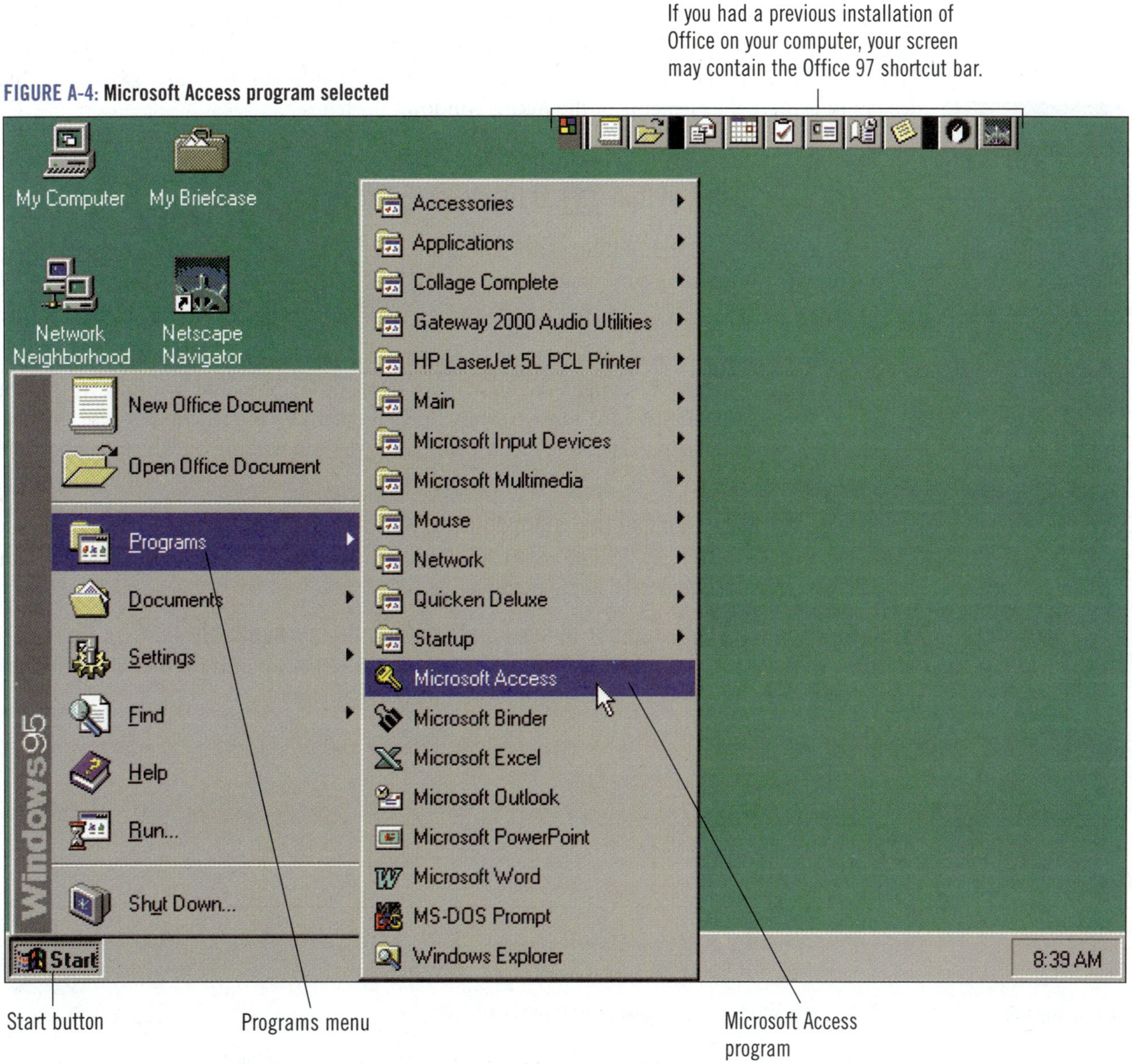

Viewing the Access Window

When you start Access, the screen displays the **startup window**, the area from which you carry out all database operations. The Access window contains many elements that help you enter and manipulate the information in your database. Some of these elements, which are described in Table A-1 and identified in Figure A-5, are common to all Windows programs. Michael decides to explore the elements of the Access window.

Steps

Trouble?

All lessons from this point on assume you have Access running. If you need help, refer to the previous lesson, "Starting Access 97," or ask your technical support person or instructor for assistance.

1. **Click the Maximize button, if the Access window does not fill the screen**
2. **Look at each of the elements shown in Figure A-5**
   You browse through the commands in the File menu.
3. **Click File on the menu bar**
   The File menu opens, as shown in Figure A-6. The File menu has commands for opening a new or existing database, saving a database in a variety of formats, and printing. At the bottom of the File menu, the four most recently opened databases are listed. Because there are so many components in a database, menu commands vary depending on which database element is currently in use.
4. **Press [Esc] twice to close the File menu**
   Pressing [Esc] once closes the File menu, but File on the menu bar is still highlighted. Pressing [Esc] the second time deselects the menu name.
5. **Review the Database toolbar to see what commands are available**
   Many of the buttons on this toolbar can be found within commands on the File menu, and the remaining buttons can be found in other menu commands.

TABLE A-1: Elements of the Access window

element	description
Menu bar	Contains menus used in Access
Startup window	Area from which database operations take place
Status bar	Displays messages regarding operations and displays descriptions of toolbar buttons
Title bar	Contains program and filename of active database
Database toolbar	Contains buttons for commonly performed tasks

CLUES TO USE

Finding out about buttons and menu commands

If you don't know what a toolbar button does, read its ToolTip—its name—by placing your mouse pointer over its button face. Even though a button is dimmed and not active in a certain window, you can still access its ToolTip.

FIGURE A-5: Access window

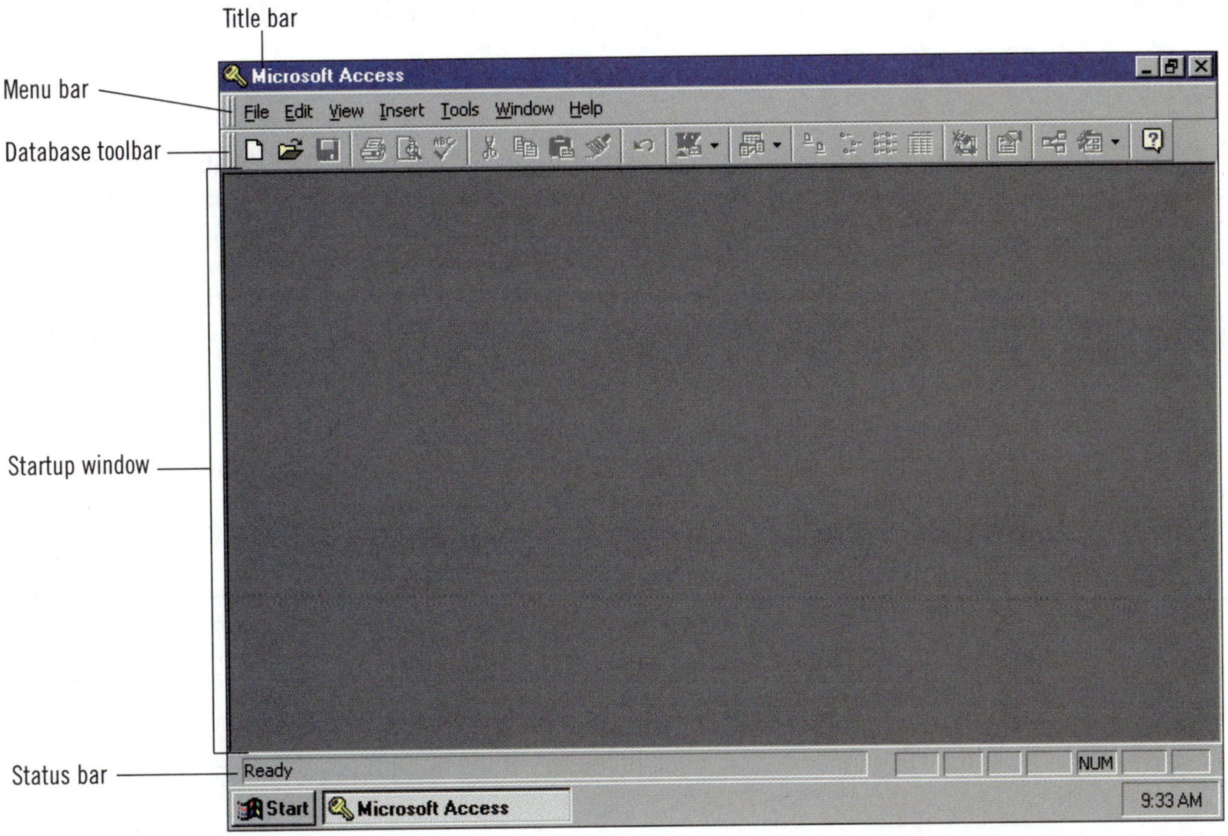

FIGURE A-6: File menu in startup window

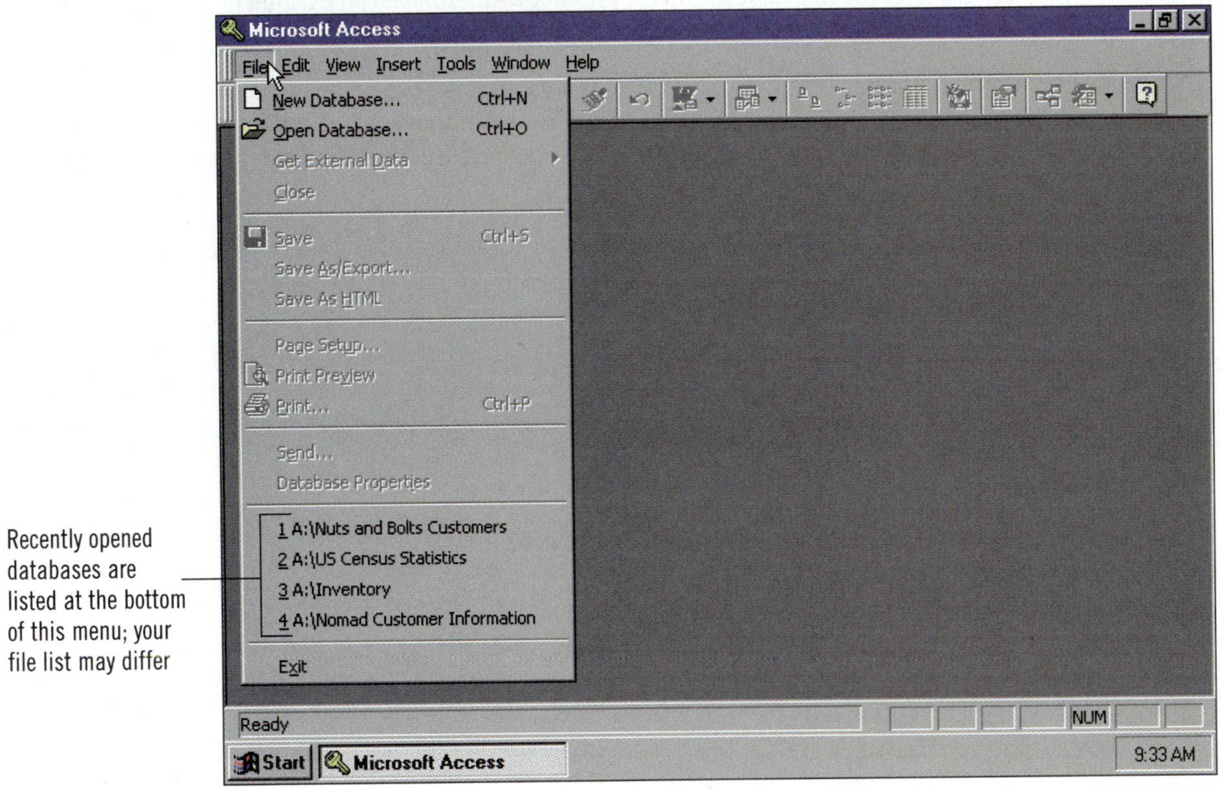

Access 97

Access 97

Opening a Database Table

After you open a database, Access displays the database window. The **database window** provides access to all objects in the database. Table A-2 describes the objects—such as tables, forms, and reports—that help you use the information in a database. A database **table** is a collection of related records within a database; a single database can contain multiple tables. Michael wants to open a database and review the table containing information about Nomad's products to see how it is structured.

Steps

QuickTip
Make a copy of your Student Disk before you use it.

1. Place your Student Disk in the appropriate drive
   To complete the units in this book, you need a Student Disk. See your instructor for a copy of the Student Disk, if you do not already have one.
2. Click the **Open Database button** on the Database toolbar
   Access displays the Open Database dialog box. Depending on the databases stored on your disk, your dialog box might look slightly different from the one shown in Figure A-7.
3. Click the **Look in list arrow**, then click the drive that contains your Student Disk
   A list of the files on your Student Disk appears in the Look in list box.
4. In the File name list box, click **Inventory** if it's not already selected

QuickTip
To open a database file quickly, you can double-click the filename in the File name list box of the Open dialog box.

5. Click **Open**
   The Database window for the file Inventory opens, as shown in Figure A-8. The top of the Database window contains the **object buttons** for the Access database objects (which are described in Table A-2). Each object button appears on its own **tab**. The Tables tab is currently the front-most tab in the dialog box. The window lists the tables in the selected database (in this case, the Inventory database contains only one table, Products). The command buttons at the right side of the window allow you to open an existing table, design your own table, or create a new table. You want to open the Products table, which is already selected.
6. Click **Open**
   A window for the Products table opens. The table contains information for 17 Nomad products. Each row is a record and the information is organized by fields arranged in columns.

TABLE A-2: Database objects

object	description
Table	Stores related data in rows (records) and columns (fields)
Query	Asks a question of data in a table; used to find qualifying records
Form	Displays table data in a layout of fields on the screen
Report	Provides printed information from a table, which can include calculations
Macro	Automates database tasks, which can be reduced to a single command
Module	Automates complex tasks using a built-in programming language

FIGURE A-7: **Open dialog box**

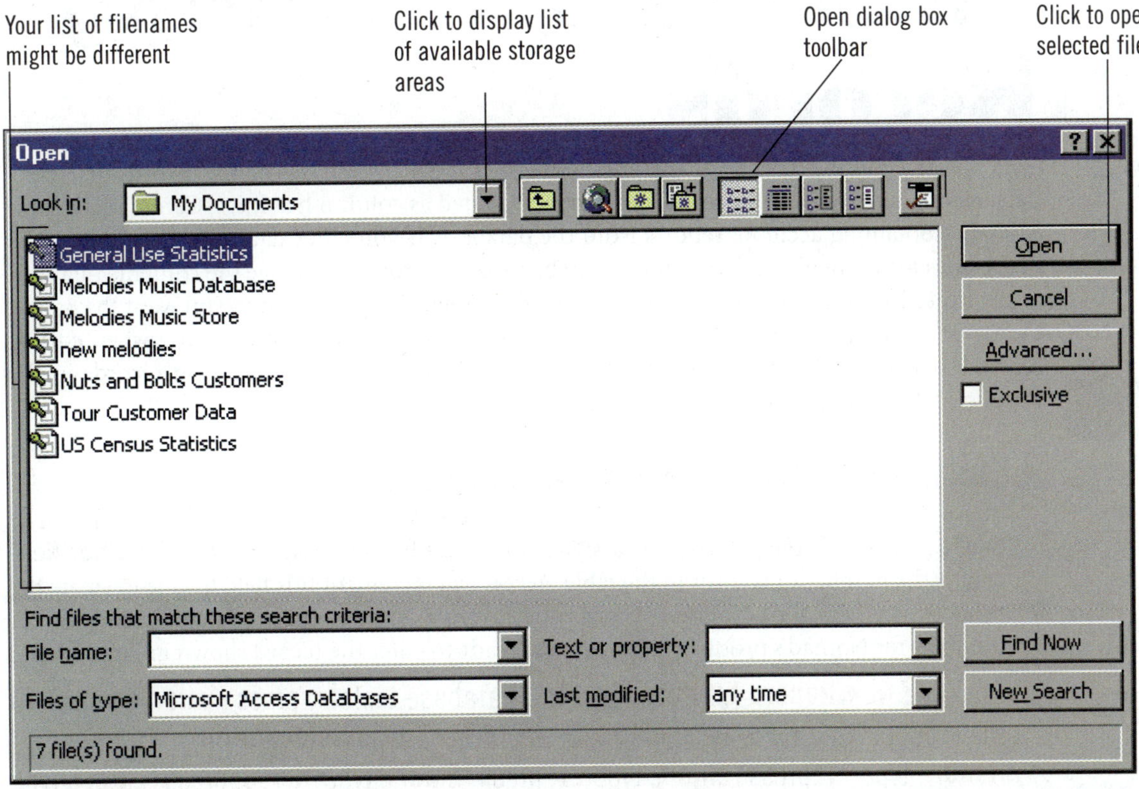

FIGURE A-8: **Database window**

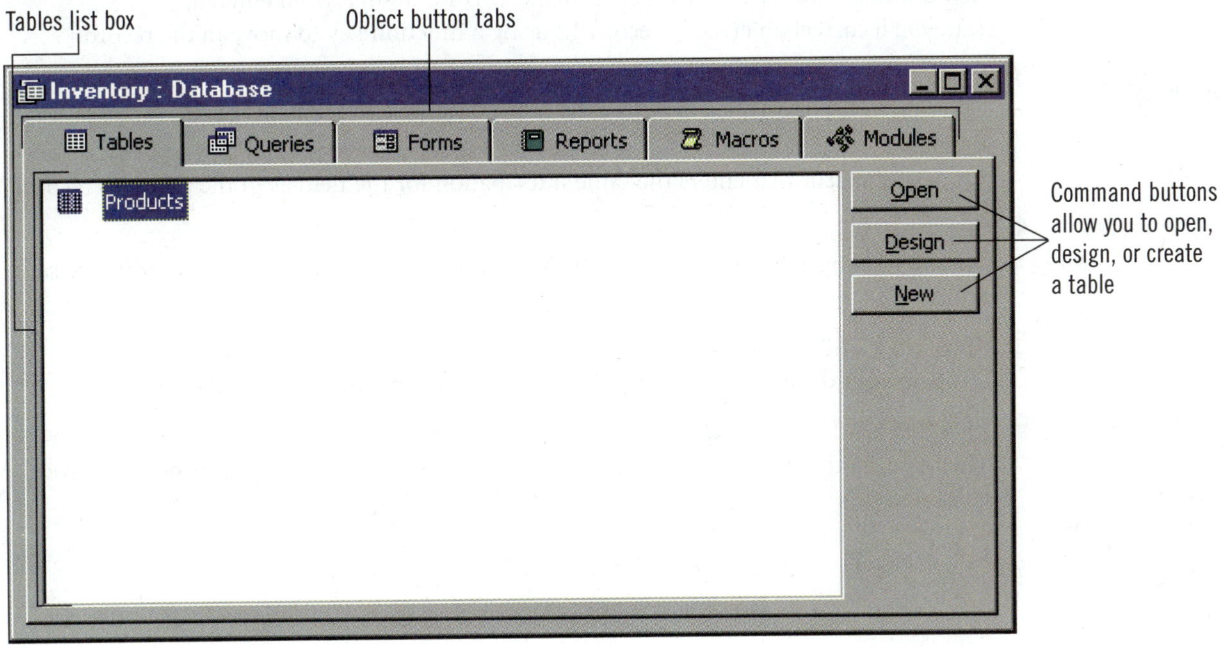

Access 97

Entering and Editing Records

Data is entered in the datasheet. A **datasheet** is a grid which contains all the records in a table. Each record is contained in a row. Field names are listed as column headings. Careful data entry is vital to obtaining accurate reports from the database. If you enter data carelessly, the results of searches for particular information might be incorrect. You can change the contents of a field at any time. To edit a field, you first click in the field, select the information you want to change, then type the corrections. Table A-3 lists several keyboard shortcuts you can use when editing records. Michael is now ready to add a new record and edit existing records in the Products table. First, he will maximize the Datasheet window.

Steps

1. Click the **Maximize button** in the Datasheet window title bar
   The word "AutoNumber" appears below the last record in the Product ID field, as shown in Figure A-9. This is the primary key assigned by Access for this table. The **AutoNumber field** counts the number of records in the table. Access will increment this field by one to create the primary key data for your new record. The Product Num column contains identification numbers for Nomad's products. Now you are ready to enter the record shown in Figure A-10.

2. Click the **New Record button** on the Database toolbar, press **[Enter]** to move to the Product Num field, type **11436**, press **[Enter]**, type **Shimano Dirt Pirates**, press **[Enter]**, type **11**, press **[Enter]**, type **27**, press **[Enter]**, type **46483**, press **[Enter]**, type **24**, press **[Enter]**, type **10**, press **[Enter]**, type **71.25**, press **[Enter]**, type **25**, press **[Enter]**, type **15**, press **[Enter]**, type **Each**, then press **[Enter]**
   Record number 18 for the product Shimano Dirt Pirates has been entered.
   Next, you'll correct an error in record 12 using a function key to move to the record.

3. Double-click in the **Units field for record 12**
   The contents of the Units field in record 12 is selected. This field should have the same contents as the field above it. You can either type the correct entry in the field, or use a keyboard shortcut that enters the same information for the field as in the previous record.

4. Press **[Ctrl][']**
   The entry changes from 'Pair' to 'Each'. Next, you'll change the Reorder Level in the same record.

5. Press **[←]** twice, then type **29**
   Compare your datasheet to Figure A-11. You save the changes made in the table.

6. Click the **Save button**
   When you modify the structure of a table or when you edit records, you need to save the table.

QuickTip

When you are entering data in a table, you can advance to the next field for that record by pressing either [Enter] or [Tab].

Trouble?

If you cannot see the column in the datasheet window, scroll to the right or left as needed to display the field you need. If you cannot see the row, scroll up or down to display the record you need.

QuickTip

When you switch views, from Datasheet to Design View, or when you close the table, any changes to the table are automatically saved.

CLUES TO USE

Moving table columns

You can reorganize the columns in a table by moving them from one location to another. To move a column, click its field name so that the entire column is selected, then drag the pointer to the column's new location. As you drag, the mouse pointer changes to . A heavy vertical line represents the new location. Release the mouse button when you have correctly positioned the column.

FIGURE A-9: Entering a record in a table

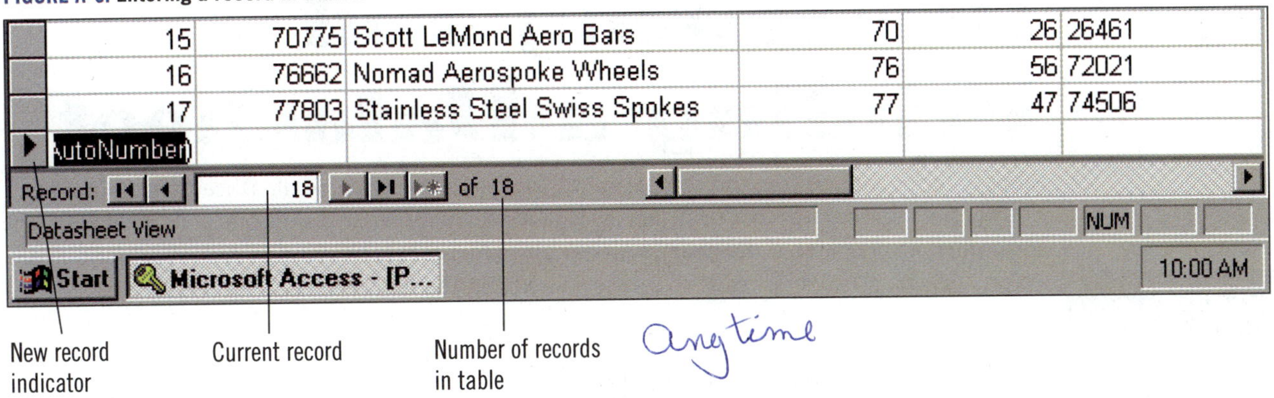

FIGURE A-10: Data in record 18

Product ID	Product Num	Product Name	Category ID	Supplier ID	Serial Number	Units in Stock	Units on Order	Unit Price	Reorder Level	Reorder Amount	Units	Disc. Status
18	11436	Shimano Dirt Pirates	11	27	46483	24	10	71.25	25	15	Each	No

TABLE A-3: Keyboard shortcuts in table

shortcut key	action
[F5]	Move to a specific record
[F6]	Move between window sections
[F7]	Open the Spelling dialog box
[Ctrl][']	Insert the value from the same field in the previous record
[Ctrl][;]	Insert the current date
[Ctrl][=]	Move to the first blank record
[Esc]	Undo changes in the current field or record
[Shift][Enter]	Save the current record

FIGURE A-11: Edited record

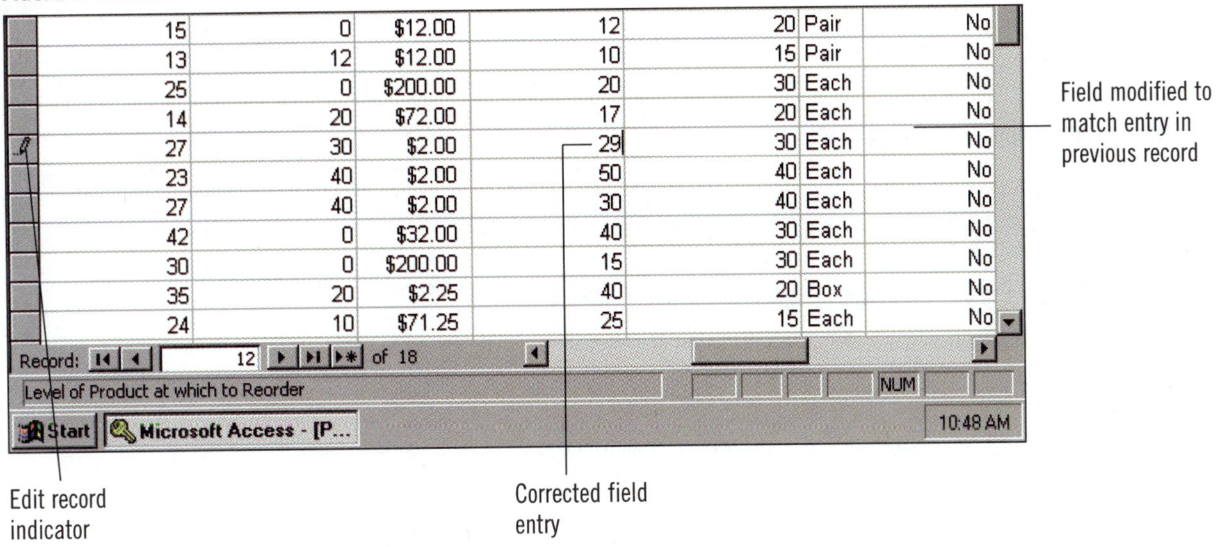

Access 97

Access 97

Previewing and Printing a Datasheet

Steps

After entering and editing the records in a table, you can print the datasheet to obtain a hard copy of the table data. Before printing, it's a good idea to preview the datasheet to see how it will look when printed and, if necessary, to make any adjustments to margins, page orientation, and so on. Michael is ready to preview and print the datasheet.

1. Click the **Print Preview button** on the Database toolbar
   The datasheet appears on a miniature page in the Print Preview window, as shown in Figure A-12, and the Print Preview toolbar appears. You decide to use the Magnifier pointer to see how the datasheet looks when magnified.
2. Click the **Magnifier pointer** anywhere in the miniature datasheet
   A magnified version of the datasheet appears. You notice that most of the fields seem to be cut off the page. You return the datasheet to its original appearance.
3. Click anywhere in the magnified datasheet
   You decide to print in landscape mode in order to see more fields on each page.
4. Click **File** on the menu bar, then click **Page Setup**
   The Page Setup dialog box opens. This dialog box provides options for the way text looks on the page.
5. Click the **Page tab**, click the **Landscape radio button**, as shown in Figure A-13, then click **OK**
   Now you can see more of the fields for the table that will print on a page.
6. Click **File** on the menu bar, then click **Print**
   The Print dialog box as shown in Figure A-15 opens, giving you several options described in Table A-4. You do not have to make any changes to this dialog box.
7. Click **OK** to print the datasheet, then click **Close** on the Print Preview toolbar to return to the datasheet
   With the datasheet printed, you are ready to save the table.
8. Click the **Save button** on the Standard toolbar

QuickTip

Click the Print button to print one copy of the entire datasheet using the default settings without making selections from the Print dialog box.

TABLE A-4: Print dialog box options

option	description
Printer	Displays the name of the selected printer and print connection
Print Range	Specifies all pages, certain pages, a range of pages to print, or selected records
Copies	Specifies the number of copies to print and whether to collate the copies
Print to File	Prints a document to an encapsulated PostScript file instead of a printer
Margins	Adjusts the left, right, top, and bottom margins (available through the Setup option)
Orientation	Specifies Portrait (the default) or Landscape paper (available through the Properties option)

FIGURE A-12: Datasheet in Print Preview (portrait orientation)

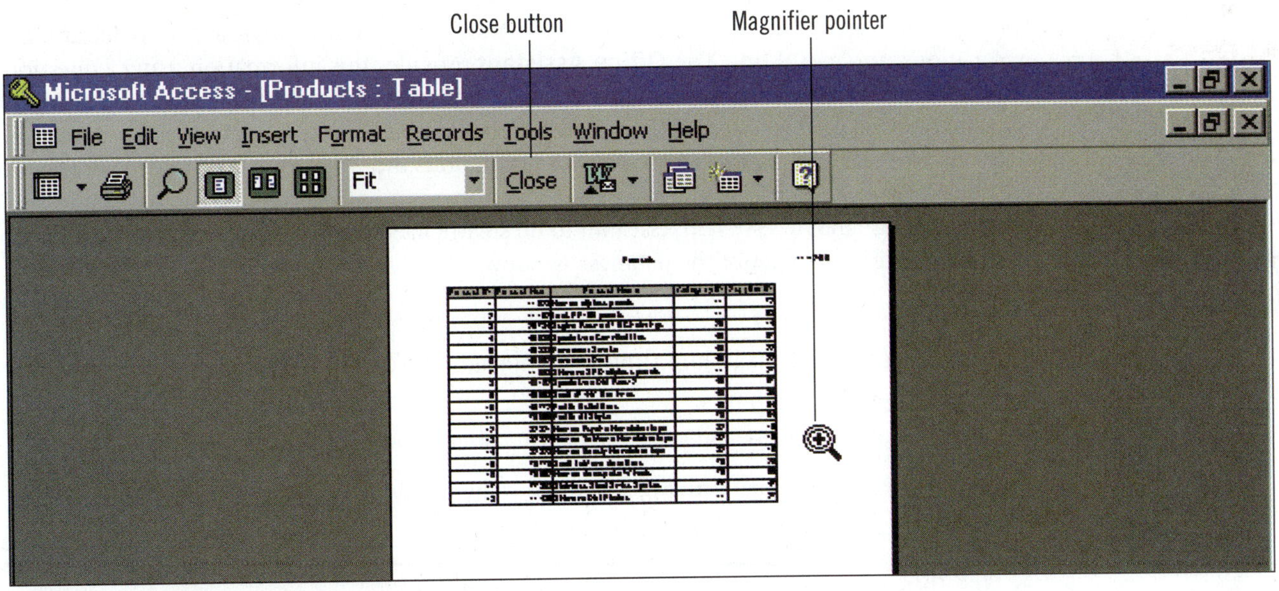

FIGURE A-13: Page Setup dialog box

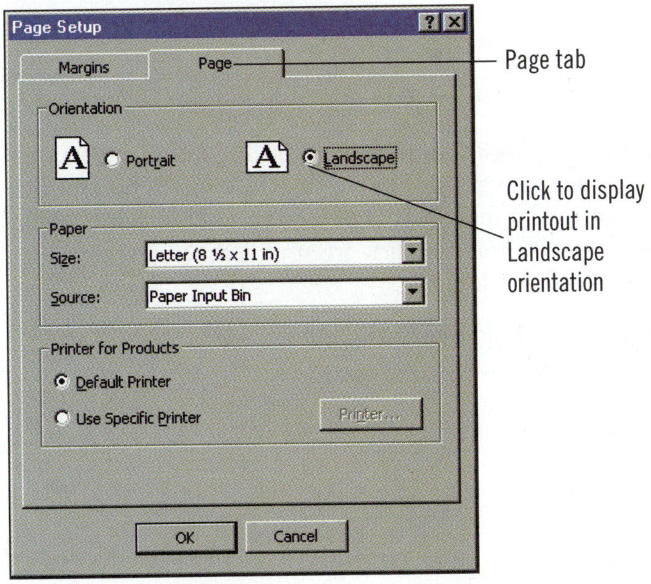

FIGURE A-14: Print dialog box

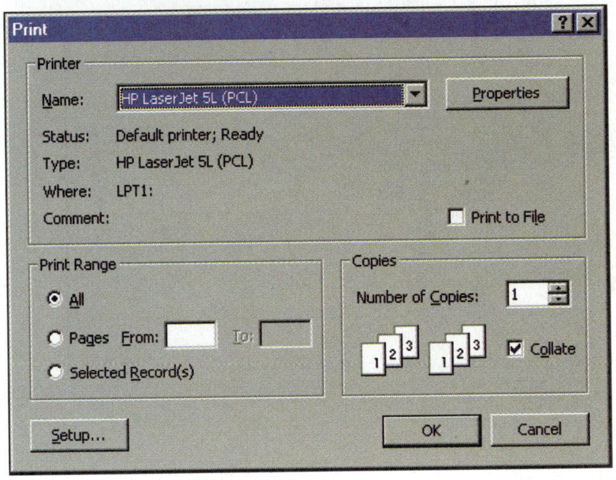

Access 97

Getting Help

Access provides an extensive on-line Help system that gives you immediate access to definitions, explanations, and useful tips. The **Office Assistant** provides this information using a question and answer format. As you are working, the Office Assistant provides tips—indicated by a light bulb you can click—in response to your own working habits. Help appears in a separate window that you can resize and refer to as you work. You can press the [F1] key at any time to get immediate help. Michael wants to find information on moving through a database table, and he decides to use the Access Help Assistant to do so. Michael decides to use the animated Office Assistant to learn more about the database window.

Steps

1. If the Office Assistant is not already displayed, click the **Office Assistant button** on the Standard toolbar
   The Office Assistant lets you get information using a question and answer format.
2. If the Office Assistant is displayed, click its window to activate the query box
   You want information on how to navigate a datasheet.
3. Type **How do I move between records in a datasheet?**
   See Figure A-16. After you ask a question, the Office Assistant displays relevant topics from which you can choose.
4. Click **Search**
   The Office Assistant displays several topics related to your question, shown in Figure A-17.
5. Click **Moving between records using navigation buttons in Datasheet or Form view**
   The help window, shown in Figure A-18, can be printed by clicking the Options button, then clicking Print Topic. When you point to text that appears as a green underlined topic, the shape of the mouse pointer changes to . You can click green underlined text to open a dialog box to get more information about that topic.
6. Click the **Close button** on the Help dialog box title bar
   The Help window closes and you return to your worksheet.

QuickTip

You can close the Office Assistant at any time by clicking its Close button.

CLUES TO USE

Changing the Office Assistant

The default Office Assistant is Clippit, but there are 8 others from which you can choose. To change the appearance of the Office Assistant, right-click the Office Assistant window, then select Choose Assistant. Click the Gallery tab, click the Back and Next buttons until you find an Assistant you want to use, then click OK. (You may need your Microsoft Office 97 CD to change Office Assistants.) Each Office Assistant makes its own unique sounds and can be animated by right-clicking its window and selecting Animate! See Figure A-15.

FIGURE A-15: Office Assistant dialog box

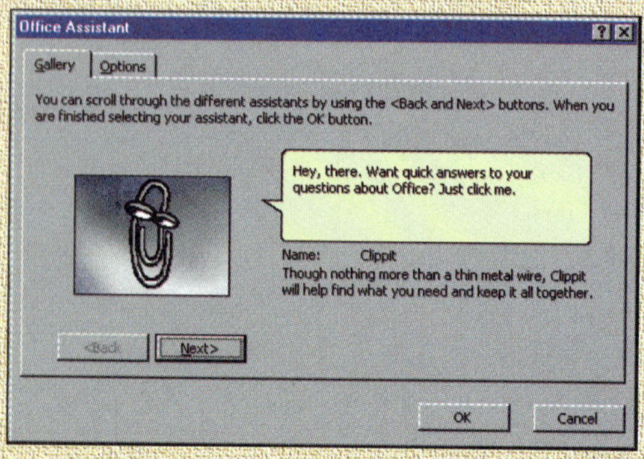

FIGURE A-16: Office Assistant

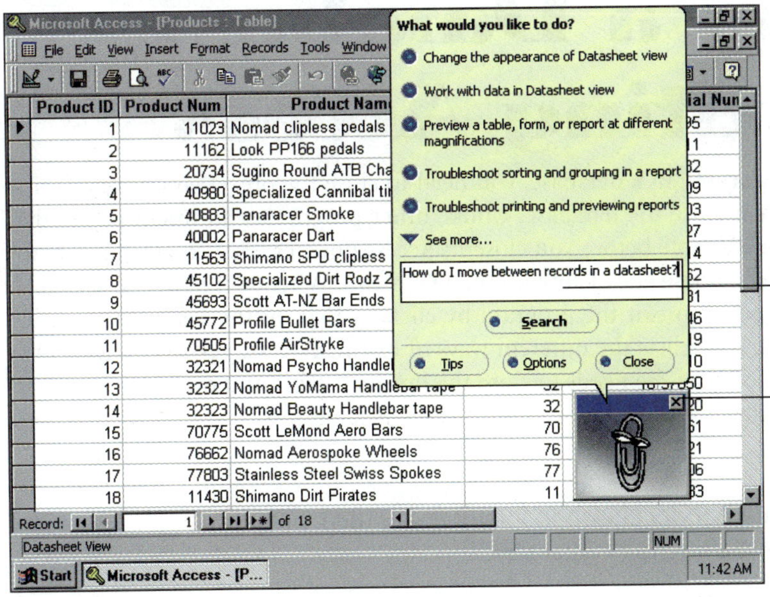

FIGURE A-17: Relevant Help Assistant Topics

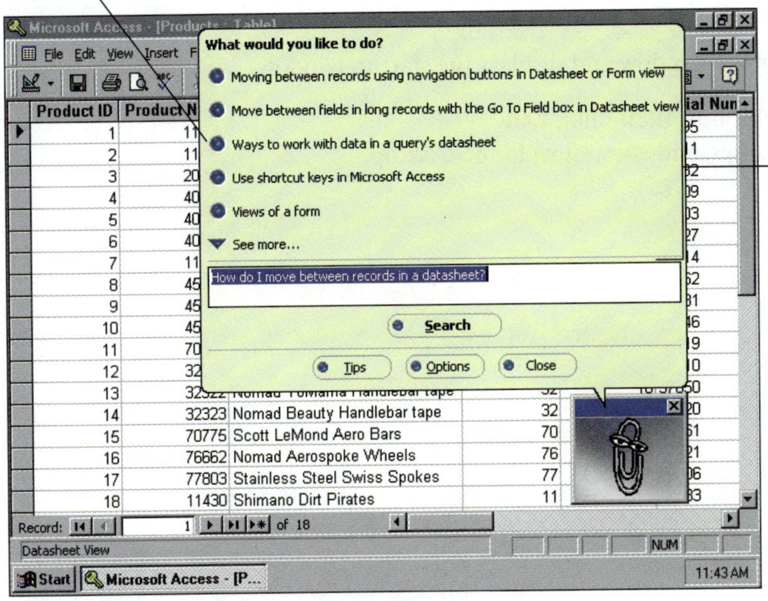

FIGURE A-18: Help window showing navigation buttons

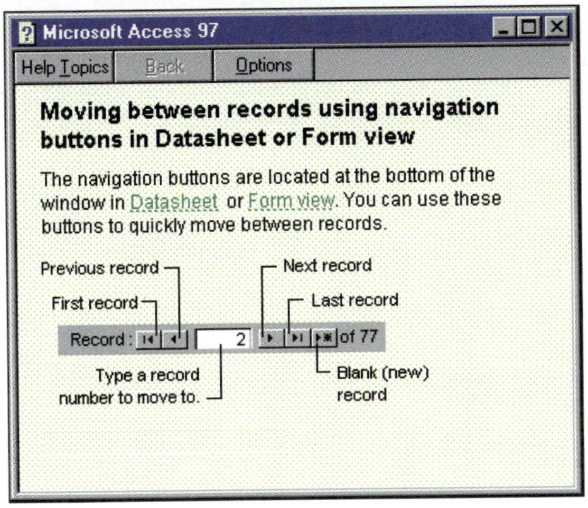

Access 97

Closing a Database and Exiting Access

When you have finished working in a database, you need to close the object you were working in, such as a table, and then close the database. Unlike other programs you might be familiar with, you don't have to save a table before you close it; Access updates your changes automatically. To close a table, or a database click Close on the File menu. When you have completed all your work in Access, you need to exit the program by clicking Exit on the File menu. Exiting closes all open objects. Table A-5 lists the different ways of exiting Access. Michael has finished exploring Access for now. He needs to close the Products table and the Inventory database, then exit Access. Michael begins by closing the Products table.

Steps

1. Click **File** on the menu bar, as shown in Figure A-19, then click **Close**

   Now you need to close the Inventory database.

2. Click **File** on the menu bar

   The File menu opens and displays a list of commands. Notice that this Database File menu has different commands than the File menu in the Table window.

3. Click **Close**

   Access closes the Database window and displays the startup window.

4. Click **File** on the menu bar, then click **Exit**

   The Access program closes, and you return to the desktop.

QuickTip

Make sure you always properly end your Access session by using the steps in this unit. Improper exit procedures can result in corruption of your data files.

FIGURE A-19:

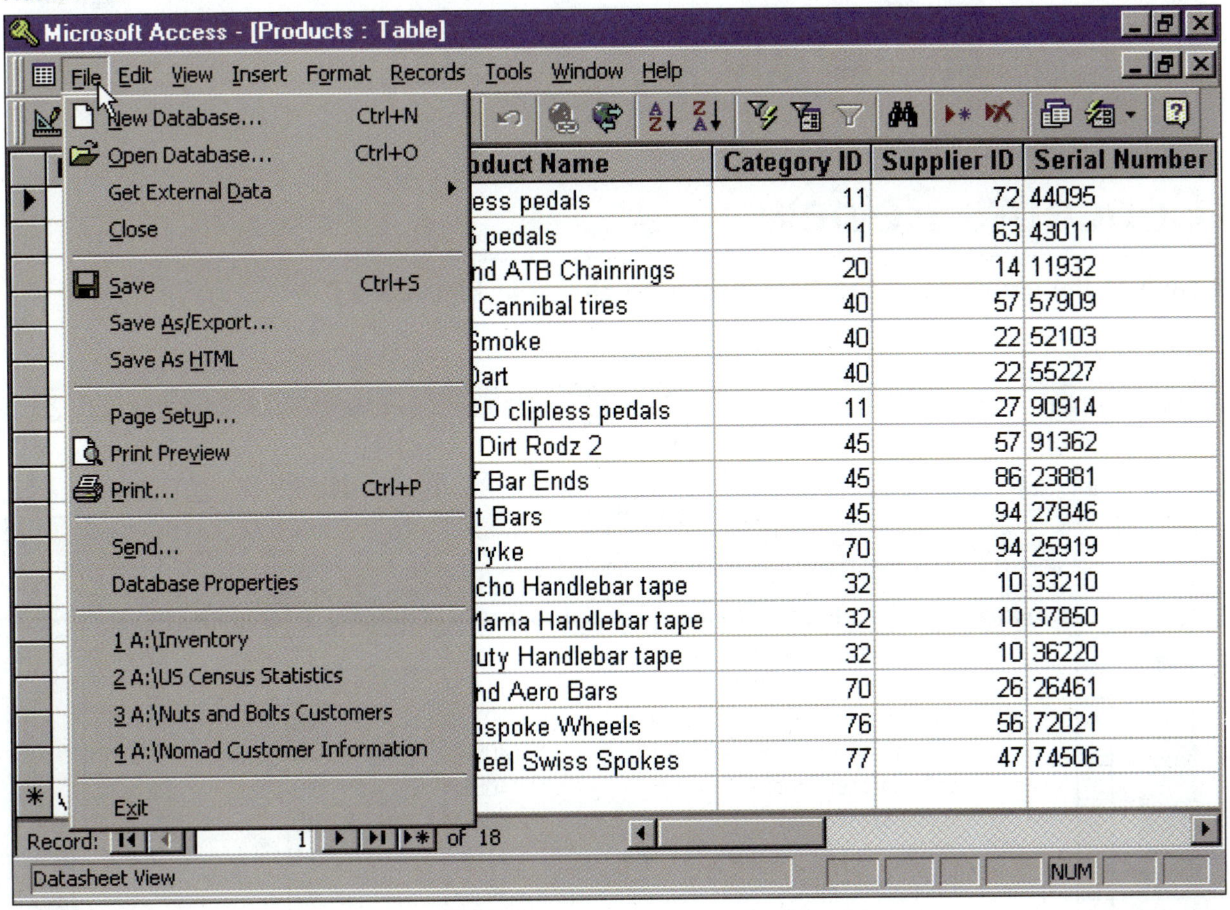

TABLE A-5: Ways to exit Access

method	key or command
Menu	Choose Exit from the File menu
Keyboard	Press [Alt][F4]
Mouse	Double-click the program control menu box

Practice

Concepts Review

Label each of the elements of the Access window shown in Figure A-20.

FIGURE A-20

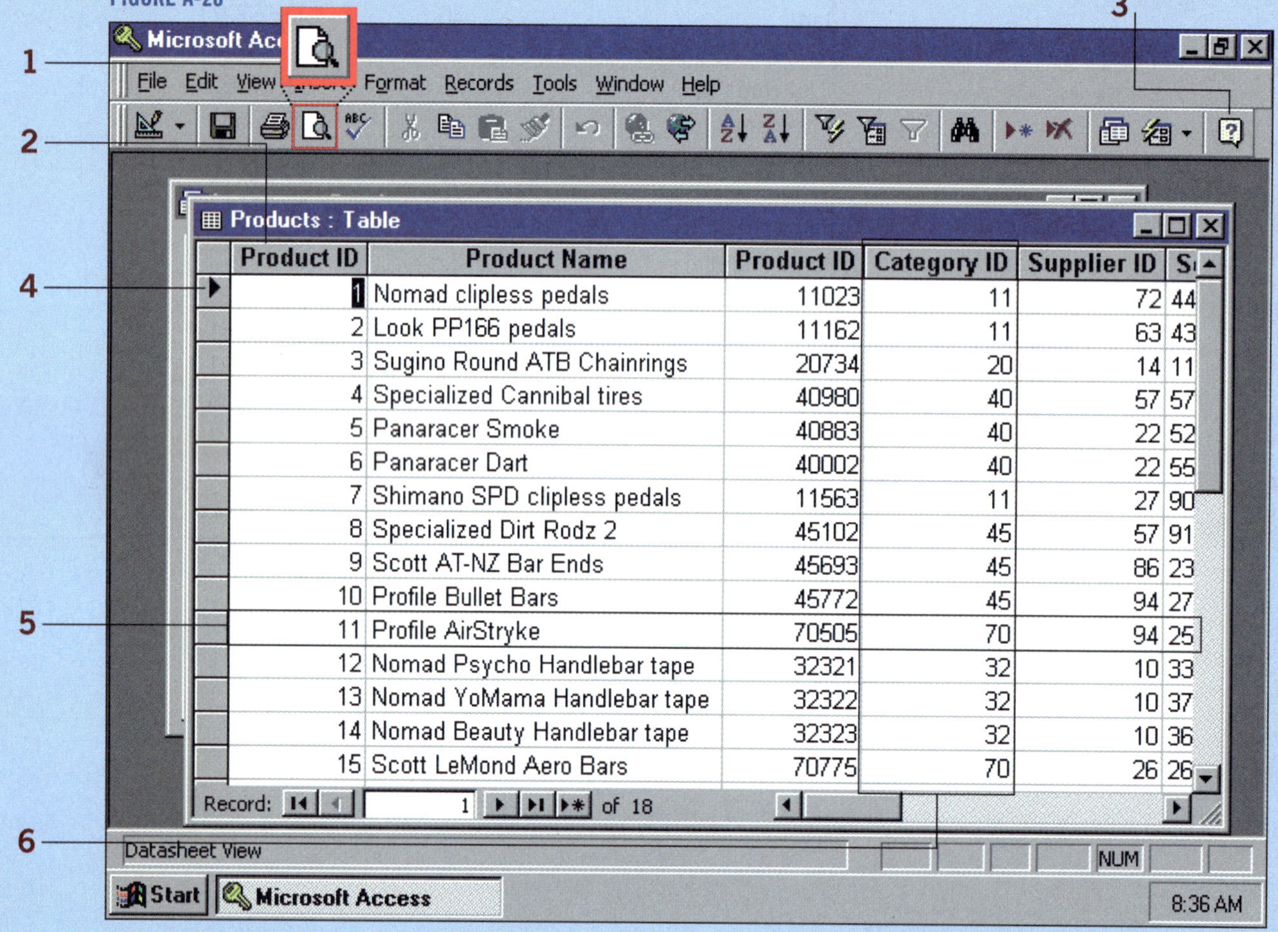

Match each of the following terms with the statement that describes its function.

7. Database window
8. Table
9. Database
10. Office Assistant
11. Shortcut keys

a. A collection of data related to a particular topic or purpose
b. Combination of keys resulting in the execution of a command
c. Area that contains all database objects
d. Stores related data in rows and columns
e. Provides information about Access

Select the best answer from the list of choices.

12. An electronic database can perform all of the following tasks, *except:*

a. Displaying information visually
b. Calculating data accurately
c. Planning database objectives
d. Recalculating updated information

13. Which of the following is NOT a database?

a. Customer information
b. Interoffice memo
c. Telephone directory
d. Dictionary

14. Which button opens an existing database?

a. 
b. 
c. 
d. 

15. Which button opens the Office Assistant?

a. 
b. 
c. 
d. 

16. You can get Help in any of the following ways, *except:*

a. Clicking Help on the menu bar
b. Pressing [F1]
c. Clicking the Help button 
d. Minimizing the Database window

▶ Skills Review

1. Start Access.
- **a.** Make sure your computer is on and Windows is running.
- **b.** Click the Start button, point to Programs, then click Microsoft Access.

2. View the Access Window.
- **a.** Try to identify as many components of the Access window as you can without referring to the unit material.

3. Open a database table.
- **a.** Make sure your Student Disk is in the appropriate disk drive.
- **b.** Click the Open Database button on the Database toolbar.
- **c.** Open the database named US Census Statistics from your Student Disk.
- **d.** Click the object tabs in the Database window to see the contents of each object.
- **e.** Open the Statistical Data table.

4. Enter and edit records.
- **a.** Click the New Record button.
- **b.** Enter the following record. State: Virginia, Region: South Atlantic, Year: 1991, Marriages: 68,771.
- **c.** Change the year in record 6 to 1991.

5. Preview and print a datasheet.
- **a.** Click the Print Preview button on the Database toolbar to display the datasheet in the Print Preview window.
- **b.** After viewing the datasheet, click the Print button on the Print Preview toolbar.
- **c.** After printing, return to the Database window.
- **d.** Save the table.

6. Get Help.
- **a.** Click the Office Assistant button on the Database toolbar.
- **b.** Ask the Office Assistant the following question: "How can I view data?"
- **c.** Click the topic "Ways to work with data in a table's datasheet."
- **d.** Click the Options button, click Print Topic, then click OK.
- **e.** Click the Close button on the Help window.
- **f.** Click the Close button on the Office Assistant.

7. Close a database and exit Access.
- **a.** Click File on the menu bar, then click Close to close the "Statistical Data" table.
- **b.** Click File on the menu bar, then click Close to close the "US Census Statistics" database file.
- **c.** Click File on the menu bar, then click Exit to exit Access.

► Independent Challenges

1. Ten examples of databases are given below. Using each of these examples, write down one sample record for each database and describe the fields you would expect to find in each.

- Telephone directory
- College course offerings
- Restaurant menu
- Cookbook
- Movie listing
- Encyclopedia
- Shopping catalog
- Corporate inventory
- Party guest list
- Members of the House of Representatives

2. Access provides online Help that explains procedures and gives you examples and demos. Help covers such elements as the Database window, the status bar, toolbar buttons, dialog boxes, and Access commands and options. Start Access then explore online Help by clicking the Office Assistant button. Ask the Office Assistant, "What is a database?" Find out about databases—what they are and how they work. Print out information you find on this topic.

FIGURE A-21

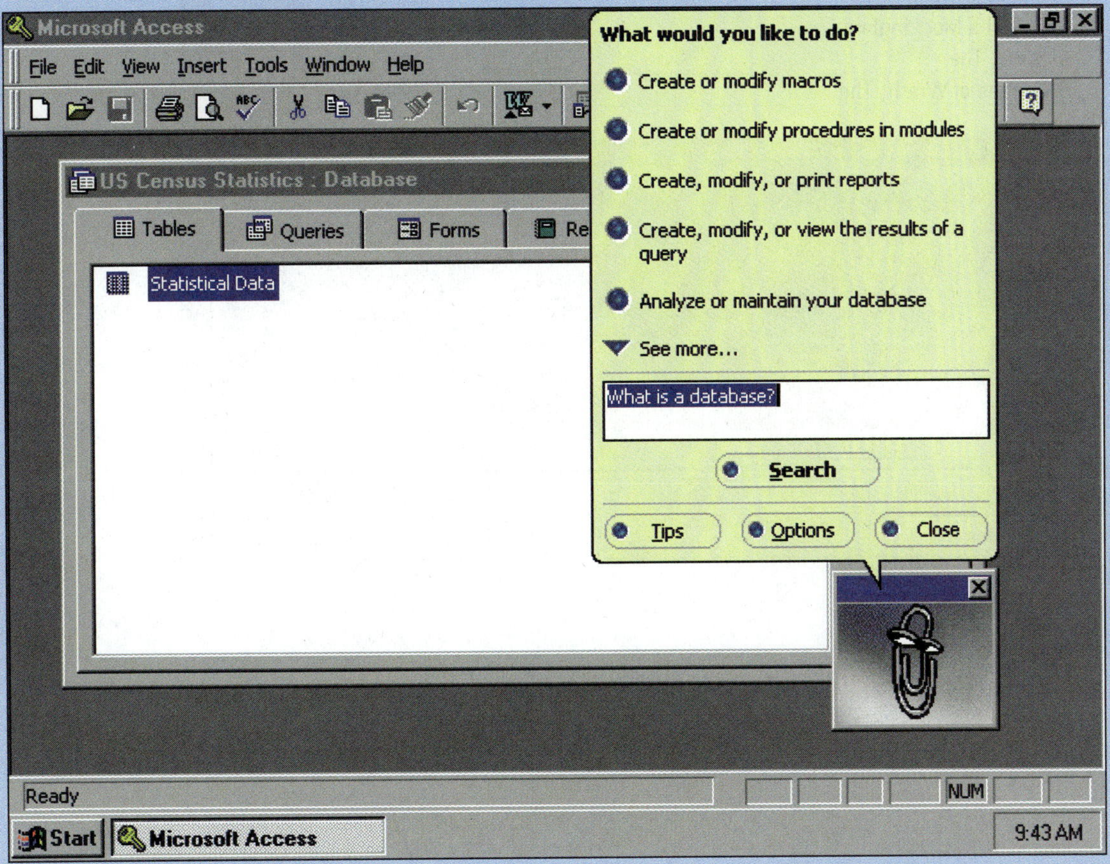

3. To become more accomplished at using databases, you've decided it would be fun to make a list of your favorite films. A database called Favorite Movies has been started. All you need to do is supply information about your favorite films.

To complete this independent challenge:

1. Open the database called Favorite Movies on your Student Disk.
2. Open the Film Favorites table.
3. Add at least ten entries. The table includes fields for up to 3 co-stars. If you don't know the year the film was released, leave the field blank, or estimate the year.
4. Preview the table, then print it in landscape mode. Submit your finished publication.

FIGURE A-22

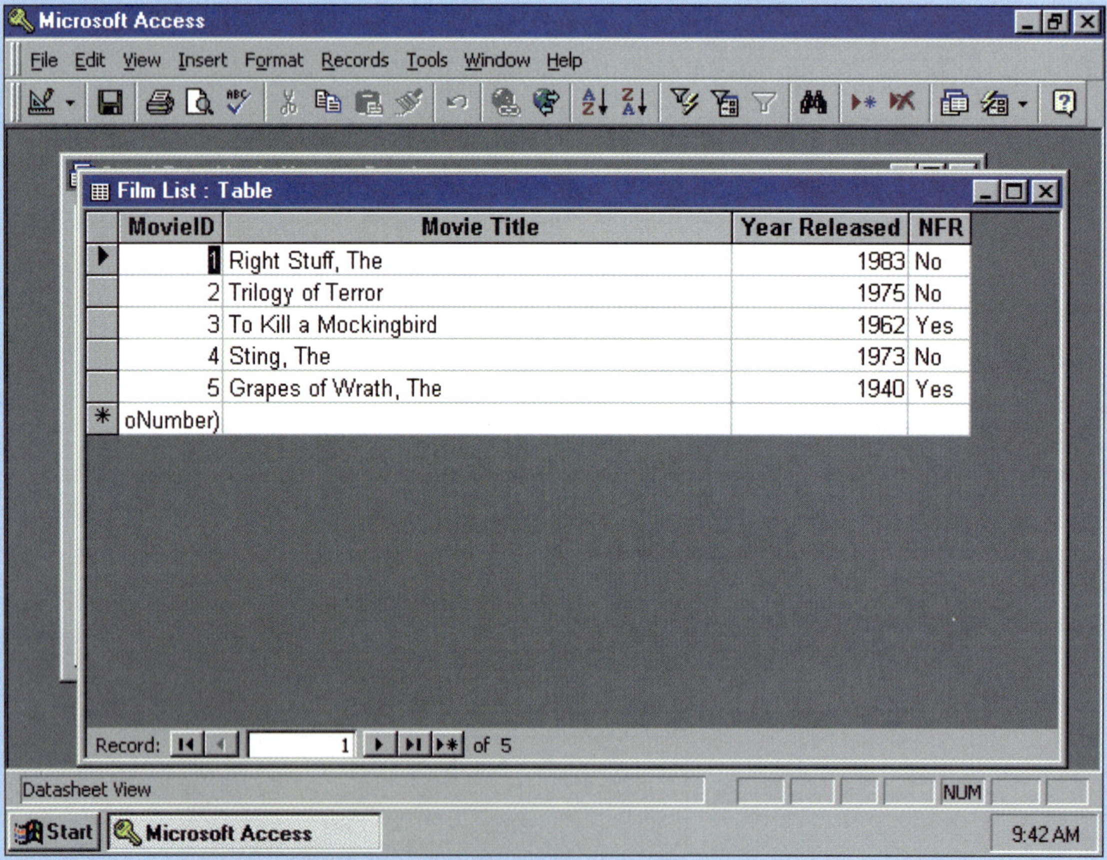

WEB WORK

4. Databases on the World Wide Web can be used to retrieve current and historical information. You work for a prestigious socialite who is interested in film preservation. She has purchased The SpeakEasy move theater where she intends to hold many festivals featuring historically important films. Using the World Wide Web, find out about the National Film Registry, which is maintained by the Library of Congress, and begin compiling films for the first festival.

To complete this independent challenge:

1. Log on to the Internet and use your browser to go to http://www.course.com. From there, click the link Student On Line Companions, then click the Microsoft Office 97 Professional Edition—Illustrated: A First Course page, then click the Access link for Unit A.
2. Use the following site to compile your data, The National Film Registry [http://1cweb.loc.gov/film/].
3. Print the National Film Registry's fact sheet.
4. Find out its current membership.
5. Using the list of films, find all the films made in the 1950's.
6. Open the SpeakEasy Movie House database on your Student Disk.
7. Open the Film List table, shown in Figure A-22.
8. Enter these films in the Film List table.
9. Save the table.
10. Preview and print the datasheet.
11. Hand in a printout of your work.

▶ Visual Workshop

Modify the existing Customers table in the Corporate Customers database on your Student Disk, then print the datasheet.

FIGURE A-23

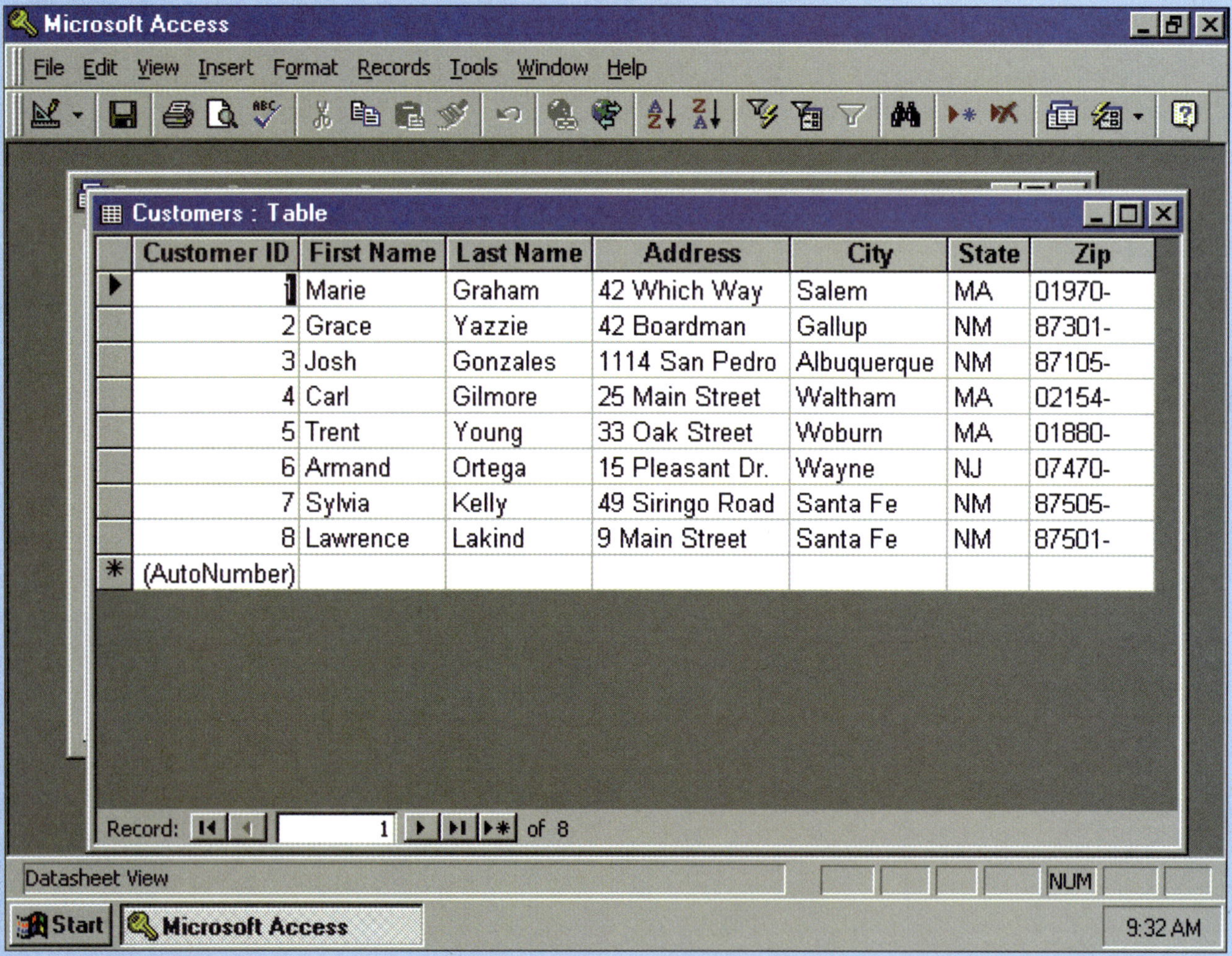

Customer ID	First Name	Last Name	Address	City	State	Zip
1	Marie	Graham	42 Which Way	Salem	MA	01970-
2	Grace	Yazzie	42 Boardman	Gallup	NM	87301-
3	Josh	Gonzales	1114 San Pedro	Albuquerque	NM	87105-
4	Carl	Gilmore	25 Main Street	Waltham	MA	02154-
5	Trent	Young	33 Oak Street	Woburn	MA	01880-
6	Armand	Ortega	15 Pleasant Dr.	Wayne	NJ	07470-
7	Sylvia	Kelly	49 Siringo Road	Santa Fe	NM	87505-
8	Lawrence	Lakind	9 Main Street	Santa Fe	NM	87501-
(AutoNumber)						

Access 97

Creating and Managing Data

Objectives

- Plan a database
- Create a table
- Modify a table
- Find records
- Sort a table
- Filter a table
- Create a simple query
- Create a complex query

Now that you are familiar with some of the basic Access features, you are ready to plan and build your own database. When you build a database, you create one or more tables containing the fields that hold the data. After you create a database, you can save, and manage the data within it. In this unit, you will learn how to find and organize data to display the results you want. You will also learn techniques for retrieving information from a table based on specified criteria. Michael wants to build and maintain a database containing information about all Nomad customers who have booked tours since 1991. The information in the database will be useful when Michael budgets for the future, plans new tours, and prepares the company's Annual Report.

Access 97

Planning a Database

Before you start entering records in the database, you need to identify the goal of the database and plan how you want data stored in it. The planning stage is when you decide how many tables the database will include and what data will be stored in each table. Although you can modify a table at any time, adding a new field after records have been entered means additional work. It's impossible to plan for all potential uses of a database, but any up-front planning makes the process go more smoothly. Michael has done some preliminary planning on how the database can be used, but he knows from experience that other Nomad employees might have additional uses for the same customer information. Michael uses the following guidelines to plan his database:

Steps

CourseHelp

The camera icon indicates there is CourseHelp available with this lesson. Click the Start button, point to Programs, point to CourseHelp, then click Access 97 Illustrated. Choose the CourseHelp that corresponds to this lesson.

1. **Determine the purpose of the database and give it a meaningful name**
   You need to store information on customers who have taken a Nomad tour. You name the database "Tour Customers," and name the table containing the customer data "Customers." You decide, for now, that the database will contain only one table because all the necessary customer information can be stored there.

2. **Determine the results, called output, that you want to see, using the information stored in the database**
   You need to sort the information in a variety of ways: alphabetically by tour name, by tour date to gauge effective scheduling dates, and by postal code for promotional mailings. You will also need to create specialized lists of customers, such as customers who took a bike tour since 1991.

3. **Collect all the information, called input, that will produce the results you want to see, talking to all the possible database users for additional ideas that might enhance the design**
   You think the current customer information form, shown in Figure B-1, is a good basis for your database table. The form provides most of the information Nomad wants to store in the database for each customer, making it a good starting point. After talking with the marketing director about targeting tours to specific age groups, you decide to add an Age field to your table.

QuickTip

Multiple database tables can be linked to one another; their information can be shared and queried.

4. **Sketch the structure of the table, including each field's data type**
   Using all the information on the original customer information form, you plan each field, the type of data each field contains (such as whether the field contains text or values to be used in calculations), and a brief description of each field's purpose. Figure B-2 is a sketch of the Customers table, which has several new fields not included in the original customer information form.

FIGURE B-1: Original customer information form

Nomad Ltd	
Customer Information Form	
Customer Name:	Ginny Braithwaite 3 Which Way, Apt. 2 Salem, MA 01970
Tour:	Road Bike
Date:	June 15, 1998

FIGURE B-2: Plan for Customers table

Fields	Data type	Description
CustomerID	Unique number for each record	Identifies each record
FirstName	Text	Customer's first name (+ optional middle initial)
LastName	Text	Customer's last name
Address	Text	Customer's street address
City	Text	Customer's city
State	Text	Customer's state
PostalCode	Text	Customer's zip code
Tour	Text	Type of tour
Date	Date/Time	Starting date of tour
Age	Number	Customer's age

CLUES TO USE

Creating a backup

The information in your database is very important. You should protect your investment of time spent planning the database and entering data in it by creating backup copies of the database file. The database file, which has the extension .MDB, should be copied to a disk or tape on a daily or weekly basis.

Creating a Table

After planning the structure of the database, the next step is to create the database file, which contains all the objects such as tables, forms, reports, and queries that will be used to enter and manipulate the data. When you create a database, you assign it a name. Once the file is created, you are ready to create the table (or tables) in the database. Access offers several methods for creating a table. It is easy to use the Access **Table Wizard**, which guides you through the process of creating a simple table, prompting you to choose the fields and options for your table. With his plan complete, Michael is ready to create the Tour Customers database file; he uses the Table Wizard to create his Customers table.

Steps 1 2 3 4

1. Start Access, click the **Blank Database option button** in the Create a New Database Using section of the dialog box, then click **OK**
   The File New Database dialog box opens.
2. Type **Tour Customers** in the File name text box, insert your Student Disk in the disk drive, click the **Save in list arrow**, click the appropriate drive, then click **Create**
   The Tour Customers database file is saved on your Student Disk. The Database window opens, displaying the new, empty database, as shown in Figure B-3.
3. In the Tour Customers: Database window, verify that the **Tables tab** is selected, then click **New**
   The New Table dialog box opens. You will use the Table Wizard to create the new table.
4. Click **Table Wizard**, then click **OK**
   The Table Wizard dialog box opens. The Table Wizard offers 25 business and 20 personal sample tables from which you can select sample fields. You will choose fields from the Customers sample table to include in your Customers table.
5. Make sure the **Business option button** is selected, click **Customers** in the Sample Tables list box, click **CustomerID** in the Sample Fields list box, then click the **Single Field button** [>]
   The CustomerID field is included in the Fields in my new table box. You proceed to add all the necessary fields for the table.
6. Repeat Step 5 to enter the following fields in the new table: **ContactFirstName**, **ContactLastName**, **BillingAddress**, **City**, **StateOrProvince**, and **PostalCode**
   Compare your Table Wizard dialog box to Figure B-4. Because you will only be entering states (not provinces) you decide to rename that field.
7. Click **StateOrProvince** in the Fields in my new table box, click **Rename Field**, type **State**, then click **OK**
8. Click **Next**
   The second Table Wizard dialog box opens. You intended to name the table "Customers," which Access suggests in this dialog box. You also want Access to set the **primary key**, a field that qualifies each record as unique. If you do not specify a primary key, Access will assign one for you.
9. Make sure the "Yes" option button is selected, click **Next**, click the **Modify the table design option button**, shown in Figure B-5, then click **Finish**
   The table opens in Design view, which allows you to add, delete, or modify the table's structure.

QuickTip

If Access is already running, you can click the New Database button on the Database toolbar to create a database.

Trouble?

If you inadvertently add the wrong sample field while in the first Table Wizard dialog box, select the field then click the Remove Field button [<].

FIGURE B-3: Tour Customers database window

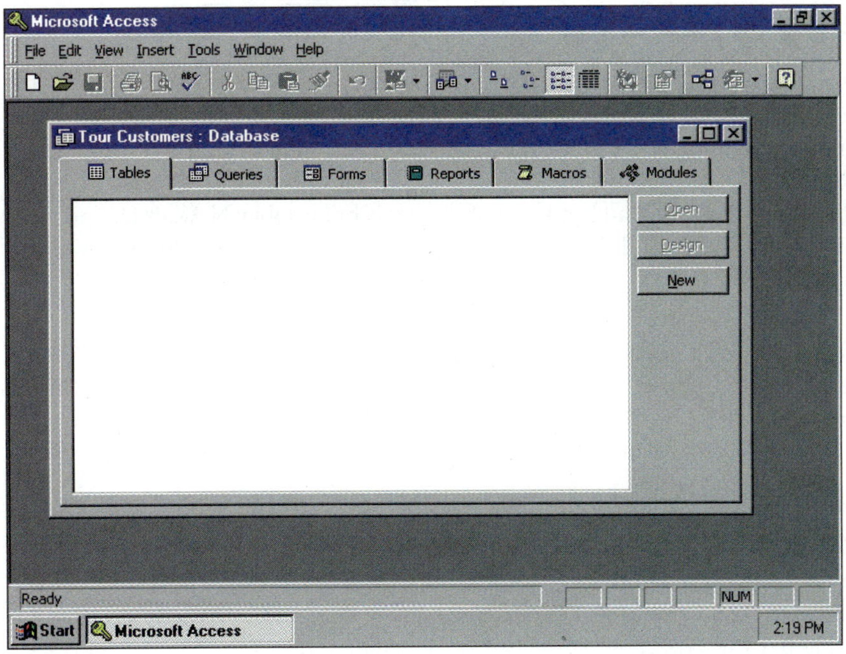

FIGURE B-4: Completed Fields in my new table list

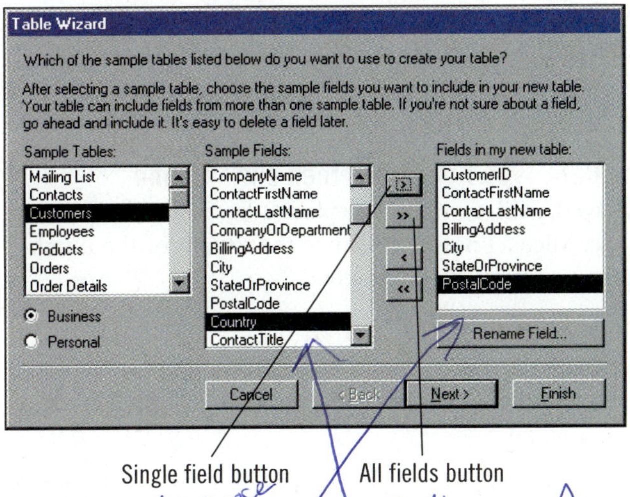

FIGURE B-5: Third Table Wizard dialog box

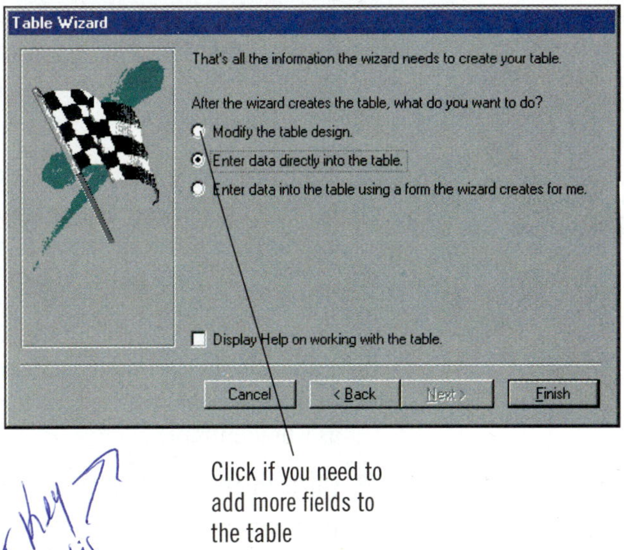

CLUES TO USE

Creating a table manually

You can create a table manually, without using the Table Wizard, by clicking the Datasheet View or Design View button in the New Table dialog box; you create the field names and their properties as you need them to store your specific data. Field names can contain up to 64 characters including letters, numbers, spaces, and some special characters. You might want to create a table manually if your application is unique or your fields are unusual.

Access 97

Access 97

Modifying a Table

After creating a table, you can modify it in **Design view**. Design view allows you to modify the structure of a table by adding and deleting fields, and adding **field descriptions** which clarify the purpose or function of a field and appear in the status bar when you enter data. You can also define other **field properties**, such as the number of decimal places in a number field. Using the Table Wizard, Michael was able to add all but three of the fields in his table. Now, in Design view, he'll add the three remaining fields, add field descriptions, and modify certain field properties.

Steps

1. Make sure the "Customers" table is open in Design view, as shown in Figure B-6
   Notice the row selectors at the left edge of the table. The selectors can contain **indicators**, such as the primary key indicator. You begin by adding a new field, "Tour," in the first available blank row. This field will identify the type of tour taken by each Nomad customer.

2. Scroll the window until the first blank row is visible, click in the **Field Name box** in this row (under PostalCode), type **Tour**, then press **[Enter]**
   The Data Type field becomes highlighted and displays the word "Text." The Tour field will contain text information, so you accept the suggested data type and enter a description for the field. See Table B-1 for a description of the available data types.

3. Press **[Enter]**, type **Type of tour** in the Description column, then press **[Enter]**
   The next field Michael enters is a date field, which will contain the date the tour was taken. A date field has a data type of Date/Time.

4. Type **Date**, press **[Enter]**, click the **Data Type list arrow**, click **Date/Time**, press **[Enter]**, type **Starting date of tour** in the Description column, then press **[Enter]**
   The last field you must enter is the Age field. This field will contain the age of the tour participant.

5. Type **Age**, press **[Enter]**, click the **Data Type list arrow**, then click **Number**
   By default, number fields are displayed with two decimal places. Because this is not an appropriate format for a person's age, Michael needs to change the format of the number. Use [F6] to move to the Field Properties section of the window.

6. Press **[F6]** to switch panes to the **Field Properties section**
   Currently the Decimal Places box displays the option "Auto," which specifies the default two decimal places. You need to change the number of decimal places so that the ages will appear as whole numbers.

7. Click in the **Decimal Places box**, click the **list arrow**, then click **0** to specify whole numbers
   Next you need to add a description for the Age field you just entered.

8. Press **[F6]** to switch panes, press **[Enter]**, then type **Enter the Customer's age at the time of the tour** in the Description column
   Next you add the descriptions for each of the remaining fields.

9. Click in the **CustomerID Description box**, type **Identification number**, then click in each of the field name Description boxes and add a description for the six fields as shown in Figure B-7

QuickTip

Type "d" in the Data Type field for a Date/Time field, type "n" in the Data Type field for a number field. See Table B-1 for other keyboard shortcuts to enter data types.

Time To

- Save
- Close

FIGURE B-6: Customers Table in Design view

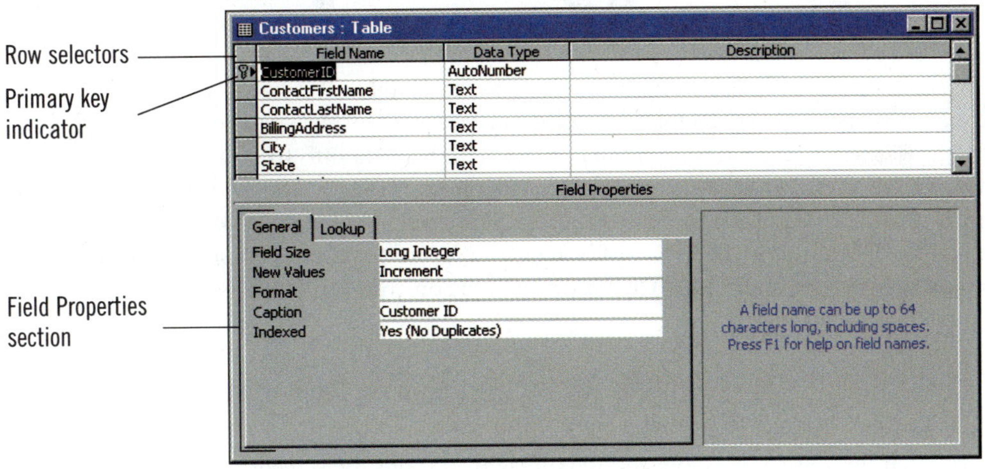

THESE Will show up as headings on your Report.

FIGURE B-7: Field descriptions for Customers Table

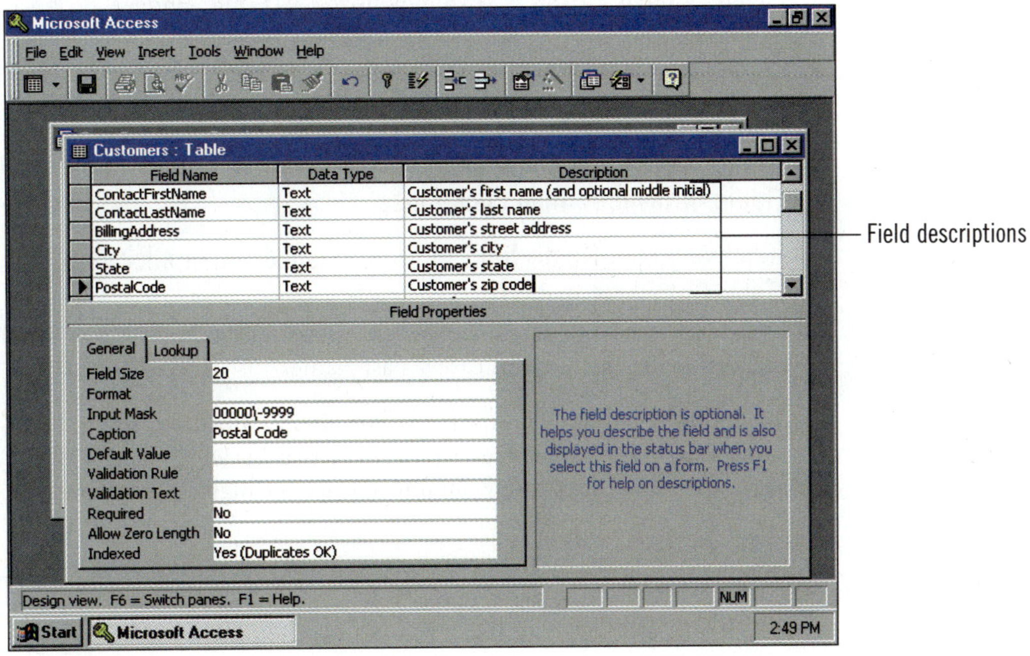

TABLE B-1: Available Data Types

data type	description	data type shortcuts
Text	Text or a combination of text and numbers that don't require calculations	T
Memo	Lengthy text or a combination of text and numbers	M
Number	Numeric data to be used in calculations	N
Date/Time	Date and time values	D
Currency	Currency values and numeric data used in calculations	C
Yes/No	Fields that can contain only one of two values	Y
OLE object	An object (such as a Word document) that is linked or embedded in an Access table	O
AutoNumber	Unique sequential number that Access assigns to each new record; can't be edited	A
Lookup Wizard	Creates a field that allows you to choose a value from another table or from a list of values	L

Finding Records

Finding records in a table is an important database task. Table B-2 lists a variety of keyboard shortcuts used to navigate a table. In addition, you can locate specific records using the datasheet. Michael has been busy entering all his data into the Customers table in the database. He also renamed the field names to take up less room on the data sheet. He wants to locate the record for Carol Smith because her name was entered incorrectly; he needs to change the last name to "Smithers." Then he needs to enter a record for a new customer. Michael's work has been saved for you in the Tour Customer Data file on your Student Disk.

Steps

1. Click the **Open Database button** on the Database toolbar, click **Tour Customer Data** on your Student Disk, then click **Open**
   Next, open the Customers table and maximize it so it fills the screen.
2. Click the **Tables tab** in the Database window, click **Customers**, click **Open**, then click the **Maximize button** to maximize the table window
   Access displays the Customers table, which contains 30 records, as shown in Figure B-8. You will use the Table Datasheet toolbar to change Carol Smith's last name to "Smithers." If the Table Datasheet toolbar is not displayed, continue to Step 3, otherwise skip to Step 4.
3. Click **View** on the menu bar, click **Toolbars** to display the Toolbars dialog box, click **Table Datasheet**, then click **Close**
4. Click any **Last Name field** in the datasheet, then click the **Find button** on the Table Datasheet toolbar
   The Find in field dialog box opens, as shown in Figure B-9. By default Access searches the current field, which in this case is Last Name.
5. Type **Smith** in the Find What text box, click **Find Next**, then click **Close**
   Access highlights the name "Smith" in record 11, which is now the current record, for the customer Carol Smith. You can now replace the highlighted name with the correct name.
6. Type **Smithers**
   Next you want to see the last record in the table before you enter the new record.
7. Click **Edit** on the menu bar, click **Go To**, then click **Last**
   The last name of the customer in the last record is selected. Next, you must enter the new record.
8. Click the **New Record button** on the Table Datasheet toolbar, press **[Tab]**, then enter the following data in record 31
   Elizabeth Michaels, Mt. Bike, 6/20/98, 57 Beechwood Drive, Wayne, NJ, 07470, 39
   The new record has been added to the table.

Time To
Save

TABLE B-2: Keystrokes for navigating a datasheet

keys	actions	keys	actions
[↑], [↓], [←], [→]	Move one field in the direction indicated	[Tab]	Move to next field in current record
[F5]	Move to Record number box on the horizontal scroll bar, then type number of record to go to	[Shift][Tab]	Move to previous field in current record
[Home]	Move to first field in current record	[Ctrl][Home]	Move to first field in first record
[End]	Move to last field in current record	[Ctrl][End]	Move to last field in last record
		[Ctrl][=]	Move to first blank record

FIGURE B-8: Customers table

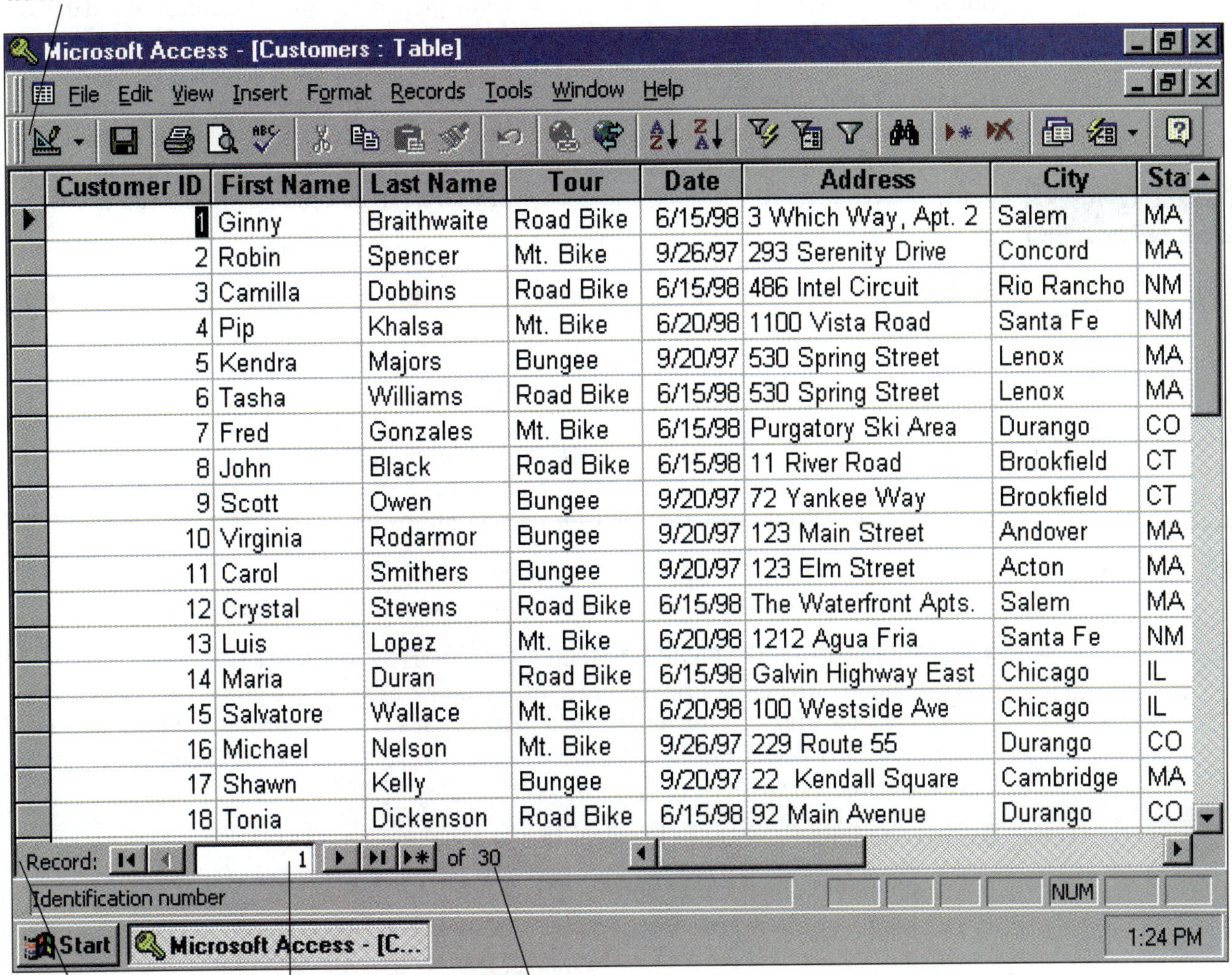

Customer ID	First Name	Last Name	Tour	Date	Address	City	Sta
1	Ginny	Braithwaite	Road Bike	6/15/98	3 Which Way, Apt. 2	Salem	MA
2	Robin	Spencer	Mt. Bike	9/26/97	293 Serenity Drive	Concord	MA
3	Camilla	Dobbins	Road Bike	6/15/98	486 Intel Circuit	Rio Rancho	NM
4	Pip	Khalsa	Mt. Bike	6/20/98	1100 Vista Road	Santa Fe	NM
5	Kendra	Majors	Bungee	9/20/97	530 Spring Street	Lenox	MA
6	Tasha	Williams	Road Bike	6/15/98	530 Spring Street	Lenox	MA
7	Fred	Gonzales	Mt. Bike	6/15/98	Purgatory Ski Area	Durango	CO
8	John	Black	Road Bike	6/15/98	11 River Road	Brookfield	CT
9	Scott	Owen	Bungee	9/20/97	72 Yankee Way	Brookfield	CT
10	Virginia	Rodarmor	Bungee	9/20/97	123 Main Street	Andover	MA
11	Carol	Smithers	Bungee	9/20/97	123 Elm Street	Acton	MA
12	Crystal	Stevens	Road Bike	6/15/98	The Waterfront Apts.	Salem	MA
13	Luis	Lopez	Mt. Bike	6/20/98	1212 Agua Fria	Santa Fe	NM
14	Maria	Duran	Road Bike	6/15/98	Galvin Highway East	Chicago	IL
15	Salvatore	Wallace	Mt. Bike	6/20/98	100 Westside Ave	Chicago	IL
16	Michael	Nelson	Mt. Bike	9/26/97	229 Route 55	Durango	CO
17	Shawn	Kelly	Bungee	9/20/97	22 Kendall Square	Cambridge	MA
18	Tonia	Dickenson	Road Bike	6/15/98	92 Main Avenue	Durango	CO

DESIGN VIEW –

S* will show all names with a beginning of "S"

SM?T = Dont use much

CLUES TO USE

Using wildcards in Find

Wildcards are symbols you can use as substitutes for characters in text to find any records matching your entry. Access uses three wildcards: the asterisk (*) represents any group of characters, the question mark (?) stands for any single character, and the pound sign (#) stands for a single number digit. For example, to find any word beginning with S, type "s*" in the Find What text box.

FIGURE B-9: Find in field dialog box

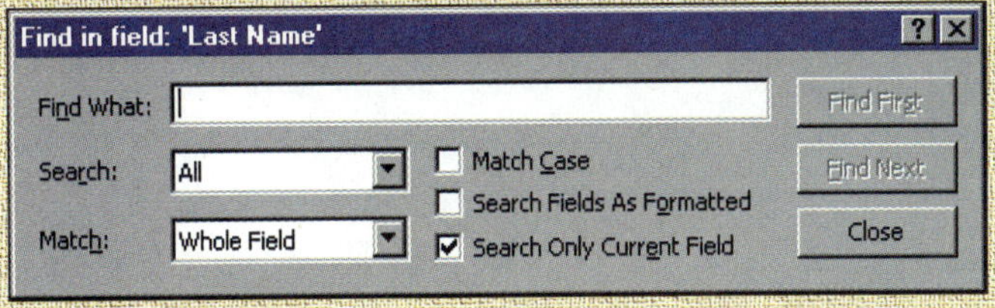

Access 97

Sorting a Table

The ability to sort information in a table is one of the most powerful features of a database. **Sorting** is an easy way of organizing records according to the contents of a field. For example, you might want to see all records in alphabetical order by last name. You can sort records in **ascending order** (alphabetically from A to Z, numerically from 0 to 9), or in **descending order** (alphabetically from Z to A, numerically from 9 to 0). Michael sorts his table in a variety of ways, depending on the task he needs to perform. His most common tasks require a list sorted in ascending order by tour, and another list sorted in descending order by date.

Steps

CourseHelp

The camera icon indicates that there is a CourseHelp available with this lesson. Click the Start button, point to Programs, point to CourseHelp, then click Access 97 Illustrated. Choose the CourseHelp entitled Sorting records.

1. Position the cursor on the **Tour field column head**, when the pointer looks like ↓, click the **Tour field name**

   The Tour column is selected. The table will be sorted by tour. In addition to clicking the Tour field name to select the field, you can also click any record's Tour field.

2. Click the **Sort Ascending button** on the Table Datasheet toolbar

   The table is sorted alphabetically in ascending order by tour name, as shown in Figure B-10. You decide to print this sorted table for reference using the default settings.

3. Click the **Print button** on the Table Datasheet toolbar

   The sorted datasheet prints. You want to return the table to its original order.

4. Click **Records** on the menu bar, then click **Remove Filter/Sort**

   The table returns to its original order in ascending order by Customer ID. You can also return a table with an AutoNumber field to its original order by sorting that field in ascending order. You decide to sort the records in descending order by the Date field to see the enrollment for each tour.

5. Click the **Date field name** to select the Date column

6. Click the **Sort Descending button** on the Table Datasheet toolbar

   The records are sorted from most recent to least recent date, as shown in Figure B-11. The sorted list shows that the mid-June bike tour has a higher enrollment than the tour a week later. You want to print the sorted table.

7. Click the **Print button** on the Table Datasheet toolbar

   Next you return the table to its original order.

8. Click **Records** on the menu bar, then click **Remove Filter/Sort**

FIGURE B-10: Table sorted in ascending order by Tour field

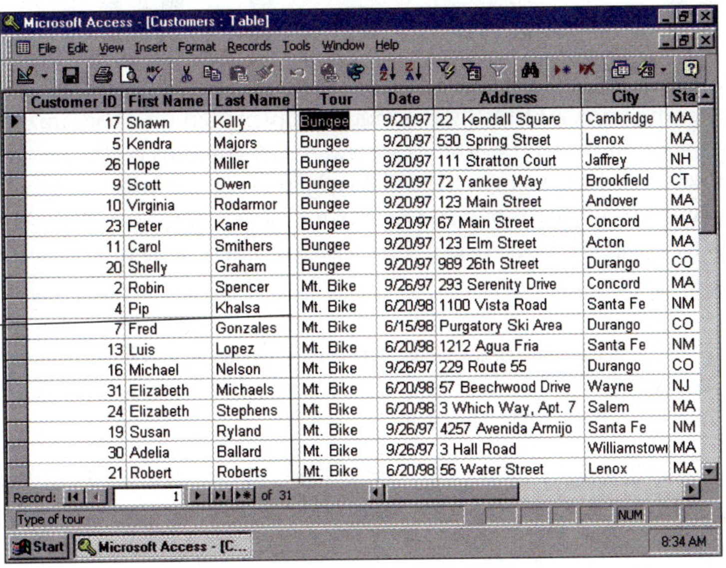

Customer ID	First Name	Last Name	Tour	Date	Address	City	Sta
17	Shawn	Kelly	Bungee	9/20/97	22 Kendall Square	Cambridge	MA
5	Kendra	Majors	Bungee	9/20/97	530 Spring Street	Lenox	MA
26	Hope	Miller	Bungee	9/20/97	111 Stratton Court	Jaffrey	NH
9	Scott	Owen	Bungee	9/20/97	72 Yankee Way	Brookfield	CT
10	Virginia	Rodarmor	Bungee	9/20/97	123 Main Street	Andover	MA
23	Peter	Kane	Bungee	9/20/97	67 Main Street	Concord	MA
11	Carol	Smithers	Bungee	9/20/97	123 Elm Street	Acton	MA
20	Shelly	Graham	Bungee	9/20/97	989 26th Street	Durango	CO
2	Robin	Spencer	Mt. Bike	9/26/97	293 Serenity Drive	Concord	MA
4	Pip	Khalsa	Mt. Bike	6/20/98	1100 Vista Road	Santa Fe	NM
7	Fred	Gonzales	Mt. Bike	6/15/98	Purgatory Ski Area	Durango	CO
13	Luis	Lopez	Mt. Bike	6/20/98	1212 Agua Fria	Santa Fe	NM
16	Michael	Nelson	Mt. Bike	9/26/97	229 Route 55	Durango	CO
31	Elizabeth	Michaels	Mt. Bike	6/20/98	57 Beechwood Drive	Wayne	NJ
24	Elizabeth	Stephens	Mt. Bike	6/20/98	3 Which Way, Apt. 7	Salem	MA
19	Susan	Ryland	Mt. Bike	9/26/97	4257 Avenida Armijo	Santa Fe	NM
30	Adelia	Ballard	Mt. Bike	9/26/97	3 Hall Road	Williamstow	MA
21	Robert	Roberts	Mt. Bike	6/20/98	56 Water Street	Lenox	MA

Records sorted by Tour

FIGURE B-11: Table sorted in descending order by Date field

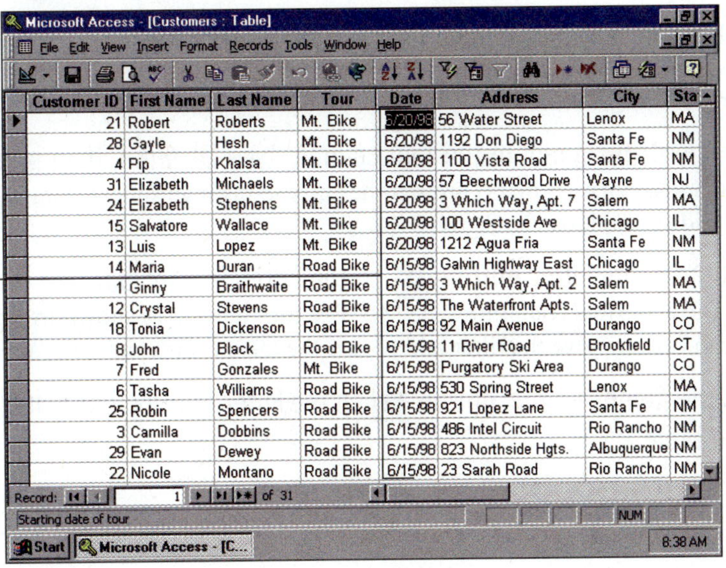

Customer ID	First Name	Last Name	Tour	Date	Address	City	Sta
21	Robert	Roberts	Mt. Bike	6/20/98	56 Water Street	Lenox	MA
28	Gayle	Hesh	Mt. Bike	6/20/98	1192 Don Diego	Santa Fe	NM
4	Pip	Khalsa	Mt. Bike	6/20/98	1100 Vista Road	Santa Fe	NM
31	Elizabeth	Michaels	Mt. Bike	6/20/98	57 Beechwood Drive	Wayne	NJ
24	Elizabeth	Stephens	Mt. Bike	6/20/98	3 Which Way, Apt. 7	Salem	MA
15	Salvatore	Wallace	Mt. Bike	6/20/98	100 Westside Ave	Chicago	IL
13	Luis	Lopez	Mt. Bike	6/20/98	1212 Agua Fria	Santa Fe	NM
14	Maria	Duran	Road Bike	6/15/98	Galvin Highway East	Chicago	IL
1	Ginny	Braithwaite	Road Bike	6/15/98	3 Which Way, Apt. 2	Salem	MA
12	Crystal	Stevens	Road Bike	6/15/98	The Waterfront Apts.	Salem	MA
18	Tonia	Dickenson	Road Bike	6/15/98	92 Main Avenue	Durango	CO
8	John	Black	Road Bike	6/15/98	11 River Road	Brookfield	CT
7	Fred	Gonzales	Mt. Bike	6/15/98	Purgatory Ski Area	Durango	CO
6	Tasha	Williams	Road Bike	6/15/98	530 Spring Street	Lenox	MA
25	Robin	Spencers	Road Bike	6/15/98	921 Lopez Lane	Santa Fe	NM
3	Camilla	Dobbins	Road Bike	6/15/98	486 Intel Circuit	Rio Rancho	NM
29	Evan	Dewey	Road Bike	6/15/98	823 Northside Hgts.	Albuquerque	NM
22	Nicole	Montano	Road Bike	6/15/98	23 Sarah Road	Rio Rancho	NM

Records sorted in descending order by Date

Access 97

CLUES TO USE

Using the menu bar to sort

In addition to using buttons on the Table Datasheet toolbar, you can also sort using the menu bar. After you select the field you want to sort, click Records on the menu bar, then click Sort. Click either Ascending or Descending on the Sort menu, shown in Figure B-12.

FIGURE B-12: Sort menu

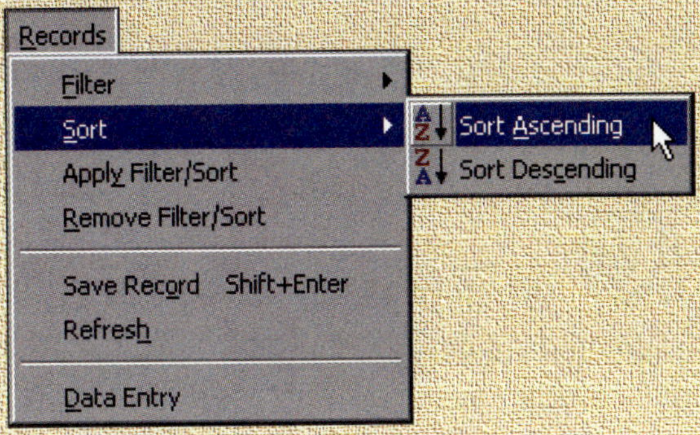

Access 97

Filtering a Table

Sorting allows you to manipulate table records in a simple way and to display them in ascending or descending order. **Filtering** is a more complex method of organizing records, where you define the fields on which the table is sorted. A sort contains all the records in a table, whereas a filter shows only those records that qualify, based on your **criteria**. Qualifying records display in a temporary view that looks and acts like a table. Often, Michael needs a list of customers by a specific tour. He can filter the Customers table to obtain this list.

Steps

1. **Make sure the Customers table is open, with all records displayed**
   You want to narrow the number of records displayed so you can see only those records for customers who took a Mt. Bike tour.

2. **Click Records on the menu bar, click Filter, click Advanced Filter/Sort, then click the Clear Grid button from the Filter/Sort toolbar to clear the grid of any preexisting criteria**
   The Filter window opens, as shown in Figure B-13. The Filter window consists of two areas: the field list on top, containing all the fields in the table, and the filter grid on the bottom, where you specify the criteria for the filter. The toolbar displayed is the Filter/Sort toolbar. You want to create a filter to show a list of all the customers who took a Mt. Bike tour.

3. **Double-click Tour in the field list**
   Access places the Tour field in the first empty Field cell in the filter grid. Next, you define the criteria for the Tour field.

4. **Click the Criteria cell in the Tour column, type Mt. Bike, then press [Enter]**
   Access adds quotation marks around the entry to distinguish text from values. Your completed filter grid should look like Figure B-14.

5. **Click the Apply Filter button on the Filter/Sort toolbar**
   Only those records containing the Mt. Bike tour appear, as shown in Figure B-15. You can now remove the filter and return the table to its original order.

6. **Click the Remove Filter button on the Filter/Sort toolbar to include all the records in the table**

Trouble?

If the grid is not cleared of any previous entries, your filter may get erroneous results.

CourseHelp

If you have trouble with the concepts in this lesson, be sure to view the CourseHelp entitled Filtering Records.

Time To

Save

Clues to Use

When to use a filter

A filter is temporary and cannot be saved; however, you can print the results of a filter just as you print any datasheet. A filter is best used to narrow the focus of the records temporarily in the current table.

FIGURE B-13: Filter window for the Customers table

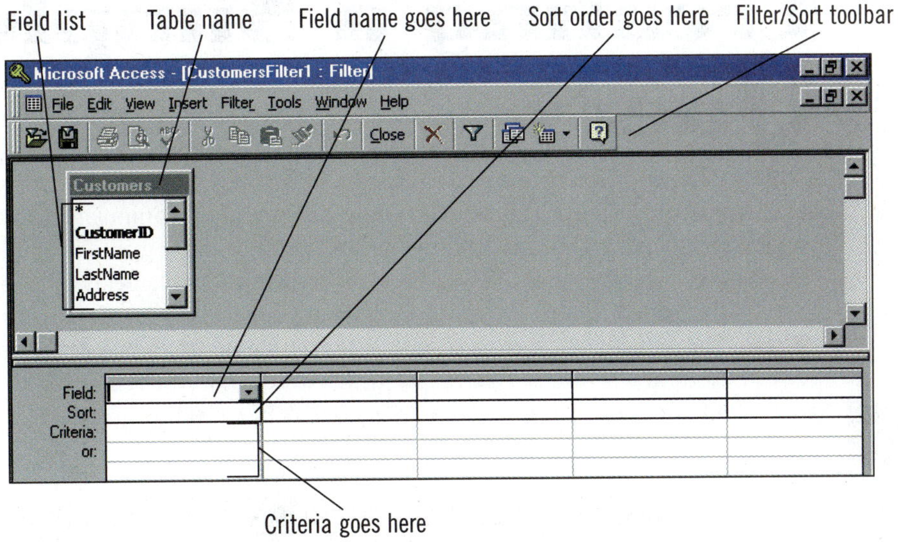

FIGURE B-14: Completed filter grid

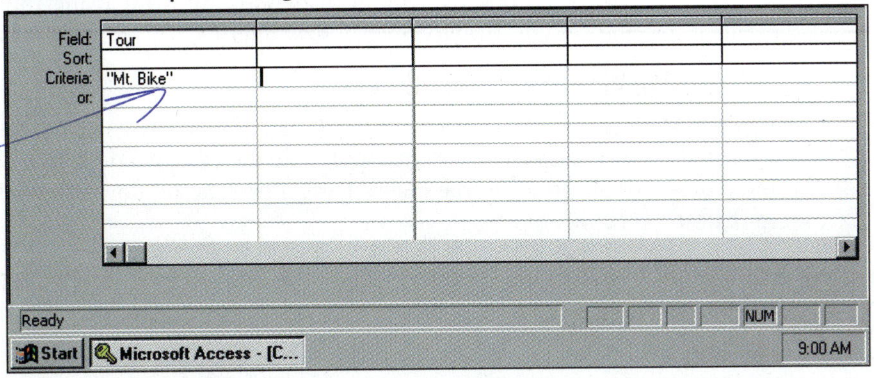

oR

M*

FIGURE B-15: Filtered table records

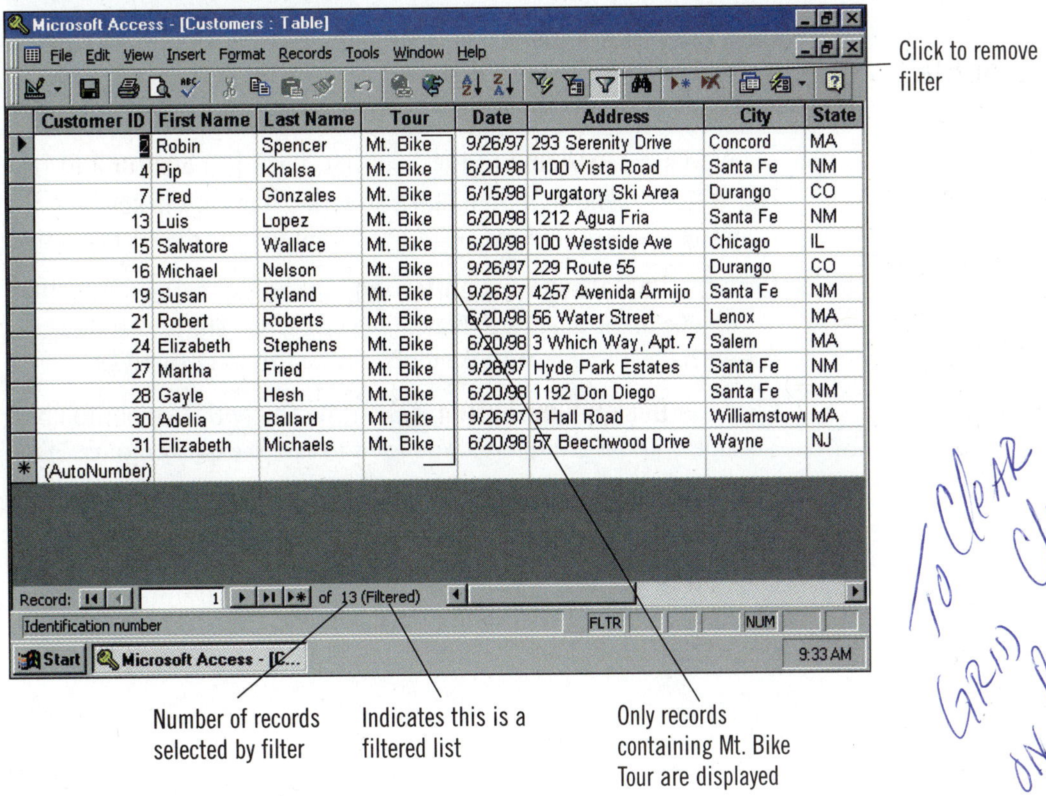

To Clear GRID click on Red X

Access 97

Access 97

Creating a Simple Query

A **query** is a set of restrictions you place on a database table by specifying criteria to retrieve qualifying records. Unlike a filter, which only allows you to manipulate data temporarily, a query can be saved so that you do not have to recreate the fields in the grid. The query results also display only the fields you have specified, rather than showing all table fields. The most commonly used query is the **select query**, in which records are collected, viewed, and can be modified later. The Nomad employee responsible for setting up Road Bike tours often asks Michael for a list of customers who have participated in these tours. Michael needs to create a query that displays only the names of all Road Bike customers in ascending order.

Steps

1. Click the **New Object button list arrow** on the Table Datasheet toolbar, then click **Query** on the pull-down palette
   The New Query dialog box opens and displays options for using the Query Wizard. You decide to use the Design View to create a new query.
2. Click **Design View**, then click **OK**
   The Select Query window opens, as shown in Figure B-16. The Query Design toolbar provides more buttons than does the Filter/Sort toolbar in the Filter window. You add the first field, sort, and criteria specifications to the Query Design grid. Scroll down the field list to display the **Tour field**.
3. Double-click **Tour** in the field list, then click the checked **Show box** in the grid to turn off the checkmark
   The Tour field name appears in the Field cell in the query grid, and the Table field displays the location of the field: the Customers table. The Show box indicates that the field will not be displayed in the query results. Next, specify the criteria for the query.
4. Click the **Criteria cell** in the Tour column, type **Road Bike**, then press **[Enter]**
   You want the query results to show the last name, in ascending order, of each customer who participated in a Road Bike tour.
5. Double-click **LastName** in the field list, click the **Sort cell** in the LastName column, type **a** (for ascending), then make sure the Show box is selected for the LastName field
   Compare your grid to Figure B-17. You want to view the results of the query.
6. Click the **Datasheet View button** on the Query Design toolbar
   The results of the query are shown in Figure B-18. The results show the last names of the 10 customers that took Road Bike tours. You return to Design View.
7. Click the **Design View button** on the Query Datasheet toolbar
   The query grid is redisplayed. You want to save the query results.
8. Click the **Save button** on the Query Design toolbar, type **Road Bike customers** in the Query Name text box of the Save As dialog box, as shown in Figure B-19, then click **OK**
   The query is saved as part of the database file.

Trouble?

If you enter a field in the query grid in error, select the field then press [Delete] to delete it.

Trouble?

For a single table query, entries in the grid are not case sensitive: it doesn't matter if you use upper or lower case characters. Field criteria entered in the query grid for linked tables, however, are case sensitive.

FIGURE B-16: Select Query window

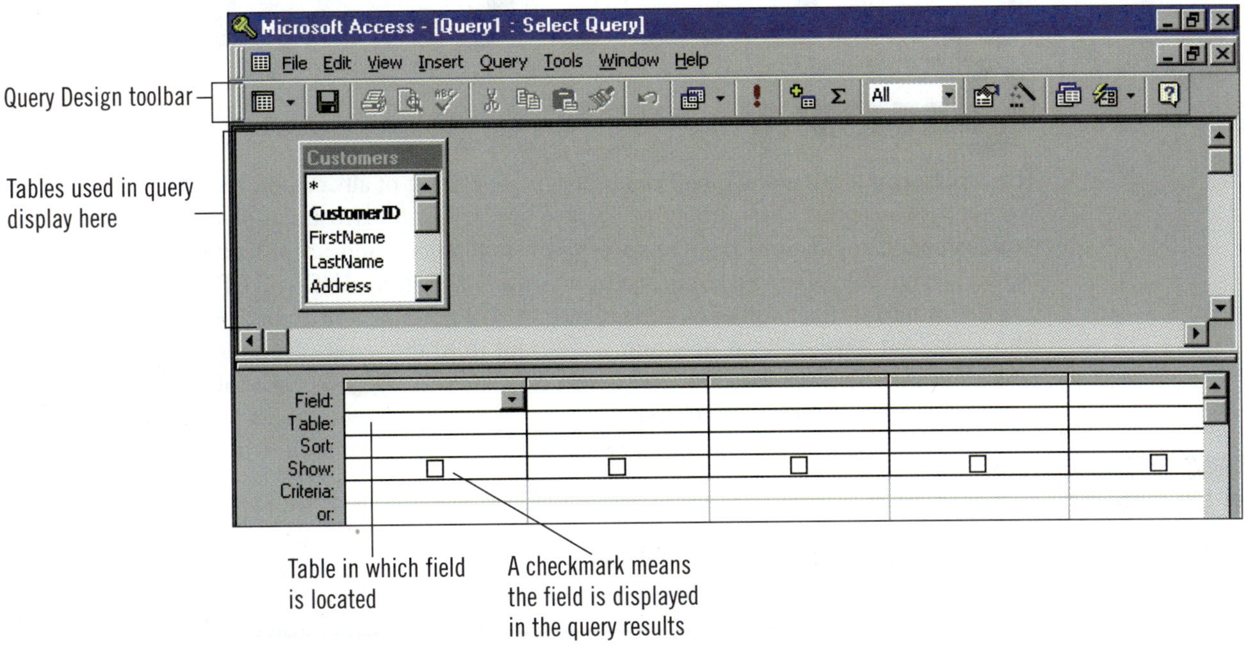

FIGURE B-17: Sample query grid

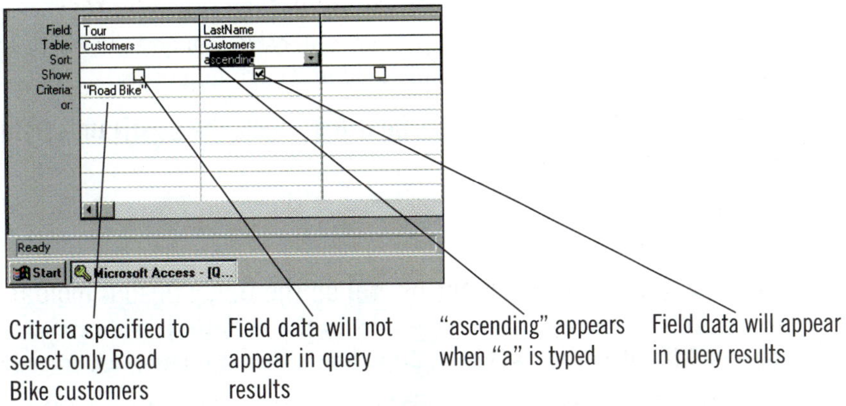

FIGURE B-18: Results of simple query

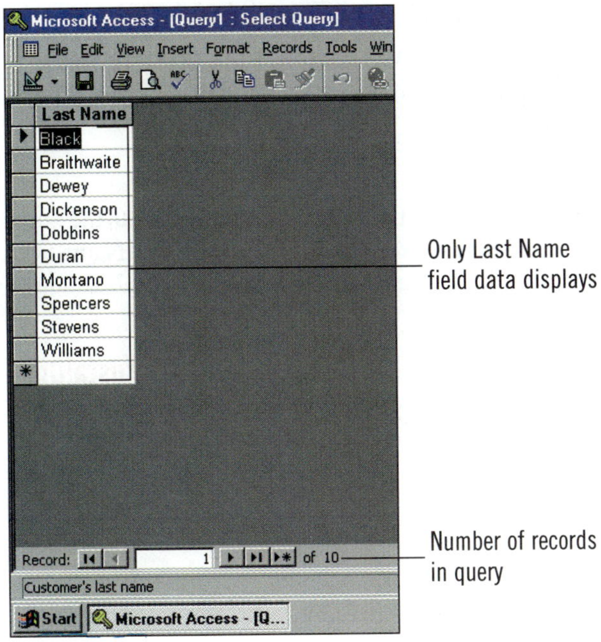

FIGURE B-19: Save As dialog box for query

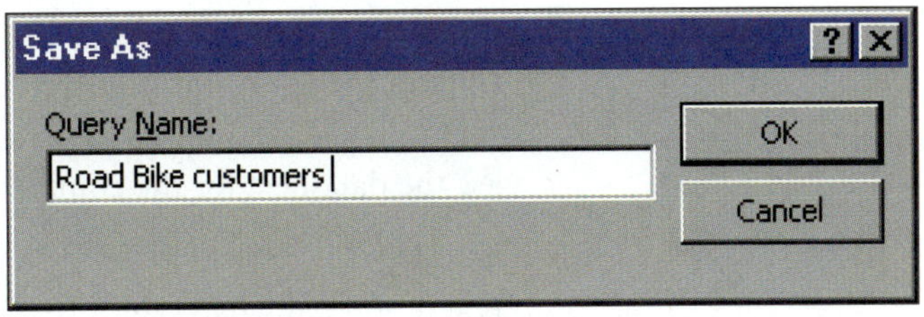

Access 97

Access 97

Creating a Complex Query

The criteria you specify for a query can be as simple as a list of all customer names, or as complex as a list of all customers over the age of 30, who live in New Mexico and took a tour in June. Using **expressions**, combinations of field names, constant values, and arithmetic operators, you can restrict the number of records returned by a query. The criteria **AND** and **OR** can also be used to broaden or narrow the number of selected records. For example, the result of a query of customers who took a Mt. Bike or Road Bike tour is different from the result of a query of customers who took a Mt. Bike or Road Bike tour and live in New Mexico. Each month, Michael wants to see a list of all customers, in descending order by last name, who took a Mt. Bike or Road Bike tour and who have a postal code greater than 50000. He decides to modify the previous query and save it as a new query.

Steps

1. Click the **Show box** for the Tour field
   You want to display the records of customers who took either a Mt. Bike or Road Bike tour, so you need to display the Tour field. You modify the current entry in the Criteria cell to include the second tour in the "or" field beneath the Criteria cell.

2. Click the **Tour field or cell**, type **Mt. Bike**, then press **[Enter]**
   The entry "Mt. Bike" appears in the "or" cell. Next, you add the FirstName to the query grid and you want to sort the LastName field in descending order.

3. Double-click **FirstName** in the field list, click the LastName field's **Sort list arrow**, then click **Descending**
   The query design changes are specified as shown in Figure B-20. You decide to view the datasheet.

4. Click the **Datasheet View button** on the Query Design toolbar
   The results of the query are displayed in the datasheet. Notice that customers who took either a Mt. Bike or Road Bike tour are listed. The last names are sorted in descending order.

5. Click the **Design View button** on the Query Datasheet toolbar
   The query grid is redisplayed. You add the PostalCode field and its criteria to the query grid.

6. Double-click **PostalCode** in the field list, click its **Criteria cell**, type **>50000**, press **[↓]** to enter the criteria in the "or" criteria cell, type **>50000**, then press **[Enter]**
   If the Tour field scrolls out of view, scroll the window to view the completed query grid. You view the datasheet for the completed query.

7. Click
   Because you wanted to view bike tour customers only with Postal codes above 50000, the query results are narrowed from 23 records to 14, and the query is being sorted by the LastName field, as shown in Figure B-21. Next, you save the modified query within the current database so you can view the results at any time.

8. Click **File** on the menu bar, click **Save As/Export**, type **Bike Tours AND PostalCode >50000** in the New Name text box as shown in Figure B-22, then click **OK**
   The new query is saved for future use. You close the query and the table and then exit Access.

9. Close and exit Access.

QuickTip

Arithmetic operators used in criteria when creating simple or complex queries are greater than (>), less than (<), equals (=), greater than or equal to (>=), less than or equal to (<=), and not equal to (<>).

QuickTip

You can save a filter as a query by choosing Save As Query from the File menu (while in the Filter window), then name the query and click [OK].

FIGURE B-20: "Or" specification in query grid

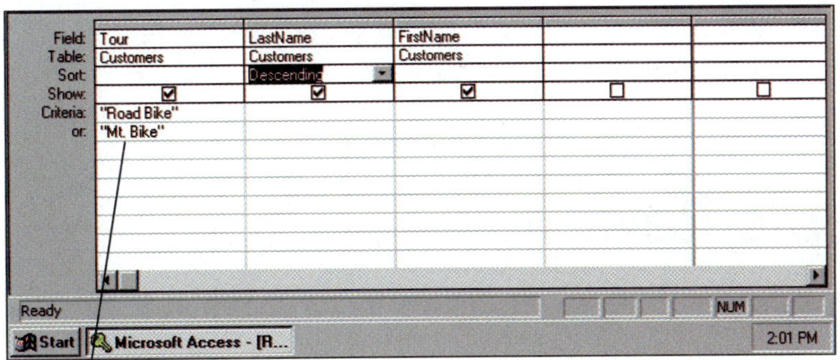

"Or" specification used in criteria

FIGURE B-21: Results of complex query

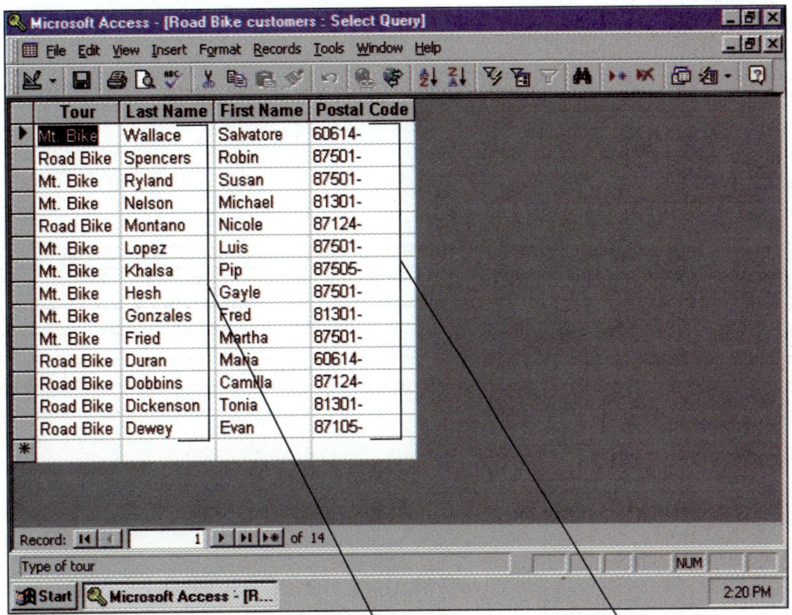

Descending order by LastName

All Postal Codes greater than 50000

FIGURE B-22: Save As/Export dialog box

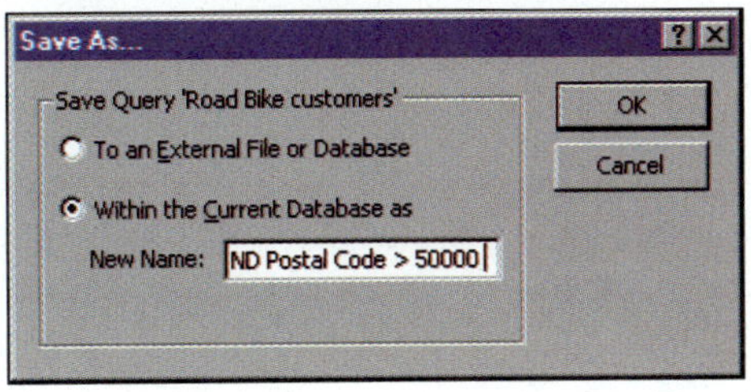

CLUES TO USE

Using And and Or to affect query results

Using the Or criteria generally results in broader query results, as either of the criteria need to be true in order for a record to be selected. The And criteria demands that both criteria be true in order for a record to be selected.

Practice

Concepts Review

Label each of the elements of the select Query window shown in Figure B-23.

FIGURE B-23

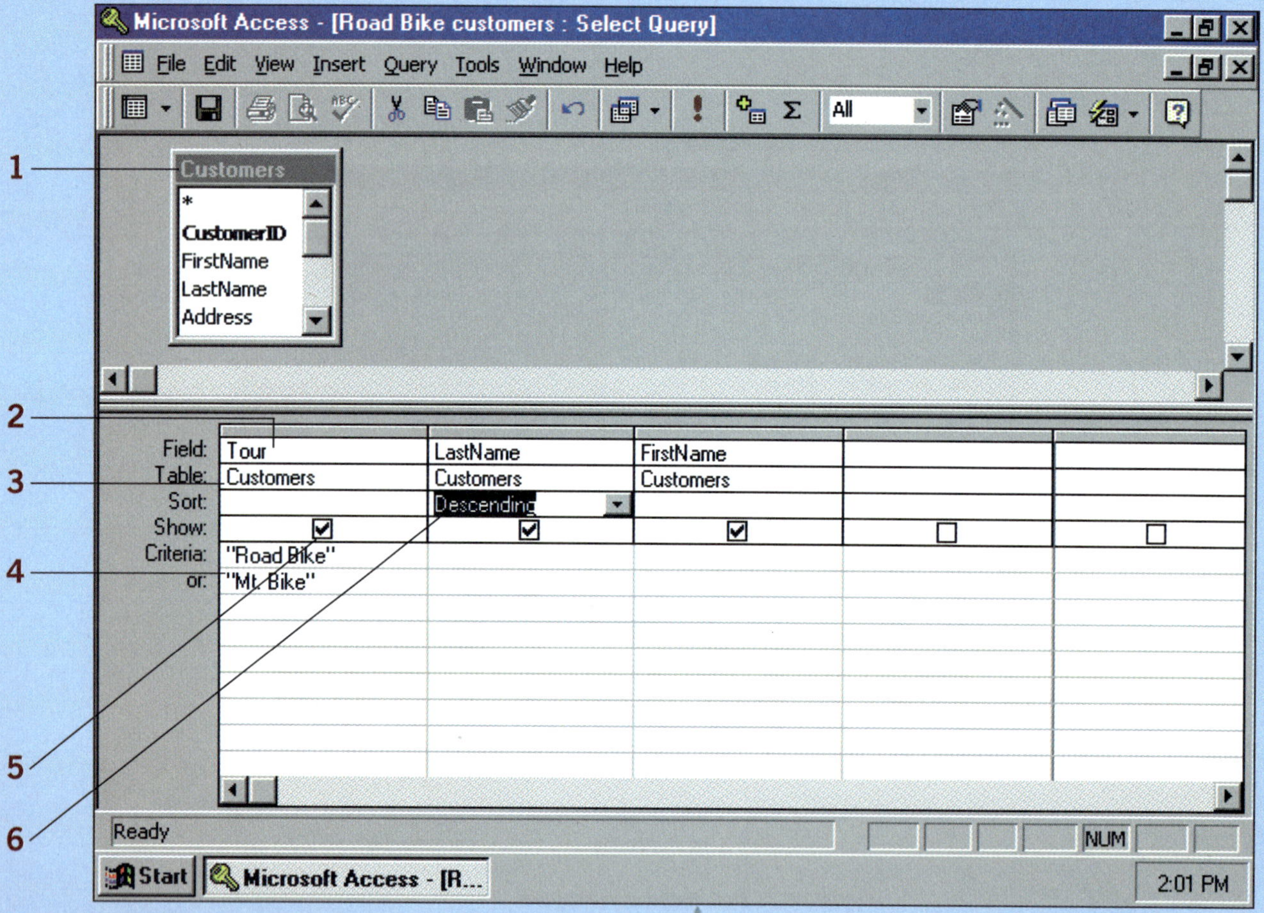

Match each button with its correct description.

7.  C
8.  e
9.  A
10.  B
11.  F
12.  D

a. Open Database
b. Print
c. New Record
d. Find
e. Datasheet View
f. Save

Select the best answer from the list of choices.

13. Which button lets you create a new object?

a.  b.  c.  d. 

14. The button that sorts a table from A to Z is

a.  b.  c.  d. 

15. The button used to add a new record to a table is

a.  b.  c.  d. 

16. Each of the following is true about a filter, *except*:

a. It creates a temporary set of records that looks like a table
b. Its contents can be sorted
c. It includes all fields in the table
d. It can be saved for future use

17. Which button is used to clear the filter grid?

a.  b.  c.  d. 

Access 97

▶ Skills Review

1. Plan a database.
- **a.** Plan a database that will contain the names and addresses of your business contacts.
- **b.** Based on your own experience, decide which fields you need to include in the database.
- **c.** Write down the necessary fields with names and descriptions for each field.

2. Create a table.
- **a.** Start Access and insert your Student Disk in the disk drive.
- **b.** Use the Blank Database option button to create a new database file.
- **c.** Save the file as "Contacts" on your Student Disk.
- **d.** Click the Tables object tab in the Database window, then click New.
- **e.** Use the Table Wizard to create the new table.
- **f.** In the Sample Tables list box, click Contacts. Make sure the Business option button is selected.
- **g.** In the Sample Fields list box, choose each of the following fields for your table:
  ContactID
  FirstName
  LastName
  Address
  City
  StateOrProvince
  PostalCode
  Birthdate
- **h.** Continue through the Table Wizard. Name the table "Business Contacts."
- **i.** Click the Modify the table design option button in the third Table Wizard dialog box, then click Finish.

3. Modify a table.
- **a.** In the first available blank row, add a new text field called "Other."
- **b.** Click the ContactID field Description box.
- **c.** Type "Unique number for Contact."
- **d.** Add appropriate descriptions for the other fields.

4. Find records.
- **a.** Open the database "Bicycle Parts" from your Student Disk. Open the "Products" table.
- **b.** Use the Find button to locate all records in all fields that match any part of a field and contain the text "bar."
- **c.** Make a note of how many occurrences there are?

5. Sort a table.
- **a.** Sort the Products table in ascending order using the "Product Num field." Print the datasheet.
- **b.** Return the datasheet to its original order.
- **c.** Create and print a list of products in descending order by "UnitsInStock."
- **d.** Return the datasheet to its original order.
- **e.** Create and print a list of products in ascending order by "ProductName."
- **f.** Return the datasheet to its original order.
- **g.** Create and print a list of products in descending order by "SupplierID."
- **h.** Return the datasheet to its original order.

6. Filter a table.

- **a.** Create a filter that shows all products on order. A product on order has a value larger than 0 in the UnitsOnOrder field. (Hint: Set the criteria in the filter grid to ">0" for Units On Order.)
- **b.** Print the datasheet.
- **c.** Return the datasheet to its original order.
- **d.** Create a filter for all non-discontinued items.
- **e.** Print the resulting datasheet.
- **f.** Return the datasheet to its original order.

7. Create a simple query.

- **a.** Create a query for all the Products On Order that shows only the ProductNum field data and the product name for the items on order. Name this query "Products on Order."
- **b.** Create a query for all non-discontinued items that shows the ProductName, SupplierID, UnitsInStock, and UnitPrice. Name this query "Non-discontinued Products."
- **c.** Create another query that lists all products with a unit price greater than $50. Name this query "Products costing >$50." (*Hint:* Do not type the $ in the criteria.)
- **d.** Use the "Non-discontinued Products" query to create a new query in which the ProductName, ProductNum, UnitsInStock, and UnitPrice field data display. Name this query "Available Products."
- **e.** Modify the existing "Non-discontinued Products" query for discontinued products. Name this new query "Discontinued Products."
- **f.** Print out the Discontinued Products query.

8. Create a complex query.

- **a.** Create a query that shows the ProductName of all products with a DiscoStatus = Yes field AND that are sold by the pair (the Units field). Sort the query in ascending order by units. Name this query "Discoed, by Unit."
- **b.** Print the datasheet for the query.
- **c.** Save the Discoed, by Unit query as "Available, by Unit." Change the DiscoStatus = Yes field to DiscoStatus = No.
- **d.** Print the datasheet for the query.
- **e.** Modify the "Products on Order" query so that the results are sorted in ascending order by the SupplierID field. Make sure the SupplierID field data is displayed. Save the modified query. Print the query results.
- **f.** Modify the "Products costing >$50" query to include the following fields: ProductNum, ReorderLevel, and ReorderAmount. Save the modified query. Print the query results.
- **g.** Modify the "Discoed, by Unit" query so that the results are sorted in descending order by units, and so that the data for the UnitPrice field is displayed. Save the modified query. Print the query results.
- **h.** Close the file and exit Access.

Independent Challenges

1. The Melodies Music Store has hired you as the customer service manager. You need to create queries in the store's music database, which is contained in the file "Melodies Music Store" on your Student Disk. The database includes one table, called Available titles.

To complete this independent challenge:

1. Start Access, open the database file "Melodies Music Store" on your Student Disk.
2. Using the Available titles table, find out how many records are in the Classic group. Should this classification be its own sub-group?
3. Sort the records by CategoryID, then by ProductName. Print the results.
4. Create a filter that examines records with a SerialNumber lower than 400000. Print this list.
5. Because musical categories overlap, group the eight classifications into three subgroups. You might, for example, group Alternative and Metal into a group called New Age; Classic, Pop, and Rock into a group called Rock N Roll; and World Music, Jazz, and Blues into a group called Easy Listening.
6. Create queries for each of the three subgroups. Each query must use an OR specification in the query grid. Name each query for its classification.
7. Query the Available titles table using each query, and print the results of each query.
8. Modify one of the subgroup queries to include a musical classification already included in another subgroup. For example, you could include Pop in Easy Listening as well as Rock N Roll. Print the results of the modified query and submit all printouts.

2. You work in the US Census Office for your city. Using the database "Census Bureau" from your Student Disk, create several queries that examine the data in the Statistical Data table. The records in the Statistical Data table contain marriage information by state.

To complete this independent challenge:

1. Add descriptions for each of the fields in the "Statistical Data" table.
2. Find the states in the same geographical area as your state. For example, if your state is Utah, other states in the Mountain Region are New Mexico, Colorado, Nevada, Montana, Arizona, Idaho, and Wyoming.
3. Create and save a query that selects records in your geographical area and sorts them in ascending order by state. Display the State and Marriages fields.
4. On paper, write down at least three additional queries that would extract meaningful data. Create and save each of these queries. Print a sample of each query's results and submit each of the samples with the handwritten work.

3. Your computer consulting firm has contracted to create a database for a special effects firm called Grand Illusions. Currently, Grand Illusions is working on five films, each having a minimum of three special effects they need to keep track of. Each special effect is created using some combination of computer imaging, prosthetics, multi-media, archived footage, and an in-house tool called Black Midnight.

To complete this independent challenge:

1. Create a database file on your Student Disk called Grand Illusions.
2. Create a table called Special Effects Register.
3. Create records for each special effect used in the five film projects. Each record should include the film name, special effect name, the Director's name, the tools used to create the effect, and the completion date of the effect.
4. Print the results of sorting the records in ascending order by film name.
5. Print the results of sorting the records in ascending order by completion date, then in ascending order by Director's name.
6. Create a query for each film which displays the completion date, Director's name, and the tools used.
7. Save the Query using the film name and Special Effects as the query name.
8. Print out each list and submit all printouts.

4. Proper use of search engines can help you find information about the elected officials in any state. The socialite for whom you work wants to be aware of who is elected to what post, and when their term is up. He has asked you to create a database based on the information you retrieve from the World Wide Web that contains this information.

1. Log on to the Internet and use your browser to go to http://www.course.com. From there click the link Student On Line Companions; then click the link to go to the Microsoft Office 97 Professional Edition—Illustrated: A First Course page, then click the Access link for Unit B.
2. Locate information about your state, and find out about your state's Federal elected officials.
3. Create a new database on your Student Disk called Elected Officials.
4. Include the following information in your table: the official's name, whether they are in the House or Senate, their official title, when their term began, when they're up for reelection, party affiliation, age, and number of years of elected service.
5. Save the table.
6. Create a query that finds Democrats, and one that finds Republicans.
7. Preview and print the datasheet.
8. Hand in a printout of your work.

Visual Workshop

Use the Customers table in the "Tour Customer Data" file on your Student Disk to create the following output using a filter.

FIGURE B-24

Customer ID	First Name	Last Name	Address	City	State	Postal Code	Tour	Date	Age
30	Adelia	Ballard	3 Hall Road	Williamstow	MA	02167-	Mt. Bike	9/26/95	42
13	Luis	Lopez	1212 Agua Fria	Santa Fe	NM	87501-	Mt. Bike	6/20/96	34
31	Elizabeth	Michaels	57 Beechwood Drive	Wayne	NJ	07470-	Mt. Bike	6/20/96	39
16	Michael	Nelson	229 Route 55	Durango	CO	81301-	Mt. Bike	9/26/95	40
2	Robin	Spencer	293 Serenity Drive	Concord	MA	01742-	Mt. Bike	9/26/95	32
24	Elizabeth	Stephens	3 Which Way, Apt. 7	Salem	MA	01970-	Mt. Bike	6/20/96	38

Creating a Form

Objectives

- Create a form
- Modify a form layout
- Change the tab order
- Use the Expression Builder
- Format controls
- Add a field to a form
- Add a graphic image to a form
- Use a form to add a record

The Datasheet View gives you an overall look at the records in a table. Often, however, the fields you need to view in the table are not all visible unless you scroll left or right. Access allows you to easily create attractive screen forms that let you determine how you view each record's fields and the records in the database. You can design a screen form to match the design of a particular paper form to facilitate data entry. Because Nomad Ltd's Travel Division has been so successful with its bicycle tours, it keeps an inventory of supplies, which it then sells to tour customers. Michael wants to create a form to make it easier to enter inventory data.

Access 97

Creating a Form

You can create a form from scratch, or you can use the **Form Wizard**. The Form Wizard provides sample form layouts and gives you options for including specific fields in a form. Currently, the Travel Division fills out a paper form for each product in its bicycle inventory. Michael needs to create an Access form for the bicycle inventory data. He wants to design the form so that it looks similar to the original paper form, displays one record at a time, and displays all but one of the table's fields .

Steps

1. Start Access and insert your Student Disk in the appropriate drive
2. Click the **Open an Existing Database radio button**, then open the database **Bike Inventory** on your Student Disk
   This database file contains the bicycle inventory data. You want to create a new form for the Bicycle Products table.
3. Click the **Forms tab** in the Database window, then click **New**
   The New Form dialog box opens, as shown in Figure C-1. You need to identify the table on which the form will be based, then you can choose the Form Wizard option to create the form.
4. Click the **Choose the table or query where the object's data comes from: list arrow**, click **Bicycle Products**, click **Form Wizard**, then click **OK**
   A dialog box opens and lists all the fields in the table, as shown in Figure C-2. This dialog box allows you to select which fields you want to include in the form, and to determine the order in which they appear in the form. Instead of selecting each field individually, you decide to select all the fields at one time, and then exclude the one you don't want to appear.
5. Click the **All Fields button** [>>], use the scroll bar in the Selected Fields box to display the top of the list, click **ProductNum**, then click the **Remove Single Field button** [<]
   All the fields except ProductNum appear in the Selected Fields box. You are ready to choose a layout for your form. You decide to accept the default style: a Columnar layout.
6. Click [Next >], then click [Next >] to accept the Columnar layout
   Next, you choose a style for your form. You decide to use the Standard style.
7. Click **Standard**, then click [Next >]
   The final dialog box suggests the table name as the title for the form. You accept the title suggestion Bicycle Products and want to see the form with data in it.
8. Click **Finish**
   The Bicycle Products form opens in Form View, as shown in Figure C-3. The fields are listed in the form organized in columns, and the data for the first record in the table is displayed. The navigation buttons at the bottom of the form allow you to move from record to record. If you can't see all the fields, the vertical scroll bar allows you to move to areas of the form that currently are not visible.

Click open Folder

Form TAB New

QuickTip

The [< Back] button in the Form Wizard dialog boxes allows you to move to the previous dialog box and make changes, as necessary, before completing the form.

FIGURE C-1: New Form dialog box

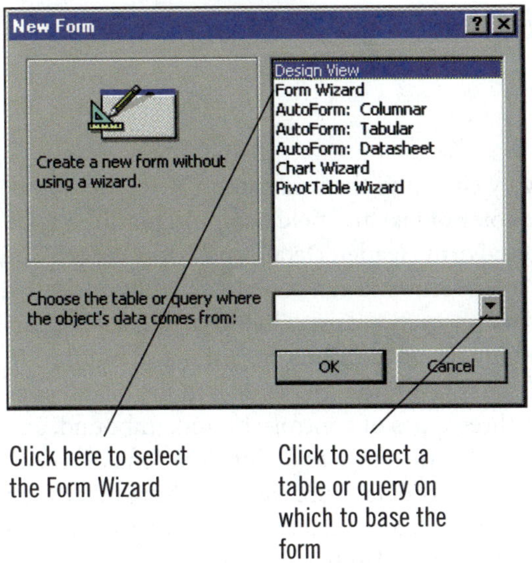

FIGURE C-2: Selecting fields in the Form Wizard dialog box

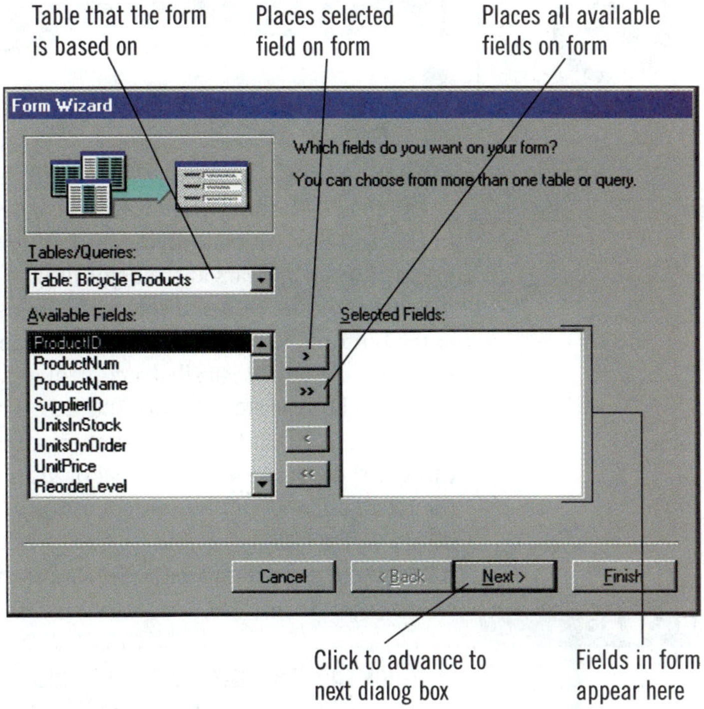

FIGURE C-3: Bicycle Products form

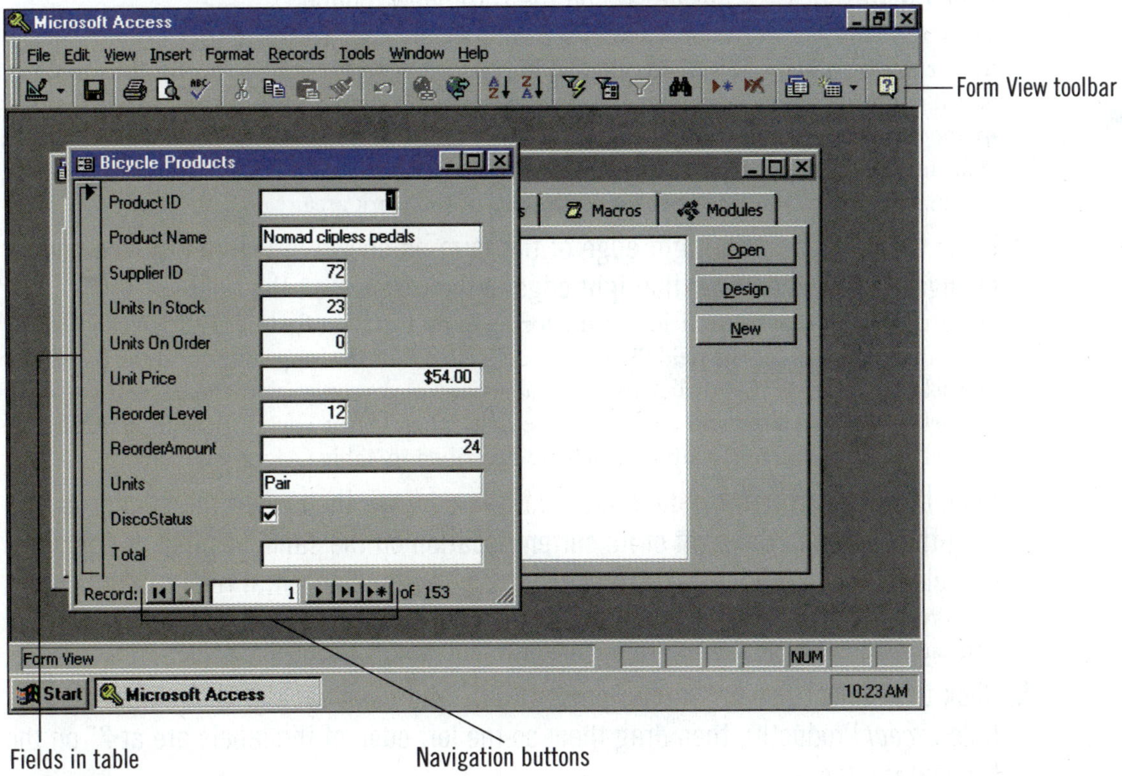

CLUES TO USE

Using AutoForm

You can create a simple form by clicking the New Object button on the Database toolbar, then clicking AutoForm from the palette. AutoForm offers no prompts or dialog boxes; it instantly creates a columnar, tabular, or datasheet form that displays all the fields in the table or query.

Access 97

Modifying a Form Layout

After you create a form, you can modify it easily by changing the locations of fields, adding or deleting fields, adding graphics, and changing the color of text and field data. You modify a form in Design View, which is divided into three sections: Form Header, Detail, and Form Footer. The **Form Header** appears at the beginning of each screen form and can contain an additional form title or logo. The **Detail** displays the fields and data for each record. The **Form Footer** appears at the bottom of each screen form and can contain totals, instructions, or command buttons. In Design View, a field is called a control. A **control** consists of the **field label** and the data it contains which is the **field value text box**. There are three types of controls: bound, unbound, and calculated. A **bound control**, such as a field, has a table or query as its information source; an **unbound control**, such as a label or graphic image, has its data source as something other than the database, and a **calculated control** uses an expression as its data source. Michael wants to reposition the fields in the form to match the design of the paper form. This will make it easier to enter data from the paper-based forms into the screen form. Figure C-4 shows a completed paper form.

Steps

1. Click the **Maximize button** to maximize the Bicycle Products form
   Next you change to Design View, where you can make modifications.
2. Click the **Design View button** on the Form View toolbar
   The screen changes to Design View, as shown in Figure C-5. The form background changes to a grid, which helps keep fields aligned horizontally and vertically. The **Toolbox toolbar**, which might appear in a different area on your screen, contains buttons you can use to modify the form. The detail section contains the field labels that identify each field; and the field value text boxes, which represent where the actual data for each field will be displayed. Before moving any fields, you want to expand the size of the work area.
3. Place the pointer on the right edge of the form as shown in Figure C-5, the pointer changes to ✛, then drag the right edge to the 6" mark on the ruler
   You are ready to reposition fields on the form. To do this, you first need to **select** a field by clicking the control for the field. Black squares, called **handles**, appear around the perimeter of a selected control. If you click the field label control you only select the label. If you click the field value text box, you also select the field label. When you work with controls, the pointer assumes different shapes, which are described in Table C-1.
4. Click the **ProductName field value text box control**, then when the pointer is ✋, drag the control to the right of its current location on the same position on the vertical ruler so the left edge of the label is at 2.5" on the horizontal ruler
   The Product Name label field is now in the middle of its original line, as shown in Figure C-6. You can select multiple controls simultaneously and modify them all together.
5. Click to deselect **ProductName**, press **[Shift]** and click each of the remaining controls *except* ProductID, then drag them so the left edge of the labels are at 2" on the horizontal ruler
6. Select the **DiscoStatus field value text box control** and drag it to the same vertical line as the ProductID control, with the left edge of its label at 2.5" on the horizontal ruler
7. Drag the **Total field value text box control** up so the bottom of the controls are at 2.5" on the vertical ruler
   Be sure your form's Design View matches the Design View displayed in Figure C-6. You might need to use the scroll bar to see the remaining controls.

QuickTip

If your Toolbox toolbar is in the way, you can drag its title bar to reposition it.

Time To

✓ Save

FIGURE C-4: Bicycle Products paper form

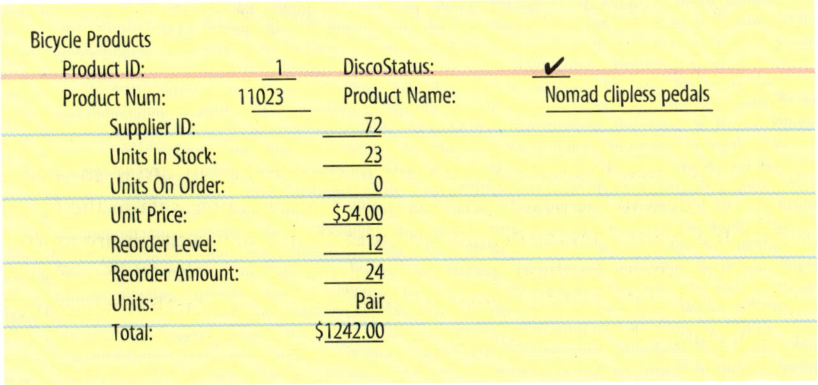

White Boxes are Bound

Shaded AREAS

Double Click to ADD FORM HEADER Footer

FIGURE C-5: Bicycle Products form in Design View

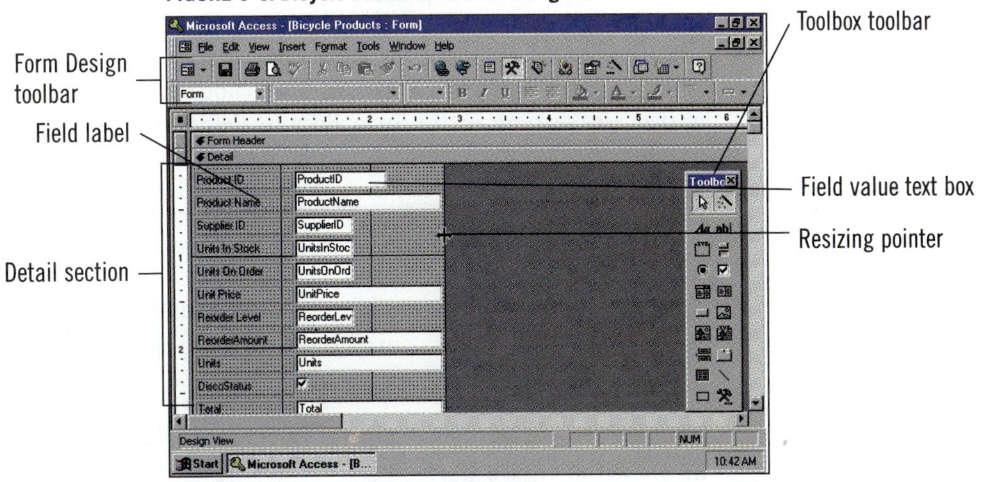

FIGURE C-6: Bicycle Products form with repositioned controls

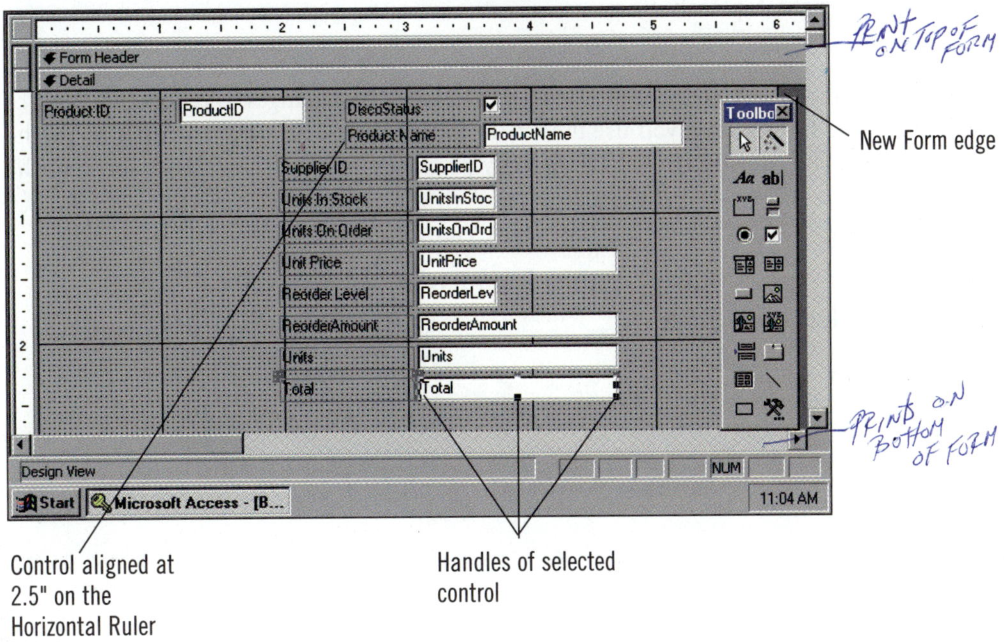

PRINT ON TOP OF FORM

PRINT ON BOTTOM OF FORM

TABLE C-1: Mouse pointer shapes

shape	action	shape	action
	Selects a control		Moves the control where pointer is currently positioned
	Moves all selected controls	↔	Changes a control's size

Access 97

Changing the Tab Order

Once the fields are moved to their new locations, you'll want to change the **tab order**, the order in which you advance from one field to the next when you press [Tab] to enter data in the form. The order of the fields in a table determines the default tab order. Even when controls are repositioned in a form, the tab order remains in the original order of the fields in the table. Michael wants the tab order to reflect the order in which the fields now appear on the form, which matches the paper form, to facilitate data entry from the paper form. He needs to modify the tab order for the form.

Steps

1. Click **View** on the menu bar, then click **Tab Order**
   The Tab Order dialog box opens. In this dialog box you can change the order of fields in any of the three sections on the form. Because fields are usually in the Detail section, this section is automatically selected. The Custom Order list box shows the current tab order, which still reflects the order of the fields in the table. You need to change the tab order so that the DiscoStatus field which indicates whether the product is currently offered or has been discontinued follows the ProductID field.
2. Click the **DiscoStatus row selector** in the Custom Order list box
   Now that the DiscoStatus control is selected, you can change its order by dragging its row to a new location.
3. Drag the **DiscoStatus row** until it is below ProductID, then release the mouse button, as shown in Figure C-7
   You can also click the Auto Order button in the Tab Order dialog box to rearrange the tab order to left-to-right, top-to-bottom.
4. Click **OK**
   Although nothing visibly changes on the form, the tab order changes to reflect the order of the fields on the form. When you use the screen form to enter data from a paper form, the order in which you move from field to field by pressing [Tab] will match the order in the paper form.
   You save your work and view the form in Form View.
5. Click the **Form View button** on the Form Design toolbar
   Compare your form to Figure C-8.
6. Save your work

Trouble?

If the pointer changes to an I you will rename the field rather than move it. Click outside the field and try again.

FIGURE C-7: Tab Order dialog box

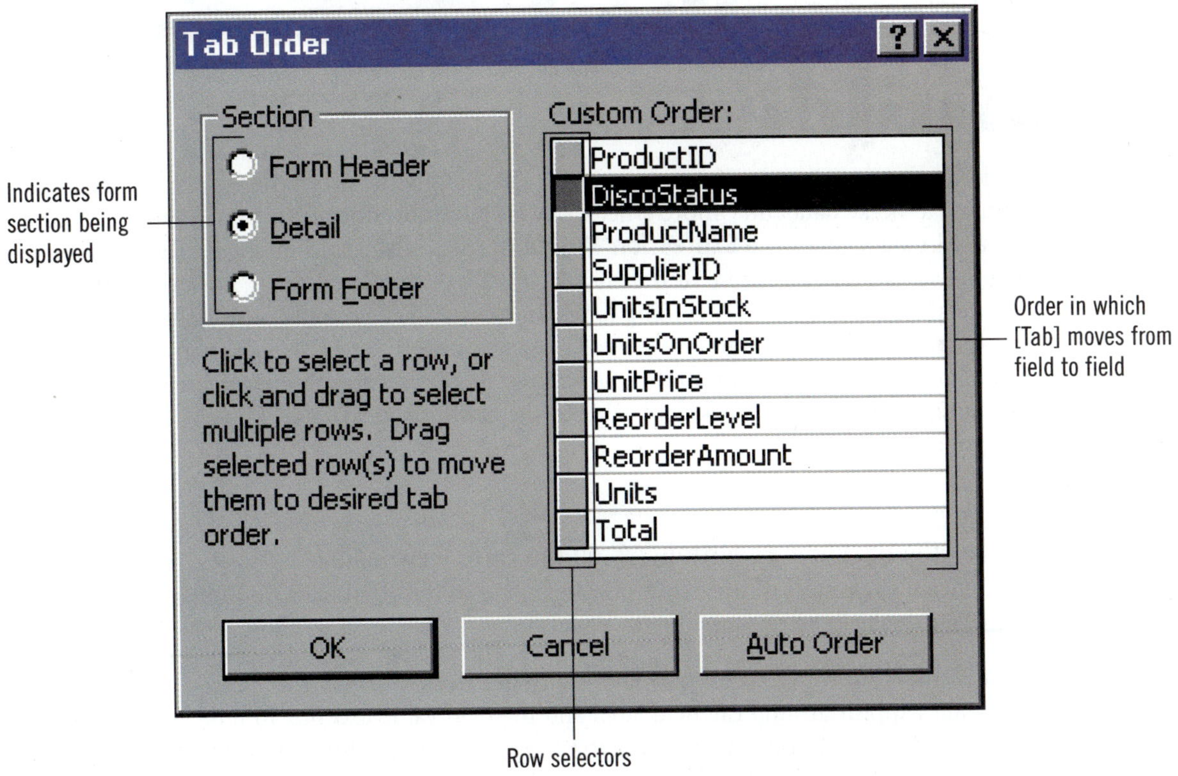

FIGURE C-8: Form displayed in Form View

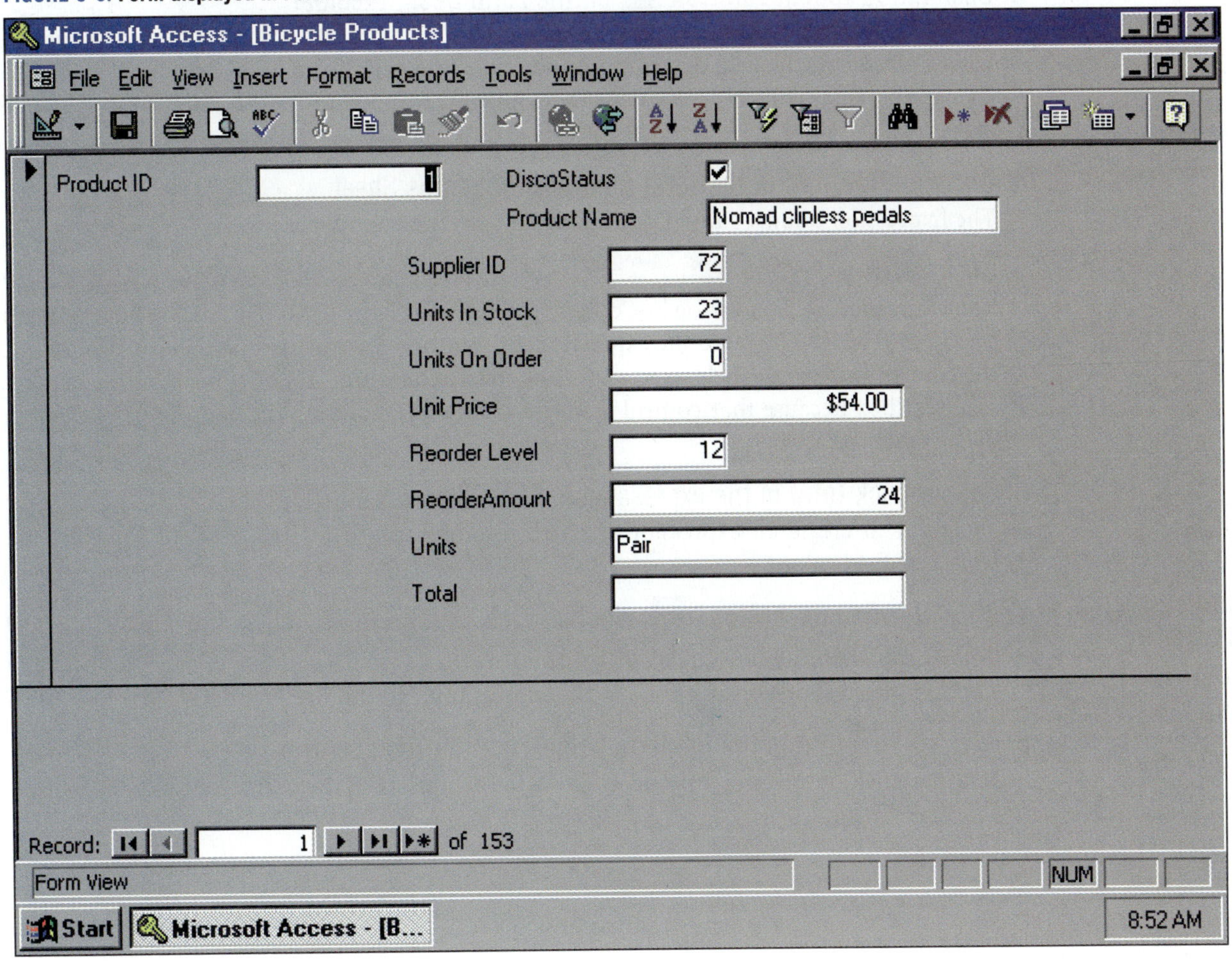

Access 97

Access 97

Using the Expression Builder

In addition to repositioning controls, you can also modify the **properties**, or characteristics, of a control to make data entry more efficient. A **calculated control** has a mathematical expression as its data source. The **Expression Builder** displays fields and mathematical symbols you can use to create an expression. By default, all controls occur as text boxes; however, you can create several types of controls, including toggle buttons and check boxes, using the Toolbox toolbar. Michael wants to create a calculated control that will display an in-stock value for each item in the inventory. To do this, he will use the Expression Builder to create an equation that multiplies the UnitsInStock field value by the UnitPrice field value. First, Michael returns to Design View.

Steps

1. **Click the Design View button on the Form View toolbar**

   You want the results of the expression to appear in the Total field. You must select the control for this field before creating the equation.

2. **Click the Total field value text box control**

   Handles appear around the field label and the field value text box to indicate that the control is selected. Although you could type an expression directly into the text box, you choose to use the Expression Builder. You access the Expression Builder through the Properties Sheet.

3. **Click the Properties button on the Form Design toolbar**

   The Properties Sheet opens for the Total control. The Properties Sheet shows the control's name and source, the field description, and other relevant information. Because you want to change the Total control to a calculated control, you need to modify the Control Source property.

4. **Click the Data tab in the Total Control's Properties Sheet**

   The Expression Builder's Build button displays, as shown in Figure C-9.

5. **Click the Build button ...**

   The Expression Builder dialog box opens, as shown in Figure C-10. This dialog box contains a section in which you build the expression, the buttons you use to build the expression, and the control fields and labels selected for the form. The word "Total" appears in the expression text box because that control was selected. Before building the expression, you must delete the word Total.

6. **Double-click Total in the expression list box, then press [Delete]**

   You need to create an expression that will multiply the UnitsInStock field value by the UnitPrice field value.

7. **Click the Equals button =, double-click UnitsInStock, click the Multiplication button *, then double-click UnitPrice**

   The completed expression appears in the expression text box. See Figure C-11.

8. **Click OK to return to the Properties Sheet for the Total control**

   Note that the Control Source property shows the expression as the source for the Total control.

Trouble?

If you enter the expression incorrectly, modify it using [Backspace], [Delete], and the arrow keys, then enter it again.

FIGURE C-9: Properties Sheet for Total control

Field name and description appear in the Format tab

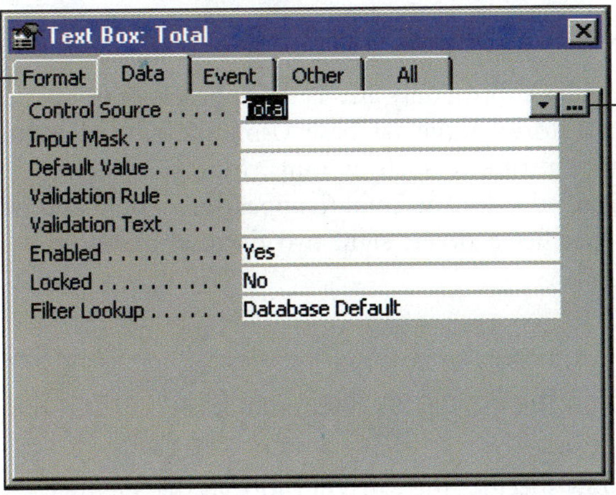

Build button

FIGURE C-10: Expression Builder dialog box

Expression appears here

Current table

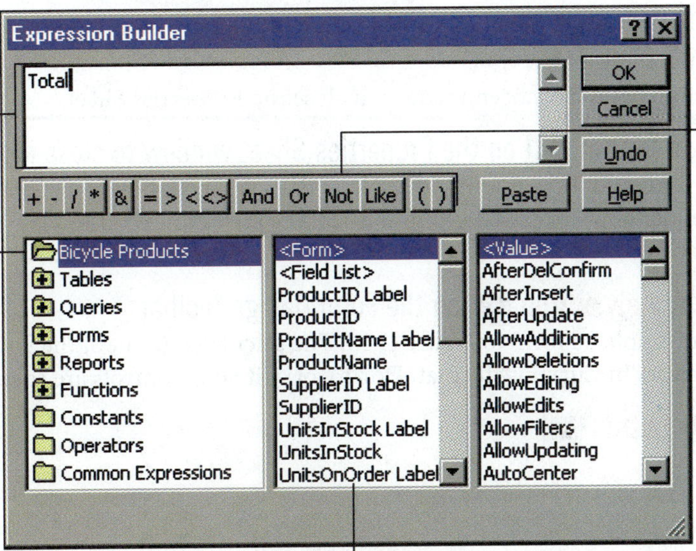

Expression buttons

Available fields in current table — you'll need to scroll to see all of them

FIGURE C-11: Completed Expression Builder dialog box

Completed expression

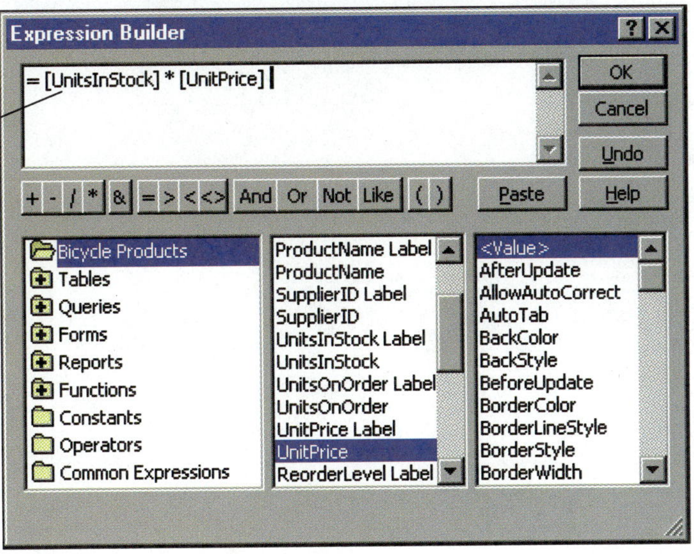

Access 97

Formatting Controls

Changing the format of a field's control only affects the appearance of the field data in the form; it does not affect how data is stored in the database. Using the Properties Sheet, you can modify numeric formatting, or text attributes such as fonts, font sizes, bolding, or italics. Michael wants the calculated value for the Total to appear extra bold and be displayed with the Currency format, which specifies a dollar sign, two decimal places, and commas separating thousands.

Steps

1. Click the **Format tab** on the Properties Sheet, click the **Format list arrow**, then click **Currency**
   The Format property now specifies the Currency format. See Figure C-12. Next, you change the format of this control to bold.

2. Scroll to display Font Weight, click the **Font Weight text box**, click the **Font Weight list arrow**, then click **Extra Bold**
   Now that these changes have been made, you close the Properties Sheet.

3. Click the **Close button** on the Properties Sheet window to close it
   The form is displayed in Design View. Note that the equation you created using the Expression Builder appears extra bold in the Total control. You want to view the completed form in Form View.

4. Click the **Form View button** on the Form Design toolbar
   Compare your completed form to Figure C-13. The calculated result of the Total field for the first record appears in Currency format. Don't worry if your controls are spaced differently.

5. Click the **Save button**

QuickTip

You can bold, italicize, or underline a control by selecting it in Design View, then click the appropriate attribute button on the Form Design toolbar.

FIGURE C-12: Completed Properties Sheet

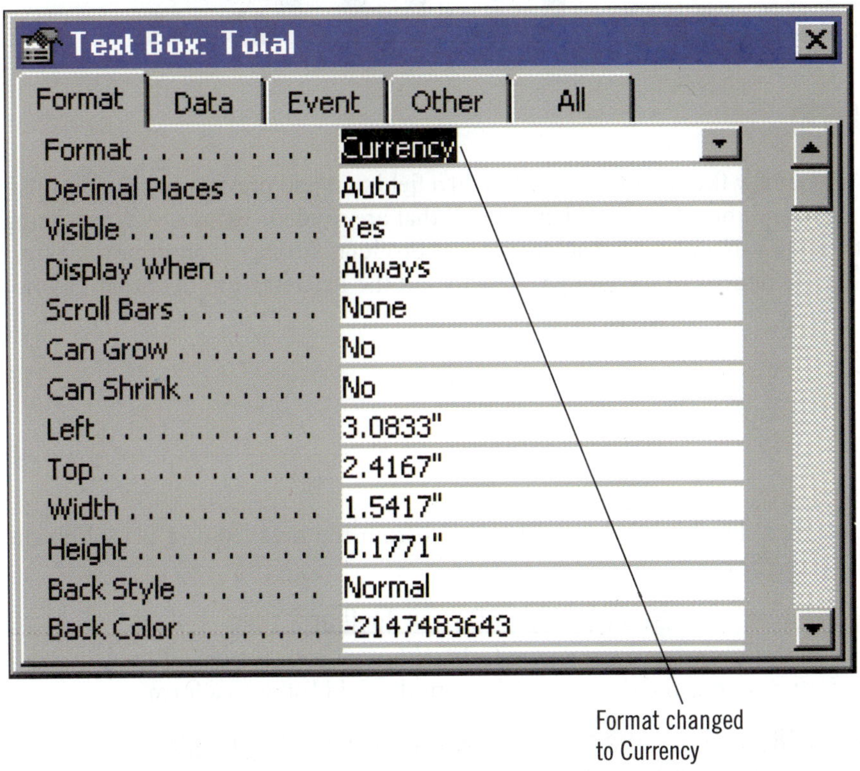

FIGURE C-13: Completed form in Form View

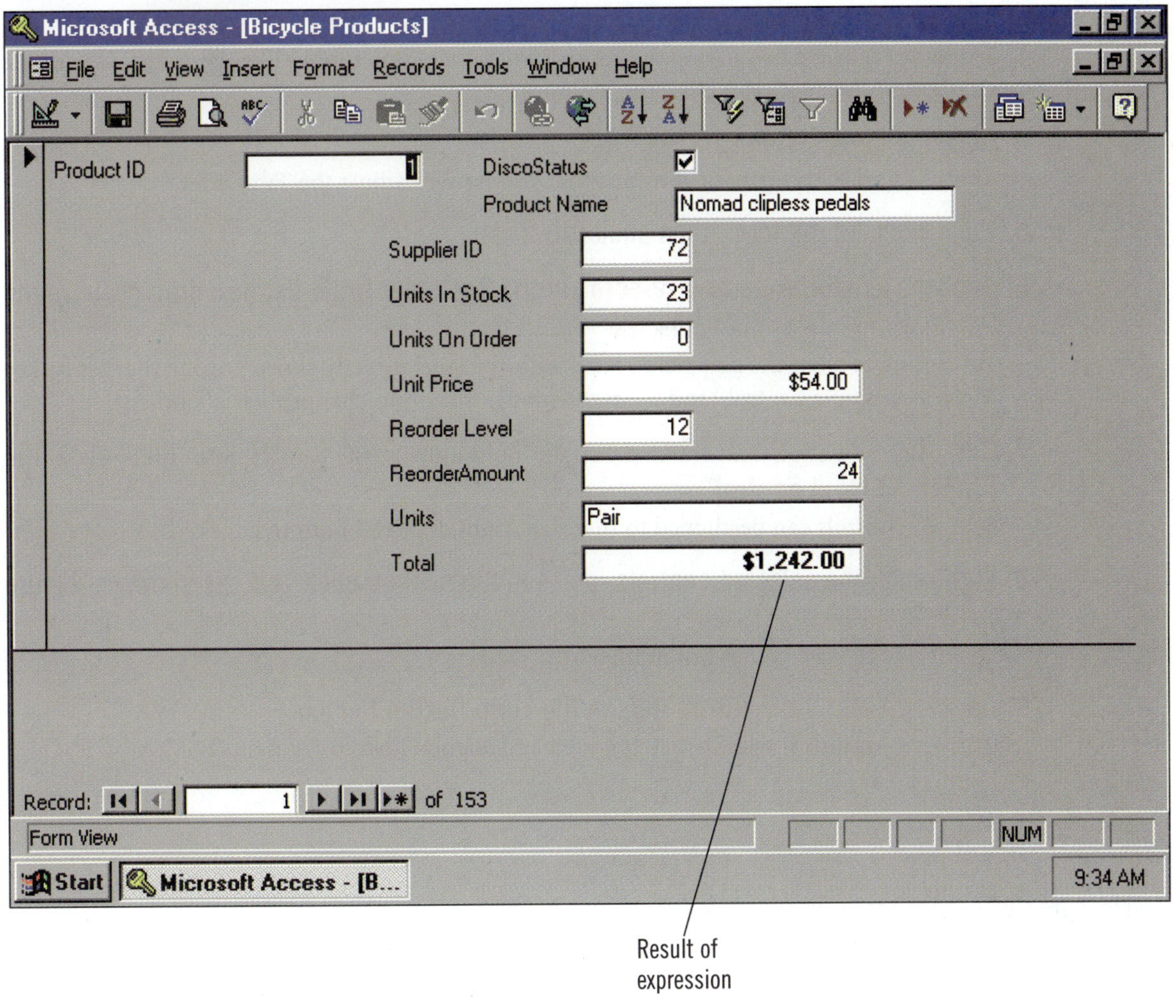

Access 97

Access 97

Adding a Field to a Form

Once a form exists, you may find that you want to add a field that had previously been omitted. You can create a form, and then add any missing fields that are needed. After speaking with the data entry staff at Nomad, Michael learns that Product Number is an important field needed in the form. He returns to the Design View to add the ProductNum field that had not been included originally.

Steps

1. **Click the Design View button**
   The field to be added, ProductNum can be selected from the field list and placed on the form. You display the field list.

2. **Click the Field List button on the Form Design Toolbar**
   The list of fields in the table display in Figure C-14, although your list may display in a different location. You can drag and drop any field from the field list onto a form.

3. **Click the ProductNum field, drag it onto the form with the pointer just beneath the currently positioned ProductID field as shown in Figure C-15, then release the mouse button**
   The field displays directly underneath the existing ProductID field. If necessary, you can reposition the field by moving the control when the pointer looks like . Satisfied with the addition of this field, you close the Field List.

4. **Click the Field List button**
   The addition of this new field means that you have to adjust the Tab Order.

5. **Right-click on the form, then click Tab Order**

6. **Click the ProductNum row selector in the Customer Order list box, drag it above the ProductName field, then click OK**
   You decide to align the new field's label with the label directly above it using the [Shift] key to select multiple controls and the right-mouse button to change their alignment.

7. **Click the ProductNum label control, hold down the [Shift] key, then click the ProductID label control**
   Selected controls can be aligned to their left, right, top, and bottom edges.

8. **Right-click the selected controls, point to Align, then click Left, as shown in Figure C-16**
   You decide to view your work in the Form View.

9. **Click the Form View button on the Form Design toolbar**
   Compare your form with its newly added and aligned field to Figure C-17.

QuickTip

You can delete a control by selecting it with the mouse, then press [Delete].

Time To

- Save the form

ADD A Field
DESIGN View
Field Box
FIND Field
Click + DRAG

FIGURE C-14: Field List displayed

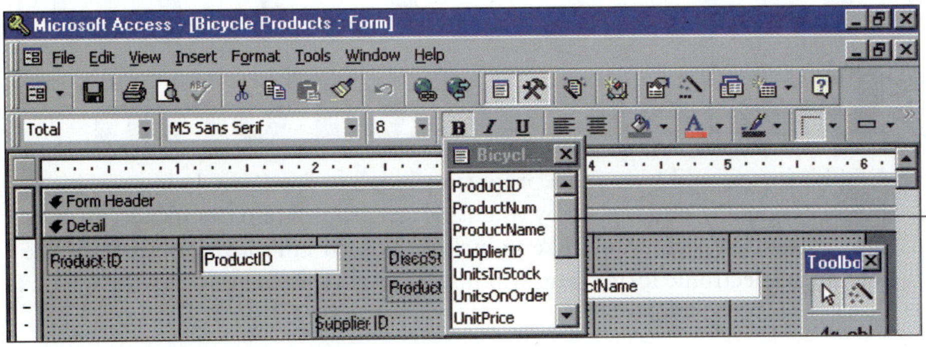

FIGURE C-15: Dragging a field to a form

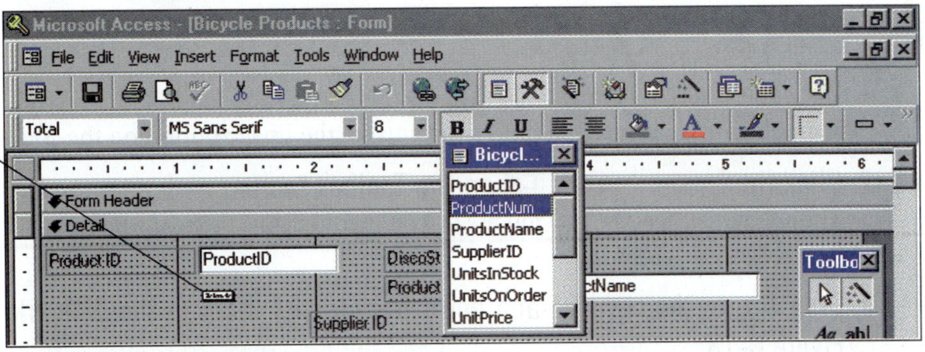

FIGURE C-16: Aligning controls

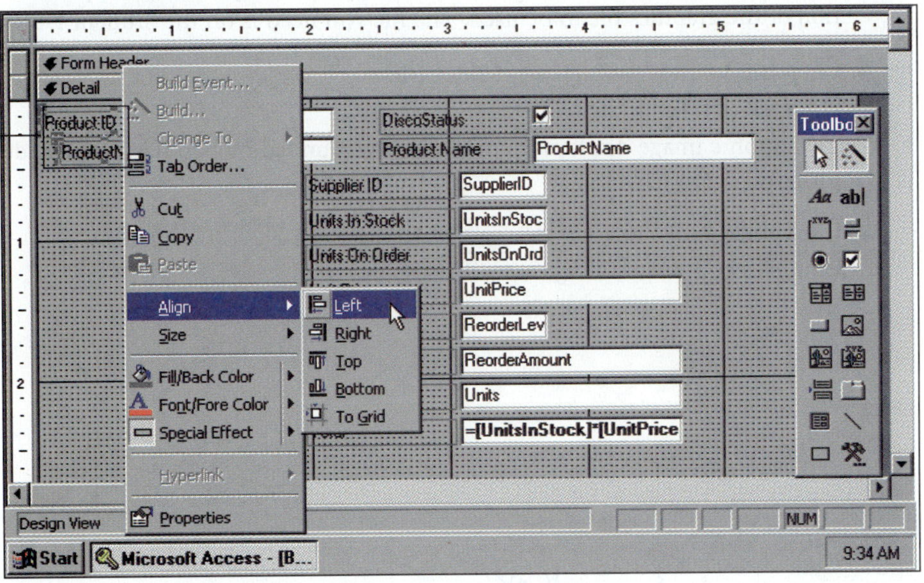

FIGURE C-17: Form with additional field

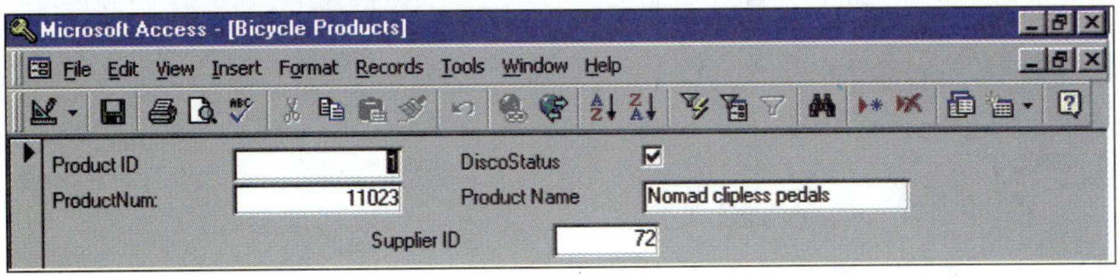

Access 97

Adding a Graphic Image to a Form

Graphic images add style and a professional look to any form. Using graphic images purchased by your company, or designed by you using any art program can make a form look more appealing. Michael would like to include Nomad Ltd's logo on his form. He already has the logo in an electronic format and will insert the graphic image using the form's Design View.

Steps

1. Click the **Design View button** on the Form View toolbar
   A graphic image is inserted onto a form using the Image button on the Toolbox toolbar.

2. Click the **Image button** on the Toolbox toolbar
   The pointer changes to +. You use this pointer to define the area where you want the image to be placed.

3. Drag + to the right 2" and down from the 1" mark to the 2" mark, as shown in Figure C-18
   Once the area is defined, the Insert Picture dialog box opens. You supply the name and location of the graphics file to be used. The file you need is on the Student Disk.

4. Click the **Look in list arrow**, select the **3½" Floppy (A:)**, click **Nomad.tif**, as shown in Figure C-19, then click **OK**
   The graphic image displays on the form, surrounded by handles. You decide to look at the form in Form View.

5. Click the **Form View button** on the Design View toolbar
   Compare your form to Figure C-20.

QuickTip

You can lock down a toolbox button (so you don't have to keep clicking it for repeated use) by double-clicking it.

QuickTip

Most commonly available graphic image types can be used in a form. These types include .BMP, .PCX, .JPG, and .TIF.

INSERT GRAPHIC
Click Tool Box
click ICON IMAGE
drag to space in
you want graphic to be
click OK

FIGURE C-18: Dragging an image's outline

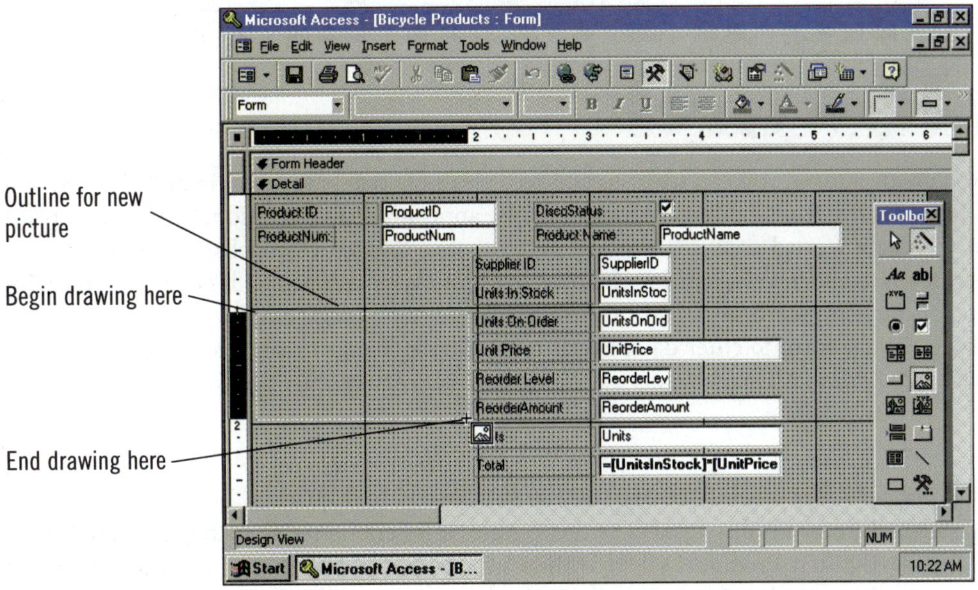

FIGURE C-19: Insert Picture dialog box

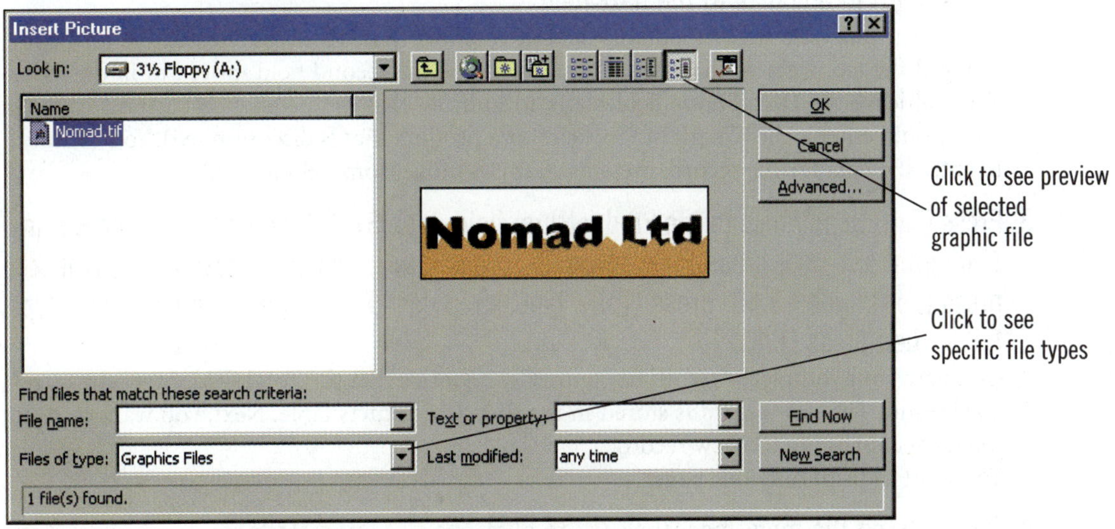

FIGURE C-20: Picture embedded in form

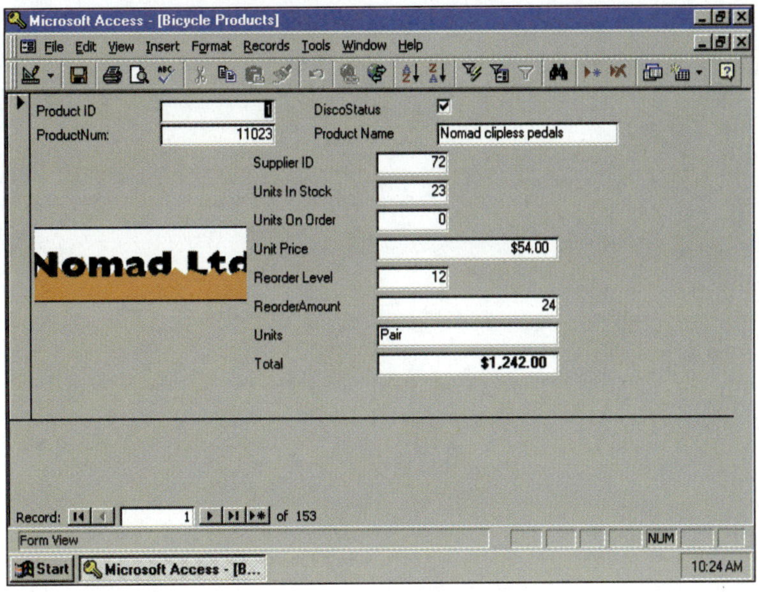

Access 97

Using a Form to Add a Record

After you create a form, you can use it to add records to the database table. To add a record you press [Tab] to move from field to field, entering the appropriate information. You can also print a form to obtain a hard copy for sharing with others. Michael will use the Bicycle Products form to add a new record to the Bicycle Products table. Then he'll print the form with the data for the new record, and distribute the form to other Nomad employees so that they can see how to use the form to enter data. Because the Bicycle Products table is already selected in the Database window, Michael begins by adding a new record to the open form.

Steps

1. **Click the New Record button on the Form View toolbar**
   A new, blank record is displayed. The text "(AutoNumber)" appears in the ProductID field. Recall that the first ProductID field is the Counter field for the table. Record 154 of 154 appears in the status bar. See Figure C-21. You begin to enter the data for the new record.

2. **Press [Tab] to advance to the next field**
   The cursor moves to the DiscoStatus field. Remember that when you created the form, you changed the tab order so that DiscoStatus would be the second field moved to in the form. You will leave the DiscoStatus field blank to indicate that the product is currently offered (you would enter a checkmark in this field for a product that is discontinued). You continue to enter the data for the record, pressing [Tab] to move from field to field.

3. **Press [Tab] to advance to the ProductNum field, type 57129, press [Tab], type Nomad FinneganFast Tire, press [Tab], type 22, press [Tab], type 14, press [Tab], type 20, press [Tab], type 15.50, press [Tab], type 15, press [Tab], type 20, press [Tab], type Each, then press [Enter]**
   Compare your completed record to Figure C-22. Notice that the Total field shows the calculated result. The new record is stored in the Bicycle Products table. Next, you want to print the form containing the new record.
   You want to print only this page.

4. **Click File on the menu bar, click Print, click the Selected Record(s) option button, then click OK**
   You close the form and return to the Database window.

Time To

- Save
- Close the form
- Exit Access

FIGURE C-21: Blank form for new record

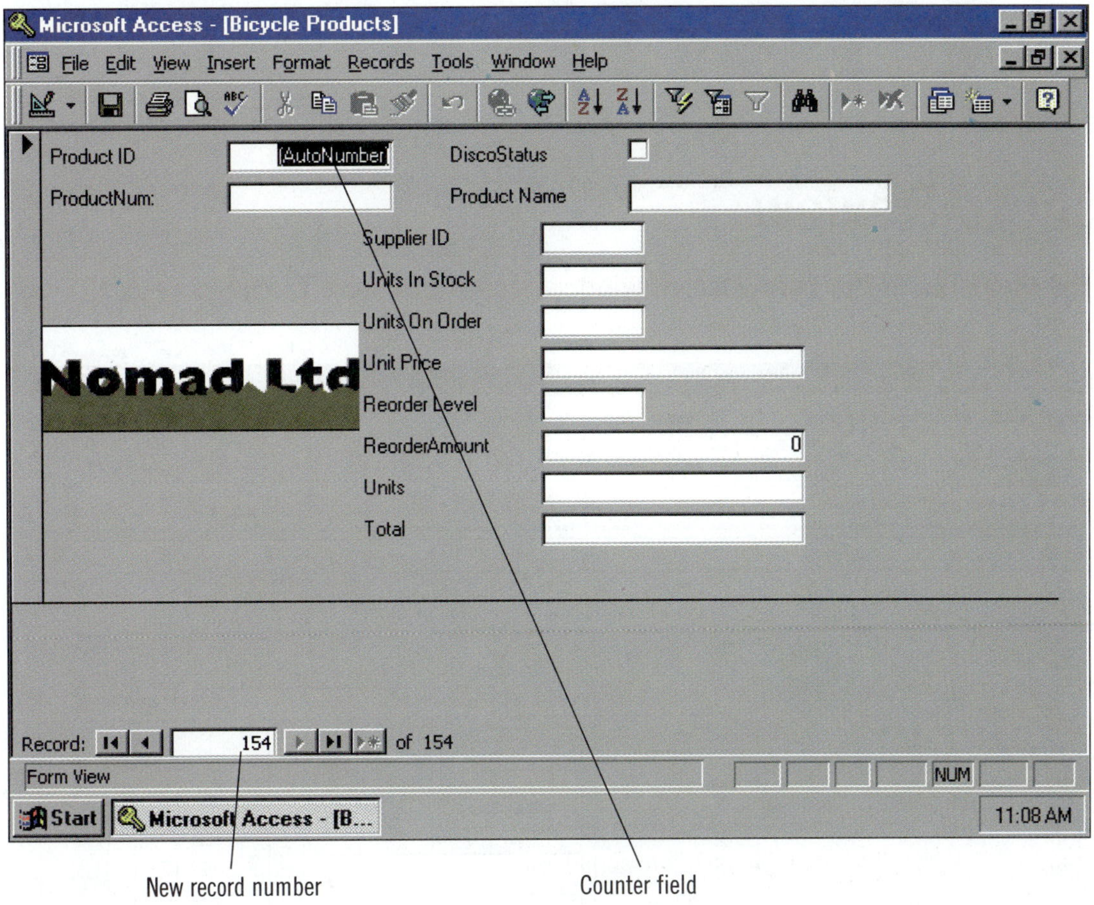

FIGURE C-22: Completed record 154

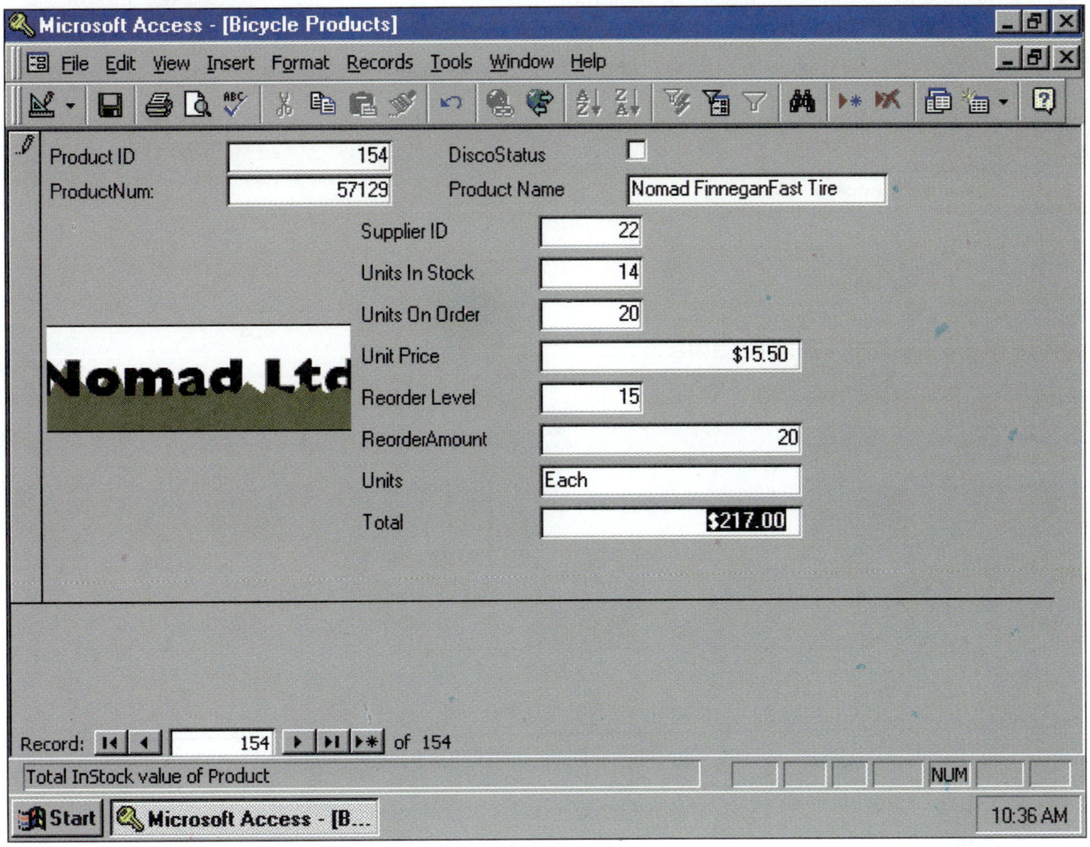

Practice

Concepts Review

Label each of the elements of the Form Design window shown in Figure C-23.

FIGURE C-23

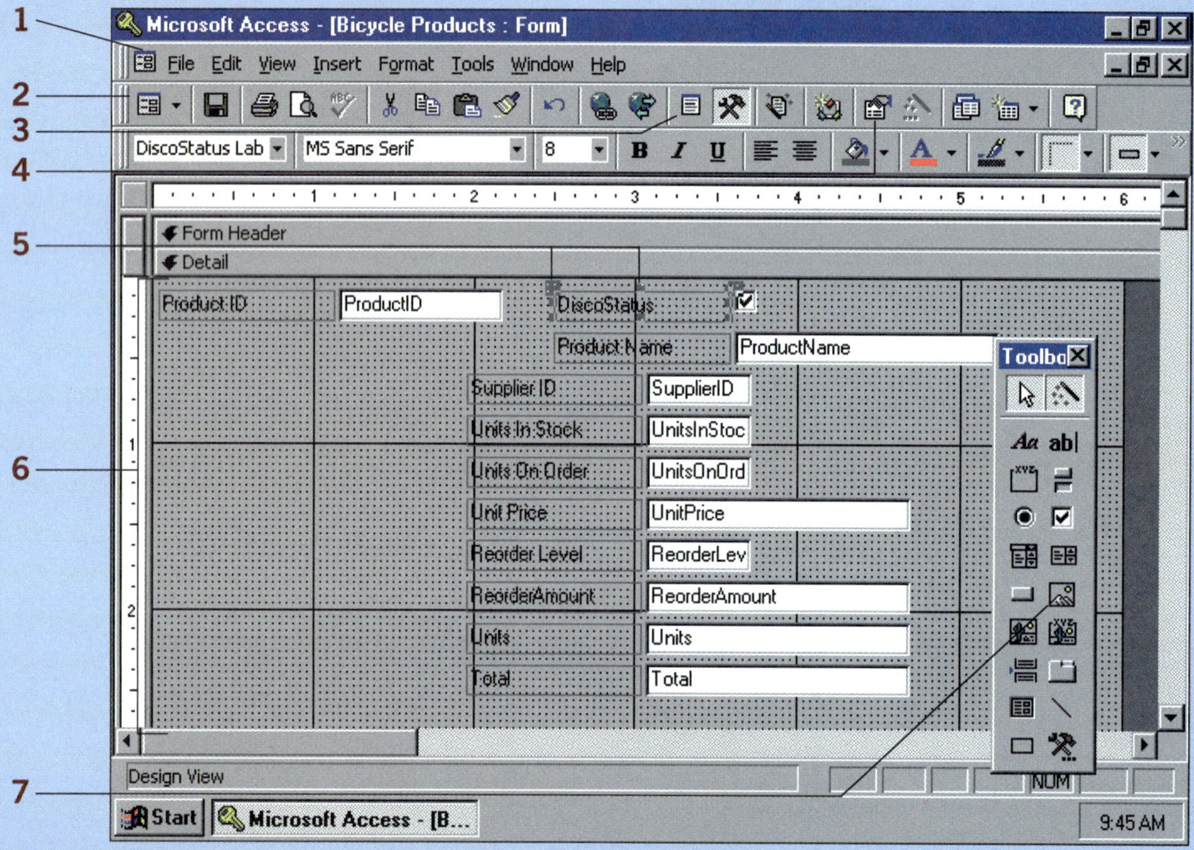

Match each button to its correct description.

8. <<
9. ...
10. 
11. >
12. 
13. 

a. Print Preview
b. Add a single field
c. Remove all fields
d. Form View
e. Design View
f. Build an expression

Select the best answer from the list of choices.

14. Objects in a form or report are called
- **a.** Properties
- **b.** Controls
- **c.** Pieces
- **d.** Handles

15. The pointer used to resize a control is
- **a.** 
- **b.** 
- **c.** 
- **d.** 

16. A control is considered to be bound when
- **a.** It is displayed in a form or report
- **b.** It is used to sort a table
- **c.** Its data source is found in a table
- **d.** Its data source is the result of an expression

17. Which button is used to add an existing field to a form?
- **a.** 
- **b.** 
- **c.** 
- **d.** 

18. Which of the following is used to change the order used to advance from field to field?
- **a.** Format tab in the Properties Sheet
- **b.** Data tab in the Properties Sheet
- **c.** Field List
- **d.** Tab Order

Skills Review

1. Create a form.
- **a.** Start Access and make sure your Student Disk is in drive A. Open the file Bike Parts from your Student Disk.
- **b.** Create a new form for the Products table.
- **c.** Include all fields except CategoryID in the form.
- **d.** Use the Form Wizard to create a columnar form.
- **e.** Use the Stone style.
- **f.** Use the title Bicycle Parts Database for the form.
- **g.** Display the form with data.

2. Modify a form layout.
- **a.** Maximize the Form window and change the form's dimensions so that it is at least 6" wide.
- **b.** Select controls and position them so that all controls are displayed on the screen in an order you feel makes sense.

3. Change the tab order.
- **a.** Modify the tab order so that pressing [Tab] moves sequentially through the fields as you have arranged them.
- **b.** Write down your new tab order, and turn the list in.

4. **Use the Expression Builder.**
   a. Click the text box button in the Toolbox, then create a calculated expression towards the bottom of the form.
   b. Calculate the cost of any product reorder. (*Hint*: multiply ReorderAmount by the UnitPrice.)
   c. Adjust the Tab Order for the new expression.
   d. Save your changes.

5. **Format controls.**
   a. Change the format of the UnitsOnOrder control so that it has one decimal place.
   b. Change the number contained in the UnitsInStock field so that it appears in italics.
   c. View the changes in Form View.
   d. Save your changes.

6. **Add a field to a form.**
   a. Display the Field List.
   b. Add the CategoryID field to the form.
   c. Modify the Tab Order for the insertion of the new field.

7. **Add a graphic image to a form.**
   a. Use the Image button on the Toolbox toolbar to define an area for a graphic image.
   b. Insert the graphic file Nomad.tif, found on your Student Disk.
   c. View the form using the Form View.

8. **Use a form to add a record.**
   a. Make sure the form is open in Form View.
   b. Enter the following new record: Product Num: 70701, Product Name: Nomad Honey Handlebar tape, Category ID: 32, Supplier ID: 10, Units In Stock: 52, Units On Order: 0, Unit Price: 2, Reorder Level: 30, Reorder Amount: 35, Units: Each, DiscoStatus: No.
   c. Save the record.
   d. Print the form containing the new record.

-Modify. Design View click + drag Text Box Properties Change Date

Independent Challenges

1. As the Customer Service Manager of the Melodies Music Store, you must continue your work on the music database. Several of the store's employees will be using the database to enter data, and you need to design a form to facilitate this data entry. The employees will be entering data from a paper-based form, shown in Figure C-24. You also need to generate reports for output requests by management as well as customers.

To complete this independent challenge:

FIGURE C-24

Product ID: Category ID:
Artist:
Product Name:
Serial Number:
Units in Stock:
Unit Price:

1. Open the file "Melodies Music Database" from your Student Disk.
2. Create a single-column form that includes all the fields in the table, then save it as Title Input.
3. The controls should be positioned so that they all fit on the screen. Make sure the tab order reflects any fields that you moved.
4. Use the newly created form to add three new records of your favorite artists.
5. Print the form containing one of the new records.
6. Add an expression that calculates a new field called OnHand that multiplies the UnitsInStock field value by the UnitPrice field value. (*Hint*: Use the text box button on the Toolbox to create a new control.)

2. You work in the U.S. Census Office for your city. The records in the Statistical Data table, which is in the database file "Census" on your Student Disk, contain marriage information by state. Each state is assigned a geographical area. Using the Statistical Data table, create a form to facilitate data entry, and create at least two reports showing different groupings of this information.

To complete this independent challenge:

1. Open the database "Census."
2. Create a single-column form containing all the fields in the table.
3. Modify the form by repositioning the controls, then adjusting the tab order.
4. Save the form using a name of your choice.
5. Preview the form after each of your modifications.
6. Create at least two forms based on information in the table. Save each form using a name of your choice.
7. In both forms, make sure the tab order reflects the order of your controls.
8. Use an expression in at least one form, and modify the formatting to include numeric formats and text attributes (bold, italics, or underlining) in both forms.

3. The medical consortium, Allied Surgeons and Physicians, are very satisfied with the database you've created, and would like you to create some customized forms for them.

Using the "Allied Surgeons and Physicians" database created by an employee of the medical group, create forms and reports that will make it easy for patient entries to be made.

To complete this independent challenge:

1. Open the database "Allied Surgeons and Physicians" on your Student Disk.
2. Create a form using the Patient Records table which displays all the fields in the table.
3. Arrange the fields in a way that seems efficient for data entry.
4. Make sure the tab order is updated to reflect the new order of fields.
5. Use the new form to add one new patient for each physician.
6. Print the form containing your new entries.
7. Add an expression that calculates each patient's current age.
8. Include formatting to make the form more attractive.
9. Obtain a graphic image—or create one yourself—and insert it on the form.
10. Submit all printouts.

WEB WORK

4. You have been asked to maintain a database of stocks for electronic and other hi-technology firms. Use the World Wide Web to gather this information, then create an attractive form you can use to enter additional records.

To complete this independent challenge:

1. Log on to the Internet and use your browser to go to http://www.course.com. From there, click the link Student On Line Companions, then click the Microsoft Office 97 Professional Edition—Illustrated: A First Course page, then click the Access link for Unit C.
2. Find information for at least 10 hi-tech or electronic company stocks, including a minimum of the stock abbreviation, the name of the parent company, and the price per share. You can add any other fields you feel are necessary.
3. Create a new database file on your Student Disk called Hi-Tech stocks.
4. Use the Table Wizard to create a table.
5. Create a new form you'll use to enter the data into the table.
6. Enter the information you retrieved from the World Wide Web.
7. Preview and print the form.
8. Hand in a printout of your work.

▶ Visual Workshop

Use the Current Product List query in the Bike Inventory database on your Student Disk to create the following form using the skills you learned in this Unit.

FIGURE C-25

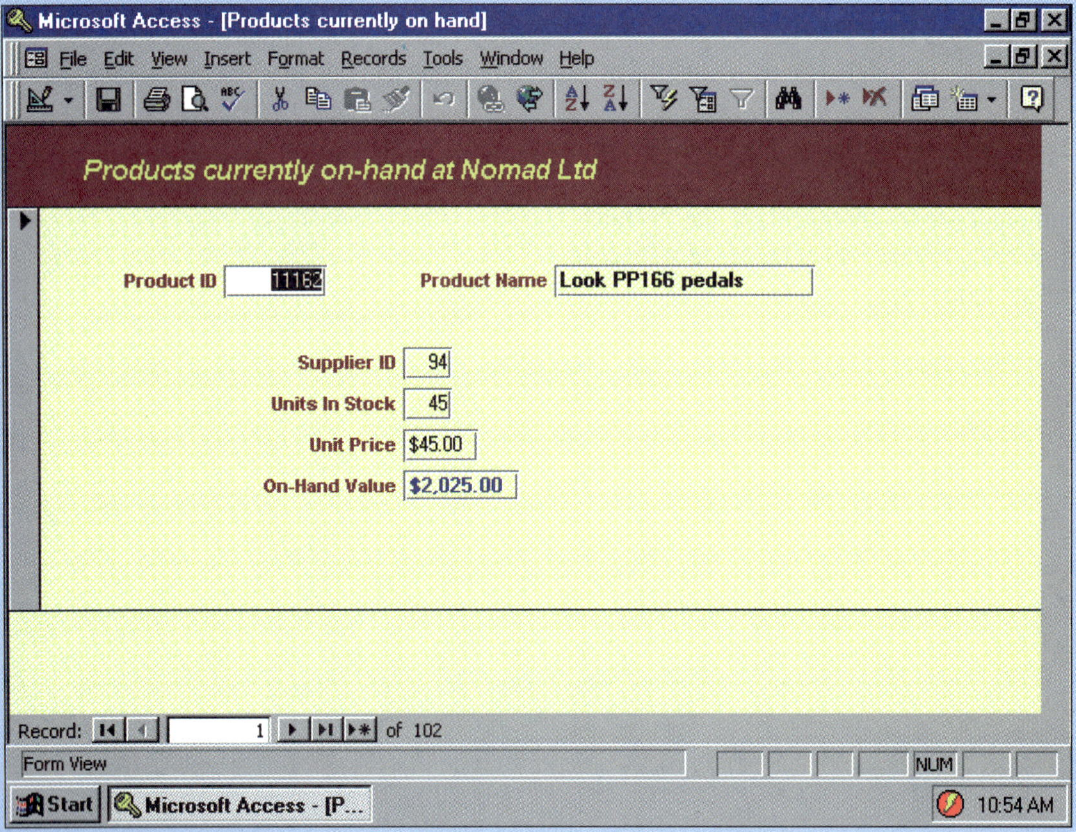

Creating
a report

Objectives

- Create a report
- Group records in a report
- Align fields
- Resize a control
- Add an expression to a report
- Create a report from a query
- Save a form as a report
- Create labels

Printed reports are an easy way of distributing information to others. Like information in a datasheet, reports can be based on a table or query, and can contain calculated expressions and sorted data. There are formatting options that let you design appealing reports that present information clearly. Michael wants to produce reports based on table data that he can distribute to other employees so they will know the status of products carried by Nomad stores.

Access 97

Creating a Report

The ability to create thoughtful, concise reports enables you to share data with others in meaningful ways. The most significant data can lose its impact if it appears in an unprofessional or poorly laid out report. You can create reports in Access from scratch or you can use the Report Wizard. The **Report Wizard** provides sample report layouts and gives you options for including specific fields in the report. As with a form, the layout of a report includes sections for a Report Header, Detail, and Report Footer. Each report also includes a section for a Page Header and a Page Footer, so you can print information on each report page. Michael wants to create a report showing all but two fields in the Bicycle Products table. He plans on distributing this report to other Nomad employees and customers.

Steps

1. Start Access, open the **Product Inventory** database on your Student Disk, click the **New Object button list arrow** on the Database toolbar, then click **Report**
   The New Report dialog box opens. You could also create a report by clicking the Reports tab in the Database window, then clicking New. You use the Bicycle Products table for this report, which you'll create using the Report Wizard.
2. Click the **Choose the table or query where the object's data comes from list arrow**, click **Bicycle Products**, click **Report Wizard**, then click **OK**
   The Report Wizard dialog box—which allows you to select which fields appear in the report—opens. You want all fields except the ProductID and Total fields to be included. Rather than individually select all but these two fields, you select all the fields and then remove the two fields you don't want.
3. Click the **All Fields button** >> in the Report Wizard dialog box
   All the fields move from the Available Fields list to the Selected Fields list. Now you can remove the fields you don't want included in the report.
4. Click **Total** in the Selected Fields list box, click the **Remove Field button** <, click **ProductID** in the Selected Fields list box, then click <
   The Report Wizard dialog box on your screen should look like the one in Figure D-1.
5. Click Next > to display the next dialog box
   This dialog box, shown in Figure D-2, determines how the data in the report will be grouped.

FIGURE D-1: Completed Selected Fields list box

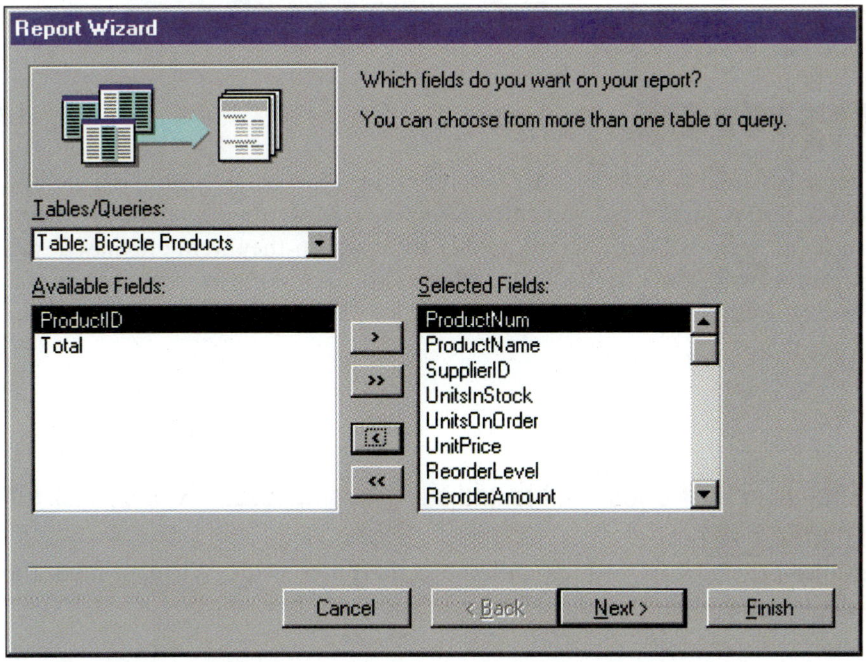

Click Reports TAB
New
Rpt WIZZARD
Click on drop down Box
Select Fields.
GROUPING click TO Be heading
Next
FIRST drop down Box DISCO STATUS

FIGURE D-2: Grouping dialog box

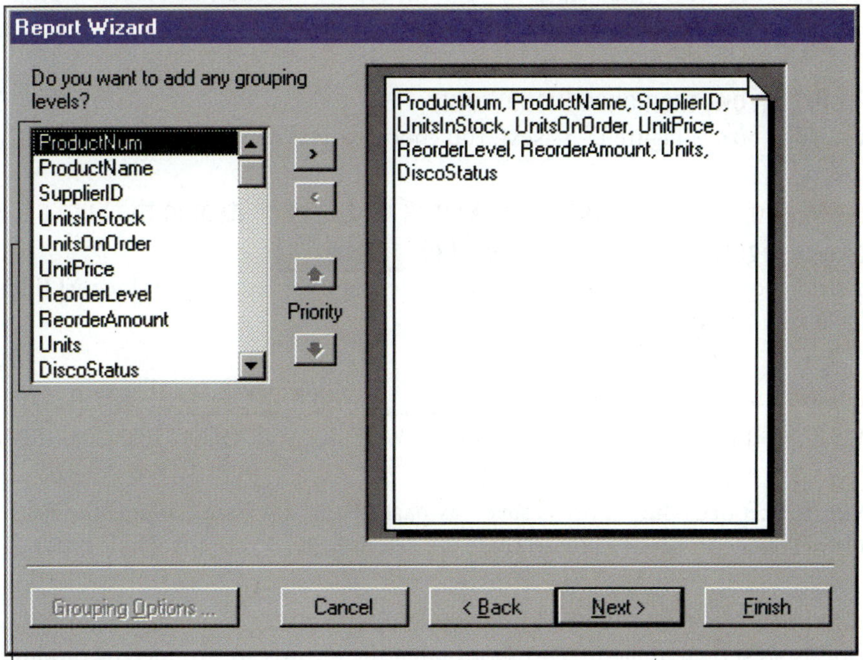

Choose how fields are grouped using available fields here

CLUES TO USE

Using AutoReport

You can create a simple report quickly by clicking the New Object button on the Database toolbar, then clicking AutoReport. AutoReport offers no prompts or dialog boxes; it instantly creates a single-column report that displays all fields in the table or query.

Access 97

Grouping Records in a Report

The grouping of records is used to make a report easier for others to read. **Grouping** is a method of organizing records, just as sorting lets you choose the way records are displayed. For example, if you wanted to see records listed by the supplier from whom they were purchased, you would group the records by the SupplierID field. Michael wants the report to display the inventory in groups by product name so that all of the data for the same products will be listed and totaled together.

Steps

1. Click **ProductName** in the **Do you want to add any grouping levels list box**, click the **Single Field button** [>]
   The ProductName field appears in blue and above the other fields. When printed, the records with all the same product names will be grouped together.

QuickTip
The Sort Order button in this dialog box is a toggle; click to change from ascending to descending order.

2. Click [Next >]
   This dialog box allows you to specify a sort order. You choose to sort by each record's DiscoStatus in ascending order (the default) so that the report will show all currently available items together and all discontinued items together.

3. Click the **first list arrow**, then click **DiscoStatus**
   Compare your dialog box to Figure D-3. Next, you choose which items will be totaled.

4. Click **Summary Options**, click to add a **checkmark** next to each item in the **Sum column**, as shown in Figure D-4, click **OK**, then click [Next >]
   The next two dialog boxes ask you to select a report style, paper orientation, and report title. You accept the default choices.

5. Click the **Landscape radio button**, click [Next >], click [Next >] again, type **Products by DiscoStatus** in the What title do you want for your report text box, then click **Finish**
   Access compiles the report. The report is saved as part of the database file and the Print Preview window is opened. You need to decrease the Zoom factor to see the whole report.

6. Click the **Zoom button** on the Print Preview toolbar
   The report appears, as shown in Figure D-5. Notice that the records are grouped by product name. You are satisfied with the report and need to preview and print your work.

Time To
Save

7. Click the **Close button** on the Print Preview toolbar
   You return to Design View. You decide to print just the first page of the report to see how it looks.

8. Click **File** on the menu bar, click **Print**, type **1** in the From text box, type **1** in the To text box, then click **OK**

FIGURE D-3: Choosing the Sort order

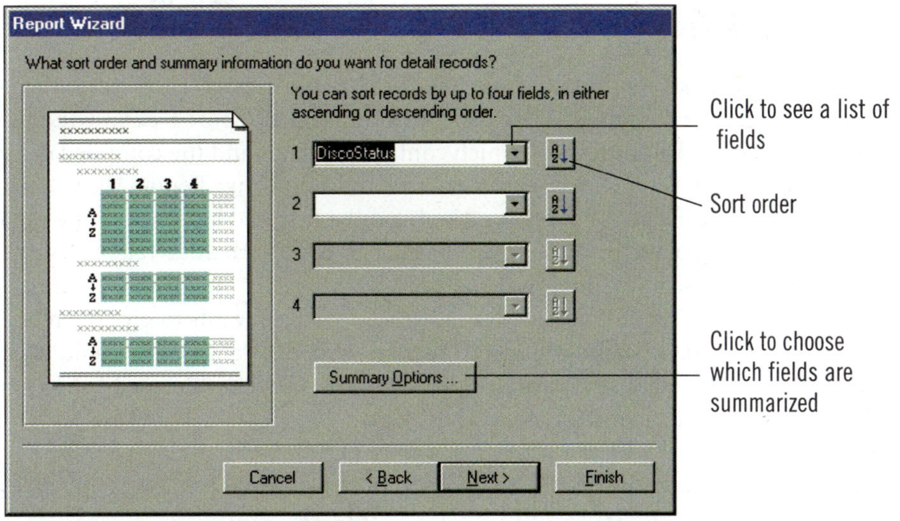

FIGURE D-4: Summary Options dialog box

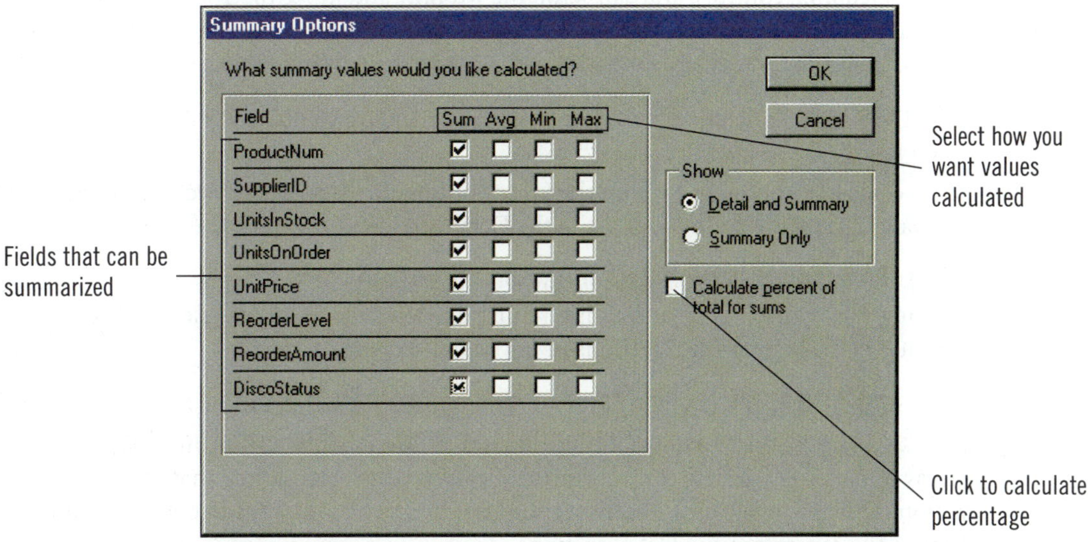

FIGURE D-5: Previewing the report

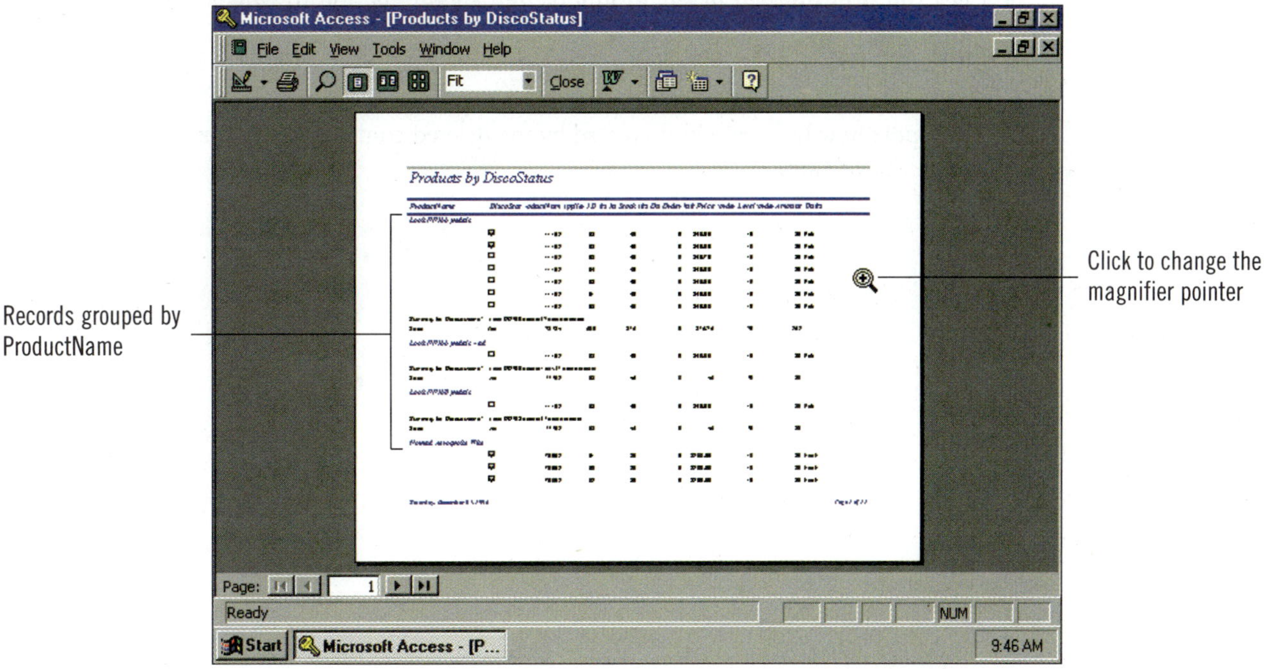

Access 97

Access 97

Aligning Fields

You can make modifications to the format of a report, such as bolding column headings or changing the alignment of fields in a column. The Report Design window is divided into seven sections: the **Detail** section, which contains controls and the compiled data from the table, and a Header and Footer section for each of the following: Report, Page, and Group. The **Report Header** and **Report Footer** print only on the first and last page of the report; the **Page Header** and **Page Footer** print on every page. The **Group Header** references the field on which each group is based (in this case, the groups are based on ProductName). Although the Products by DiscoStatus report is adequate, Michael wants to give the report a more professional look. The field headings are not aligned with the data below them, as shown in Figure D-6. Because Michael's screen is already in Design View, he can easily align the field headings with their data to format the report.

Steps

1. Press and hold **[Shift]**, click each of the **control headings** in the Page Header section, *except* ProductName, then release **[Shift]**
   You selected nine controls. You can scroll the window and move the Toolbox toolbar to select all the desired controls. Each selected control has handles surrounding it. First you center the selected controls and decrease the font size to make the text less crowded.
2. Click the **Center button** on the Formatting toolbar, click the **Font Size list arrow**, then click **8**
   Access centers the headings for the selected controls in the Page Header section. See Figure D-7. You want to center align the controls in the Detail section of the report.
3. Select the **ProductNum control** in the Detail section
   Selecting this control without holding [Shift] deselects the previously selected controls. You continue to make multiple selections in the Detail section.
4. Press and hold **[Shift]**, click **each of the controls** in the Detail section, *except* the DiscoStatus control, release **[Shift]**, then click on the Formatting toolbar
   Access centers the selected controls in the Detail section. You decide that the current information in the ProductName Footer section is unnecessary and want to delete it, but first you deselect the controls in the Detail section.
5. Click the **first control** in the ProductName Footer section to select it
6. Press and hold **[Shift]**, click **each of the controls** in the ProductName Footer section, release **[Shift]**, then press **[Delete]**
   The report now has a gap in it created by the deleted controls. Later, you will add an expression in this section.

QuickTip

You can select all the controls in a single section by moving the mouse to the left of the section and clicking when the pointer turns to ➡. Press [Shift] and click to deselect individual selected controls.

FIGURE D-6: Unedited Products by DiscoStatus report

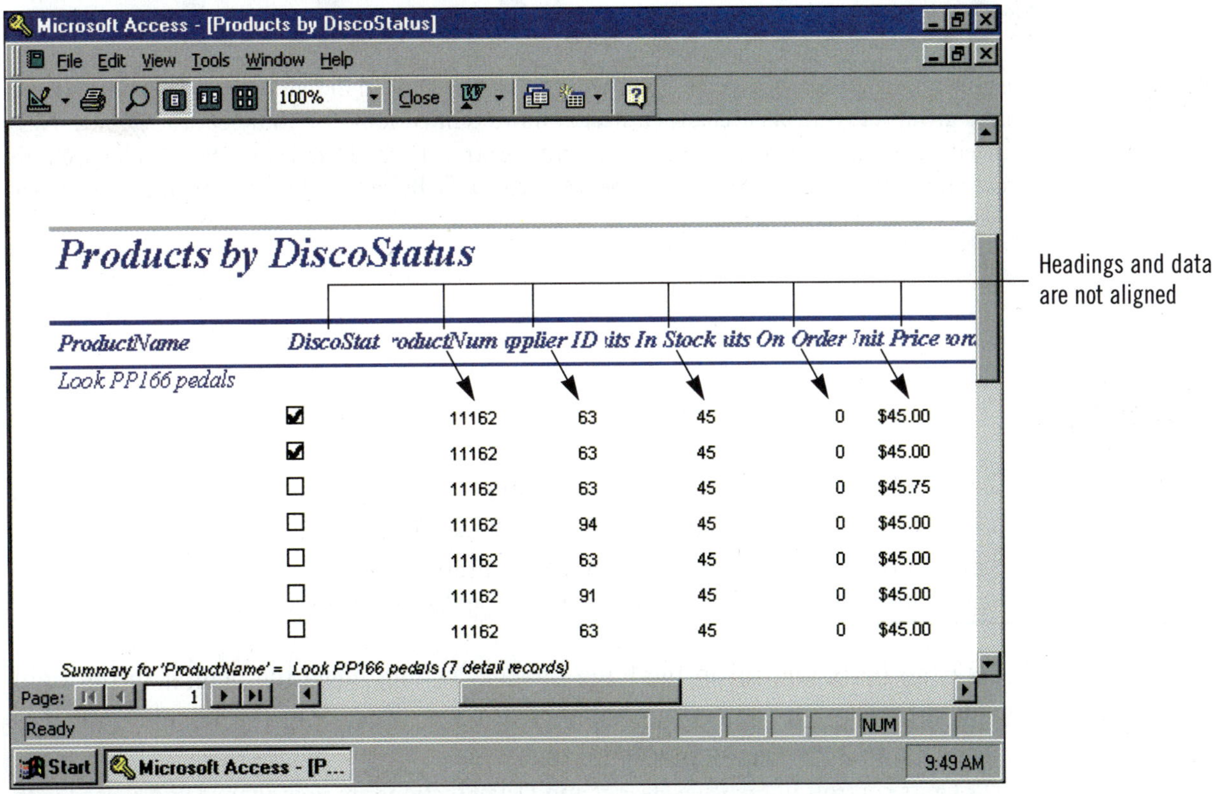

FIGURE D-7: Centered controls in the report

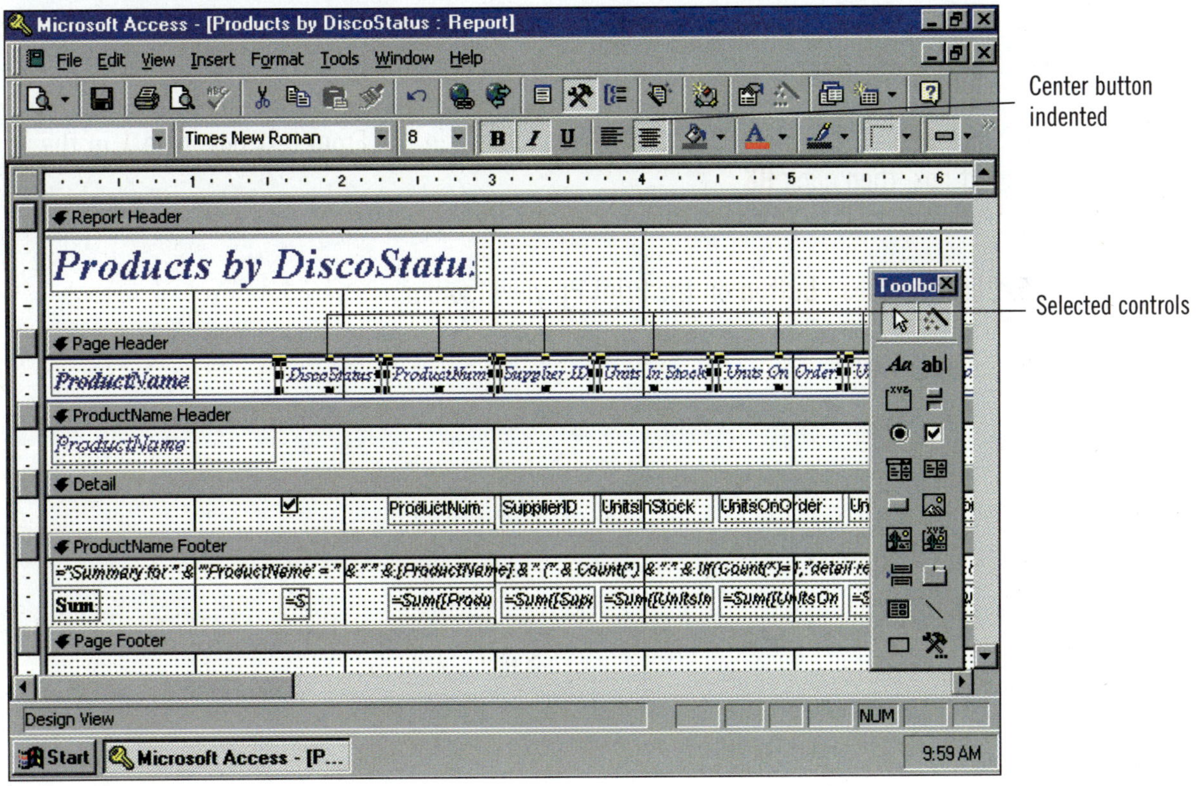

Access 97

Access 97

Resizing a Control

The position of controls, as well as their widths, can be changed individually or in groups. If you resize a group of controls it creates a neater, more unified look for your report. Next Michael decides to resize the width of the Units controls in the Detail and Page Header sections because they take up more space than the other controls. By resizing these controls, Michael will be able to tighten up the right side of the report.

Steps

1. Click the **Units control** in the Detail section, move the pointer to the right middle handle until the pointer changes to ↔, then drag the handle until it is aligned with 8.25" on the horizontal ruler, as shown in Figure D-8
   Repeat this procedure for the Units control in the Page Header section.

2. Click the **Units control** in the Page Header section, move the pointer to the right middle handle until the pointer changes to ↔, then drag the handle until it is aligned with 8.25" on the horizontal ruler
   The Units controls in the Page Header and Detail sections are now aligned and resized with each other. You want to preview the report and print a sample page.

3. Click the **Print Preview button** on the Report Design toolbar
   The controls in the report are aligned, as shown in Figure D-9.

4. Click **File** on the menu bar, click **Print**, type **1** in the From text box, type **1** in the To text box, then click **OK**
   You close the Print Preview window and save the report.

5. Click the **Close button** on the Print Preview toolbar

6. Save your work

FIGURE D-8: Resizing a control

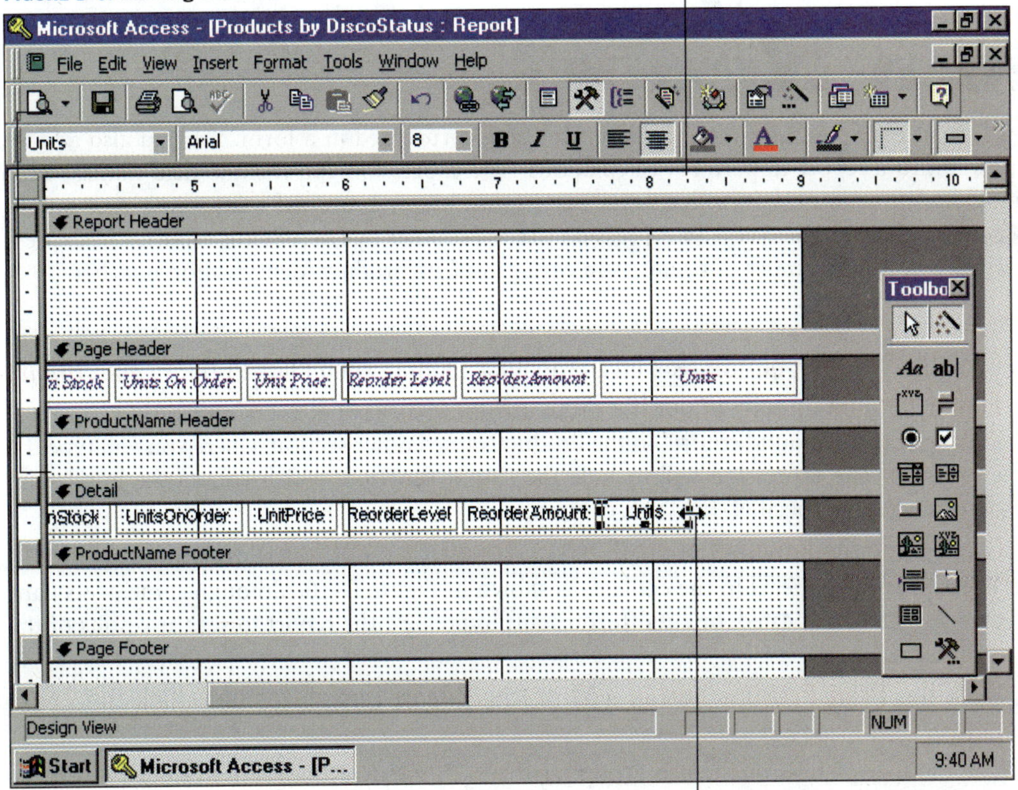

Change HEADER
click BOX -
Type in new
name

FIGURE D-9: Report in Print Preview

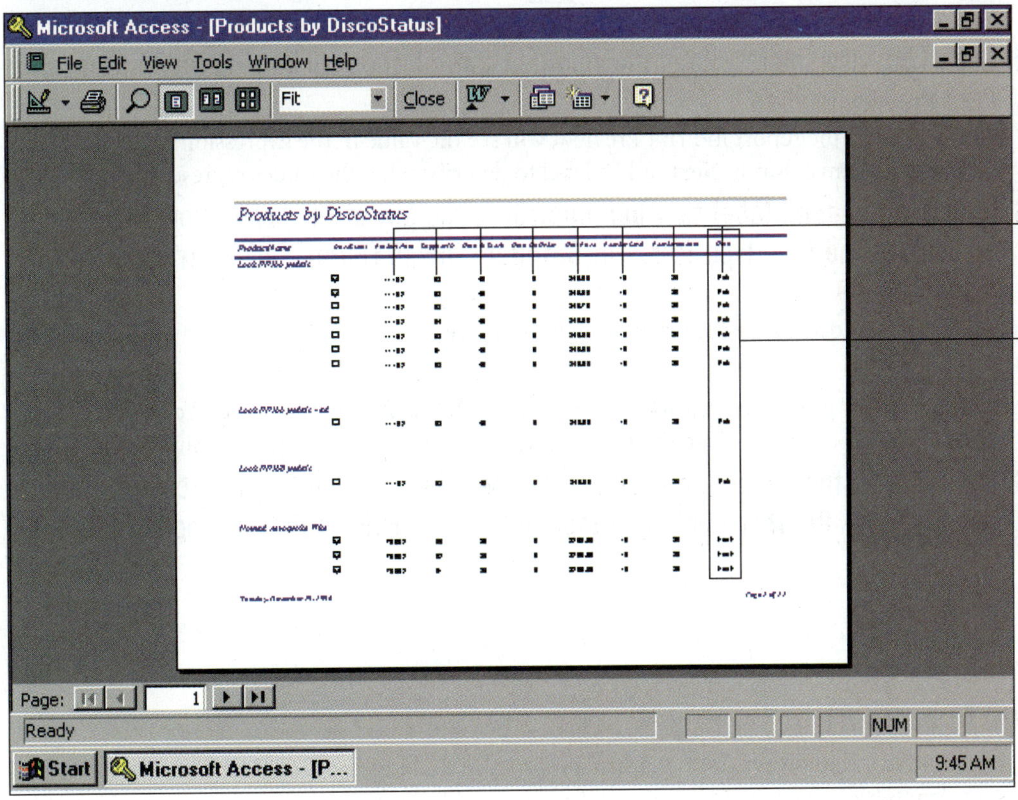

Access 97

Access 97

Adding an Expression to a Report

You have already seen how an expression can be incorporated in a form. You can also add an expression to a report to perform calculations. The expression can include field names, table names, and functions. A **function** is an easy-to-use preprogrammed mathematical equation. Michael wants to add an expression to the Products by DiscoStatus report. The expression will count the number of products in each group, by product identification number.

Steps

QuickTip

In addition to Count, Access provides many other functions for use in expressions. Ask the Office Assistant how you can use functions in expressions for more information.

1. Click the **Text box button** abl on the Toolbox toolbar, then click in the **ProductName Footer section** directly under the ProductNum control at the **2¼"** mark
   This places an unbound control in the ProductName Footer section, where you will type the expression. The expression will include the Count function, which counts the number of occurrences of a specified field in a column.
2. Click inside the **unbound control**, type **=Count([ProductNum])**, then press **[Enter]**
   The expression appears in the control, as shown in Figure D-10, although some of its contents might be truncated, or cut off. You want to preview the report to see the results of the expression.
3. Click the **Print Preview button** on the Report Design toolbar, click the **Zoom button** if necessary
   The number of records in each group has been counted, although the values need to be aligned with the values in the ProductNum column and it needs a descriptive label.
4. Click the **Close button** on the Print Preview toolbar, then with the expression still selected, click the **Align Left button** on the Report Design toolbar
   You decide to preview the report again to check the results of this modification.
5. Click , view the results of the modified control, then click the **Close button** on the Print Preview toolbar
   When viewing the report in Print Preview, you see the value in the expression is left-aligned in the ProductNum column. Next, add a label to describe what the values represent in the report.
6. Click the **unbound label text box control** to the left of the expression, double-click the **text in the box**, type **Items in Category**, press **[Enter]**, click the **Font Size list arrow**, click **9**
   The label is added to the report as shown in Figure D-11. You again preview the report.
7. Click
   Compare your previewed report with Figure D-12. Use Zoom as needed. You print the first page of the report, then close the Print Preview window and save the modifications.
8. Click **File** on the menu bar, click **Print**, type **1** in the From text box, type **1** in the To text box, click **OK**, then click the **Close button** on the Print Preview toolbar

Time To

- Save
- Close the report

CLUES TO USE

Adding a field to a report

In addition to adding expressions, you can always add existing fields to a report. Any tables whose fields are available in the table can be dragged to areas within a report by clicking the Field List button on the Report Design toolbar, then dragging a field to an area of the report.

FIGURE D-10: Truncated expression in control

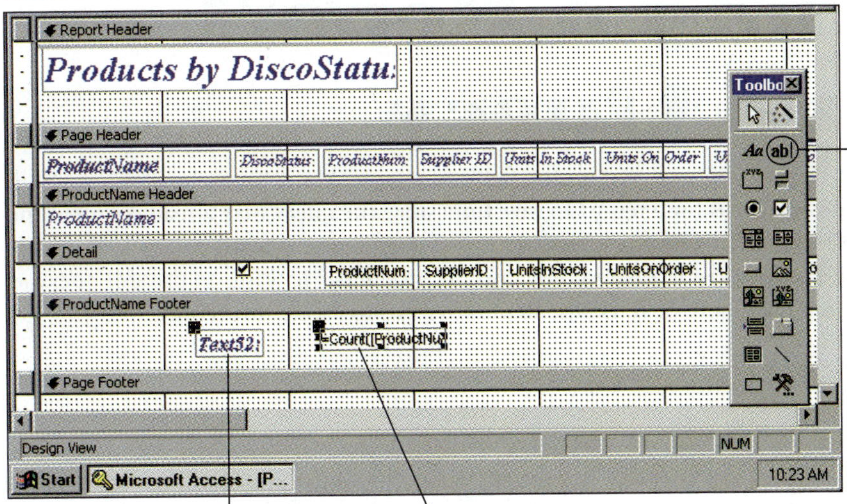

Text box button

Default label text

Expression indicating Count function

FIGURE D-11: Descriptive label added to expression

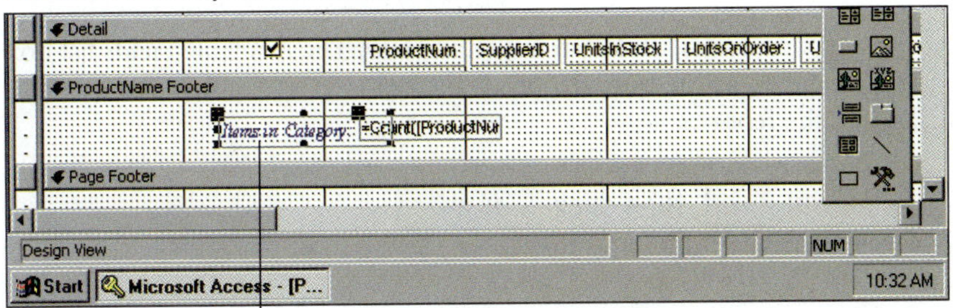

Label identifies results of expression

FIGURE D-12: Completed report with expression and label

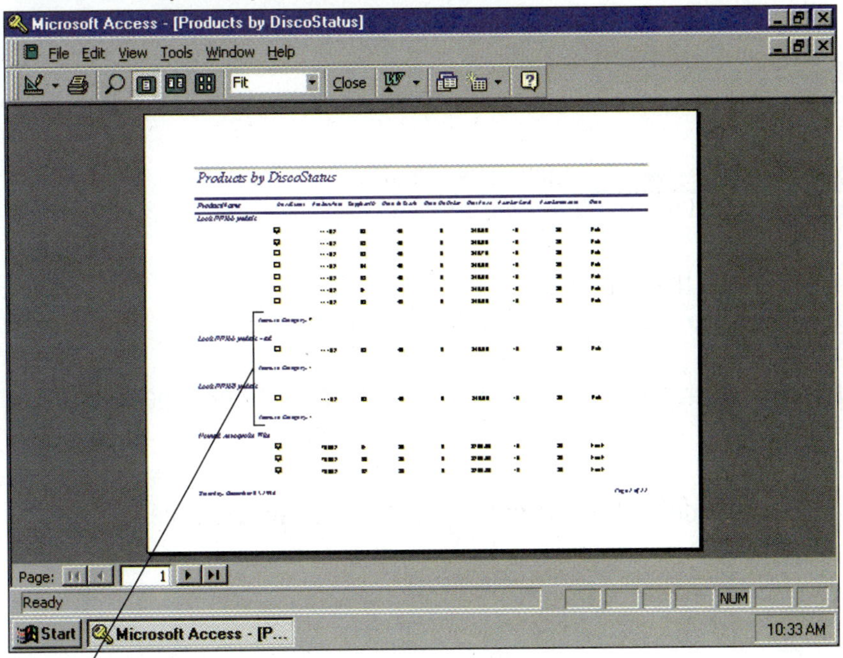

Labels and results of expression

Access 97

Creating a Report from a Query

You've seen how to create a report based on the fields in a table. Many times, however, you will want to use a query as the basis for a report to save time since the query may already contain the information you want printed. Michael has created a query for the Bicycle Products table called Current Product List to display only current products. He wants to use this query as the basis for a new report. Again, he'll use the Report Wizard to create this report.

Steps

1. Click the **New Object button list arrow** on the Database toolbar, then click **Report**, click the **Choose the table or query where the object's data comes from list box**, click the **Current Product List** then click **Report Wizard**
   Compare your New Report dialog box with Figure D-13.

2. Click **OK**
   The Report Wizard dialog box opens, as shown in Figure D-14. The Available Fields list box displays all the available fields in the query (not all the fields in the table). You want to include all these fields in the report.

3. Click the **All Fields button** [>>], then click [Next >]
   You want the records grouped by ProductName.

4. Click **ProductName**, then click the **Single Field button** [>]
   The records will be grouped by the ProductName field, as shown in Figure D-15. You need to advance to the next dialog box which lets you determine the sort order. You decide that you don't need to sort by any other fields and accept the default.

5. Click [Next >], click [Next >] again
   Next, you decide to accept the default layout and orientation, style, and report title.

6. Click [Next >], click [Next >], then click **Finish**
   Access creates the report and displays it in Print Preview.

7. Click the **Close button** on the Print Preview toolbar
   Satisfied with the report, you decide to print the first page as a sample.

8. Click **File** on the menu bar, click **Print**, type **1** in the From text box, type **1** in the To text box, then click **OK**

9. Save the report using the default report name **Current Product List**, then close it

QuickTip

When basing a report on a query, give the report the same name as the query name; this will remind you that the report and the query are related.

FIGURE D-13: New Report dialog box

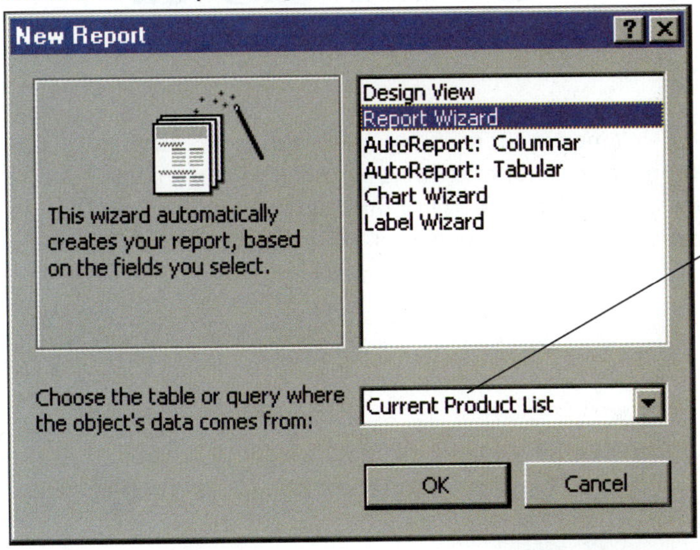

Query to be used in the report

PAGE D10 Shows how ADD Footer

FIGURE D-14: Report Wizard dialog box

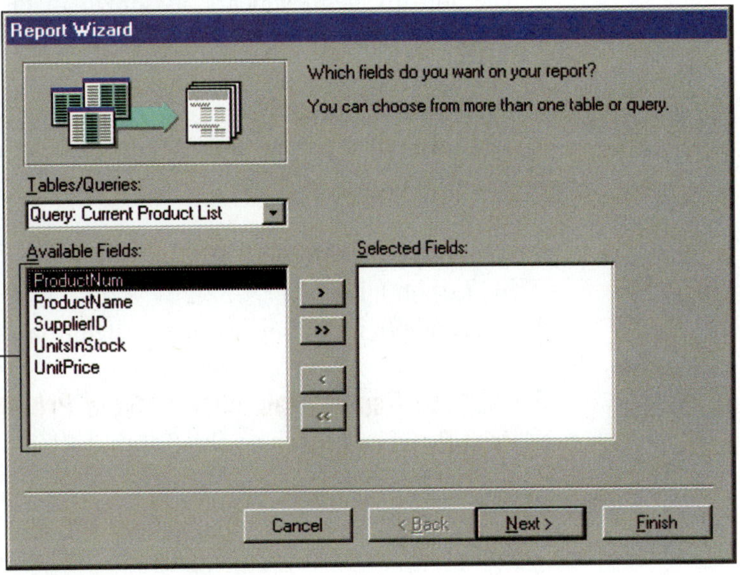

Fields available in the query

Expression always starts to (=)

always has to have ( )

FIGURE D-15: Grouping records in the Report Wizard dialog box

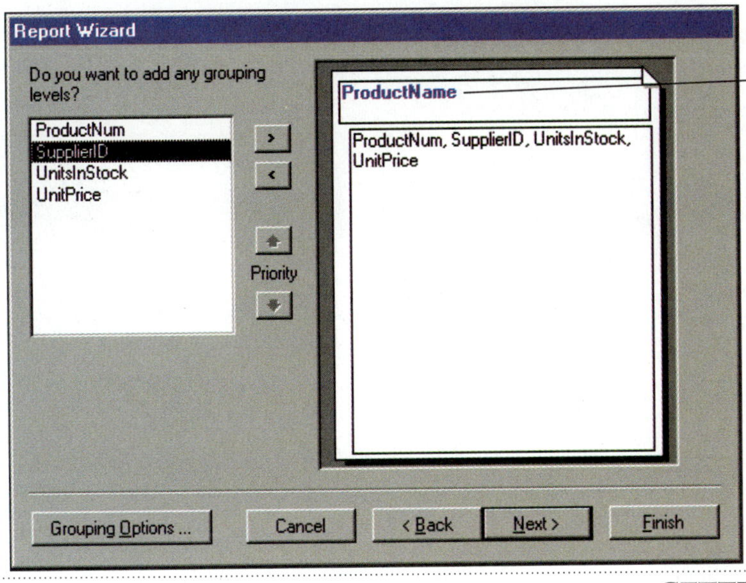

Records will be grouped by this field

Access 97

Access 97

Saving a Form as a Report

If you already have a form designed that meets your needs, you can work more efficiently by saving a form as a report. This can be an efficient way of creating a familiar-looking report, because your co-workers will already have seen the form. To save a form as a report, open the form in Design View, click File on the menu bar, click Save As Report, then supply a new name for the report. Michael creates a report from the Bicycle Products form.

Steps

1. Click the **Forms tab**, then make sure the **Bicycle Products form** is selected
   Once the form is selected, you can save it as a report using the context-sensitive pop-up menu.

2. Right-click the **Bicycle Products form**
   The pop-up menu appears, as shown in Figure D-16. You select the Save As Report command.

3. Click **Save As Report**
   You can keep the same name used in the form, but you choose to change the name for the report.

4. Type **Bicycle Products - from Form** in the Report Name text box, as shown in Figure D-17, then click **OK**
   You decide to preview the report created from the form.

5. Click the **Reports tab**, click **Bicycle Products - from Form report**, then click the **Print Preview button** on the Database toolbar

6. If necessary, click the **Maximize button** and scroll to see all the records in the report
   Compare your report to Figure D-18. Satisfied with the new report, you close the Preview window.

7. Click the **Close button** on the Print Preview toolbar

8. Close the report

FIGURE D-16: Pop-up menu

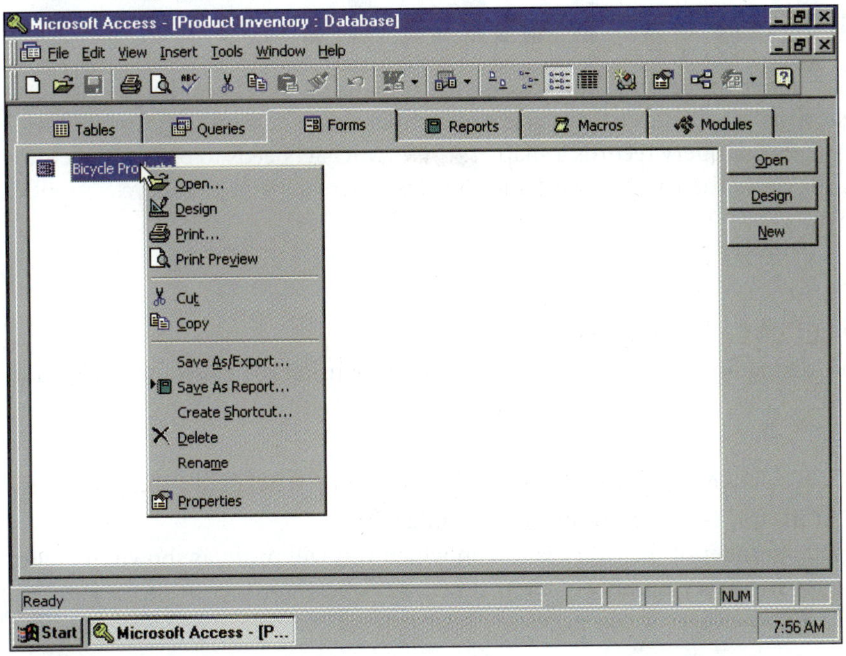

FIGURE D-17: Save Form As Report dialog box

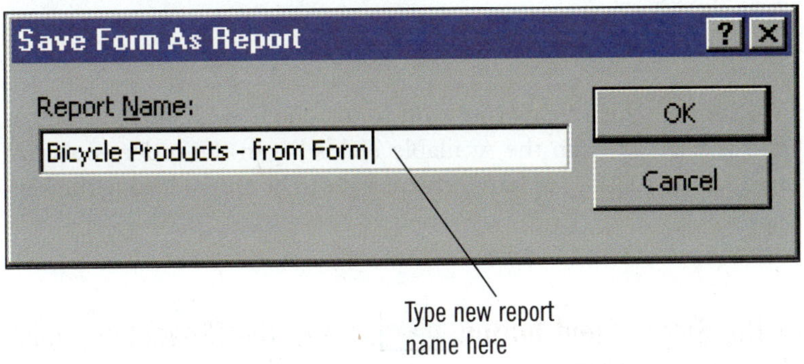

FIGURE D-18: Preview of report created from form

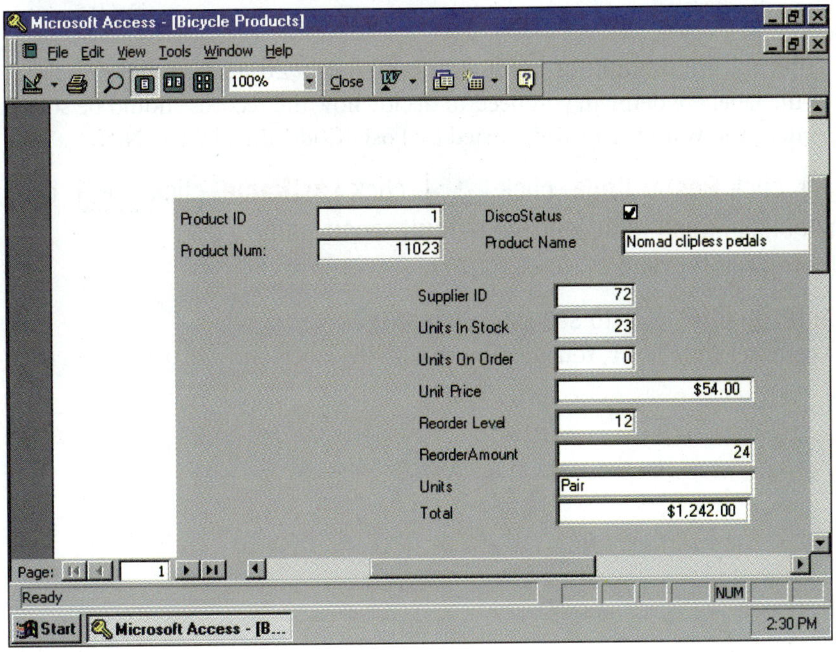

Access 97

Access 97

Creating Labels

Labels are a necessity in any office, and they are easy to create using the Access Label Wizard. If you use Avery labels, you'll be able to find the size and style label you currently use, making creating labels based on table or query records a snap. Michael needs to prepare labels for Nomad customers. He'll use the Label Wizard and the Customers table in the Bicycle Supplies database.

Steps

1. **Click the New button on the Reports tab**
   The New Report dialog box opens. You'll create your labels using the Customers table and the Label Wizard.

2. **Click Label Wizard, click the Choose the Table or query where the object's data comes from list arrow, click Customers, then click OK**
   Next, you select the number of the Avery labels on which you will print, as shown in Figure D-19. You decide to use Avery number 5160, that prints 3 labels across each sheet.

3. **Click 5160, then click Next >**
   The third dialog box allows you to change the font, font size, and other text attributes. You choose to accept the default values.

4. **Click Next >**
   In the next dialog box, you choose which fields you want to include in each label, as well as their placement. Each field is selected from the Available Fields list in the order you want them on the label. Any spaces, punctuation, or hard returns have to be entered using the keyboard.
   Enter the information for the first line in the label.

5. **Click FirstName, click the Single Field button >, press the [Spacebar], click LastName, click >, then press [Enter]**
   Next, you'll enter the fields for the information containing the address, city, state, and postal code.

6. **Repeat step 5 entering the remaining fields using Figure D-20 as a guide**
   Once the fields in the label are defined, you need to decide how the records should be sorted when they are printed. You want the records sorted by PostalCode, then by LastName.

7. **Click Next >, click Postal Code, click >, click LastName, click >, click Next >, then click Finish to accept the default report name**
   The labels display in Print Preview.

8. **Click the magnifier pointer to see the whole page**
   Compare your screen to Figure D-21. You are pleased with the labels and will print them later.

QuickTip

Double-click the field name in the Available Fields list to move it to the Prototype label text box.

Time To

- Close
- Exit

FIGURE D-19: Second Label Wizard dialog box

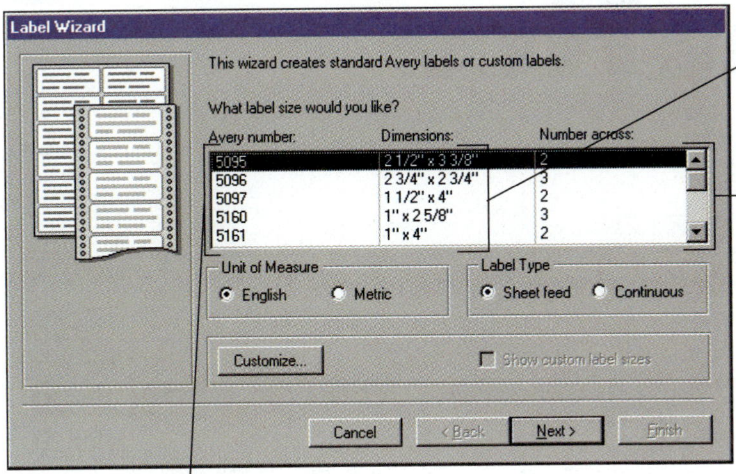

FIGURE D-20: Defining fields in a label

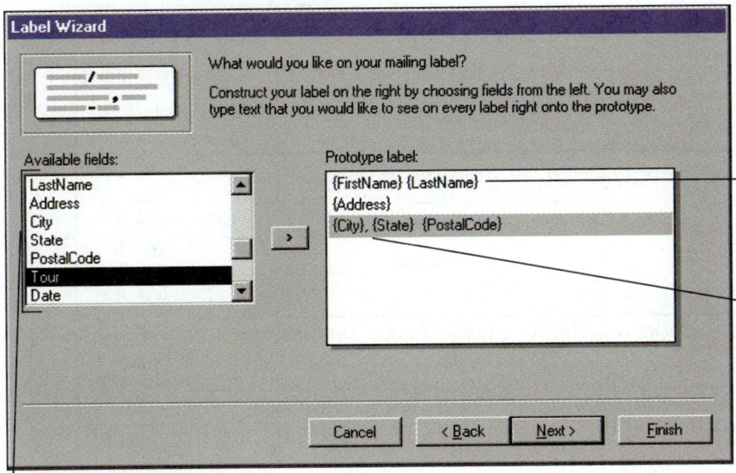

FIGURE D-21: Completed labels

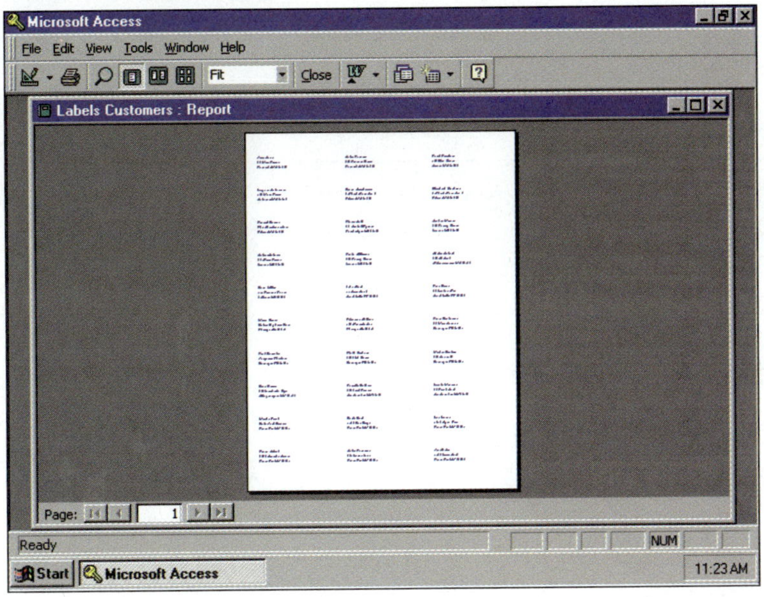

Access 97

Practice

► Concepts Review

Label each of the elements of the Report Design window shown in Figure D-22.

FIGURE D-22

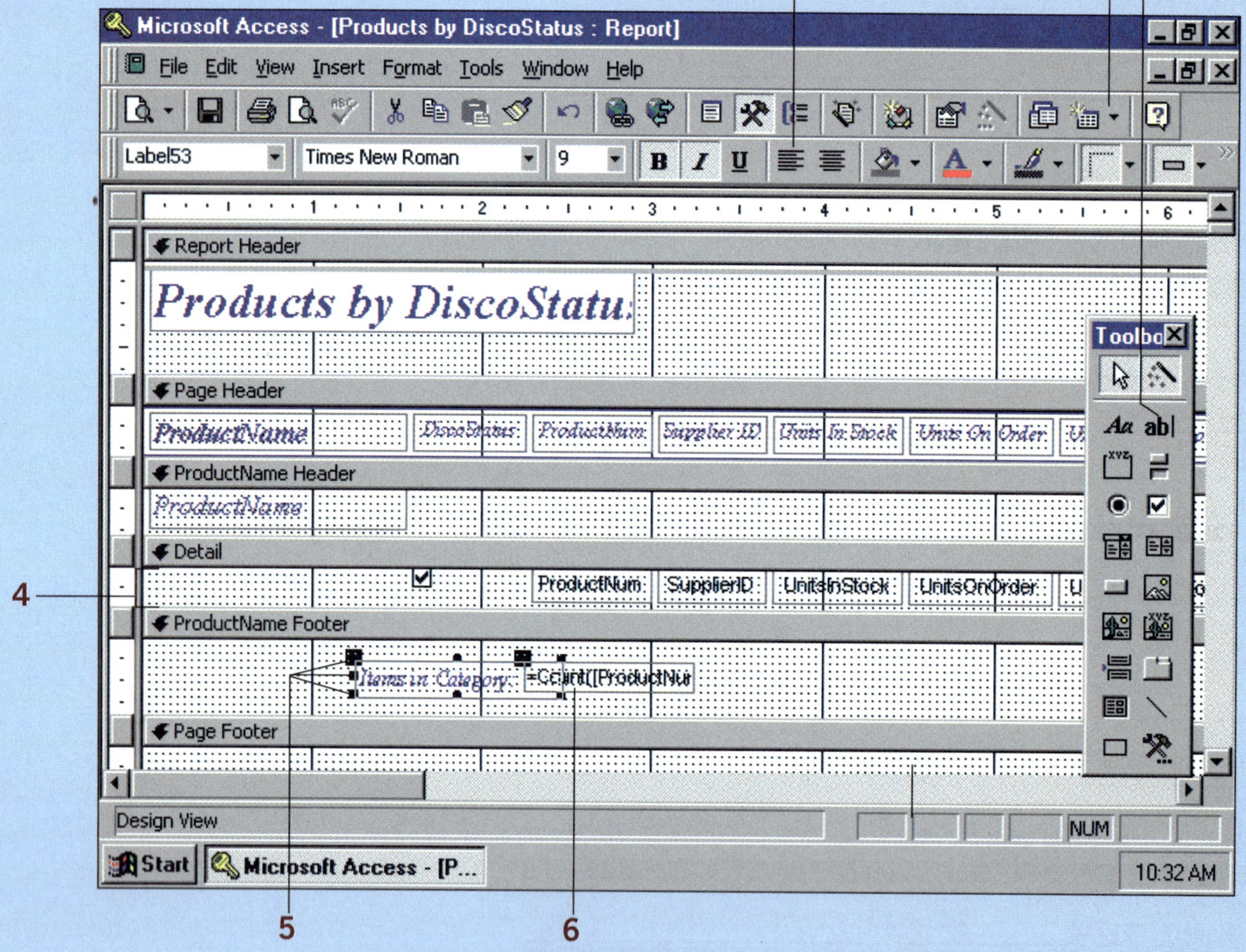

Match each button to its correct description.

7. [button]
8. ab|
9. <
10. [button]
11. [button]
12. >

a. Print Preview
b. Zoom
c. New Object
d. Select field
e. Remove field
f. Text box

Practice

Select the best answer from the list of choices.

13. Which key do you press to select multiple controls?

a. [Ctrl] **b.** [Alt] **c.** [Shift] **d.** [Tab]

14. The __________ section contains controls and compiles data.

a. Detail **b.** Report Header **c.** Group Header **d.** Report Footer

15. Which button is used to add an unbound control to a report?

a. [button] **b.** [button] **c.** Aa **d.** ab|

16. Which of the following is true about report expressions?

a. They can contain mathematical functions.
b. In Design View, the contents may appear truncated.
c. The label text can be customized.
d. All of the above.

17. How can labels be created?

a. Click [button], then click Labels
b. Click Reports from the menu bar, then click Label Wizard
c. Click New from the Reports tab, then click Label Wizard
d. Click [button] from the Database toolbar

Skills Review

1. Create a report.
   a. Open the Parts List database on your Student Disk.
   b. Create a Groups/Totals report based on the Products table using the Report Wizard.
   c. Include all the fields in the report.

2. Group records in a report.
   a. Group the report by UnitsinStock.
   b. Sort the report in ascending order by ProductName.
   c. Summarize three fields, get an average for unit price and a sum for the reorder amount and units on order fields.
   d. Accept the default report layout.
   e. Use the Formal style.
   f. Save the report as Products by Units in Stock.
   g. Preview the report with the data in it.
   h. Print the report.

3. Align fields.
   a. Align the fields so that the values are centered with the headings above them.
   b. Delete the reorder amount summary which detracts from the report.
   c. Preview and print the report.
   d. Save your changes.

4. Resize a control.
   a. Change the font size of the Page Header controls to 8.
   b. Move the ReorderAmount controls closer to the edge of the page.
   c. Resize the ReorderAmount control so it takes up only enough room to display its label.
   d. Save your modifications.
   e. Preview the report.

5. Add an expression to a report.
   a. Create an expression in the Detail section under ProductName that subtracts ReorderLevel from UnitsinStock. (*Hint*: Drag the section divider to make room for the new expression)
   b. Add the descriptive label "Reorder if Negative" to the left of the expression.
   c. Adjust the fonts sizes and control locations to create a professional-looking report.
   d. Preview and print the report.
   e. Save your changes.

6. Create a report from a query.
- **a.** Use the Report Wizard and create a report using the Products sold as "Each" query.
- **b.** Group the report by UnitsinStock.
- **c.** Sort the report by ProductName.
- **d.** Accept the default layout, style, and name for the report.
- **e.** Preview the report with the data.
- **f.** Move the controls and align the fields as necessary to create a professional-looking report.
- **g.** Print the report.

7. Save a form as a report.
- **a.** Save the Bicycle Parts Database form as a report. Name the new report: Parts List Database - from Form.
- **b.** Print the first page of the new report.

8. Create labels.
- **a.** Use the Label Wizard and the Products table to create stock room shelf labels using Avery 5160 labels.
- **b.** The first line of the label should include the ProductNum and the ProductName.
- **c.** The second line of the label should include the ReorderLevel and the ReorderAmount.
- **d.** The third line of the label should include the UnitPrice.
- **e.** Sort the labels by the ProductName.
- **f.** Name this report "Shelf Labels."
- **g.** Save your work.
- **h.** Print the page of labels.

Control Enter to Change

Reorder Point to Reorder Point

► Independent Challenges

1. You have been using the "Music Store" database for several weeks, and now need to design several reports that can be printed on a weekly basis. Four reports are needed: one that lists all the items in the Available titles table, and one for each of the existing queries.

To complete this independent challenge:

1. Open the file "Music Store" from your Student Disk.
2. Create a report using the Available titles table that displays all the table's fields, grouped by Artist and sorted in descending order by TitleName.
3. The UnitsInStock field should be summed, and the UnitPrice field should be averaged.
4. Use the Outline1 report layout and the Casual style.
5. Name this report Complete titles list.
6. Preview the report.
7. Modify the font size of the heading controls so all the column labels are visible.
8. Save your changes.
9. Preview and print the first page of the report.

► Independent Challenges

2. You have determined that shelf labels would make inventory control much more efficient at your music store. On a weekly basis, the inventory is checked against the cash register receipts and the shelves are restocked. Use the Available titles table in the "Music Store" database to design a shelf label.

To complete this independent challenge:

1. Open the file "Music Store" from your Student Disk.
2. Use the Label Wizard and the Available titles table to create shelf labels. Use Avery 5160 labels and red semi-bold, italics text.
3. The first line should say "Artist: ", then display the Artist name, the second line should display the TitleName, and the third line should display the SerialNumber, UnitsInStock, and UnitPrice.
4. Sort the labels by Artist, then by TitleName.
5. Name the report Available Titles Shelf Labels.
6. Save, preview and print report.

▶ Independent Challenges

3. The database you created for the Allied Surgeons and Physicians is very successful. In fact, they would like you to create a report based on the "Patient Records" table.

To complete this independent challenge:

1. Open the file "ASP Database" from your Student Disk.
2. Create a report using the following fields in the Patient Records table: ID, FirstName, LastName, DateofBirth. Gender, Telephone, KnownAllergies, MostRecentVisit, and PhysicianLastName.
3. Group the records by PhysicianLastName.
4. Sort the records by LastName, then FirstName.
5. Use the Outline2 report layout and the Compact style.
6. Name this report All Patients list.
7. Preview the report.
8. Make sure all the column labels are visible.
9. Save your changes.
10. Preview and print the first page of the report.

▶ Independent Challenges

WEB WORK

4. Use your knowledge and skills navigating the World Wide Web to create attractive reports of information about colleges and universities. Locate information about institutions that offer programs in computer use, create a database containing this information, then design reports that display this data.

To complete this independent challenge:

1. Create a new database called "Colleges" on your Student Disk. Include any fields you feel are important, but make sure you include the institution's name, state, and whether it is a 4 or 2-year school.
2. Log on to the Internet and use your browser to go to http://www.course.com. From there, click the link Student On Line Companions, then click the Microsoft Office 97 Professional Edition—Illustrated: A First Course page, then click the Access link for Unit D. Search the World Wide Web for schools that offer programs in computer science using any available search engines.
3. Compile a list of at least 15 institutions.
4. Enter the information in your database.
5. Create a report that includes all the fields in the table, and use the default grouping.
6. Sort the records by the state, then by the institution's name.
7. Save, preview and print the report.
8. Hand in a printout of your work.

▶ Visual Workshop

Use the Products table in the Parts List database to create these labels. Use the settings for Avery label 5161. Sort the labels by SupplierID, then by ProductName, and name the report "Warehouse Labels."

FIGURE D-23

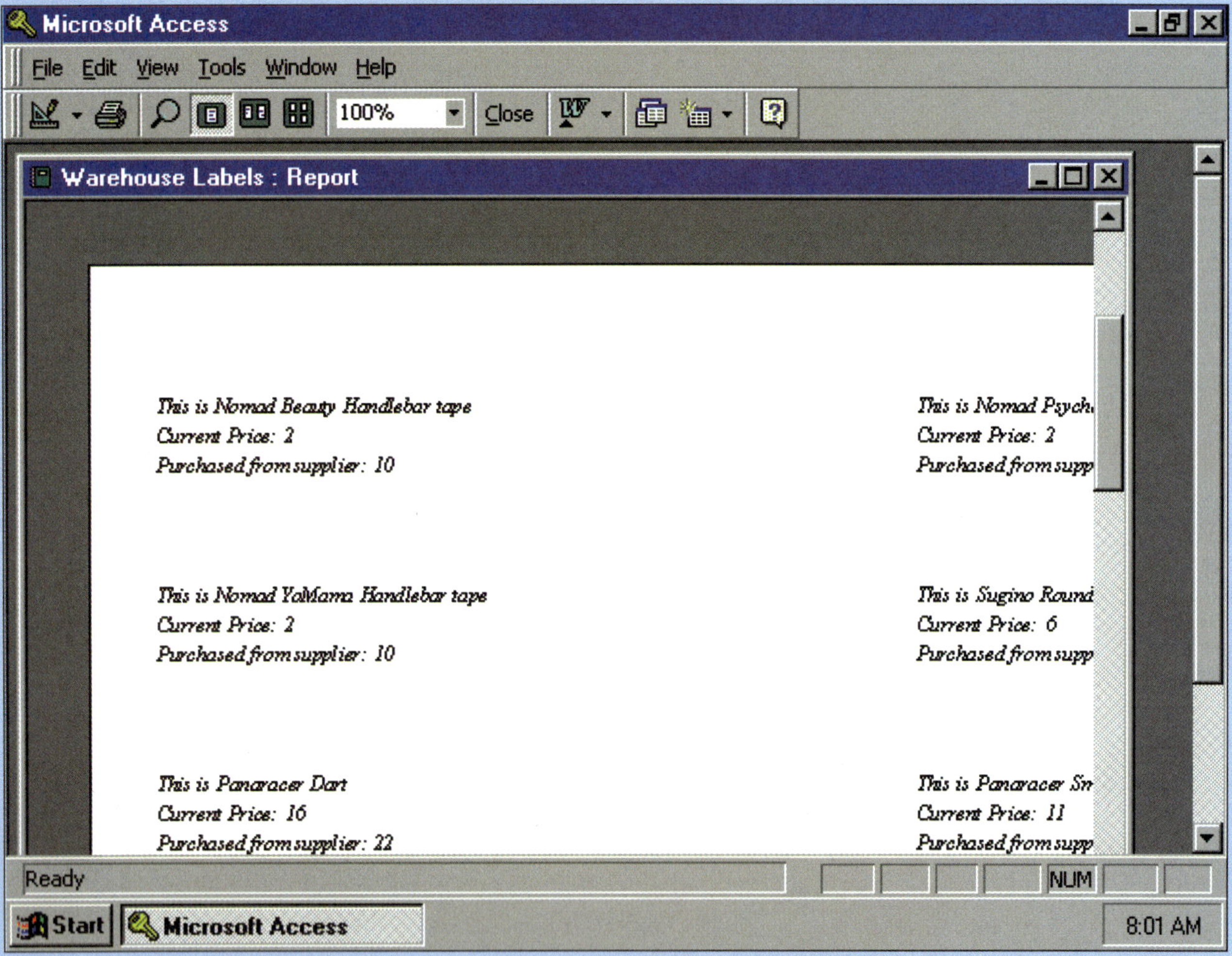

Modifying
a Database Structure

Objectives

- Examine relational database requirements
- Plan a table
- Create new tables
- Create one-to-many relationships
- Delete fields
- Define field properties
- Define date/time field properties
- Define field validation properties

In this unit, you will add new tables to an existing database and link them in one-to-many relationships to create a relational database. You will also modify several field **properties** such as field formatting and field validation to increase data entry accuracy. Michael Belmont has decided to expand the use of Access within Nomad to track customer, tour, and sales information. Because a single table database will not meet all of his needs, he will use multiple tables of data and link them together to create a relational database.

Access 97

Examining Relational Database Requirements

A **relational database** is a collection of related tables that share information. The goals of a relational database are to satisfy dynamic information management needs and to eliminate duplicate data entry wherever possible. After analyzing Nomad's sales transactions, Michael begins to see repeat customers. The Customers table shown in Figure E-1 allows Michael to sort and retrieve specific information on customers and tours very quickly, but does not have an easy way to track more than one sale to the same customer. The following list of database concepts will guide Michael's actions as he moves from a single table of data to the powerful relational database capabilities provided by Access.

Details

A relational database is based on multiple tables of data. Each table should be based on only one subject.

Right now the Customers table in the Nomad database actually contains three subjects: Customers, Tours, and Sales. Michael knows that duplicate data across records of a table is a clue that a database needs to be redesigned into multiple tables. By breaking out each of these subjects into its own table, Michael will eliminate redundant data and increase the flexibility of his database.

Each record in a table should be uniquely identified with a key field or key field combination.

A **key field** is a field which contains unique information for each record. Typically, a customer table contains a Customer Identification (CustID) field to uniquely identify each customer. While using the customer's last name as the key field might accommodate a small database, it would be a poor choice and bad database design because it won't allow the user to enter two customers with the same last name.

Tables in the same database should be related, or linked, through a field common to each table in a one-to-many relationship.

To tie the information from the Customers table to the Sales table, the CustID field would need to be in both tables. Because the CustID field is a key field in the Customers table, this side of the relationship is the "one" side. Because the CustID field may be listed many times in the Sales table to record multiple sales to the same customer, this side of the relationship is the "many" side. Linking tables together with a common field in this manner is called creating a **one-to-many relationship** and is shown in Figure E-2.

FIGURE E-1: The datasheet of the Customers table

Customers : Table

CustID	First	Last	Street	City	State	Zip	Tour	Date	Birth Date
1	Ginny	Braithwaite	3 Which Way	Salem	MA	01970	Road Bike	6/15/96	1/10/60
10	Virginia	Rodarmor	123 Main Street	Andover	MA	01810	Bungee	9/20/96	1/6/70
11	Kristen	Reis	4848 Ashley	Fontanelle	IA	50810	Big Sky	1/10/97	3/18/68
12	Tom	Reis	4848 Ashley	Fontanelle	IA	50810	Big Sky	1/10/97	7/3/65
13	Mark	Eagan	987 Lincoln	Schaumberg	IL	44433	Big Sky	1/10/97	1/29/60
14	Peg	Fox	125 Maple	Des Moines	IA	50625	Big Sky	1/10/97	4/10/59
15	Ron	Fox	125 Maple	Des Moines	IA	50625	Big Sky	1/10/97	8/28/87
16	Amanda	Fox	125 Maple	Des Moines	IA	50625	Big Sky	1/10/97	1/30/88
17	Rebecca	Gross	123 Oak	Bridgewater	KS	50837	Road Bike	6/15/96	9/20/62
2	Robin	Spencer	293 Serenity Dr.	Concord	MA	01742	Mt. Bike	9/26/96	1/30/52
3	Camilla	Dobbins	486 Intel Circuit	Rio Rancho	NM	87124	Road Bike	6/15/96	3/15/65
4	Pip	Khalsa	1100 Vista Road	Santa Fe	NM	87505	Mt. Bike	9/26/96	4/16/69
5	Kendra	Majors	530 Spring Street	Lenox	MA	02140	Bungee	9/20/96	5/4/70
6	Tasha	Williams	530 Spring Street	Lenox	MA	02140	Road Bike	6/15/96	5/8/71
7	Fred	Gonzales	Purgatory Ski Area	Durango	CO	81301	Mt. Bike	6/15/96	6/10/60
8	John	Black	11 River Road	Brookfield	CT	06830	Road Bike	6/15/96	7/15/65
9	Scott	Owen	72 Yankee Way	Brookfield	CT	06830	Bungee	9/20/96	3/15/65

Record: 1 of 17

FIGURE E-2: A relational database with two tables

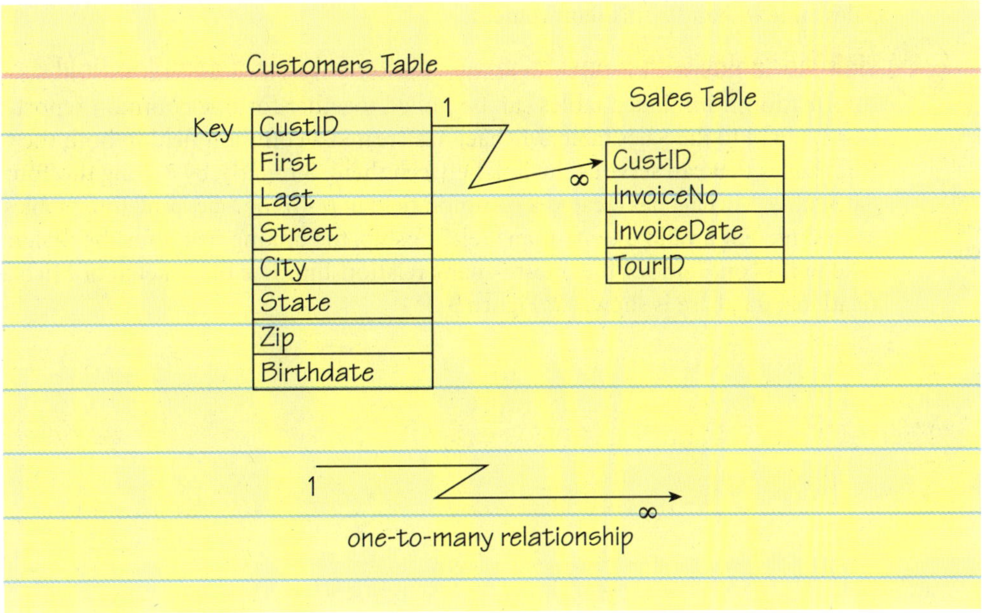

Planning a Table

Careful planning is crucial to successful relational database design and creation. Not only is duplicated data error-prone, but it limits the query and reporting capabilities of the overall database. Once you understand the concepts and goals of a relational database, you'll often need to redistribute the fields of the database into new tables. Michael realizes that the current single-table database provides no way to track additional sales to existing customers without duplicating all of the customer's demographic data such as name and address. Michael decides to get some advice on how to redesign his database from a database expert.

Details

List all of the fields of data that need to be tracked

Typically, these fields are already present in existing tables or paper reports. Still, it is a good idea to document each field on a single sheet of paper in order to examine all fields at the same time. This is the appropriate time to determine if there are additional fields of information that do not currently exist on any report, but that should be tracked for future purposes. Michael decides that in addition to the existing fields in the Customers table he would also like to start tracking tour cost, tour sales price, invoice date, tour handicap accessibility, and tour difficulty.

Group fields together in subject matter tables

The new Nomad database will track sales to customers, a common use for a relational database in business. It will contain three tables: Customers, Tours, and Sales.

Identify key fields that exist in tables

Each table should include a key field or key field combination in order to uniquely identify each record. Each customer, tour, and sale must be uniquely identified. Michael will use the CustID field in the Customers table, the TourID field in the Tours table, and the InvoiceNo field in the Sales table to handle this requirement.

QuickTip

The linking field should be the only field that is duplicated in two tables. For clarity, give the linking field the same name in both tables.

Link the tables with a one-to-many relationship via a common field

Information from linked tables can be pulled together for one common report. By adding the CustID field to the Sales table, Michael has created a common field in both the Customers and Sales tables that can serve as the link between them. Similarly, by adding the TourID field to the Sales table, Michael has created a common field in both the Sales and Tours tables that can serve as the link. For a valid one-to-many relationship, the linking field must be designated as the key field in the "one" side of the one-to-many relationship. The final sketch of Michael's redesigned relational database is shown in Figure E-3.

FIGURE E-3: Final sketch of the redesigned relational database

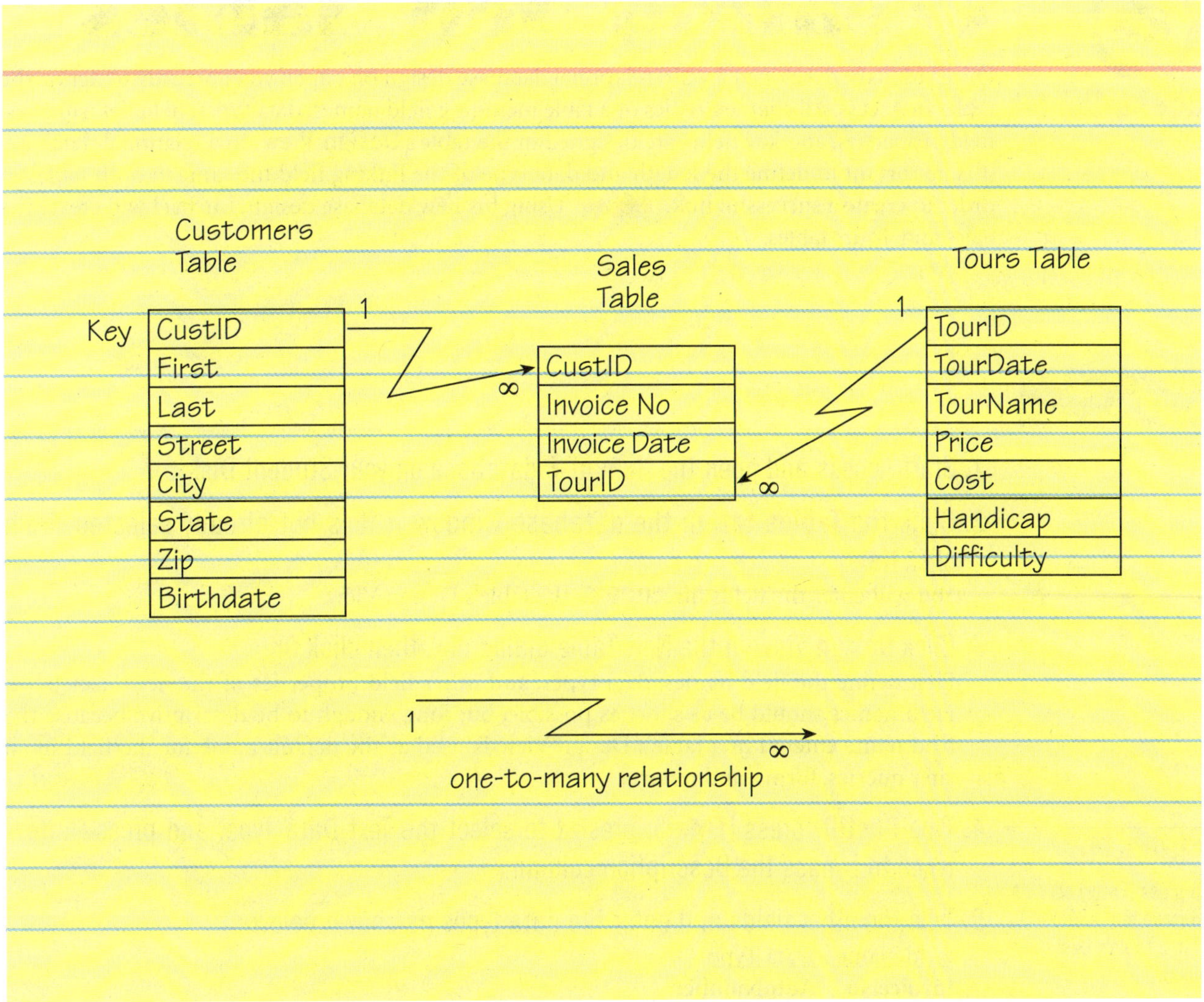

Access 97

CLUES TO USE

Key field combinations

Identifying a single key field may be difficult in some tables. Examine, for instance, a table that records employee promotions over time that includes three fields: employee number, date, and pay rate. None of the fields individually could serve as a valid key field because none are restricted to unique data. The employee number and date together, however, could serve as a valid **key field combination** since the employee number and date together would uniquely identify the record.

Access 97

Creating New Tables

Once you have developed a valid relational database design on paper, you are ready to define the tables in Access. All characteristics of a table including field names, data types, field descriptions, field properties, and key fields are designed in the table's **Design View**. In a relational database, it is important to define the length and data type of the linking field the same in both tables in order to create a successful link. Using his new database design, Michael will create the Sales and Tours tables.

Steps

1. Start Access and open the **Nomad-E** database on your Student Disk
2. Click the **Tables tab** in the database window if it is not already selected, then click **New**
   You will enter the fields directly into the table's Design View.
3. Click **Design View** in the New Table dialog box, then click **OK**
   First define the field names, data types, and other field properties of the new Sales table. Field names should be as short as possible, but long enough to be descriptive because the field name entered in a table's Design View is used as the default name for the field in all later queries, forms, and reports.
4. Type **CustID**, press **[Enter]**, press **t** to select the Text Data Type, and press **[Enter]** twice to bypass the Description column
5. Type the other fields and enter the data types as shown below:

Field Name	Data Type
InvoiceNo	**AutoNumber**
InvoiceDate	**Date/Time**
TourID	**Text**

6. Click **InvoiceNo** in the Field Name column, then click the **Primary Key button** on the Table Design toolbar
   The completed table Design View for the Sales table is shown in Figure E-4. Next, name, save, and close the Sales table.
7. Click the **Save button** on the Table Design toolbar, type **Sales** in the Table Name text box in the Save As dialog box, click **OK**, then click the **Close button** in the Sales: Table Design View window
   Sales is now displayed in the Tables tab, and it is a table in the Nomad-E database.
8. Click **New**, click **Design View**, click **OK**, then design the **Tours** table using the field information for the Tours table shown in Figure E-5
   Now that you have entered all the field information for the Tours table, name and save the table.
9. Click , type **Tours** in the Table Name text box in the Save As dialog box, click **OK**, then click the **Close button** in the Tours : Table Design View window
   Sales and Tours are now displayed in the Tables tab in the Nomad-E database.

QuickTip

You can press [Enter] or [Tab] to move to the next column in a table's Design View window.

Trouble?

If you clicked the Access program window Close button rather than the table's Close button, you closed the entire Nomad-E database. To continue work, simply start Access, open Nomad-E, and resume work.

FIGURE E-4: Design View for the Sales table

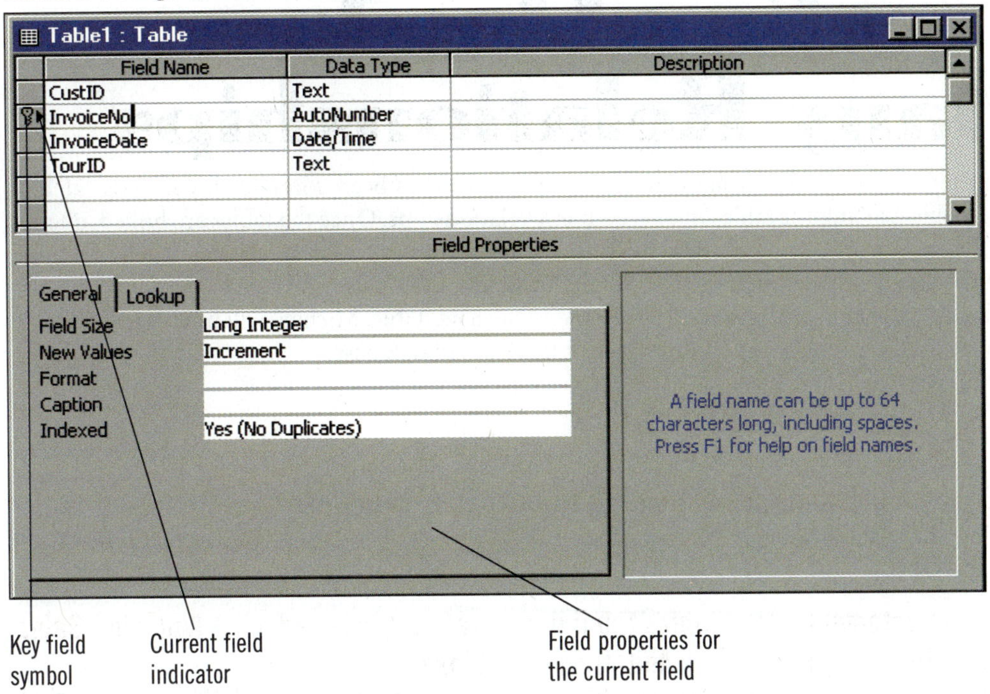

FIGURE E-5: Design View for the Tours table

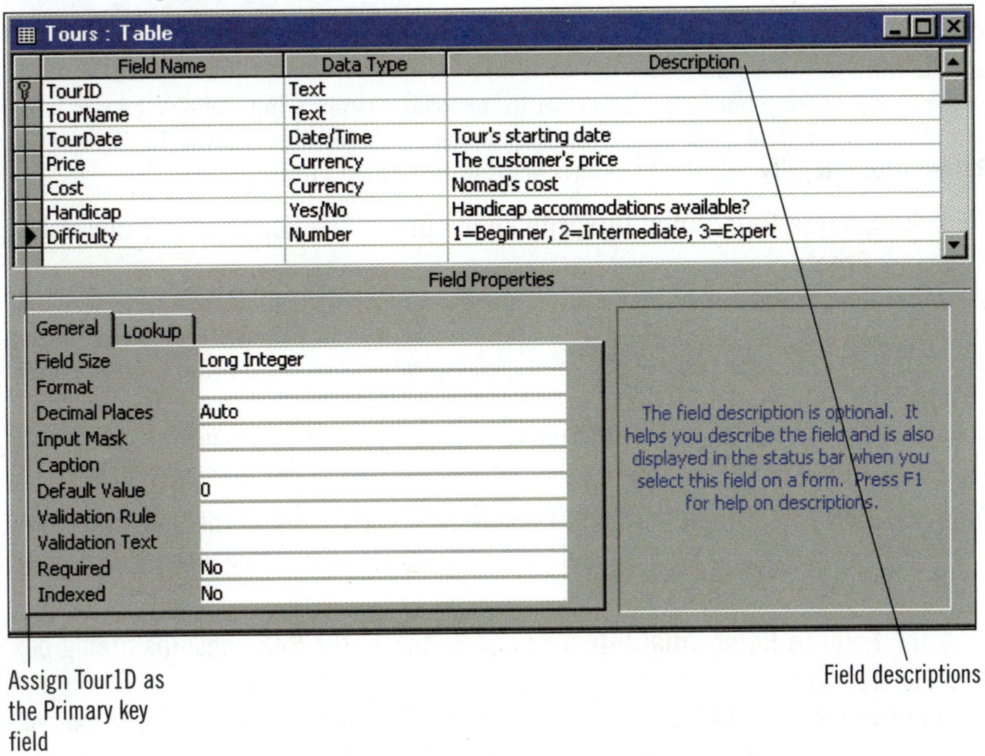

CLUES TO USE

Linked tables

A **linked table** is a table created in another database product, or another application such as Excel, that is stored in a file outside of the open database. You can add, delete, and edit records in a linked table from within Access but you can't change its structure. An **imported table** creates a copy of the information from the external file, and places it in a new Access table in your database.

Access 97

Creating One-to-Many Relationships

Once the initial database design and table entry phase has been completed, you must identify which fields will link the tables in one-to-many relationships. Once the tables are linked, queries, reports, and forms can be designed with fields from multiple tables. Michael's initial database sketch revealed that the CustID field will link the Customer table to the Sales table and that the TourID field will link the Tours table to the Sales table. Michael will now define the one-to-many relationships between the tables of the Nomad database.

Steps

Trouble?
If the Show Table dialog box is not open, click the Show Table button on the Relationships toolbar.

Trouble?
If all of a table's field names are not displayed in the Relationships window, drag the bottom border of the table window until the scroll bar disappears and all fields are visible.

QuickTip
To delete a table from the Relationships window, click the table and press [Delete].

QuickTip
To print a copy of the Relationships window, press [Print Screen] while viewing the window, start an empty word processing document, paste, then print the document.

1. Click the **Relationships button** on the Database toolbar
   The Show Table dialog box opens and lists all three tables in the Nomad database on the Tables tab.
2. Click **Customers** on the **Tables tab** if it is not already selected, click **Add**, click **Sales**, click **Add**, click **Tours**, click **Add**, then click **Close**
   The field lists of all three tables have been added to the Relationships window with key fields in bold. Now Michael can create links between the tables.
3. Maximize the window, then drag the **CustID field** from the Customers table to the **CustID field** in the Sales table
   Dragging a field from one table to another in the Relationships window links the two tables with the chosen field and opens the Relationships dialog box shown in Figure E-6. **Referential integrity** between the tables helps insure data accuracy.
4. Click the **Enforce Referential Integrity check box** in the Relationships dialog box, then click **Create**
   The **one-to-many line** shows the linkage between the CustID field of the Customers table and the Sales table. The "one" side of the relationship is the unique CustID for each record in the Customers table. The "many" side of the relationship is identified by an infinity symbol pointing to the CustID field in the Sales table. This relationship allows repeat customer sales to be recorded in the Sales table without duplicating any of the static customer data in the Customers table. The only field that is duplicated is the data in the linking CustID field.
5. Drag the **TourID field** from the Tours table to the **TourID field** in the Sales table
   The TourID field will link the Sales table to additional information about each tour in the Tours table.
6. Click the **Enforce Referential Integrity check box** in the Relationships dialog box, then click **Create**
   The finished Relationships window with all of the field names displayed should look like Figure E-7. Close the Relationships window and save the layout changes.
7. Click the **Close button** in the Relationships window, then click **Yes**
   Michael is finished with the database today, so he'll close it.
8. Click the **Close button** in the Nomad-E : Database window

FIGURE E-6: Creating table relationships

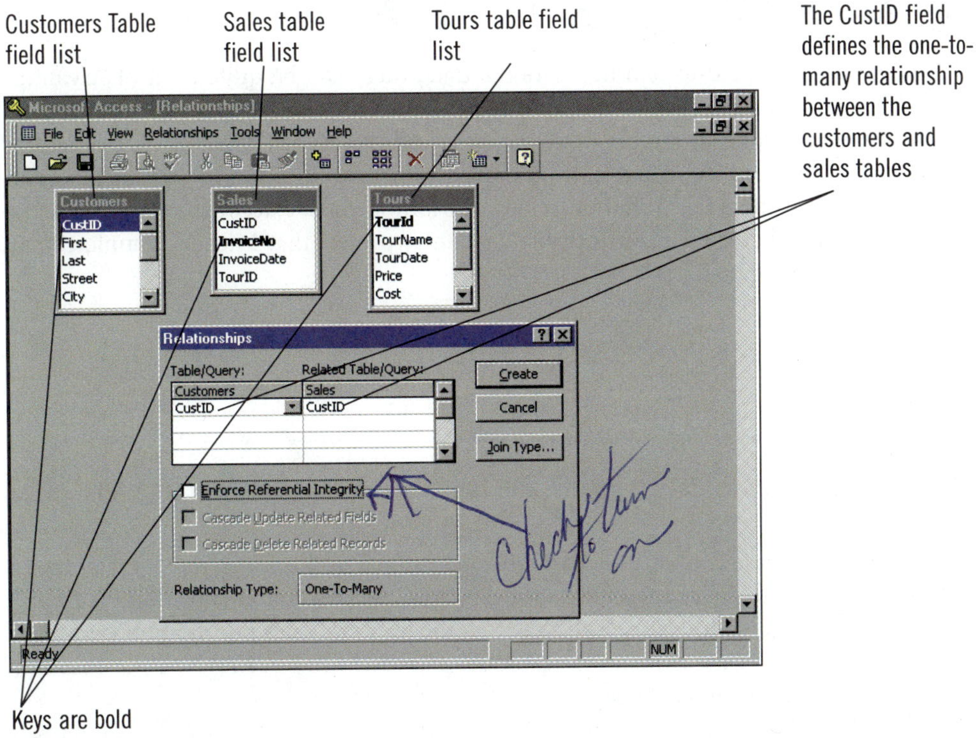

FIGURE E-7: The final Relationships window

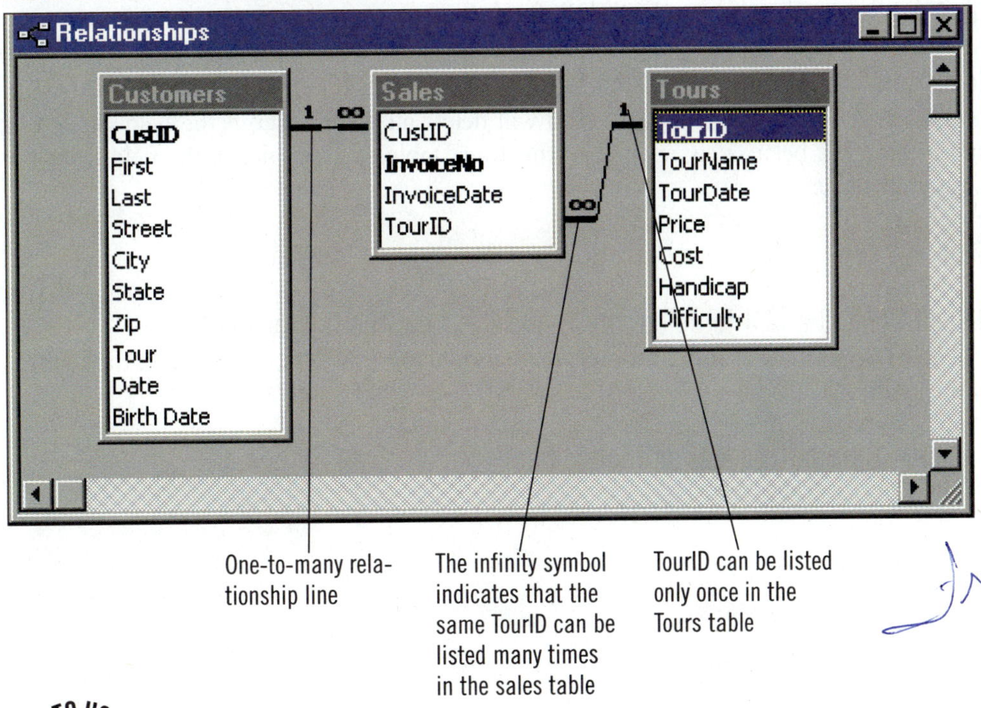

CLUES TO USE

Why enforcing referential integrity is important

By using the **Enforce Referential Integrity** option, you are enforcing a set of rules to help maintain the accuracy of your database. In this case, referential integrity would not allow you to enter a CustID in the Sales table that had not already been entered in the Customers table. Similarly, you could not enter a TourID in the Sales table that had not already been entered in the Tours table. That way, you cannot record a sale to an unidentified customer or nonexistent tour.

Access 97

Deleting Fields

Once a database is redesigned to handle relational data, there can be quite a bit of "cleanup" work to do. Changes to a table such as adding new fields, deleting unnecessary fields, or changing field properties are done in a table's Design View. When Michael redesigned his database, he moved the Tour information from the Customers table to the Tours table. In addition, he started tracking new fields that describe each tour such as Price, Cost, Handicap, and Difficulty. These changes created a considerable data entry project that Michael completed and saved as the database Nomad-E2.

Steps

1. Click the **Open Database button** on the Database toolbar and open the **Nomad-E2** database

   The Nomad-E2 database contains the data Michael entered in the Tours and Sales tables. In order to verify his work, he printed the datasheets from the Tours table shown in Figure E-8 and the Sales table shown in Figure E-9. Now that the tour and sales information is saved in the appropriate tables of the Nomad-E2 relational database, you can eliminate the Tour and Date fields from the Customers table.

2. Click the **Tables tab** in the Nomad-E2 : Database window if it is not already chosen, click the **Customers table**, then click **Design**

3. Scroll down the field names, click the **Tour field selector**, then press **[Delete]**

   Access warns you that deleting this field will delete all of the data in the field. Since this information has been safely entered in the Tours table, you can delete the field from the Customers table.

4. Click **Yes**

5. Repeat steps 3 and 4 to delete the **Date field** from the Customers table

   The new Design View of the Customers table should look like Figure E-10. Save the changes to the table.

6. Click the **Save button** on the toolbar

Trouble?

If the entire row isn't highlighted, you selected the field name rather than the field selector button to the left of the field name.

Trouble?

If you delete the wrong field, you can undo the action by clicking the Undo button. You can only undo your last action, however, so you must act immediately once the mistake occurs.

FIGURE E-8: Datasheet for the Tours table

Current record indicator symbol

Current record

Total number of records

Tours : Table

TourID	TourName	TourDate	Price	Cost	Handicap	Difficulty
Bigs0197	Big Sky	1/10/97	$258.00	$150.00	☐	3
Bung0996	Bungee	9/20/96	$175.00	$100.00	☐	2
Bung0997	Bungee	9/15/97	$240.00	$120.00	☐	2
Cave0597	Caves of Missouri	5/1/97	$240.00	$125.00	☑	1
Grea1096	Great Plains	10/1/96	$216.00	$95.00	☑	1
Mtbi0996	Mt. Bike	9/26/96	$200.00	$105.00	☐	2
Mtbi0997	Mt. Bike	9/30/97	$240.00	$135.00	☑	2
Road0696	Road Bike	6/15/96	$100.00	$60.00	☑	1
Texa1196	Texas Star	11/3/96	$174.00	$85.00	☑	1
*			$0.00	$0.00	☐	0

Record: 1 of 9

FIGURE E-9: Datasheet for the Sales table

Sales : Table

CustID	InvoiceNo	InvoiceDate	TourID
1	1	5/1/96	Road0696
2	2	8/1/96	Mtbi0996
3	3	8/2/96	Bung0996
4	4	8/2/96	Mtbi0996
5	5	8/2/96	Bung0996
6	6	8/2/96	Bung0996
7	7	8/2/96	Mtbi0996
8	8	8/5/96	Mtbi0996
9	9	8/5/96	Bung0996
10	10	8/5/96	Mtbi0996
11	11	12/2/96	Bigs0197
12	12	12/2/96	Bigs0197
13	13	12/3/96	Bigs0197
14	14	12/3/96	Bigs0197
15	15	12/4/96	Bigs0197
16	16	12/4/96	Bigs0197
11	17	2/3/97	Bung0997
13	18	2/3/97	Bung0997
14	19	2/4/97	Mtbi0997
15	20	2/4/97	Mtbi0997
*	(AutoNumber)		

Record: 1 of 20

These sales represent repeat customers

FIGURE E-10: Design View of the final Customers table

Field selector button

Tour and Date fields have been deleted from the Customers table

Customers : Table

Field Name	Data Type	Description
CustID	Text	
First	Text	
Last	Text	
Street	Text	
City	Text	
State	Text	
Zip	Text	
Birth Date	Date/Time	

Field Properties

General | Lookup

Format	
Input Mask	
Caption	
Default Value	
Validation Rule	
Validation Text	
Required	No
Indexed	No

A field name can be up to 64 characters long, including spaces. Press F1 for help on field names.

Access 97

Access 97

Defining Field Properties

Field properties are the characteristics that apply to each field in a table, such as field size, default value, or field formats. Modifying these properties helps insure database accuracy and clarity. Michael decides to make three field property changes in the Customers table. He will alter the field size, format, and default value properties for the State field.

Steps

QuickTip

Most field properties are optional, but if they require an entry, Access provides a default value.

QuickTip

The < (the less than sign) in the Format property forces all characters in the field to be lowercase letters.

1. Click each of the **field names** while viewing the Field Properties panel
   The Field Properties panel of a table's Design View changes to display the properties of the selected field. For example, when a field with a Text data type is selected, the Field Size property is visible. When a field with a Date/Time data type is selected, Access controls the Field Size property and therefore doesn't display it for the user.
2. Click the **State field name**
   Shorten the length of the Field Size for the State field in the Customers table to two characters since every state will be identified by its two-letter abbreviation.
3. Double-click **50** in the **Field Size Field Property text box** in the Field Properties panel, then type **2**
   Fifty is the default field size for a text field, but now the State field is limited to only two characters to prevent some keying errors. You will also force each entry in the State field to be uppercase letters, regardless of how the entry is typed.
4. Click in the **Format Field Property text box**, then type **>** (the greater than sign)
   The greater than sign forces all entries to be converted to uppercase characters. Since the majority of Nomad's new customers live in Iowa, designate IA as the default value for the State field.
5. Click in the **Default Value Field Property text box**, then type **IA**
   The Design View of the Customers table should now look like Figure E-11. Notice that the State field is chosen in the upper half of the window, and the Field Properties panel displays the properties that you have just changed.
6. Click the **Save button** on the Standard toolbar, then click **Yes** to continue when warned about losing data
   Since none of the entries in the State field were longer than two characters, you won't actually lose any data. Display the Customers table datasheet to see the effect of his property changes.
7. Click the **Datasheet View button** on the Table Design toolbar
   Notice that IA is entered as the default property for the next new record as shown in Figure E-12.

FIGURE E-11: The State field property changes

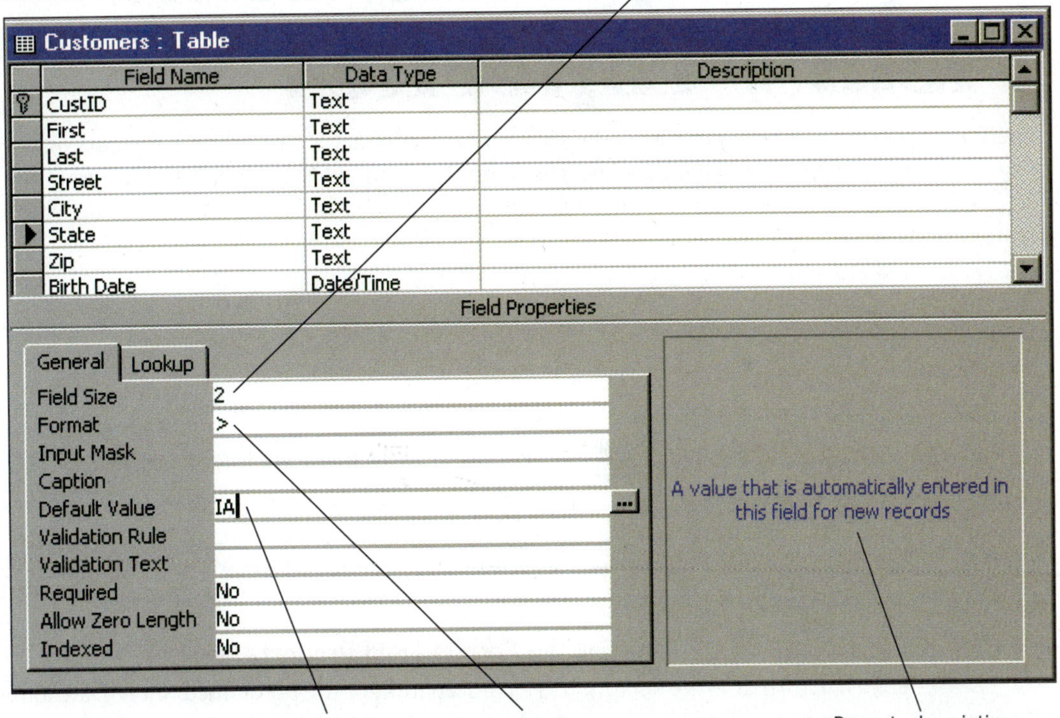

FIGURE E-12: The Customers table datasheet

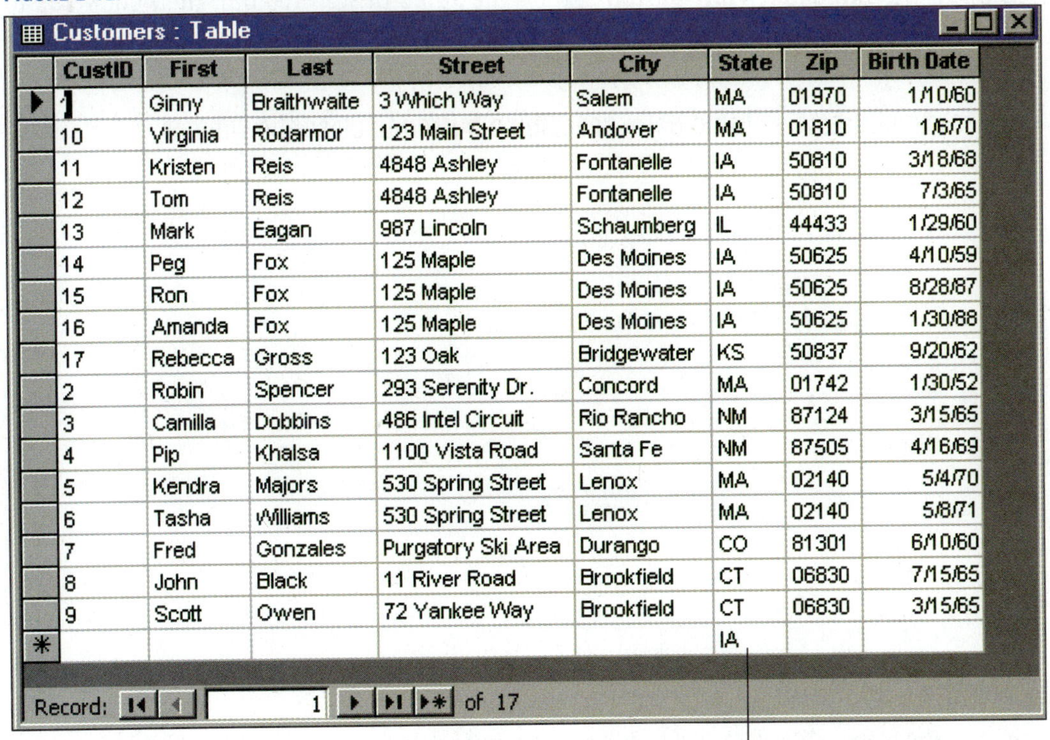

CustID	First	Last	Street	City	State	Zip	Birth Date
1	Ginny	Braithwaite	3 Which Way	Salem	MA	01970	1/10/60
10	Virginia	Rodarmor	123 Main Street	Andover	MA	01810	1/6/70
11	Kristen	Reis	4848 Ashley	Fontanelle	IA	50810	3/18/68
12	Tom	Reis	4848 Ashley	Fontanelle	IA	50810	7/3/65
13	Mark	Eagan	987 Lincoln	Schaumberg	IL	44433	1/29/60
14	Peg	Fox	125 Maple	Des Moines	IA	50625	4/10/59
15	Ron	Fox	125 Maple	Des Moines	IA	50625	8/28/87
16	Amanda	Fox	125 Maple	Des Moines	IA	50625	1/30/88
17	Rebecca	Gross	123 Oak	Bridgewater	KS	50837	9/20/62
2	Robin	Spencer	293 Serenity Dr.	Concord	MA	01742	1/30/52
3	Camilla	Dobbins	486 Intel Circuit	Rio Rancho	NM	87124	3/15/65
4	Pip	Khalsa	1100 Vista Road	Santa Fe	NM	87505	4/16/69
5	Kendra	Majors	530 Spring Street	Lenox	MA	02140	5/4/70
6	Tasha	Williams	530 Spring Street	Lenox	MA	02140	5/8/71
7	Fred	Gonzales	Purgatory Ski Area	Durango	CO	81301	6/10/60
8	John	Black	11 River Road	Brookfield	CT	06830	7/15/65
9	Scott	Owen	72 Yankee Way	Brookfield	CT	06830	3/15/65
					IA		

Access 97

Access 97

Defining Date/Time Field Properties

The Date/Time format property allows the user to use predefined date and time formats or use custom formats. Michael is concerned about dates past the year 1999. He wants the database to display all dates with four digits for the year so there is no confusion regarding which century is being displayed. Michael will first make this change to the Customers table.

Steps

1. Click the **Design View button** on the Table Datasheet toolbar to return to the table's Design View
   You have to use a custom format for the Birth Date field because none of the predefined Date/Time formats match the format you want. For more information on predefined Date/Time formats, refer to Table E-1.
2. Click the **Birth Date field**, then click the **Format Field Property text box**
   The General Date format is the default. It is a combination of the predefined Short Date and Long Time settings. See Table E-1.
   To define a custom format, enter symbols that represent how you want the date to appear in the Format property text box.
3. Type **mm/dd/yyyy** as shown in Figure E-13
   Display the Customers table datasheet to see the effect of his property changes.
4. Click the **Datasheet View button** on the Table Design toolbar, then click **Yes** to save the changes
   Notice that all of the dates now display four digits as shown in Figure E-14.
5. Click the Customers table datasheet **Close button** to close the window

QuickTip

Press [F6] to move between the upper and lower parts of a table's Design View window.

Clues to Use

Planning for the 21st Century

The General Date format assumes that dates between 1/1/30 and 12/31/99 are twentieth century dates (1930–1999), and those between 1/1/00 and 12/31/29 are twenty-first century dates (2000–2029). If you wish to enter dates outside these ranges, you must enter all four digits of the date.

FIGURE E-13: The Birth Date field property change

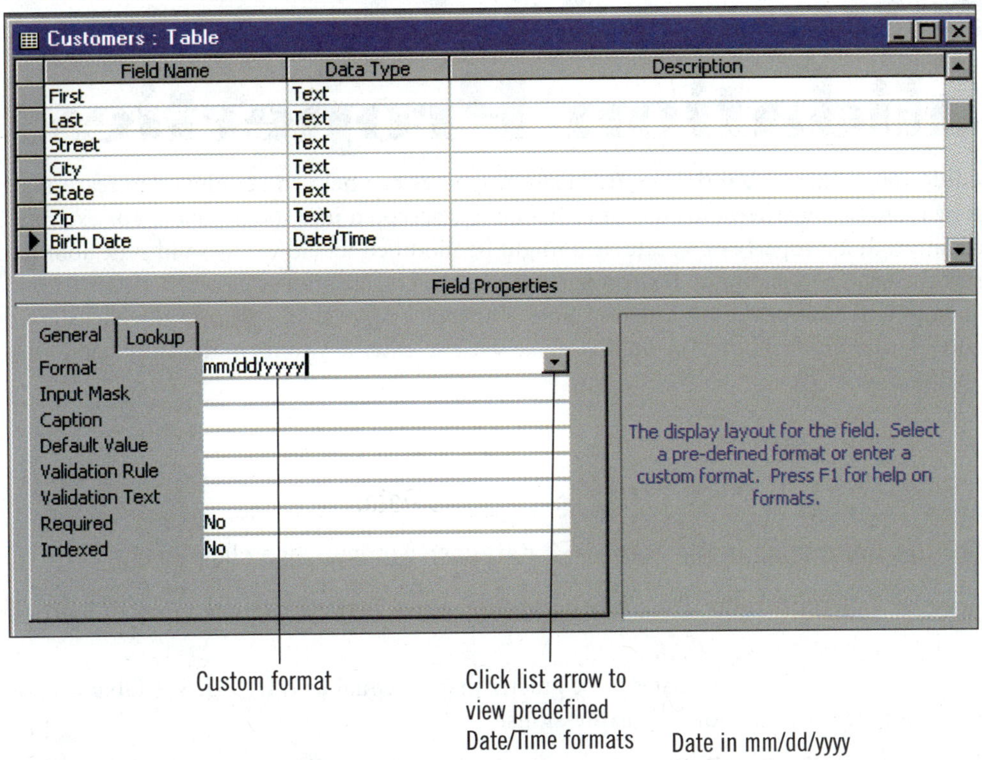

FIGURE E-14: The Customers table datasheet

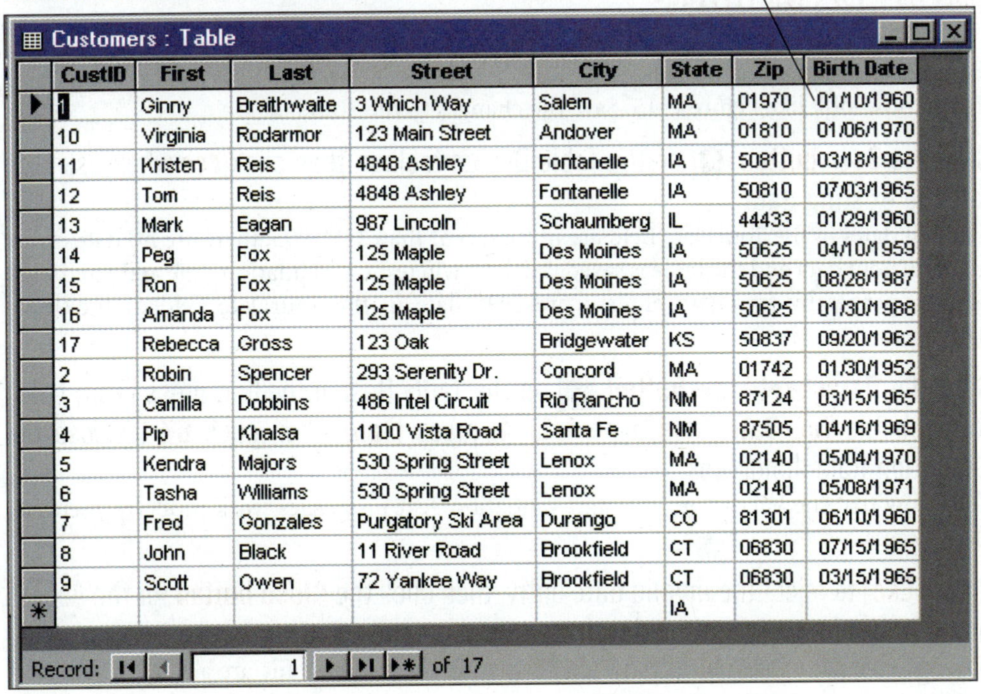

CustID	First	Last	Street	City	State	Zip	Birth Date
1	Ginny	Braithwaite	3 Which Way	Salem	MA	01970	01/10/1960
10	Virginia	Rodarmor	123 Main Street	Andover	MA	01810	01/06/1970
11	Kristen	Reis	4848 Ashley	Fontanelle	IA	50810	03/18/1968
12	Tom	Reis	4848 Ashley	Fontanelle	IA	50810	07/03/1965
13	Mark	Eagan	987 Lincoln	Schaumberg	IL	44433	01/29/1960
14	Peg	Fox	125 Maple	Des Moines	IA	50625	04/10/1959
15	Ron	Fox	125 Maple	Des Moines	IA	50625	08/28/1987
16	Amanda	Fox	125 Maple	Des Moines	IA	50625	01/30/1988
17	Rebecca	Gross	123 Oak	Bridgewater	KS	50837	09/20/1962
2	Robin	Spencer	293 Serenity Dr.	Concord	MA	01742	01/30/1952
3	Camilla	Dobbins	486 Intel Circuit	Rio Rancho	NM	87124	03/15/1965
4	Pip	Khalsa	1100 Vista Road	Santa Fe	NM	87505	04/16/1969
5	Kendra	Majors	530 Spring Street	Lenox	MA	02140	05/04/1970
6	Tasha	Williams	530 Spring Street	Lenox	MA	02140	05/08/1971
7	Fred	Gonzales	Purgatory Ski Area	Durango	CO	81301	06/10/1960
8	John	Black	11 River Road	Brookfield	CT	06830	07/15/1965
9	Scott	Owen	72 Yankee Way	Brookfield	CT	06830	03/15/1965
*					IA		

TABLE E-1: Predefined Date/Time Formats

setting	examples	setting	examples
General Date (default)	4/3/97 5:34:00 PM	**Long Time**	5:34:23 PM
Long Date	Saturday, April 3, 1997	**Medium Time**	5:34 PM
Medium Date	3-Apr-97	**Short Time**	17:34
Short Date	4/3/97		

Access 97

Access 97

Defining Field Validation Properties

The **Validation Rule** and **Validation Text** field properties can help you eliminate unreasonable entries by establishing criteria for the entry before it is accepted into the database. For example, the Validation Rule property of a State field might be modified to allow only valid state abbreviations as entries. The Validation Text property is used to display a message when a user tries to enter data that doesn't pass the Validation Rule property for that field. Michael started his business in 1995. Therefore, it wouldn't make sense to enter any tours in the Tours table with dates earlier than 1995.

Steps

QuickTip

You must use the # (pound sign) to identify date criteria and use the double quote character to identify text criteria in a Validation Rule expression.

1. Click the **Tours table** in the Nomad-E2 database window, then click **Design**
2. Click the **TourDate field**, click the **Validation Rule text box** in the Field Properties panel, then type **>=#1/1/95#**
   This property forces all tour dates to be greater than or equal to 1/1/1995. See Table E-2 for more examples of validation rule expressions.
3. Click in the **Validation Text text box** in the Field Properties panel, then type **Date must be later than 1/1/1995**
   The Validation Text property will appear on the screen when the field entry does not pass the criteria specified in the Validation Rule property. The Design View of the Tours table should now look like Figure E-15. Save the changes to the Tours table.
4. Click the **Save button** on the Table Design toolbar, then click **Yes** when asked to test the existing data
   Since all dates in the TourDate field are more recent than 1/1/1995, there are no date errors in the current data and the table is saved. Michael will test the Validation Rule and Validation Text properties by trying to enter a pre-1995 date in the TourDate field of the Tours datasheet.
5. Click the **Datasheet View button** on the Table Design toolbar, press **[Tab]** twice to reach the **TourDate field**, type **1/1/94**, press **[Tab]**, then click **OK** to close the Validation Rule dialog box
   You know that the Validation Rule and Validation Text properties work properly, therefore close Access.
6. Press **[Esc]** to reject the invalid date entry, then click the **Close button** for the Access program window to close the database and program
   Since all changes to the objects and records within the database file are already saved, exiting the application does not open a Save dialog box.

FIGURE E-15: **The TourDate field validation properties**

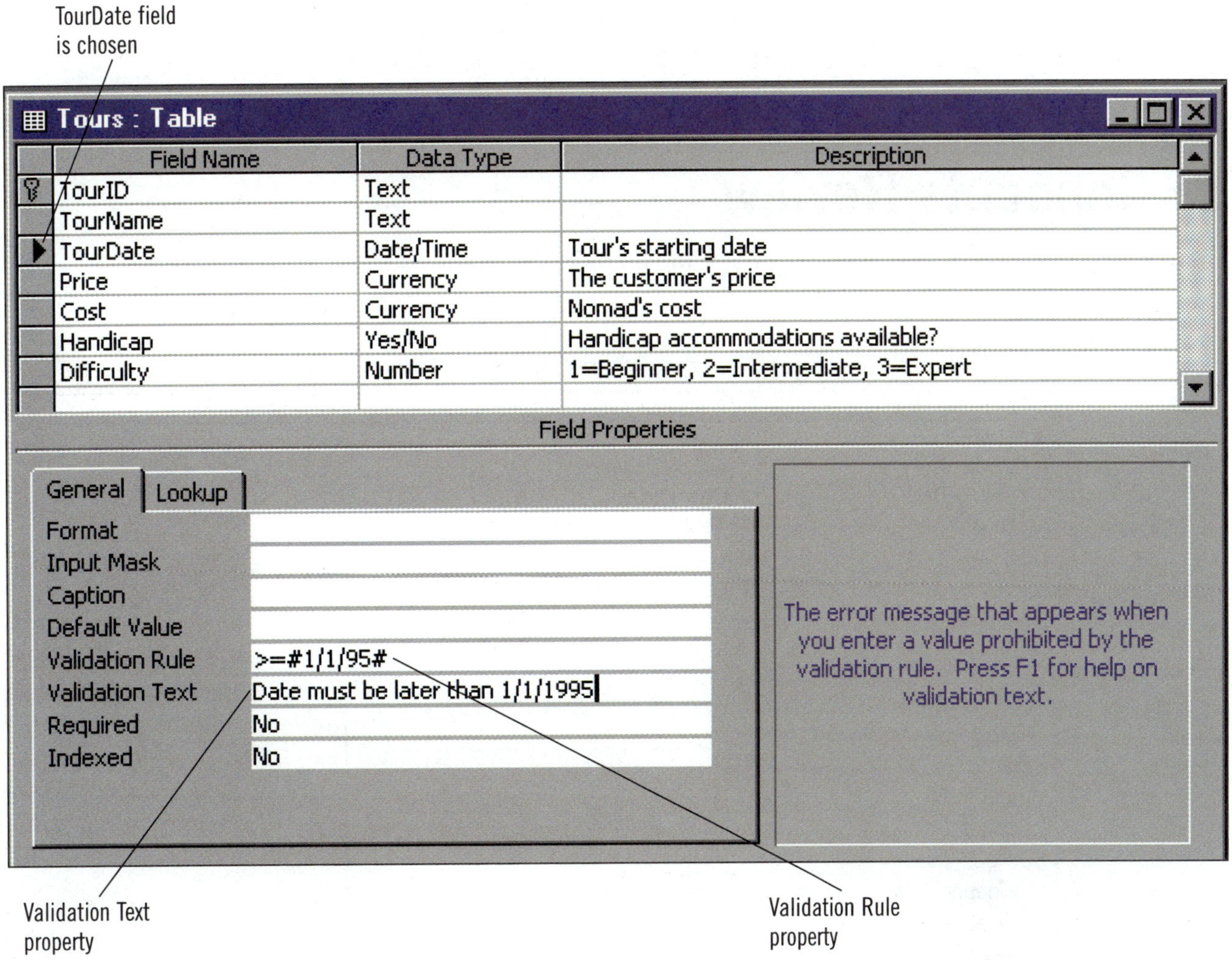

Access 97

TABLE E-2: **Validation Rule Expressions**

data type	validation rule expression	description
Number or Currency	>0	The number must be positive
Number or Currency	>10 And <100	The number must be between 10 and 100
Number or Currency	10 Or 20 Or 30	The number must be 10, 20, or 30
Text	"IA" Or "NE" Or "MO"	The entry must be IA, NE, or MO
Date/Time	>=#1/1/93#	The date must be on or after 1/1/1993
Date/Time	>#1/1/80# And <#1/1/90#	The date must be between 1/1/1980 and 1/1/1990

CLUES TO USE

Validation property rules

The Validation Rule property and Validation Text properties go hand in hand. If you omit the Validation Rule, no data validation is performed and the Validation Text property is meaningless. If you set the Validation Rule property, but not the Validation Text property, Access displays a standard error message when the validation rule is violated.

Practice

► Concepts Review

Identify each element of a table's Design View shown in Figure E-16.

FIGURE E-16

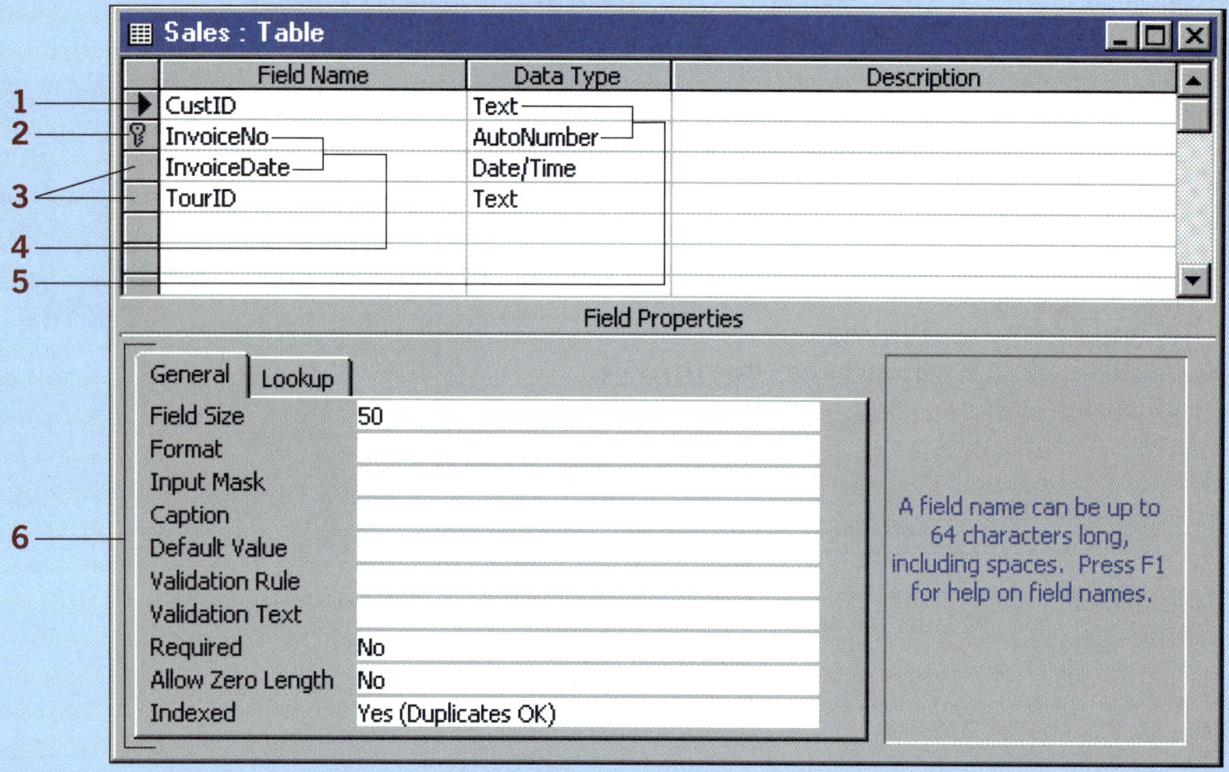

Match each term with the statement that describes its function.

7. Several tables linked together in one-to-many relationships
8. A field that holds unique information for each record in the table
9. Where all characteristics of a table including field names, data types, field descriptions, field properties, and key fields are defined
10. Characteristics that apply to each field of a table, such as field size, default values, or field formats
11. Helps you eliminate unreasonable entries by establishing criteria for the entry

a. Primary Key
b. Field Properties
c. Design View
d. Validation Rule and Validation Text
e. Relational database

Practice

Select the best answer from the list of choices.

12. Which of the following steps would probably help eliminate fields of duplicate data in a table?
- **a.** Redesign the database and add more tables.
- **b.** Redesign the database and add more fields.
- **c.** Change the formatting properties of the field in which the duplicate data existed.
- **d.** Change the validation properties of the field in which the duplicate data existed.

13. Which of the following is NOT defined in the table's Design View?
- **a.** Key fields
- **b.** Duplicate data
- **c.** Field lengths
- **d.** Data types

14. Which of the following is NOT a common Data Type?
- **a.** Text
- **b.** Alpha
- **c.** Number
- **d.** Date/Time

15. Which feature helps the database designer make sure that one-to-many relationships are preserved?
- **a.** Validation Text property
- **b.** Validation Rule property
- **c.** Field formatting
- **d.** Referential Integrity

16. Which character is used to identify dates in a validation expression?
- **a.** " (double quote)
- **b.** ' (single quote)
- **c.** # (pound sign)
- **d.** & (ampersand)

17. Which Format Property Option displays all characters in the field as uppercase?
- **a.** <
- **b.** >
- **c.** !
- **d.** @

Skills Review

1. Examine relational database requirements.
- **a.** Examine your address book.
- **b.** Write down the fields you will need.
- **c.** Examine which fields contain duplicate entries.

2. **Plan a table.**
   a. Start Access.
   b. Use the Blank Database option button to create a new database file.
   c. Save the file as "Addresses-E" on your Student Disk.
   d. Click the Tables tab in the Database window, then click New.

3. **Create new tables.**
   a. Use Design View to create the new table with the following fields with the given data types.

First	Text
Last	Text
Street	Text
City	Text
State	Text
Zip	Text
Birthday	Date/Time

   b. Close the table, name, and save it as "Names".
   c. Do not define a primary key for Names.
   d. Reconsider what fields will contain duplicate data.
   e. Click the Tables tab in the Database window, then click New.
   f. Use Design View to create another new table with the following Text fields.
      Zip
      City
      State
   g. Identify Zip as the primary key.
   h. Close the table, then save it as "Zips".

4. **Create one-to-many relationships.**
   a. Click the Relationships button on the Database toolbar.
   b. Add both the Names and the Zips tables to the Relationships window.
   c. Drag the Zip field from the Zips table to the Zip field of the Names table to create a one-to-many relationship between these fields of the tables.
   d. Enforce referential integrity between the linking fields of the tables.
   e. Close the Relationships window, saving your layout changes.

5. **Delete fields.**
   a. Open the Names table in Design View.
   b. Click the City field selector button and delete the City field.
   c. Click the State field selector button and delete the State field.
   d. Close the Names table, saving the changes.

6. **Define text field properties.**
   a. Open the Zips table in Design View.
   b. Click the State field name and change the Field Size property to 2.
   c. Click the State field names Format property text box, then type > (greater than sign) to force all entries to uppercase letters.
   d. Close the Zips table, saving the changes.

7. **Define date/time field properties.**
   a. Open the Names table in Design View.
   b. Click the Birthday field names Format property text box, then type MM/DD/YYYY to display all dates with four-digit years.
   c. Close the Names table, saving the changes.

8. **Define field validation properties.**
   a. Note that this address listing will contain contacts from only three states: IA, KS, and MO.
   b. Open the Zips table in Design View.
   c. Click the State field name, click the Validation Rule property text box, then type ="IA" OR "KS" OR "MO".
   d. Note that this validation rule could be extended to accept more valid entries for all 50 states.
   e. Click the Validation Text text box, then type "State must be IA, KS, or MO".
   f. Close the Zips table, saving the changes.
   g. Print a copy of each table's datasheet in the Addresses-E database.

Independent Challenges

1. As the president of a civic organization, you have decided to launch a recycling campaign. Various clubs will gather recyclable trash and make deposits at recycling centers. You need to develop a relational database that tracks how much material has been taken to each of the centers, as well as the club that is responsible for the deposit. The following fields will be tracked in this database:

Club Information:
Name, Street, City, State, Zip, Phone, Club Number (a unique number to identify each club)
Deposit Information:
Date, Weight, Deposit Number (a sequential number for each drop off)
Recycle Center Information:
Name, Street, City, State, Zip, Phone, Center Number (a unique number to identify each recycling center)

To complete this independent challenge:

1. Plan the database.
   a. Sketch how the fields will be organized into three tables: Clubs, Deposits, and Recycling Centers.
   b. Determine if there are key fields in the tables.
   c. Determine how the tables should be linked using one-to-many relationships. This may involve adding a linking field to a table to establish the connection.
2. Create and save a database called "Cleanup-E".
3. Create the three tables in the Cleanup-E database using appropriate field names, data types, and key fields.
4. Create one-to-many relationships to link the tables. Be sure to enforce referential integrity as appropriate.
5. Print the Relationships window of the database using the [Print Screen] technique. Be sure that all fields of each table are visible.
6. Add a Validation Rule property to the Date field that only allows dates of 1/1/97 or later to be entered into the database. The property entry is >=#1/1/97#.
7. Add a Validation Text property to the Date field that states "Dates must be later than 1/1/1997".

2. You want to document the books you've read in a relational database. The following fields will be tracked:
Book Information:
Title, Category (such as Biography, Mystery, or Science Fiction), Rating (a numeric value from 1–10 that indicates how satisfied you were with the book), Date Read
Author Information (Note: If a book has more than one author, enter the name of the author listed first.):
First Name, Last Name, Author Number (a unique number to identify each author)

To complete this independent challenge:

1. Plan the database.
   a. Sketch how the fields will be organized into two tables: Books and Authors.
   b. Determine if there are key fields in the tables.
   c. Determine how the tables should be linked using one-to-many relationships. This may involve adding a linking field to a table to establish the connection.
2. Create and save a database called "Readings-E".
3. Create the three tables in the Readings-E database using appropriate field names, data types, and key fields.
4. Create the one-to-many relationship to link the tables. Be sure to enforce referential integrity as appropriate.
5. Print the Relationships window of the database using the [Print Screen] technique discussed in the Quick Tip of the "Creating one-to-many relationships" lesson. Be sure that all fields of each table are visible.
6. Change the field size of the author's First Name field and Last Name field to 25.

3. You work for a large medical clinic and wish to track the time physicians are spending on civic activities such as the Rural Outreach Program and the Low Income Health Screening Program. The database should track the date and number of hours each physician has logged with each program. The following fields will be tracked in this database:
Physician Information:
First Name, Last Name, Physician Number (a unique number to identify each physician)
Activity Information:
Date, Hours
Program Information:
Name, Program Number (a unique number to identify each program)

To complete this independent challenge:

1. Plan the database.
   a. Sketch how the fields will be organized into three tables: Physicians, Activities, and Programs
   b. Determine if there are key fields in the tables (*Hint*: The Activities table does not have a Key field.)
   c. Determine how the tables should be linked using one-to-many relationships. This may involve adding a linking field to a table to establish the connection.
2. Create and save a database called "Doctors-E".
3. Create the three tables in the Doctors-E database using appropriate field names, data types, and key fields.
4. Create one-to-many relationships to link the tables. Be sure to enforce referential integrity as appropriate.
5. Print the Relationships window of the database using the [Print Screen] technique discussed in the Quick Tip of the "Creating one-to-many relationships" lesson. Be sure that all fields of each table are visible.

4. You wish to find and document nine-digit ZIP codes for several addresses in a database. You know that nine-digit ZIP codes make the mail service more efficient because the nine digits specify the specific street address in addition to the city and state of the addressee.

To complete this independent challenge:

1. Log on to the Internet and use your browser to go to http://www.course.com. From there, click Student Online Companions, click Microsoft Office 97 Professional Edition – Illustrated: A Second Course, click the Access link for Unit E, then click the link for the United States Postal Service.
2. Read the homepage and click hypertext links to find the interactive ZIP+4 lookup service. (*Hint*: Finding the interactive ZIP+4 lookup service should take about two hypertext links.)
3. Use the Zip+4 Code Lookup page to find the ZIP+4 code for at least four addresses of friends or acquaintances and jot them down.
4. Plan a database to handle address information with ZIP+4 ZIP codes.
   a. Sketch how the fields will be organized into two tables: Names and Zips.
   b. Determine if there are key fields in the tables.
   c. Determine how the tables should be linked using one-to-many relationships. This may involve adding a linking field to a table to establish the connection.
5. Create and save a database called "Addresses9-E".
6. Create the two tables in the Addresses9-E database using appropriate field names, data types, and key fields. Recognize that this relational database is extremely similar to the one you created in the Skills Review with one exception: a ZIP code extension field needs to be added to the Names table.
7. Create the one-to-many relationship to link the tables. Be sure to enforce referential integrity as appropriate.
8. Print the Relationships window of the database using the [Print Screen] technique discussed in the Quick Tip of the "Creating one-to-many relationships" lesson. Be sure that all fields of each table are visible.
9. Open the Zips table in Datasheet View and enter the four ZIP codes, cities, and states that you researched on the Internet.
10. Print the Zips datasheet.
11. Open the Names table in Datasheet View and enter the four addresses that you researched on the Internet.
12. Print the Names datasheet.

Visual Workshop

Create a new database that includes the two tables, Alumni and Donations, shown in Figures E-17 and E-18. Give each of the fields a text Data Type, except for Value (use Currency) and Date (use Date/Time). Make sure that the Social Security Number is the key field in the Alumni table and links the Alumni table with the Donations table in a one-to-many relationship. Enforce referential integrity for the linking Social Security Number field between the tables. (*Hint:* The Donations table does not have a Key field.) Enter the records for both tables, then save and name the database "VW-E" on your Student Disk. Print the datasheets of both tables.

FIGURE E-17

Alumni : Table

First	Last	Street	City	State	Zip	Phone	SSN
Doug	Allen	888 Maple	Ames	IA	50010	515-555-8888	444-44-4444
Lisa	Eagan	777 Oak	Johnston	IA	50015	515-777-9999	111-11-1111
Kelsey	Wambold	555 Elm	Fontanelle	IA	50846	515-888-1111	222-22-2222
Aaron	Washington	222 Apple	Bridgewater	IA	50837	515-222-4444	333-33-3333

Record: 4 of 4

FIGURE E-18

Donations : Table

Value	Date	Type	SSN
$100.00	5/1/97	Art	111-11-1111
$200.00	5/1/97	Cash	222-22-2222
$500.00	5/2/97	Stock	333-33-3333
$50.00	6/2/97	Cash	111-11-1111
$1,000.00	6/2/97	Cash	444-44-4444
$500.00	6/2/97	Stock	333-33-3333
$500.00	7/1/97	Cash	444-44-4444
$500.00	7/1/97	Cash	333-33-3333
$0.00			

Record: 8 of 8

Access 97

Creating Multiple Table Queries

Objectives

- Create select queries
- Sort a query on multiple fields
- Develop AND queries
- Develop OR queries
- Develop calculated fields
- Add calculations on groups of records
- Develop crosstab queries
- Create update queries

In this unit, you will create **queries**, database objects that answer questions about the data by pulling fields and records that match specific criteria into a single datasheet. A **select query** retrieves data from one or more linked tables and displays the results in a datasheet. Queries can also be used to sort records, develop new calculated fields from existing fields, or develop summary calculations such as the sum or average of the values in a field. **Crosstab queries** present information in a cross tabular report, and **update queries** quickly change existing data in a table. Michael Belmont redesigned the Nomad database into multiple tables to eliminate redundant data entry. Michael will create select, crosstab, and update queries to display and change the data in his database.

Access 97

Creating Select Queries

Queries are developed by using the Query Wizard or by directly specifying requested fields and query criteria in **Query Design View**. The resulting query datasheet is not a duplication of the data that resides in the original table's datasheet, but rather, a logical view of the data. If you change or enter data in a query's datasheet, the data in the underlying table (and any other logical view) is updated automatically. Queries are often used to present and sort a subset of fields from multiple tables for data entry or update purposes. Michael creates a query to answer the question, "Who is buying what?" He pulls fields from several tables into a single query object which displays a single datasheet.

Steps

1. Start Access and open the **Nomad-F** database
2. Click the **Queries tab** in the Nomad-F: Database window, click **New**, click **Design View** in the New Query window, then click **OK**
   Use the Show Table dialog box to add the Tours table and the Customers table to the Query Design View. You also need to include the Sales table because it contains the linking fields that match specific customers to the specific tours they have purchased.
3. Click **Customers**, click **Add**, click **Sales**, click **Add**, click **Tours**, click **Add**, then click **Close**
   The Query Design View displays **field lists** for the three tables. Each table's name is in its field list title bar. Key fields are bold, and often serve as the "one" side of the one-to-many relationship between two tables. Relationships are displayed with **one-to-many join lines** between the linking fields as shown in Figure F-1. View the customer's last name in the query datasheet.
4. Drag the **Last field** in the Customers table field list to the Field cell in the first column of the Query design grid
   The order in which the fields are placed in the **Query design grid** will be their order in the datasheet. Select the First field from the Customers table, then add the TourName and TourDate fields from the Tours table.
5. Drag the **First field** from the Customers table to the Field cell in the second column, drag the **TourName field** from the Tours table to the Field cell in the third column, then drag the **TourDate field** from the Tours table to the Field cell in the fourth column
   You sort the datasheet by TourDate.
6. Click the **Sort cell** of the **TourDate field** in the Query design grid, click the **Sort list arrow**, then click **Ascending**
   The resulting Query design grid should look like Figure F-2.
7. Click the **Datasheet View button** on the Query Design toolbar
   The records of the datasheet are now listed in chronological order by TourDate as shown in Figure F-3. You scroll through the datasheet and notice that Mark Egan purchased two tours, and that his name has been incorrectly entered in the database. Change "Eagan" to the correct spelling "Egan" directly within the query datasheet.
8. Scroll and click before the **first letter A** of either **Eagan** in the Last column in the datasheet, press **[Delete]**, then click any other record in the datasheet
   The update shows that you are using a properly defined relational database and that any change to the data is automatically applied to all other occurrences of the customer's name.
9. Click the **Query datasheet Close button**, click **Yes** when prompted to save the changes, type **Customer Purchases** in the Query Name text box, then click **OK**
   The query is now saved and listed on the Queries tab in the Nomad-F: Database window.

Trouble?

Click the Show Table button on the Query Design toolbar to add table field lists to Query Design View. To delete a field list click the list and press [Delete].

QuickTip

Double-click the table's title bar to select all fields then drag them as a group to the grid if you want all fields in the resulting datasheet.

FIGURE F-1: Query Design View

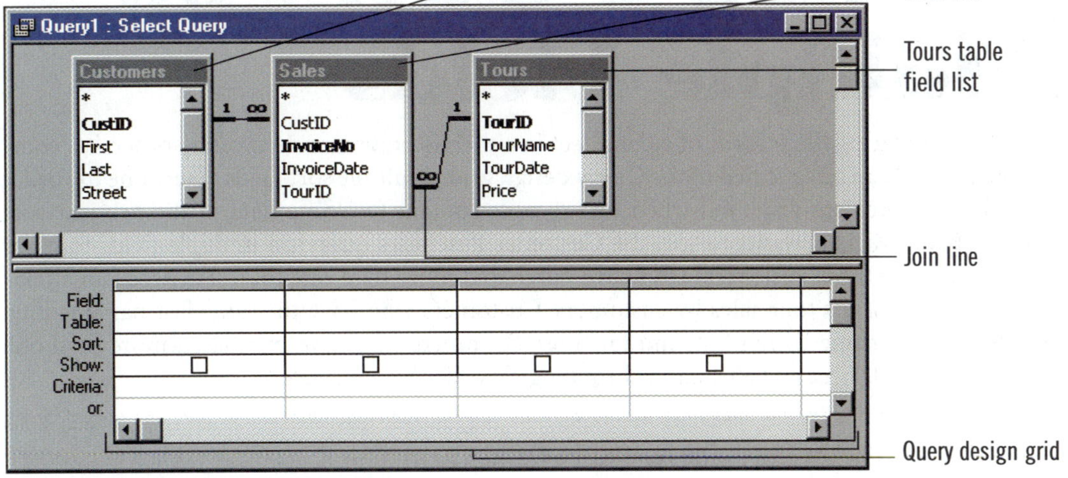

FIGURE F-2: Completed Query design grid

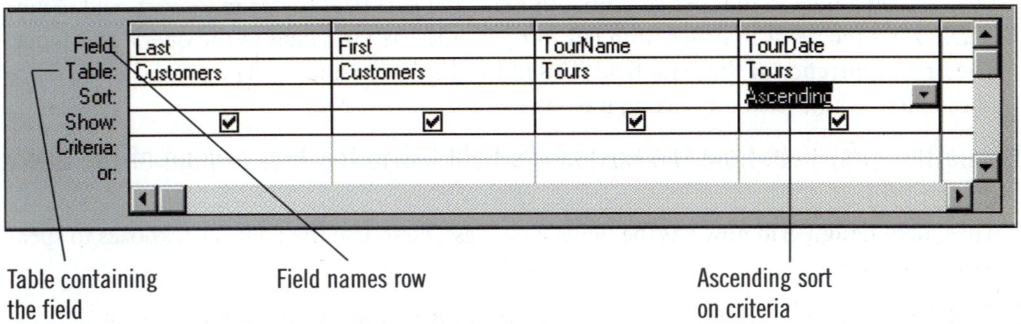

FIGURE F-3: Datasheet sorted in ascending order by TourDate

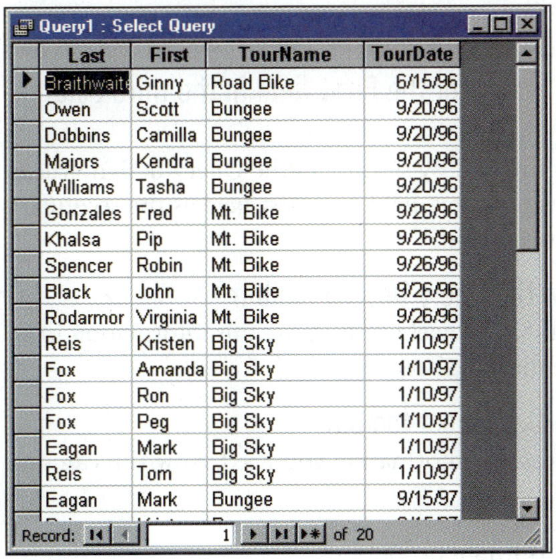

Last	First	TourName	TourDate
Braithwaite	Ginny	Road Bike	6/15/96
Owen	Scott	Bungee	9/20/96
Dobbins	Camilla	Bungee	9/20/96
Majors	Kendra	Bungee	9/20/96
Williams	Tasha	Bungee	9/20/96
Gonzales	Fred	Mt. Bike	9/26/96
Khalsa	Pip	Mt. Bike	9/26/96
Spencer	Robin	Mt. Bike	9/26/96
Black	John	Mt. Bike	9/26/96
Rodarmor	Virginia	Mt. Bike	9/26/96
Reis	Kristen	Big Sky	1/10/97
Fox	Amanda	Big Sky	1/10/97
Fox	Ron	Big Sky	1/10/97
Fox	Peg	Big Sky	1/10/97
Eagan	Mark	Big Sky	1/10/97
Reis	Tom	Big Sky	1/10/97
Eagan	Mark	Bungee	9/15/97

CLUES TO USE

The difference between queries and filters

Use a filter to temporarily view or edit a subset of records when viewing a datasheet. Use a query to view the subset of records without first opening a specific table, to choose fields from multiple tables for the query, to control which fields from the subset of records appear in the results, or to perform calculations on values in fields.

Sorting a Query on Multiple Fields

Sorting, or placing the records of a datasheet in either ascending or descending order, is a common task and can be specified in the Query design grid. Multiple sort fields determine the order in which records are displayed when two records contain the same data in the primary sort field. Michael wants to sort the Customer Purchases query on multiple fields to more clearly identify those customers who have purchased more than one tour. He needs an alphabetical listing of his tour sales by customers. Customers who have the same last name will be sorted by first name within last, and for those customers who have purchased more than one tour, the records need to be listed in chronological order by TourDate.

Steps

1. Click the **Queries tab** in the Nomad-F : Database window if necessary, click **Customer Purchases**, then click **Design**

   The Query Design window of the Customer Purchases - Select Query opens. You want to show the First field in the first column, but make the Last field the primary sort field. Since Access sorts the fields in order from left to right, add the First field to the query grid twice. The first occurrence of the First field is used for display purposes. The second occurrence of the First field is used for sorting purposes.

2. Drag the **First field** from the Customer's field list to the first column of the Query design grid

   The Query design grid now has the fields First, Last, First. Use the Show checkboxes to specify this sorting.

3. Click the **First field Show checkbox** in the third column to deselect it

   Now that the grid includes all the fields needed to accommodate this datasheet, add the sort criteria.

4. Click the **Sort cell** of the **Last field** in the second column, click the **Sort list arrow**, click **Ascending**, then click the **Sort list arrow** for the **First field** in the third column, then click **Ascending**

   The new Query design grid is shown in Figure F-4. By setting up the Query design grid in this way, you specify the Last field as the primary sort field, the First field as the secondary sort field, and the TourDate field as the third sort field.

5. Click the **Datasheet View button** on the Query Design toolbar

   The resulting datasheet is shown in Figure F-5. Michael wants to use this information in an upcoming sales meeting, so print a copy of the datasheet.

6. Click the **Print button** on the Query Datasheet toolbar

   You review the printout, and verify that it has the information you need. Now you can save the Customer Purchases query.

7. Click the **Save button** on the Query Datasheet toolbar

Trouble?

If you drag a field from a Field list to the wrong column of the Query design grid, click the column selector and drag the column to its new location. Existing fields shift to make room for the inserted column.

FIGURE F-4: Query design grid for a sort order that doesn't follow the order of the fields on the datasheet

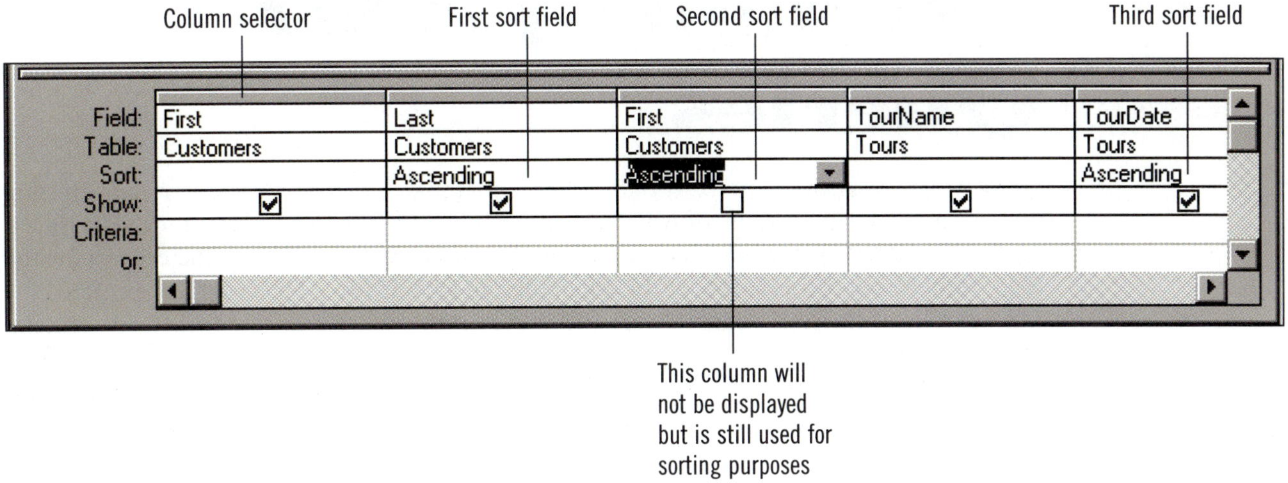

FIGURE F-5: Customer Purchases query with three sort fields

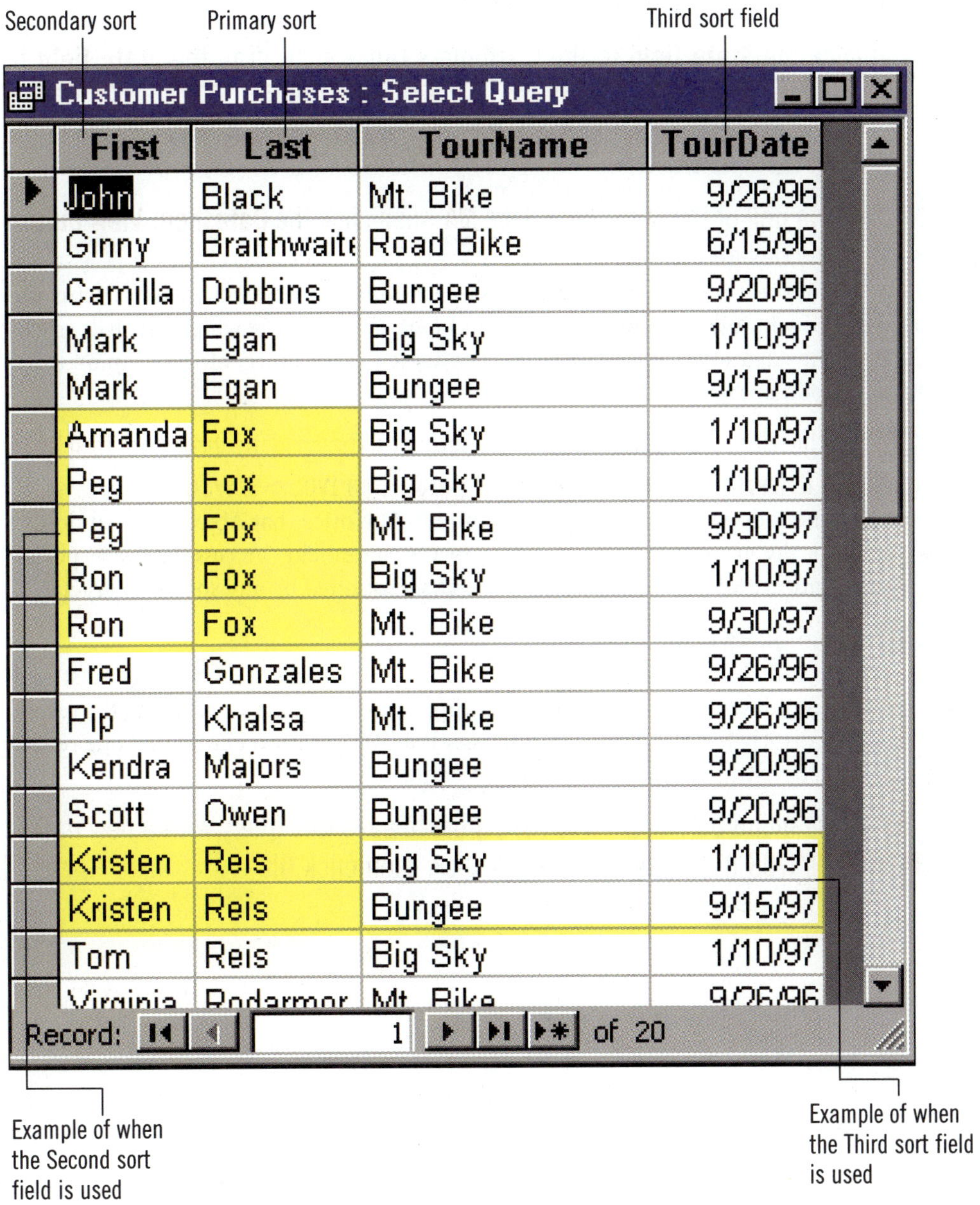

Access 97

Developing AND Queries

Using Access you can query for specific records that match two or more criteria, or limiting conditions. **Criteria** are tests for which the record must be true to be selected for a datasheet. To create an **AND query** in which two or more criteria are present, enter the criteria for the fields on the same Criteria row of the Query design grid. If two AND criteria are entered for the same field, the AND operator separates the criteria in the Criteria cell for that field. Michael wants to send a special mailing to a subset of his customers who have recently purchased tours in Massachusetts. He creates an AND query because the State field must equal Massachusetts and the TourDate field must be greater than 09/01/96.

Steps

1. Click the **Design View button** on the Query Datasheet toolbar
   Instead of creating a query from scratch, modify the Customer Purchases query. The only additional field you have to add to the query is the State field.
2. Scroll and click the **State field** in the Customers table, then drag the **State field** to the fourth column in the Query design grid after the First field
   The TourName and TourDate fields move to the right to accommodate the new field in the grid. Next, enter the state criterion.
3. Click the **Criteria cell** of the **State field**, type **MA**, then click the **Datasheet View button** on the Query Design toolbar
   The resulting datasheet in Figure F-6 shows five customers from Massachusetts. Return to the Query design window to complete the second part of this query which involves selecting only those tour dates that are after 9/1/96. See Table F-1 for more information on using special comparison operators.
4. Click on the Query Datasheet toolbar, scroll in the grid to view the **TourDate field**, click the **Criteria cell** of the **TourDate field**, then type **>9/1/96**
   The resulting Query design grid is shown in Figure F-7. Notice that Access entered double quotes automatically around the text criterion in the State field. Access enters # (pound signs) around date criteria. Numeric criteria aren't surrounded by any special character.
5. Click on the Query Design toolbar
   Multiple criteria added to the same line of the Query design grid (AND criteria) must *each* be true for the record to be displayed in the resulting datasheet, therefore causing the resulting datasheet to display fewer records. In this case, the date criterion eliminated one record in the datasheet. Save this query with a different name.
6. Click **File** on the menu bar, click **Save As/Export** to save this query with a new name, type **MA after 9/1/96** in the New Name: text box, then click **OK**

QuickTip

To resize a column in the Query design grid, click the right boundary of the column selector then drag it left or right.

FIGURE F-6: Datasheet for MA query

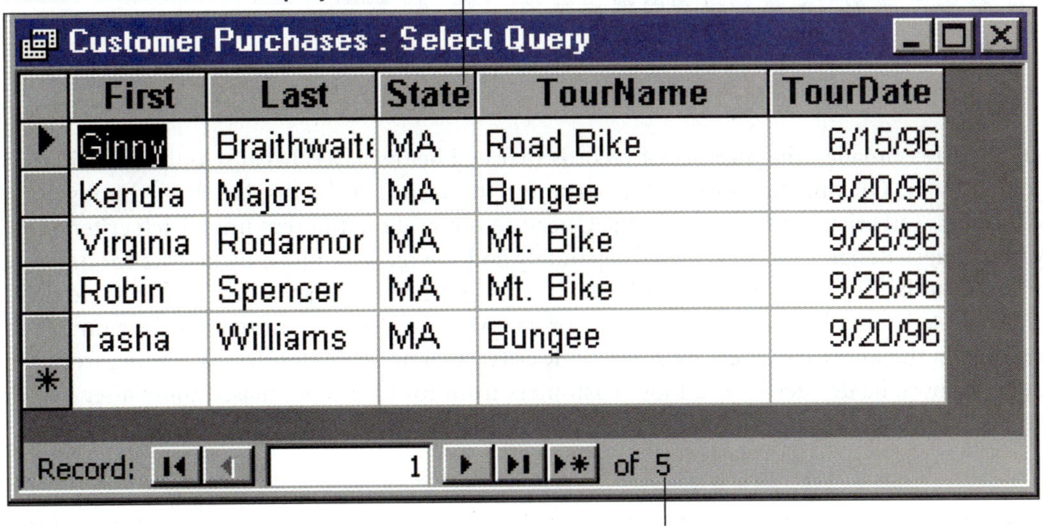

FIGURE F-7: Query design grid for AND query

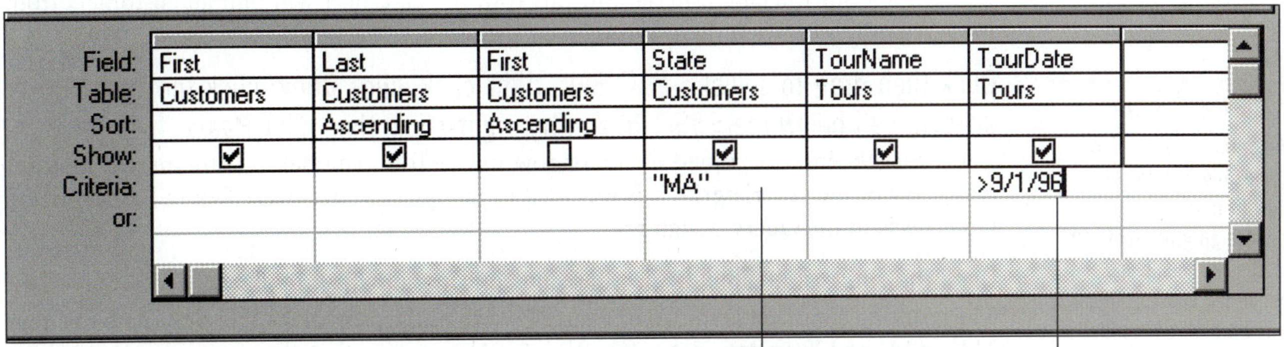

TABLE F-1: Comparison operators for the Criteria row of the Query design grid

operator	description	example	result
>	greater than	>50	Value exceeds 50
>=	greater than or equal to	>=50	Value is 50 or greater
<	less than	<50	Value is less than 50
<=	less than or equal to	<=50	Value is 50 or less than 50
<>	not equal to	<>50	Value is any number other than 50
Between...And	finds values between two numbers or dates	Between #2/2/95# And #2/2/98#	Dates between 2/2/95 and 2/2/98
In	finds a value that is one of a list	In(IA,KS,NE)	Value equals IA or KS or NE
Null	finds records which are blank	Null	No value has been entered
Is Not Null	finds records which are not blank	Is Not Null	Any value has been entered
Like	finds records that match the criteria	Like "A"	Value equals A
Not	finds records that do not match the criteria	Not "2"	Numbers other than 2

Developing OR Queries

OR queries broaden the number of records that will be displayed because only one criterion joined by an OR operator needs to be true for the record to be displayed on the resulting datasheet. OR criteria are entered in the Query design grid on different lines. Each criteria line of the Query design grid is evaluated separately and the record must only be true for one row in order to be displayed in the datasheet. If two OR criteria are specified for the same field, they are separated by the **OR operator**. Michael decides to broaden the number of records in the query datasheet by adding OR criteria. Since new business is coming from the state of Iowa, he decides to add those customers from Iowa who purchased tours after 9/1/96 to his existing query.

Steps

1. Click the **Query Design View button** on the Datasheet toolbar
   To add OR criteria, enter criteria in the 'or' row of the Query design grid.
2. Click the **or State criteria cell** below the **MA** entry, then type **IA**
   If you don't put the date criteria into this row, the datasheet will pull all customers from Iowa, regardless of when their tour date occurred.
3. Click then drag to select **>#9/1/96#**, right-click, click **Copy**, click the **TourDate** or **criteria cell** below the **>#9/1/96#** entry, right-click, then click **Paste**
   The >#9/1/96 entry is copied to the or row in the TourDate field. If the record matches *either* row of the criteria grid, it is included in the query's datasheet. Figure F-8 shows the OR criteria in the Query design grid.
4. Click the **Datasheet View button** on the Query Design toolbar
   The resulting datasheet is shown in Figure F-9. All of the records contain State data of either MA or IA, and TourDate data after 9/1/96. Also, notice that the sort order (Last, First, TourDate) is still in effect. Save this query as a separate database object as well.
5. Click **File** on the menu bar, click **Save As/Export**, type **MA and IA after 9/1/96**, then click **OK**
   You have completed this query. Close the datasheet.
6. Click the **MA and IA after 9/1/96 datasheet Close button**
   The Nomad-F database Queries tab displays the new queries that you created.

QuickTip

If the criterion expression becomes too long to completely fit in a cell of the Query design grid, right-click the cell then click Zoom on the shortcut menu. The Zoom dialog box provides space to enter lengthy criteria expressions.

FIGURE F-8: Query design grid for OR query

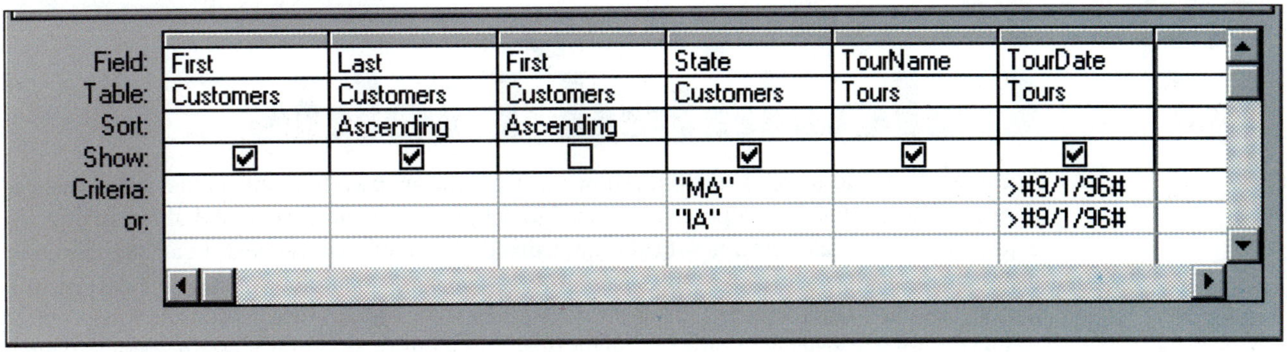

Field:	First	Last	First	State	TourName	TourDate
Table:	Customers	Customers	Customers	Customers	Tours	Tours
Sort:		Ascending	Ascending			
Show:	☑	☑	☐	☑	☑	☑
Criteria:				"MA"		>#9/1/96#
or:				"IA"		>#9/1/96#

FIGURE F-9: Datasheet for OR query

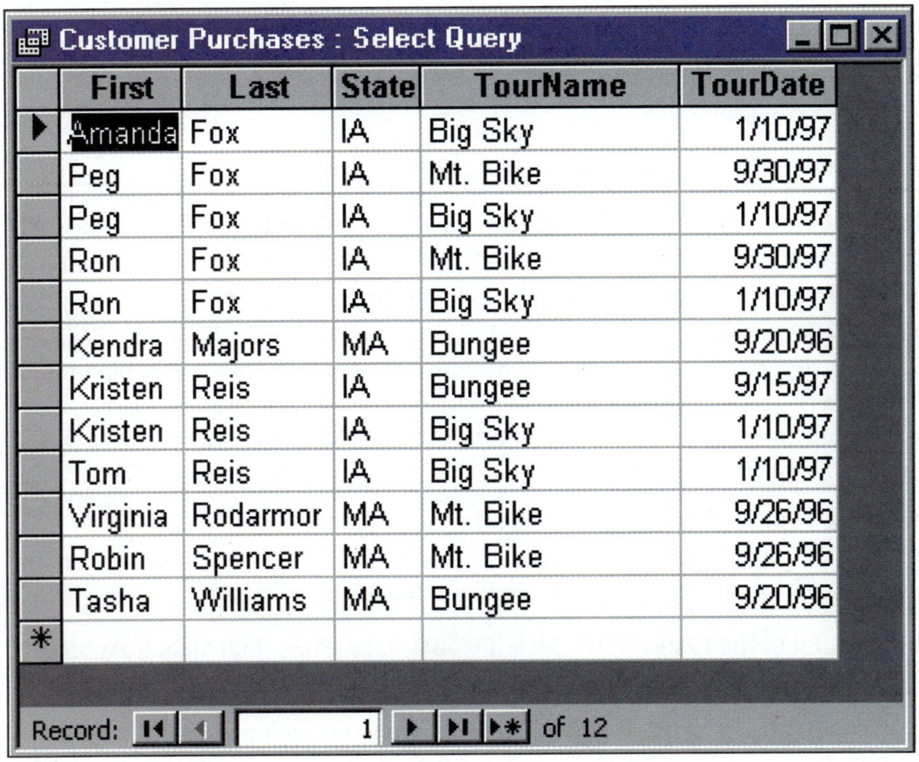

Customer Purchases : Select Query

First	Last	State	TourName	TourDate
Amanda	Fox	IA	Big Sky	1/10/97
Peg	Fox	IA	Mt. Bike	9/30/97
Peg	Fox	IA	Big Sky	1/10/97
Ron	Fox	IA	Mt. Bike	9/30/97
Ron	Fox	IA	Big Sky	1/10/97
Kendra	Majors	MA	Bungee	9/20/96
Kristen	Reis	IA	Bungee	9/15/97
Kristen	Reis	IA	Big Sky	1/10/97
Tom	Reis	IA	Big Sky	1/10/97
Virginia	Rodarmor	MA	Mt. Bike	9/26/96
Robin	Spencer	MA	Mt. Bike	9/26/96
Tasha	Williams	MA	Bungee	9/20/96

Record: 1 of 12

F* Show All 'F' people.

OR Like "F"

CLUES TO USE

Using wildcard characters in query criteria

To search for a pattern, use a ? (question mark) to search for any single character and an * (asterisk) to search for any number of characters. Wildcard characters are often used with the Like operator. For example, the criterion Like "10/*/97" would find all dates in October of 1997 and the criterion Like "F*" would find all values that start with the letter F.

Access 97

Developing Calculated Fields

Arithmetic operators such as the ones shown in Table F-2 are used to create mathematical calculations in a query. Often these operators are used to develop a completely new field of information in a query. If you can calculate a new field of information based on existing fields in a database, never define it as a separate field in the table's Design View. The query method of creating the data ensures that the new field contains accurate, up-to-date information. Michael has decided to track profit (the difference between his cost and his price) per tour. To accomplish this, he creates a query that tells him how much profit he has realized for each tour booked.

Steps

1. Click the **Queries tab**, if necessary, click **New**, click **Design View**, then click **OK**
   You need the InvoiceNo, TourName, TourDate, Price, and Cost fields from the Sales and Tours tables to develop this query.
2. Click **Sales**, click **Add**, click **Tours**, click **Add**, then click **Close**
3. Drag the **InvoiceNo field** from the Sales table to the **first Field column** of the Query design grid, drag the **TourName field** from the Tours table to the **second Field column**, then drag the **TourDate field** from the Tours table to the **third Field column**
   A **calculated field** is created by entering a field name followed by a colon in the Field cell of the Query design grid followed by an expression. An **expression** is a combination of operators such as + (plus), - (minus), * (multiply), or / (divide), raw values (such as numbers or dates), functions, and fields that produce a result. Field names used in an expression are surrounded by square brackets.
4. Click the blank **Field cell** of the fourth column, then type **Profit:[Price]-[Cost]**
   The Query design grid should now look like Figure F-10. You further decide to sort the records from the most profitable sales transaction to the least profitable.
5. Click the **Sort cell** of the **Profit field**, click the **Sort list arrow**, then click **Descending**
   View this query to see the results of your work.
6. Click the **Datasheet View button** on the Query design toolbar
   The query's datasheet appears with the calculated field, Profit. The records are sorted from the highest to the lowest profit as shown in Figure F-11. You cannot enter information directly into the datasheet of a calculated field. The data shown in the Profit field is totally dependent upon the underlying fields of Price and Cost which are not displayed in this datasheet. To use this query at a meeting, print the resulting datasheet.
7. Click the **Print button** on the Query Datasheet toolbar
   You are done with this query. Close the datasheet.
8. Click the **Datasheet Close button**, then click **Yes** when prompted to save changes
9. Type **Profit by Sale** as the query name, then click **OK**

QuickTip

Double-click the thin black vertical line separating field names in the Query design grid or datasheet to make the column width automatically adjust to the widest entry in the column.

CLUES TO USE

Functions in calculated expressions

Functions can be used in expressions. You can develop a function to calculate information based on data in a record, or use a "built-in" function available within Access. The Date built-in function, for example, returns today's date and can be used in an expression or custom function to determine the number of days between today and another date.

FIGURE F-10: A calculated field

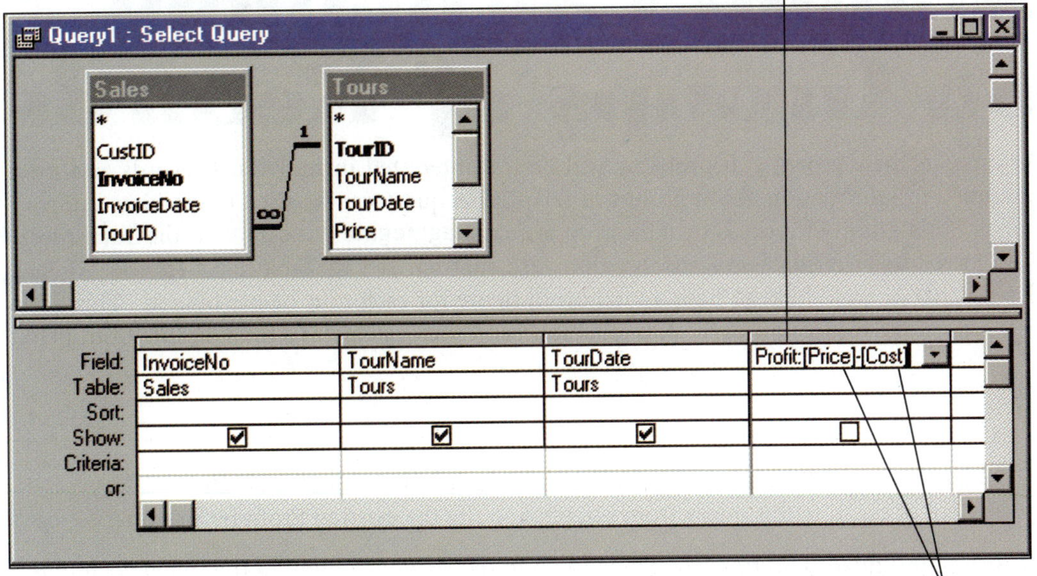

Type Profit in Blank field then : (Price) - (Cost)

FIGURE F-11: Datasheet sorted in descending order by Profit

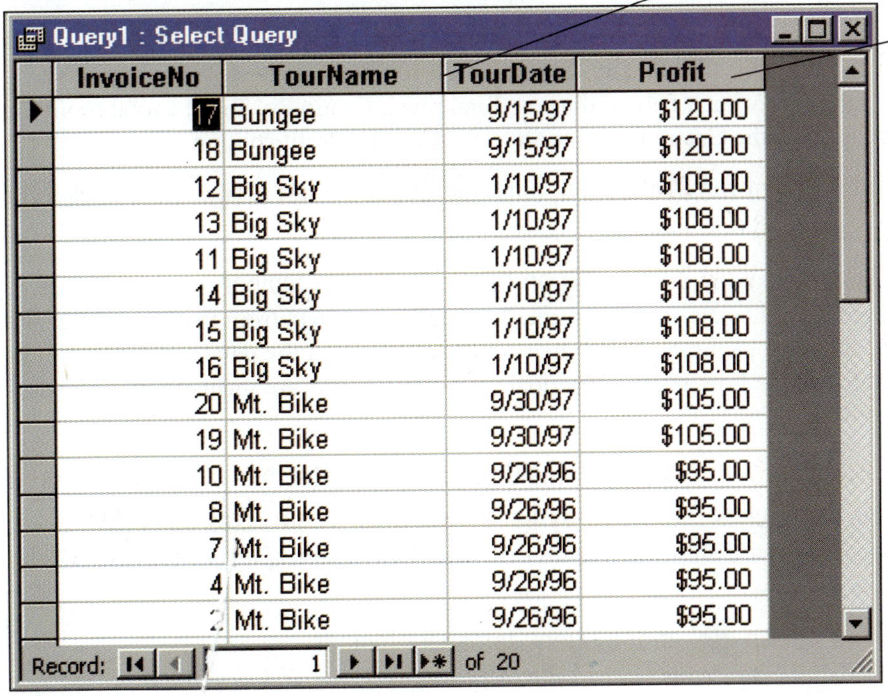

TABLE F-2: Arithmetic operators

operator	description
+	Addition
-	Subtraction
*	Multiplication
/	Division
^	Exponentiation

Access 97

Adding Calculations on Groups of Records

As your database grows, you probably will be less interested in individual records and more interested in information about groups of records. A query can be used to calculate information about a group of records by adding appropriate **aggregate functions** to the Total row of the Query design grid. Aggregate functions are summarized in Table F-3. Michael decides that he would like to have a total profit figure for each tour he has offered. This query first groups the records for each individual tour, and then calculates a total on the Profit field.

Steps

1. Click the **Profit by Sale** query on the Queries tab, then click **Design**
   Instead of creating this query from scratch, modify the existing Profit by Sale query.
2. Drag the **TourID field** from the Sales table to the second column of the Query design grid
   The fields move to the right to accommodate the move. The records will be grouped by TourID and summarized by Profit. The InvoiceNo field is not required for this query.
3. Click the **InvoiceNo field column selector**, then press **[Delete]**
   Deleting the field from the Query design grid does not affect the data in the underlying table. Next, add the Total row to the Query design grid.
4. Click the **Totals button** Σ on the Query Design toolbar
   By default, the entry for each field of the new Total row is Group By. To get a total profit for each TourID, change the Group By function to Sum for the Profit column.
5. Click the **Total cell** of the **Profit field**, click the **Group By list arrow**, then click **Sum**
   The Query design grid now looks like Figure F-12.
6. Click the **Datasheet View button** on the Query Design toolbar
   As you can see from the resulting datasheet, Michael netted $648 from the 1/10/97 Big Sky tour. It was the most profitable tour when summarized across the database. Add a Count function to determine how many individual sales transactions are included in each summarized profit figure.
7. Click the **Design View button** on the Query Datasheet toolbar, click the **Total cell** of the **TourID field**, click the **Group By list arrow**, click **Count**, then click
   The resulting datasheet is shown in Figure F-13 and shows that six Big Sky tours were sold. Print the query.
8. Click the **Print button** on the Query Datasheet toolbar
   You add this datasheet to your Nomad file of printouts. Close and save the Profit by Sale query.
9. Click the **Profit By Sale Close button**, then click **Yes** to save the changes

QuickTip

Click the list arrow of the Top Values button on the Query design toolbar to quickly narrow the number of records in the resulting datasheet to the top 5, 25, 100, 5%, or 25% of the total records.

FIGURE F-12: Query design grid with Total row

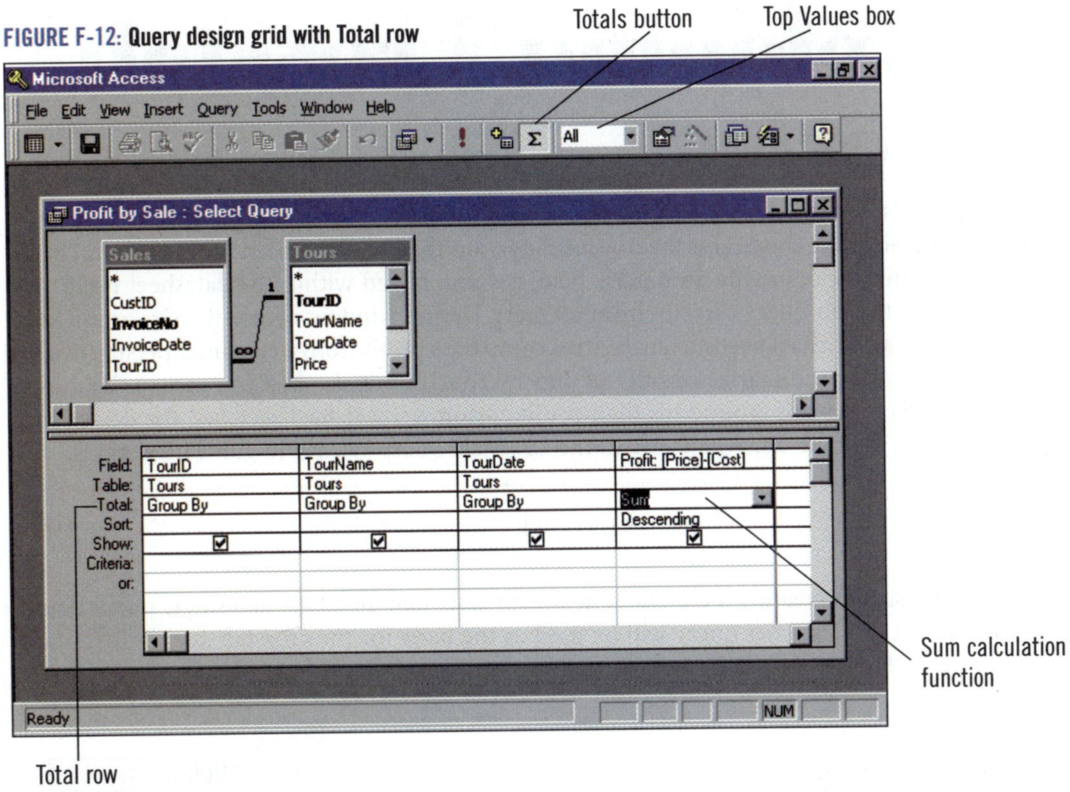

FIGURE F-13: Datasheet with Count and Sum functions

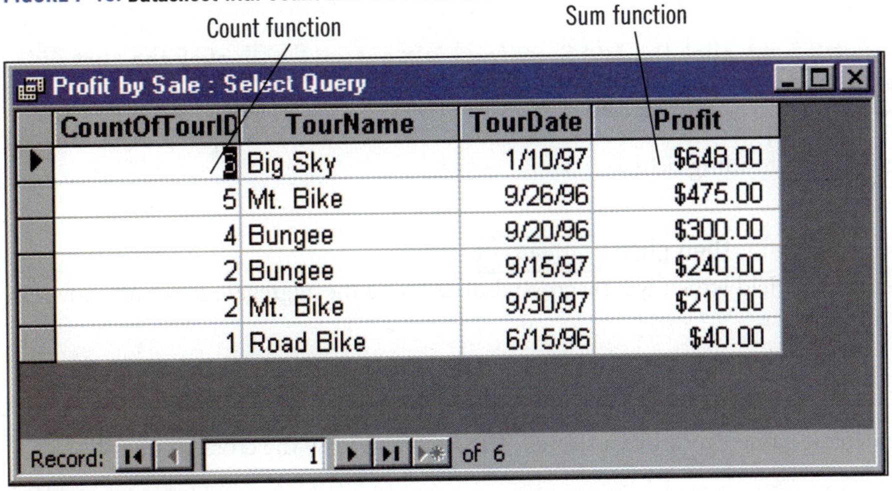

TABLE F-3: Aggregate functions

aggregate function	used to find the
Sum	total of values in a field
Avg	average of values in a field
Min	minimum value in the field
Max	maximum value in the field
Count	number of values in a field (not counting null values)
StDev	standard deviation of values in a field
Var	variance of values in a field
First	field value from the first record in a table or query
Last	field value from the last record in a table or query

Access 97

Developing Crosstab Queries

Crosstab queries provide another method to summarize data by creating a datasheet in which one or more fields are chosen for the row headings, another field is chosen for the column headings, and a third field, usually a numeric field, is summarized within the datasheet itself. You can create a crosstab query directly from a Query Design window or use the Crosstab Query Wizard. Michael needs to analyze his company's profit from a customer perspective. He creates a query that summarizes profit not only by TourID, but also by Customer so that he can develop marketing plans around his high-profit customers. Michael sketched the design for a final report in Figure F-14. Michael uses the Crosstab Query Wizard to guide his actions.

Steps

1. Click the **Queries tab** if necessary, click **New**, click **Crosstab Query Wizard**, then click **OK**
   The first step to creating a crosstab query is to assemble the fields in a single query object. The Profit by Customer query will be used as the basis for the crosstab query. It contains the needed fields of CustID, Last, TourID, and Profit.

QuickTip

You can make any query into a crosstab query by choosing the Crosstab option from the Query type button on the Query toolbar.

2. Click the **Queries option button**, click **Profit by Customer**, then click [Next >]
   Identify the CustID and Last fields as row headings.

Trouble?

If the Crosstab Wizard has been recently used, you may see different default options in each dialog box. Be sure to check each option as you move through the dialog boxes. Click the Back button to review previous dialog boxes. Be sure to double-check the query name and modify the default option if necessary.

3. Click the **CustID field**, click the **Add Selected Field button** [>], click the **Last field**, click [>], then click [Next >]
   The sample pane displays the results of your choices as you build the query. Next Michael identify the column heading field.
4. Click the **TourID field**, then click [Next >]
   Finally, identify the field which will be crosstabulated, and the aggregate function shown in Figure F-15.
5. Click **Profit**, click **Sum** in the Functions column, then click [Next >]
   Accept the default name Profit by Customer_Crosstab and view the crosstab query
6. Click [Finish], then click the datasheet **Maximize button** if necessary
   The resulting datasheet for the Crosstab query is shown in Figure F-16. You could switch to Query Design View and sort this query by Profit or enter limiting criteria as with any other query. In this case though, just print a copy of the crosstab datasheet for a future meeting.
7. Click the **Print button** on the Query Datasheet toolbar, click the **Crosstab query datasheet Close button**

CLUES TO USE

Types of Query Wizards

The Simple Query Wizard is another way to create a select query rather than use the Query Design View. The Find Duplicates Query Wizard is used to determine whether a table contains duplicate values in one or more fields. The Find Unmatched Query Wizard is used to find records in one table that don't have related records in another table.

FIGURE F-14: Sketch of a crosstab query

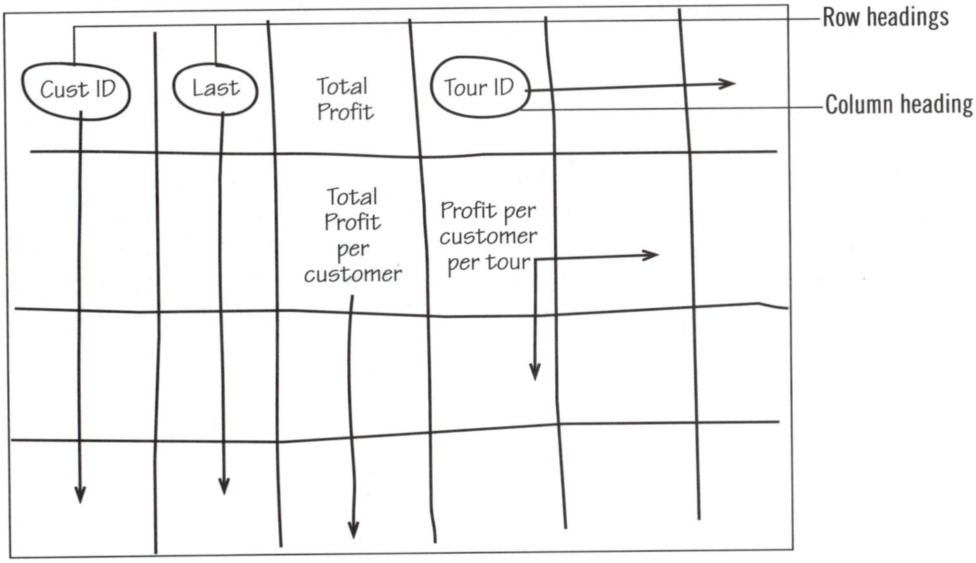

FIGURE F-15: Crosstab Query Wizard

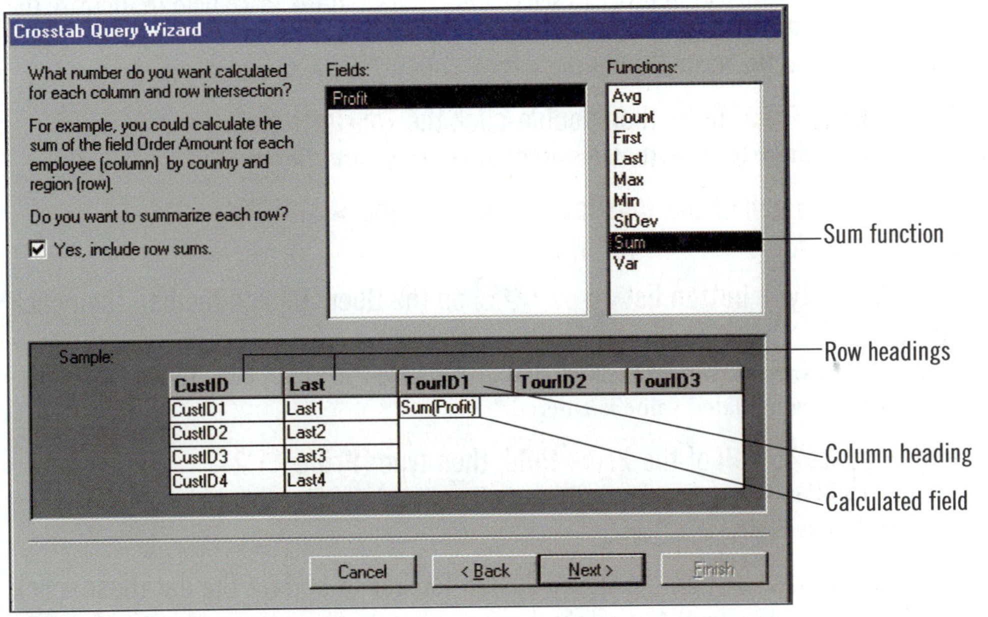

FIGURE F-16: Crosstab query datasheet

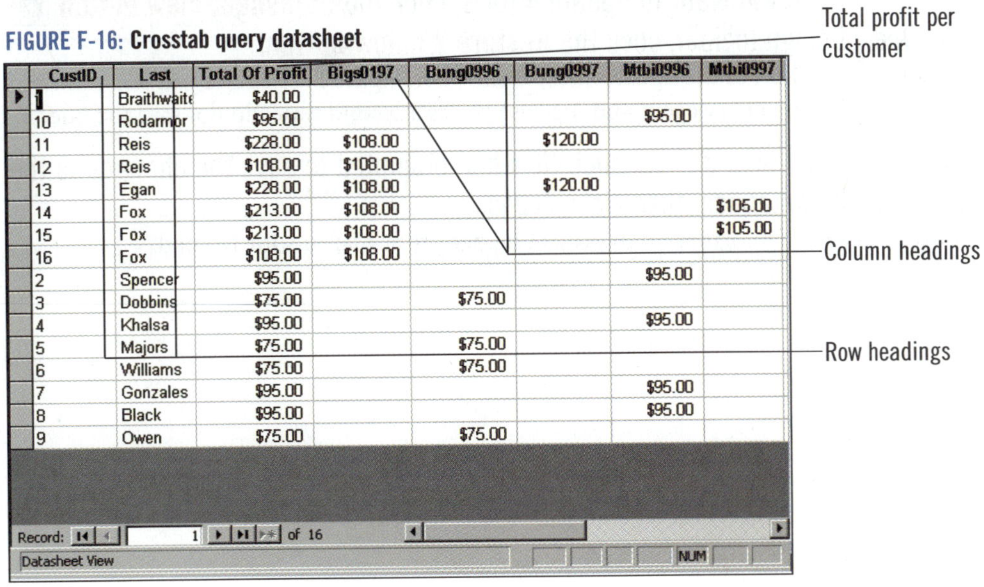

CustID	Last	Total Of Profit	Bigs0197	Bung0996	Bung0997	Mtbi0996	Mtbi0997
1	Braithwaite	$40.00					
10	Rodarmor	$95.00				$95.00	
11	Reis	$228.00	$108.00		$120.00		
12	Reis	$108.00	$108.00				
13	Egan	$228.00	$108.00		$120.00		
14	Fox	$213.00	$108.00				$105.00
15	Fox	$213.00	$108.00				$105.00
16	Fox	$108.00	$108.00				
2	Spencer	$95.00				$95.00	
3	Dobbins	$75.00		$75.00			
4	Khalsa	$95.00				$95.00	
5	Majors	$75.00		$75.00			
6	Williams	$75.00		$75.00			
7	Gonzales	$95.00				$95.00	
8	Black	$95.00				$95.00	
9	Owen	$75.00		$75.00			

Creating Update Queries

Update queries allow you to select a group of records then update all of them with one action. For example, you may wish to delete a group of records with a **Delete** query, change the value of a field with a basic Update query, or add several records to an existing table with an **Append** query. An update query starts as a select query with an Update to row added to the Query design grid. Table F-4 shows examples of update formulas. Michael wants to increase the prices of all 1997 tours by 20%.

Steps

1. **Click the Queries tab, click New, click Design View, then click OK**
   The only table you need for this update query is the Tours table.

2. **Click Tours, click Add, then click Close**
   You need the TourDate field in order to select 1997 tours and the Price field to increase the data in that field by 20%. You have to insert the Price field in the first column in the Query design grid, and the TourDate field in the second column in the Query design grid.

3. **Double-click the Price field, then double-click the TourDate field**
   Specify that only those tours with dates on or after 1/1/97 are chosen.

4. **Click the Criteria cell of the TourDate field, then type >=1/1/97**
   Change the select query into an update query.

5. **Click the Query Type button list arrow on the Query Design toolbar, then click Update Query**
   The Sort and Show rows of the Query design grid changes to an Update To row where the formula for the new updated value is entered.

6. **Click the Update To cell of the Price field, then type [Price]*1.2**
   This formula will update the current prices of all tours selected by 20%. The Query Design grid now looks like Figure F-17.

7. **Click the Run button on the Query Design toolbar to update the database, click Yes when asked if you want to update 4 rows, click the Datasheet View button on the Query Design toolbar, click the Restore Window button.**
   The resulting datasheet of the update query is shown in Figure F-18. Since you don't want to inadvertently run the query again and increase prices a second time, do not save the query.

8. **Click the Access Close button, click No when prompted to save the changes to the query, close the database, then close Access**
   Michael can use this information to project higher profit margins for Nomad.

Trouble?

Don't click the Run button twice or you will update the Price field of the chosen records by 20% a second time.

FIGURE F-17: Query Design View of an update query

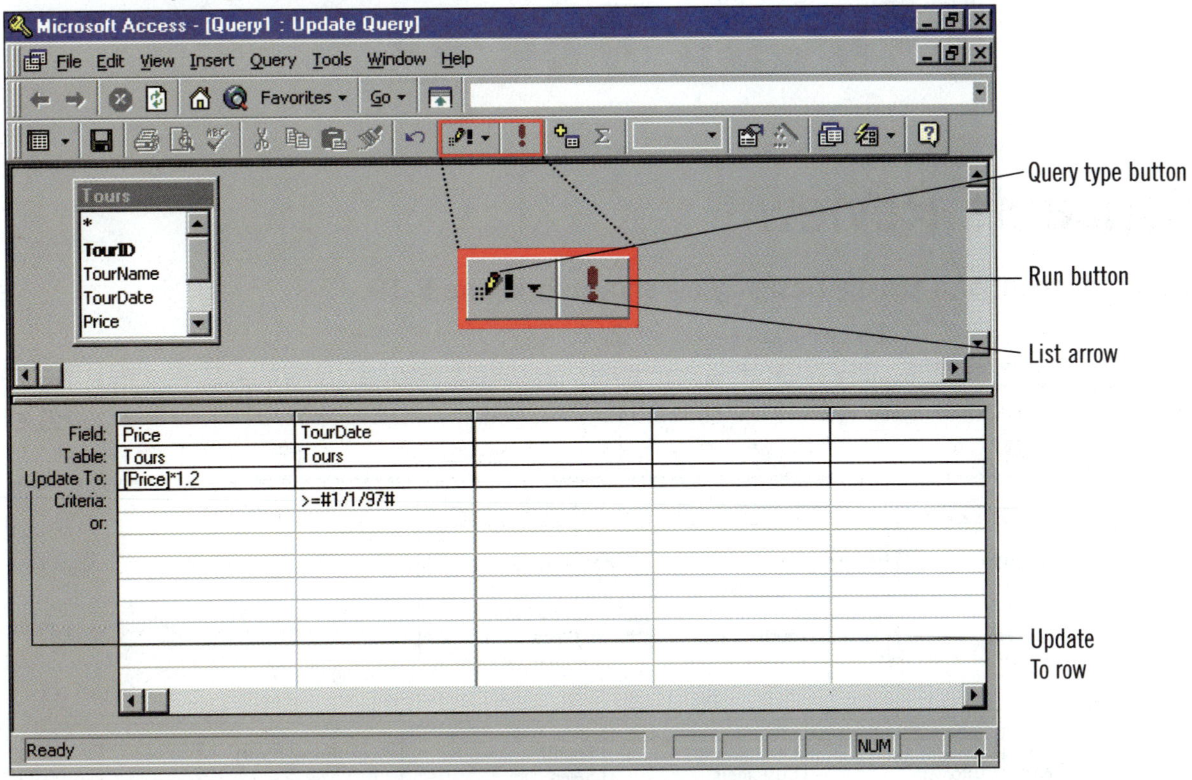

FIGURE F-18: Datasheet of an update query after running the update

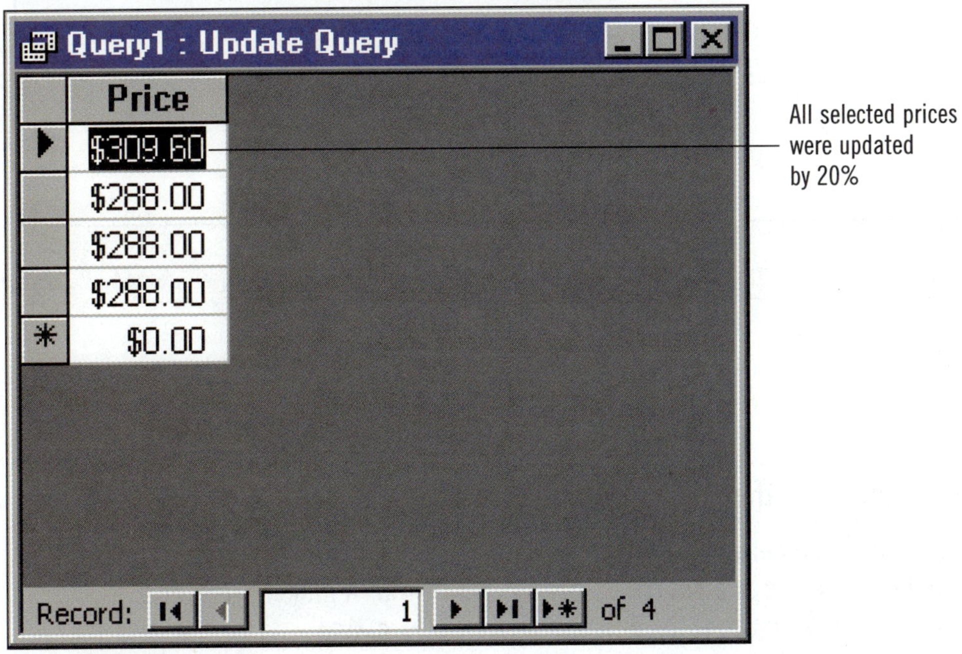

TABLE F-4: Update query formulas and results

update formula	result
"Vice President"	Changes the values of the chosen field to the text Vice President
#1/1/98#	Changes the values of the chosen field to the date 1/1/98
7	Changes the values of the chosen field to 7
[Cost]*1.05	Updates the values of the chosen field to five percent more than the current value of the Cost field

Practice

Concepts Review

Identify each element of a table's Design View shown in Figure F-19.

FIGURE F-19

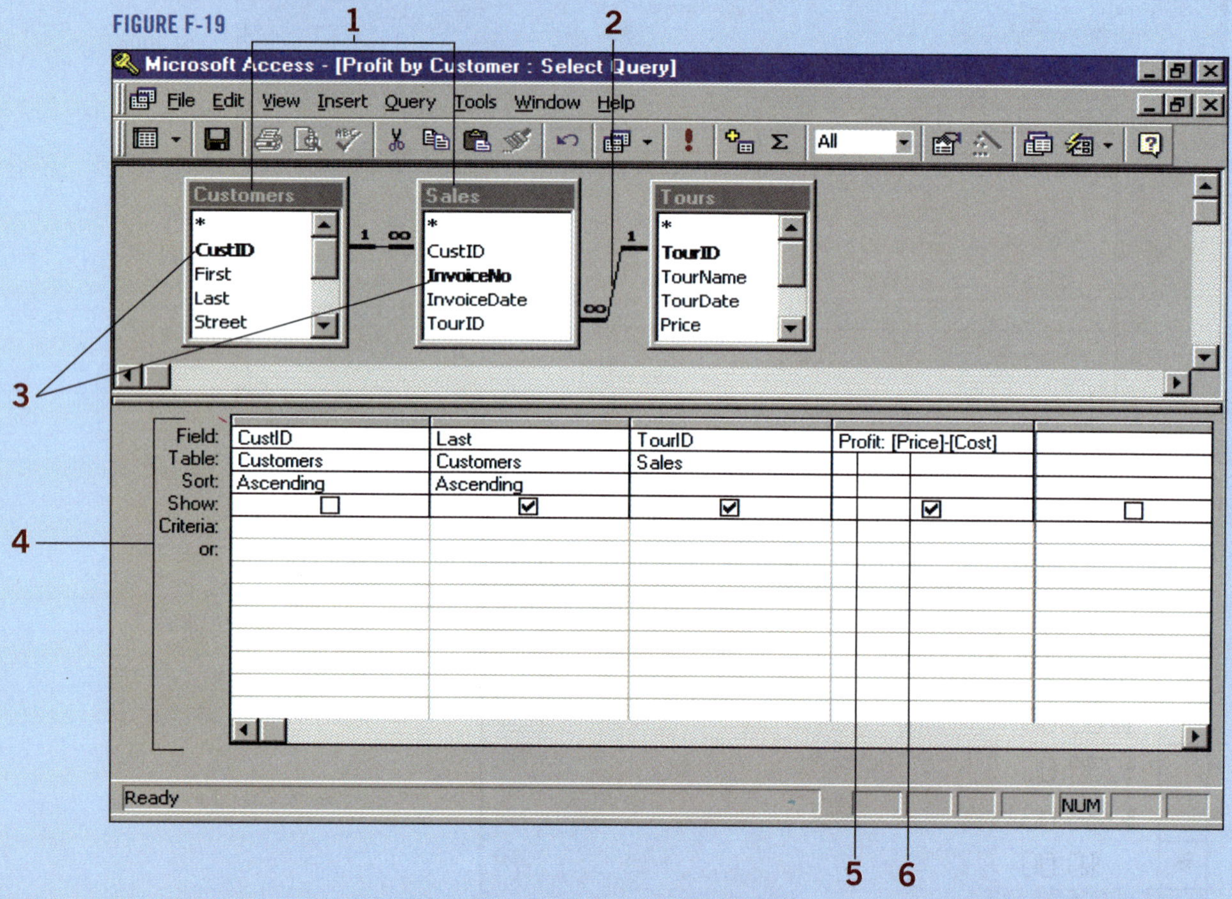

Match each term with the statement that describes its function.

7. Placing the records of a datasheet in a certain order
8. Used to create mathematical calculations in a query
9. A database object that answers questions about the data
10. Conditions that select only certain records
11. Operator used to combine two expressions

a. Query
b. Arithmetic operators
c. And
d. Sorting
e. Criteria

Select the best answer from the list of choices.

12. The query datasheet can best be described as:
- **a.** A duplication of the data in the underlying table's datasheet.
- **b.** A logical view of the selected data from an underlying table's datasheet.
- **c.** A separate file of data.
- **d.** A second copy of the data in the underlying tables.

13. Queries are often used to:
- **a.** Create copies of database files.
- **b.** Eliminate the need to build multiple tables.
- **c.** Create option boxes and list boxes from which to choose field values.
- **d.** Present a subset of fields from multiple tables.

14. When you update data in a table that is displayed in a query:
- **a.** You must also update the query.
- **b.** You must relink the query to the table.
- **c.** The data is automatically updated in the query.
- **d.** You have the choice whether you want to update the data in the query or not.

15. To assemble several fields from different tables, use a(n):
- **a.** Select Query.
- **b.** Update Query.
- **c.** Delete Query.
- **d.** Append Query.

16. The order in which records are sorted is determined by:
- **a.** The order in which the fields are listed in the underlying table.
- **b.** The alphabetic order of the field names.
- **c.** The left-to-right position of the fields in the Query grid.
- **d.** Ascending fields are sorted first in the Query grid. Descending fields are sorted second.

17. Crosstab queries are used to:
- **a.** Summarize information based on fields in the column and row headings of the report.
- **b.** Update several records at the same time.
- **c.** Select fields for a datasheet from multiple tables.
- **d.** Calculate price increases on numeric fields.

▶ Skills Review

1. Create select queries using multiple tables

a. Start Access and open the database Addresses-F.
b. Create a new select query using Design View using both the Names and Zips tables.
c. Add the following fields to the Query design grid in this order:
First, Last, Street, and Zip from the Names table
City and State from the Zips table
d. Save the query as "Basic Address List", view the datasheet, print the datasheet, then close the query.

2. Sort a query on multiple fields

a. Think about how you would modify the "Basic Address List" query so that it is sorted in ascending order by Last, then by First, but do not change the order of the fields in the resulting datasheet.
b. Add another First field to the right of the Last field in the Query design grid to make the first three fields in the Query design grid First, Last, and First.
c. Add the ascending sort criteria to the second column and third column fields, and uncheck the Show check-box in the third column.
d. Save the query as "Sorted Address List", view the datasheet, print the datasheet, then close the query.

3. Develop AND queries

a. Think about how you would modify the "Basic Address List" query so that only those people from IA with a last name that starts with "F" are chosen.
b. Enter F* (the asterisk is a wildcard) as the criterion for the Last field to choose all people whose last name starts with F. Enter IA as the criterion for the State field.
c. Be sure to enter the criteria on the same line in the Query design grid to make the query an AND query.
d. Save the query as "Iowa F Names", view the datasheet, print the datasheet, and close the query.

4. Develop OR queries

a. Modify the "Iowa F Names" query so that only those people from IA with a last name that starts with "F" or "B" are chosen.
b. Enter the OR criterion B* on the or row for the Last field in the Query design grid. Access will assist you with the syntax for this type of criterion and enters "Like B*" in the cell when you click elsewhere in the grid.
c. Be sure to reenter the IA criterion on the or row for the State field in the Query design grid to make sure that your query doesn't display all names that start with B, but only those who live in Iowa.
d. Save the query as "Iowa B or F Names", view the datasheet, print the datasheet, then close the query.

5. Develop calculated fields

a. Plan how you might create a new select query using Design View using just the Names table to determine the number of days old each person is based on the information in the Birthday field.
b. Add the following fields from the Names table to the Query design grid in this order:
First, Last, Birthday
c. Create a calculated field called "Days Old" in the fourth column of the Query design grid with the expression
Days Old:Date()-[Birthday]
(Note: Date() is an Access function that always represents today's date.)
d. Save the query as "Days Old", view the datasheet, print the datasheet, then close the query.

6. Add calculations on groups of records
   - **a.** Create a new select query using Design View, then add the Names and Zips tables.
   - **b.** Add the following fields:
     Zip from the Names table
     City and State from the Zips table
   - **c.** Add the Total row to the Query design grid and change the function from Group By to Count for the Zip field
   - **d.** Save the query as "Count Zip", view the datasheet, print the datasheet, then close the query.

7. Develop crosstab queries
   - **a.** Use the Crosstab Query Wizard to create a new crosstab query that counts the number of people who live in each City and State.
   - **b.** Use the Basic Address List query as the basis for the new crosstab query.
   - **c.** Select City as the row heading and State as the column heading.
   - **d.** Count the First field for the calculation within the crosstab datasheet.
   - **e.** Name the query "Crosstab of Cities and States".
   - **f.** View, Save, print, then close the datasheet.

8. Create update queries
   - **a.** Think about how you would create a new select query using Design View to update the city "Overland Park" to the correct post office designation of "Shawnee Mission."
   - **b.** Use Design View to design a new query.
   - **c.** Add just the Zips table to the Query design grid.
   - **d.** Add the City field from the Zip table to the query.
   - **e.** Click Query on the menu bar, then click Update Query.
   - **f.** In the Criteria cell, enter "Overland Park".
   - **g.** In the Update To cell, enter "Shawnee Mission".
   - **h.** Run the query to update the record that contains the Overland Park entry in the City field.
   - **i.** Save the query as "Shawnee Mission".
   - **j.** Close the database, then exit Access.

Independent Challenges

1. As the president of a civic organization, you have developed a database that tracks donations of recyclable material called Cleanup-F. Now that several deposits have been made and recorded, you wish to query the database for several different listings that are needed for the next meeting.

To complete this independent challenge:

1. Start Access and open the database Cleanup-F.
2. Create a query that pulls the following fields into a datasheet and print the datasheet.
   Name (of Clubs), Deposit Date, Weight, Name (of Recycle Centers)
   Call the query "Deposits by Club".
3. Modify Deposits by Club so that it is sorted ascending by club Name, and then ascending by Deposit Date. Print the datasheet and save the query as "Deposits Sorted by Club then Date".
4. Modify Deposits Sorted by Club then Date to eliminate both the deposit Date and Name (of Center) fields. Then, group the records by club Name and total the Weight. Print the datasheet and save the query as "Total Weight by Club".

5. Modify Total Weight by Club so that the records are sorted from the highest total deposit weight to the lowest. Print the datasheet and save the query as "Sorted Total Weight by Club".
6. Create a new query that pulls the following fields with the given criteria into a datasheet.
   Fields: Name (of Center), deposit Date, Weight
   Criteria: Recycle Center Name = East Side
   Sorting: Sort ascending by deposit Date
7. Save the query with the name "East Side Deposits", view, then print the datasheet.
8. Close the database and exit Access.

2. Now that you've developed a relational database that documents the books you've read called Readings-F, your friends are starting to ask for recommended reading lists. You wish to query your book database to satisfy the requests of your friends.

To complete this independent challenge:

1. Start Access and open the database Readings-F.
2. Create a query that pulls the following fields into a datasheet:
   Title, Category, Rating, and Last Name
   Print the datasheet, save, and name the query "Books I've Read".
3. Modify Books I've Read so that it is sorted in a descending order on Rating and then in an ascending order by Last Name. Print the datasheet and name the query "Books I've Read Sorted by Rating and Author".
4. Use the Crosstab Query Wizard and the Books I've Read query to find out how many books you've read within each category by each author. Use Last Name as the row heading field, Category as the column heading field, and count the Title field within the body of the Crosstab report. Print the datasheet and name the query "Crosstab of Authors and Categories".
5. Modify the Books I've Read Sorted by Rating and Author query so that only fiction books with a rating of 7 or above are displayed.
6. Save the query as "Top Fiction Books", then print the datasheet.
7. Close the database and exit Access.

3. You have recently helped the medical director of a large internal medicine clinic put together and update a database called Doctors-F that tracks extra-curricular activities. You wish to query the database for specific listings of information to present to the committee responsible for philanthropic activities.

To complete this independent challenge:

1. Start Access and open the database Doctors-F.
2. Create a query that pulls the following fields into a datasheet:
   First Name, Last Name, Date, Hours, and Name (of Program)
   Save the query as "Physician Activities", then print the datasheet.
3. Modify Physician Activities so that it is sorted ascending by Last Name and then ascending by Date. Print the datasheet and name the query "Physician Activities Sorted by Name and Date".
4. Modify the Physician Activities Sorted by Name and Date query to eliminate the Date and Name fields. Then, group the records by Last Name and First Name and subtotal them by Hours. Print the datasheet and save the query as "Total Physician Hours".
5. Modify Total Physician Hours so that the records are listed from the physician who has volunteered the most time to the least. Print the datasheet and save the query as "Total Physician Hours Sorted from High to Low".

6. Create a new query that pulls the following fields with the given criteria into a datasheet:
   Fields: Name (of program), Last Name, Date, Hours
   Criteria: Hours are greater than 2 and Program equals "Heart Healthy" or Hours are greater than 2 and Program equals "Diabetes Campaign"
   Sorting: Sort ascending by Name then Last Name
7. Save the query as "Heart and Diabetes", then print the datasheet.
8. Create a new query that pulls the Program Name field from the Programs table and updates any occurrences of "Elderly Outreach" to "Senior Outreach".
9. Save the query as "Elderly to Senior".
10. Create a new query that pulls the First Name field and Last Name field from the Physicians table. Make the First Name field the first column and the Last Name field the second column. Sort by Last Name, then by First Name.
11. Add the Hours field to the third column of the grid of the new query.
12. Add a calculated field to the fourth column of the grid that calculates the total time spent by the staff during the activity. The total time is calculated as three times the hours spent by the physician to account for the hours spent by the physician, the nurse, and the aide. The entry in the fourth column should be as follows: Total Staff:[Hours]*3
13. Save the query as "Total Time."
14. Close the database and exit Access.

WEB WORK

4. You are interested in finding out about technical jobs currently available at IBM. Using information about job openings posted at IBM's Web site, you have started an Access database that you can query for the opportunities that most interest you.

To complete this independent challenge:

1. Log on to the Internet and use your browser to go to http://www.course.com. From there, click Student Online Companions, click the link for this textbook, then click the Access link for Unit F.
2. Use the IBM Employment site to find out what jobs are posted on the web page, and print at least two pages of the web site.
3. Open the IBM-F database.
4. Using the information you printed from IBM's site, enter two new records into the Job Titles table.
5. Create a new query that first displays the Category field from the Job Categories table, second displays the Job Title from the Job Titles table, and third shows the Job Reference # field from the Job Titles table.
6. Having recently read an article about job prospects for developers, you decide to determine how many of the job postings in the database match this title. Modify the query by entering "Developers" in the Criteria cell of the Job Title field.
7. Sort the records ascending by the Category field.
8. Resize the columns of the resulting datasheet so that all the information in each column is displayed.
9. Save the query as "Developers Query", print the datasheet, close the datasheet and database, then exit Access.

▶ Visual Workshop

Open the VW-F database and create a new query as shown in Figure F-20. Notice that the records are sorted alphabetically by last name and the total value of their donations is summarized in the SumOfValue field. Save the query as "Summarized Donations" then print the datasheet.

FIGURE F-20

Query1 : Select Query

Last	SSN	City	State	SumOfValue
Allen	444-44-4444	Ames	IA	$1,500.00
Eagan	111-11-1111	Johnston	IA	$150.00
Wambold	222-22-2222	Fontanelle	IA	$200.00
Washington	333-33-3333	Bridgewater	IA	$1,500.00

Record: 1 of 4

Developing

Forms with Subforms

Objectives

- Create a form from multiple tables
- Move and resize controls
- Add labels and format controls
- Sort records within a form
- Find records within a form
- Filter records within a form
- Change the default value of a form control
- Add list boxes

Adding new records or modifying existing data in a database must be easy and straightforward. A datasheet is often too cumbersome or complex for extensive data entry purposes. A **form** overcomes these obstacles by allowing you to present fields in any logical or useful screen arrangement. Also, forms allow you to add **controls** such as field labels, field text boxes, list boxes, and option buttons to help identify the data on the form. Michael wants to develop forms that match Nomad's source documents, the paper documents on which data is initially recorded. Entering data through well-designed forms will encourage fast, accurate data entry and will shield the data entry person from the complexity of tables, queries, and datasheets.

Access 97

Creating a Form from Multiple Tables

A form displays the fields of a table or query in an arrangement that you design, and can be based on one of five general layouts: Columnar, Tabular, Datasheet, Chart, and PivotTable. See Table G-1 for more information on the different form layouts. Once the form is created, the design can be changed. Michael will develop a sales transaction form that Nomad employees can use to record additional tour sales including customer and invoice information at the time of the sale. The form requires fields from both the Customers and Sales tables in the Nomad database.

Steps

1. Start Access and open the **Nomad-G** database
2. Click the **Forms tab** in the Nomad-G : Database window, click **New**, click **Form Wizard** in the New Form dialog box, then click **OK**
   The **Form Wizard**, as shown in Figure G-1, prompts you to select the fields, layout, and style of the form. You use the Form Wizard to select all the fields from both the Customers and Sales tables which are not currently gathered in any single query object.
3. Click the **Select all fields button** [>>] to select all fields from the Customers table, click the **Tables/Queries list arrow**, click **Table: Sales**, click the **Select all fields button** [>>], then click [Next >]
   Next, you must decide how to view the data. Arranging the form by Customers places the customer information at the top of the form, and places invoice and tour information in a subform. A **subform** links multiple records from one table (Sales) to a single record of another table (Customers). It is especially effective when you want to show data from tables with a one-to-many relationship.
4. If necessary, click **by Customers**, click the **Form with subform(s) option button**, then click [Next >]
   Next, choose a tabular form layout then choose a Standard style in the following dialog box.
5. Click the **Tabular option button**, click [Next >], click **Standard**, then click [Next >]
   Form names appear on the Forms tab and should be descriptive so you can identify the forms at a later time. Change the default form name and accept the default subform name.
6. Type **Customer Form** in the Form: text box, click [Finish], then click the **Customer Form Maximize button**
   The form is shown in Figure G-2. By placing the customer information in the main form and the sales information in the subform, you can show multiple sales transactions for the same customer on the same form.

CLUES TO USE

Using AutoForm

The **AutoForm** option creates the specified type of form for the chosen table or query. To quickly create a columnar form, click the table or query object with the fields you wish the form to contain, click the New Object button on the Database toolbar, then click AutoForm.

FIGURE G-1: Form Wizard

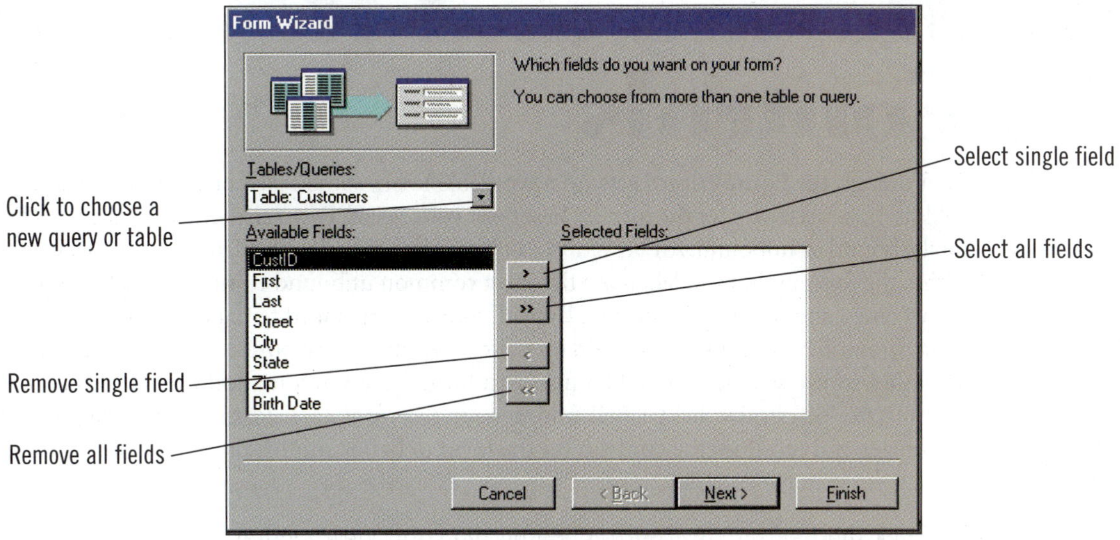

FIGURE G-2: Customer Form

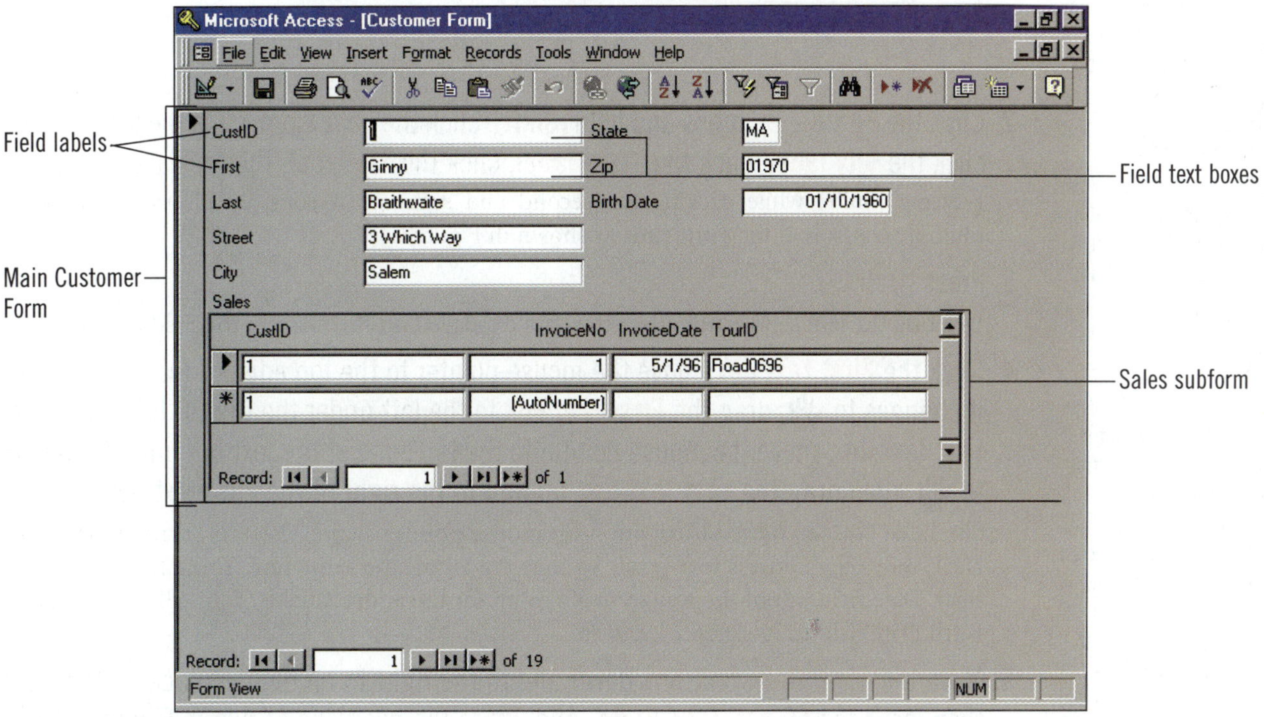

TABLE G-1: Form layouts

layout	description
Columnar	Each field appears on a separate line with a label to its left, one record for each screen
Tabular	Each field appears as a column heading and each record as a row; displays multiple records just like a datasheet, but provides more design control and flexibility; for example, you could change elements such as colors, fonts, headers, or footers
Datasheet	Each field appears as a column heading and each record as a row; the datasheet layout displays multiple records, but formatting options, except for resizing columns, are limited
Chart	Numeric fields are present in a chart (graph) format
PivotTable	Fields are chosen for column and for row headings, and a field is summarized in the intersection of the appropriate column and row in a cross-tabular format

Access 97

Moving and Resizing Controls

Even though the Form Wizard sets up a workable form, some rearrangement and resizing of the fields is often necessary for the form to best meet your needs. Form elements are called **controls** and can be bound or unbound. An **unbound control** is not linked to the data of any table; it exists only within the form itself. Field labels are the most common unbound control, but other types include clipart, lines, and instructional labels. **Bound controls** are linked to data in underlying tables. The most common bound control is a field text box. Check boxes, list boxes, and option buttons can also be bound controls. When you add a field to a form, Access automatically adds both an unbound control (the descriptive field label) and a bound control (a field text box). Michael rearranges and modifies the controls on the form to better suit his data entry needs.

Steps 1 2 3 4

Trouble?

If the Toolbox covers the form, drag the Toolbox title bar to the right edge of the window so the entire form is visible.

Trouble?

If you select the wrong label, click it again while holding [Shift] to deselect it and retain the other selections.

QuickTip

The Object list box on the left edge of the Formatting (Form/Report) toolbar always displays which control is currently selected on the form. In addition, you can select a control by clicking the Object list arrow, then clicking the desired control from the list.

QuickTip

You can press and hold [Ctrl] while pressing an arrow key to move objects very small distances (less than a grid mark).

Time To

- Save
- Close

1. **Click the Design View button on the Form View toolbar**

   Use Design View to move, delete, or add any elements to the form. The fields from the Customer table appear in the upper half of the form, and a large control to designate the size and position of the Sales Subform appears in the lower half. Delete the unnecessary labels from the form.

2. **Click the First label, press and hold [Shift], click the Last label, click the Street label, click the City label, click the State label, click the Zip label, then release [Shift]**

   Pressing [Shift] while clicking the second and subsequent controls allows you to select multiple controls at the same time as shown in Figure G-3.

3. **Press [Delete]**

   Deleting the labels does not affect the data displayed on the form in the field text boxes.

4. **Click the First text box, move the mouse pointer to the top edge of the text box until it changes to ✋, drag the First text box to the left under the CustID label, click the Last text box, move the mouse pointer to the top edge of the text box until it changes to ✋, then drag the Last text box up and to the right of the First text box**

   See Table G-2 for more information on mouse pointer shapes used in Form Design View. Next, move the address text boxes so they are all on the same line. You have to move the Birth Date field out of the way to make room for the address fields. You will then move the Birth Date field to its correct location.

5. **Move the Birth Date text box down and to the right to an empty space on the form, then move the Street, City, State, and Zip to the positions shown in Figure G-4**

   You want the Birth Date field label and text box next to the CustID field.

6. **Click the Birth Date text box, move the mouse pointer to the top edge of the text box until it changes to ✋, then drag the Birth Date text box to the right of the CustID field**

   The CustID and Zip text boxes are wider than necessary.

7. **Click the CustID text box, press and hold [Shift], click the Zip text box, move the mouse pointer to the middle resize handle on the right side of the Zip text box; drag ↔ to the left to the 4.5" mark on the ruler**

   The new form design organizes the information logically, without the unnecessary labels.

8. **Click the Form View button on the Form Design toolbar**

   Compare your screen to the form shown in Figure G-5. Now you can save and close the new form.

FIGURE G-3: Form Design View

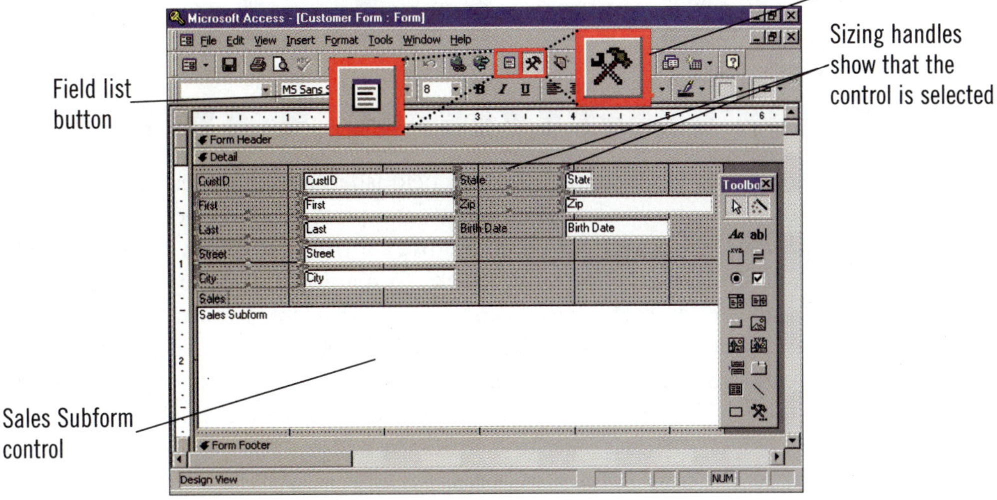

FIGURE G-4: Customer Form after fields are moved

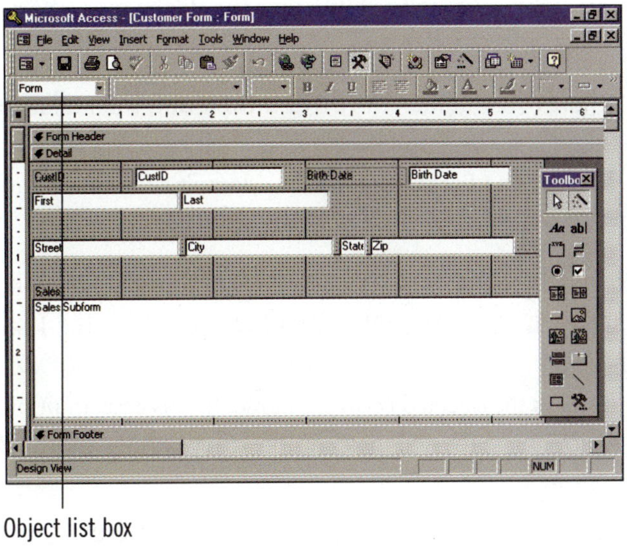

FIGURE G-5: Final Customer Form

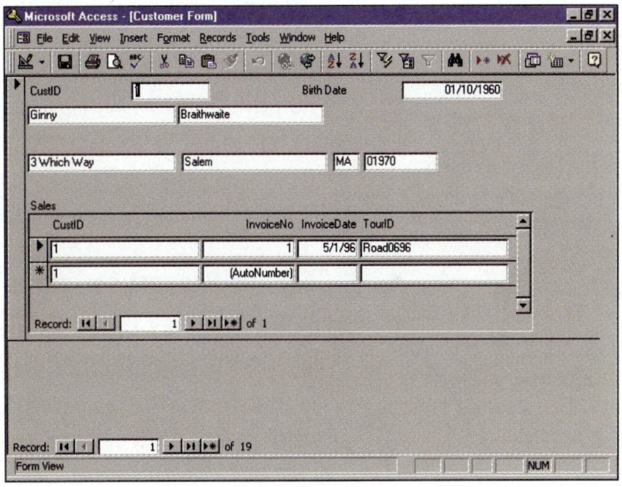

TABLE G-2: Mouse pointer shapes used in Form Design View

pointer	used to
	Select controls
	Move multiple controls
	Move one control
	Resize a control horizontally
	Resize a control vertically
and	Resize a control diagonally (horizontally and vertically at the same time)
	Resize sections of a form

Access 97

Adding Labels and Formatting Controls

Even though unbound controls such as field labels and lines help identify and organize related information on a form, sometimes more descriptive labels are necessary. Formatting, enhancing the appearance of controls, can also improve a form's readability. The **Formatting** (Form/Report Design) toolbar provides the most popular formatting options for changing a label's border, font name, font size, or color. Formatting options that are not available on the toolbar must be changed through the control's property sheet. Michael decides to add a label to the Detail section of the form. See Table G-3 for more information on form sections. He will also change the label alignment so labels are positioned closer to the field text boxes they describe. His first step will be to add a label to identify the address information, then he'll realign the labels closer to their corresponding text boxes.

Steps

1. Click **Customer Form** on the Forms tab if necessary, click **Design**, click the **Label tool** in the Toolbox, click above the **address text fields at 1/8" on the ruler**, then type **Address Information:**

   Select both the CustID and Birth Date labels so that you can change the alignment property on both labels at the same time.

2. Click the **CustID label**, press and hold **[Shift]**, click the **Birth Date label**, then release **[Shift]**

   You want to right-align these labels. Since the Formatting toolbar doesn't contain a right-alignment button, make the change on the property sheet for these controls.

3. Click the **Properties button** on the Form Design toolbar, click the **Format tab**, scroll to display the **Text Align property**, click the **Text Align text box**, click the **Text Align list arrow**, then click **Right**

   The title bar of the property sheet displays the selected control's name. In this case, multiple controls are selected. The Customer Form should look like Figure G-6. Close the property sheet and view this form.

4. Click the **Properties button** on the Formatting toolbar, then click the **Form View button** on the Formatting toolbar

   The CustID and Birth Date labels are right aligned on the form.

5. Click the **Save button** on the Form View toolbar

   The final Customer Form should look like Figure G-7.

QuickTip

Click the Properties button to toggle the form property sheet on or off.

Trouble?

If you move, resize, or change a property of the wrong control, click the Undo button to undo your last action.

TABLE G-3: Form sections

section	description
Detail	Appears once for every individual record
Form Header	Appears at the top of the form and often contains a label with the form's title
Form Footer	Appears at the bottom of the form and often contains a label with instructions on how to use the form
Page Header	Appears at the top of a printed form with information such as page numbers or dates. The Page Header and Page Footer sections can be added to the form by clicking View on the menu bar, then clicking Page Header/Footer
Page Footer	Appears at the bottom of a printed form with information such as page numbers or dates

FIGURE G-6: Customer Form with label and alignment changes

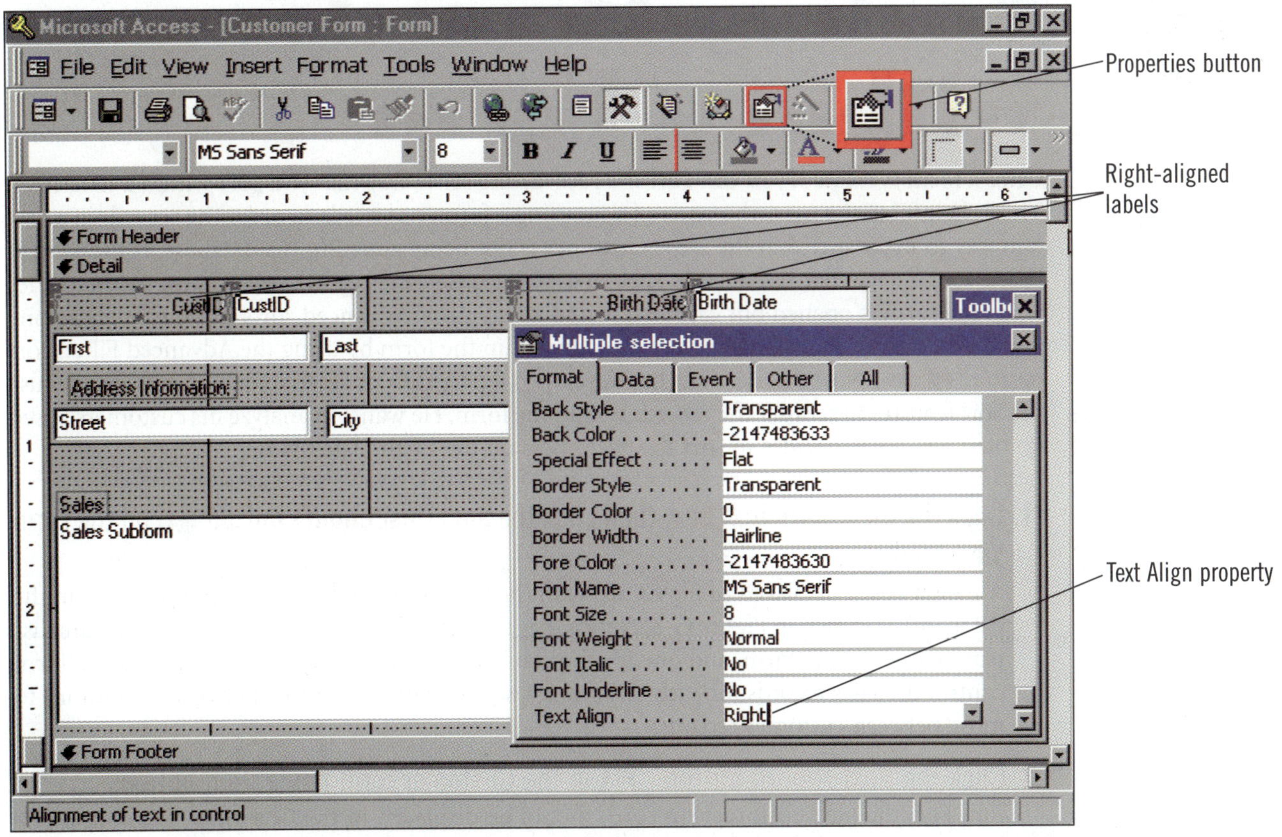

FIGURE G-7: Customer Form

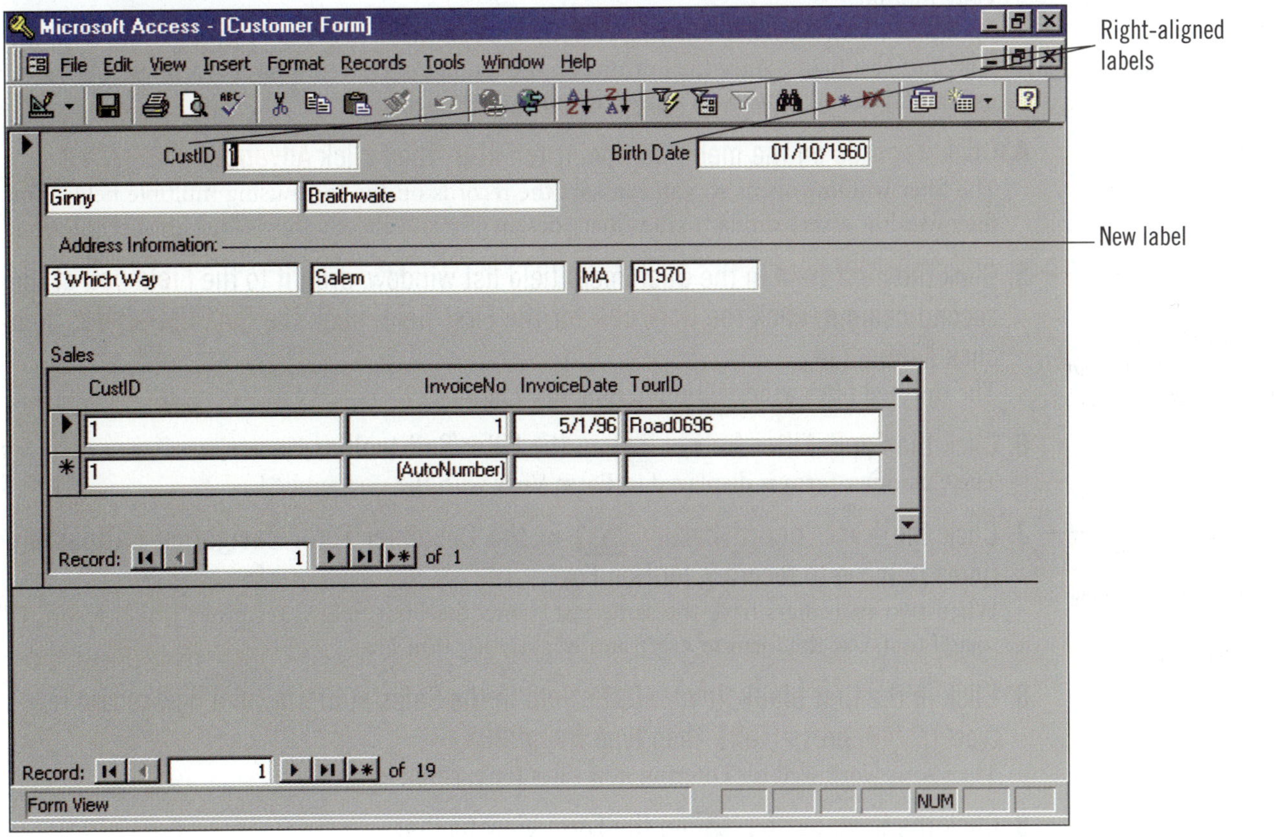

Access 97

Access 97

Sorting Records within a Form

Once a form is created, you can **sort** the records the same way that you sort within a datasheet. This is helpful to the user who entered data using a form, but needs to order the records in a certain way to make sure that the same customer is not being added to the database. If the form is based on a query that has already specified a sort order, the records will appear in that order when the form is opened but can be resorted at any time. Advanced sorts using more than one field in the sort order can be applied directly within the form by using the Advanced Filter/Sort option. Now that Michael has developed the Customer Form to record sales, he will use the Sort features to reorder the records within the form. He wants to analyze his customers based on their age, so he decides to sort the customers on the Birth Date field.

Steps

1. Click the **Birth Date text box**, then click the **Sort Descending button** on the Form View toolbar
   Amanda Fox is displayed as the record with the highest birth date (she is the youngest in the database) as shown in Figure G-8. Notice that two sets of **record navigation buttons** are displayed, one for the form, and one for the subform. The navigation buttons for the subform control the sales records for each customer. Use the main form record navigation buttons to move between customer records.
2. Click the **Next record button** in the Customer form navigation buttons
   Ron Fox, the next customer's record, should be displayed in the Customer Form. Ron Fox has two sales records in the Sales subform. Sort the records by name.
3. Click the **Last text box (Fox)**, then click the **Sort Ascending button** on the Form View toolbar
   John Black is displayed as the first record. You can further sort the records using both the First and Last fields. Since the buttons on the toolbar only accommodate a single-field sort, use the Advanced Filter/Sort option to sort on two fields.
4. Click **Records** on the menu bar, point to **Filter**, then click **Advanced Filter/Sort**
   The filter window opens so you can sort the records on the form using multiple fields. The filter window is very similar to the Query design grid and already shows the Last sort criterion.
5. Click the **First field** in the Customers field list window, drag it to the **Field cell** of the second column, click the **Sort cell** for the First field, click the **Sort list arrow**, then click **Ascending**
   The finished filter window should look like Figure G-9.
6. Click the **Apply Filter button** on the Filter/Sort toolbar
   The Customer form is displayed in Form View with the sort applied.
7. Click the **Next record button** in the Customer Form navigation buttons six times to move to record 7 for Ron Fox
   When two customers have the same last name, the First field determines which record is sorted first. Use the form to enter another sale for Ron Fox.
8. Click in the first blank **InvoiceDate field** in the Sales subform (in a new record row), type **7/1/98**, press **[Tab]**, then type **Bung0998**
   The forms work well for entering new sales for existing customers.
9. Click the **Save button** on the Form View toolbar

QuickTip

Double-click a field in the field list to move it to the next available column in the grid.

QuickTip

Type a record number in the record indicator box and press [Enter] to quickly move to that record in the database.

FIGURE G-8: Form sorted descending by Birth Date

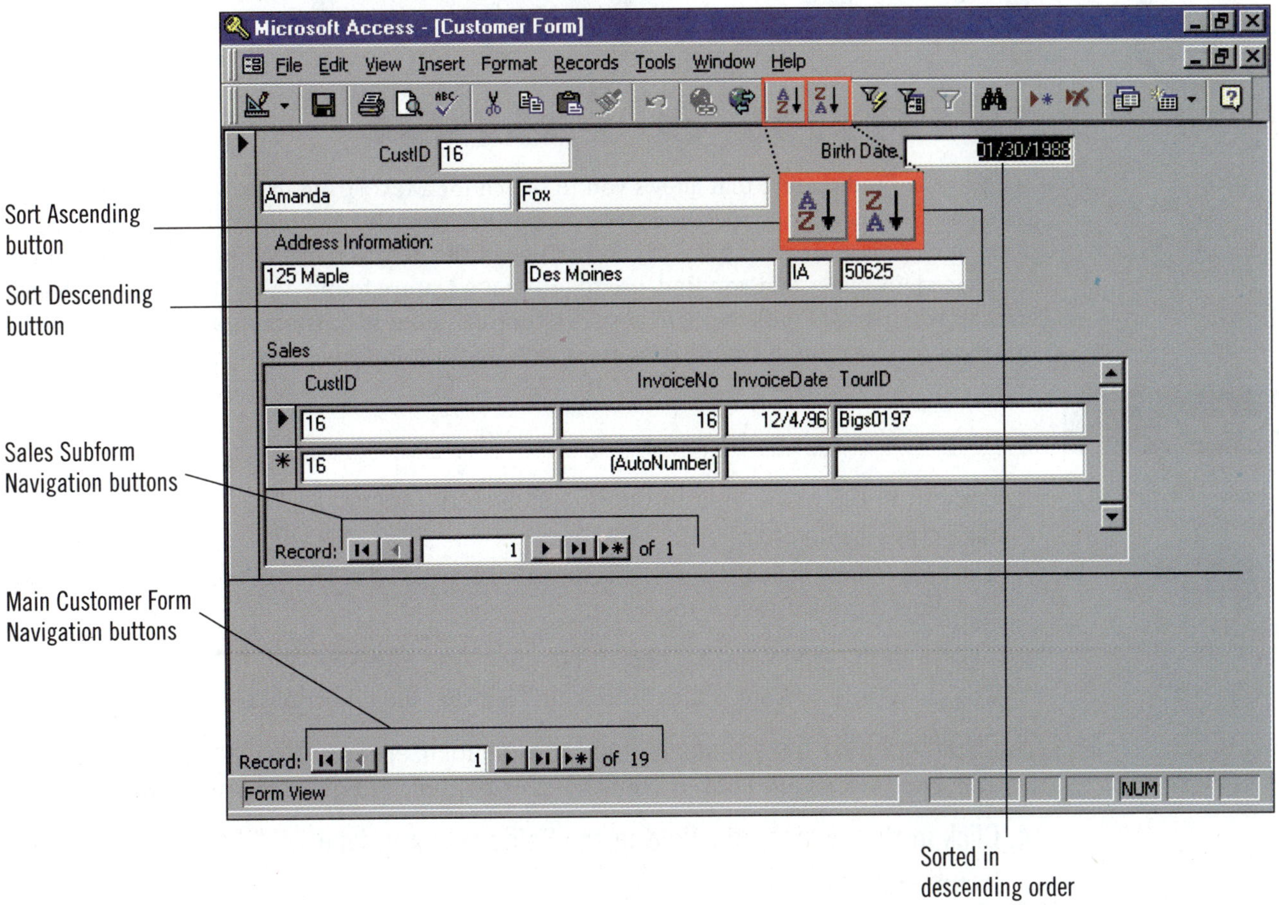

FIGURE G-9: Filter window

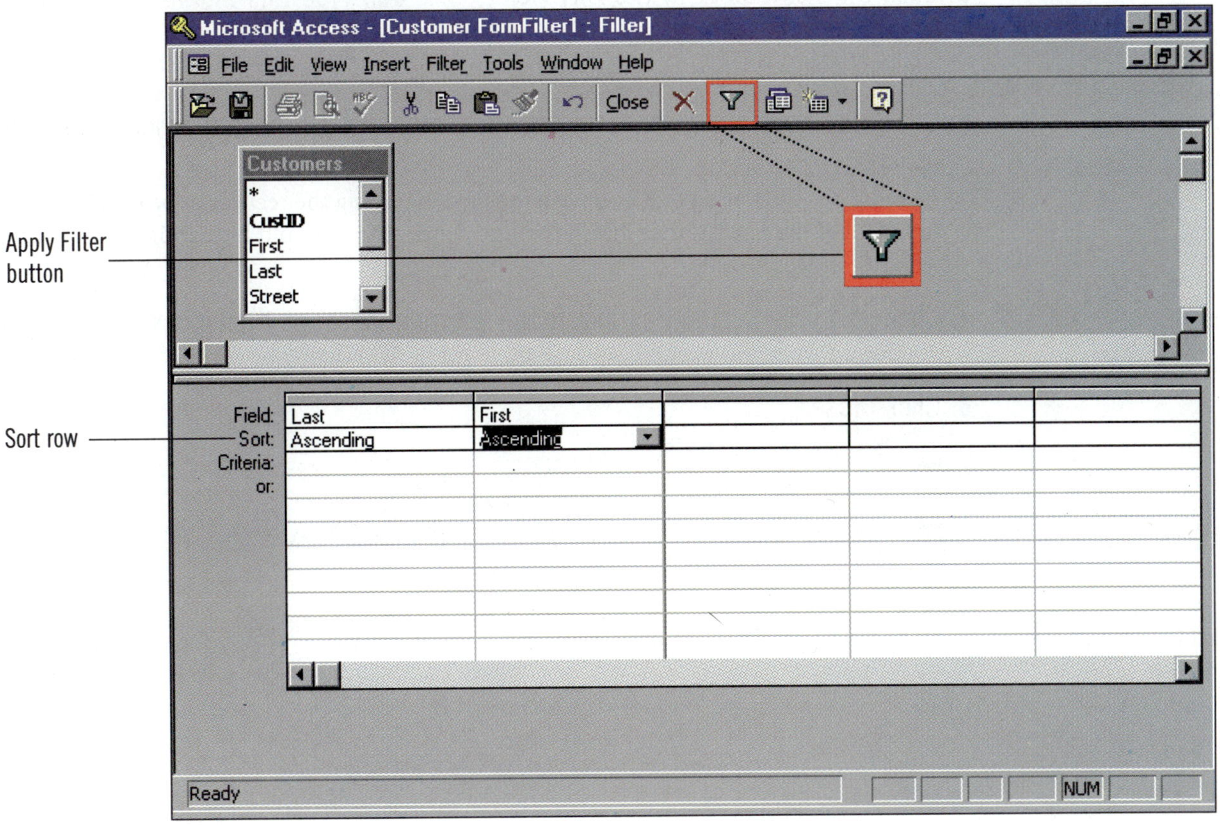

Access 97

Access 97

Finding Records within a Form

Access has a **Find** feature that allows you to search for a text string in any field. With the Find dialog box, you can locate specific records or find certain values within fields. You can navigate through records as Access finds each occurrence of the item you're looking for. If you want to replace certain values that you find, use the **Replace** feature found on the Edit menu. Michael will use the Find feature to answer questions about his customers and sales. Michael is making a presentation in Des Moines, Iowa, and wants to find all customers from that state.

Steps

1. Click **IA** in the **State field** in the Customer Form, then click the **Find button** on the Form View toolbar
   The Find in field dialog box opens as shown in Figure G-10. The options in the Find dialog box allow you to customize the search.
2. Type **IA** in the Find What text box, then click **Find First**
   The Amanda Fox record is the first one that matches the find criteria.
3. Click **Find Next** three times to find Fritz Friedrichsen's record, then click **Close**
   Fritz Friedrichsen just booked a tour, so record the sale to Fritz in the subform.
4. Click in the **InvoiceDate field** in the Sales subform, type **7/1/98**, press **[Tab]**, then type **Bung0998** in the TourID text box
   The sale is recorded as shown in Figure G-11. Next, find all customers who live in Des Moines.
5. Click the **Fontanelle** in the City field, click , type **Des Moines**, then click **Find First** in the Find dialog box
   Amanda Fox is the first customer in the database who lives in Des Moines.
6. Click **Find Next**, then view each found record until you have reached the end of the records
   A dialog box indicating that you have finished searching the records appears when you have found all of the records that match the find criteria. You should have found three customers who live in Des Moines.
7. Click **OK** in the Search item not found warning message dialog box
   You found what you needed, so close the Find in field dialog box.
8. Click **Close**

FIGURE G-10: Find dialog box

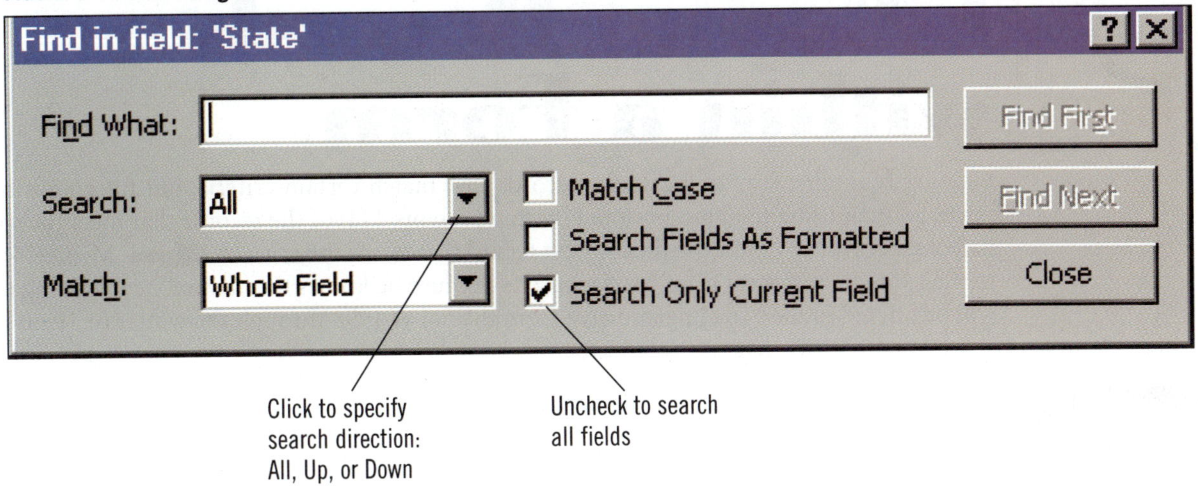

FIGURE G-11: Adding a sale using the Customer Form

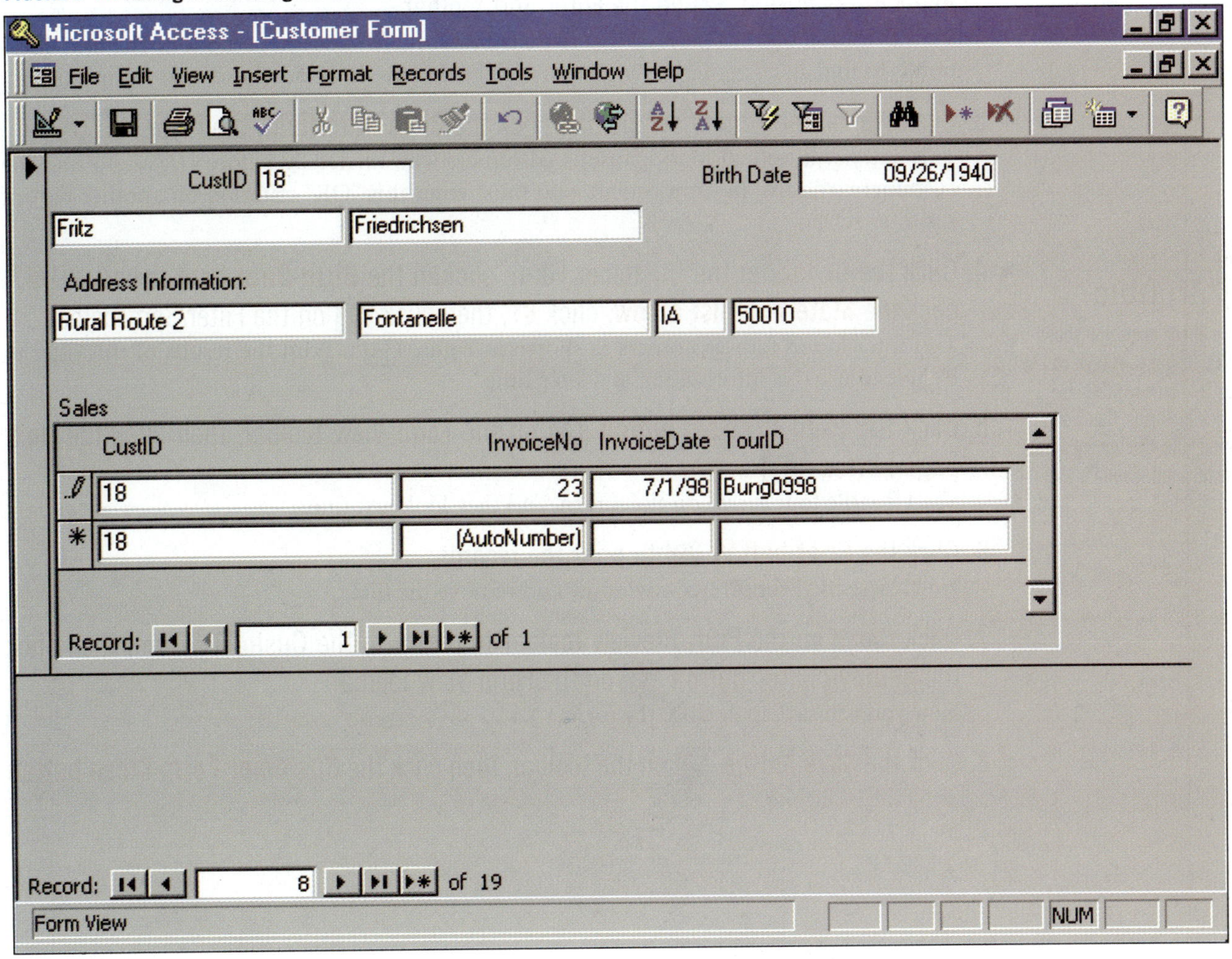

Access 97

Filtering Records within a Form

Filtering is another way to locate the records that match certain criteria, but filtering is more powerful than using the Find button. Filtering presents ALL of the records that meet the specified criteria instead of just the first or next record that meets the criteria. Michael wants to filter for all customers from Massachusetts because he knows that several new exciting tours will be offered in the New England area from the fall of 1998 through the winter of 1999.

Steps

QuickTip

Click the Filter by Selection button to apply a filter that finds the records based on the information in the current field.

Trouble?

If this filter does not show four customers, return to the Filter by Form window to see if a criterion has been entered into the wrong field. Be sure to check each Or tab as well.

1. Click the **Filter By Form button** on the Form View toolbar
   The Filter by Form window opens as shown in Figure G-12. Filter by Form allows you to filter the record using criteria in one or many fields. Filter for all the customers who live in Massachusetts.
2. Click the blank **State field**, click the **State field list arrow**, click **MA**, then click the **Apply Filter button** on the Filter/Sort toolbar
   The navigation buttons indicate that five customers match this filter criterion. The next question is to find all customers over 30 years of age that live in Massachusetts or Connecticut.
3. Click on the Form View toolbar, click the **Birth Date field**, then type **<1/1/67**
   This entry will find all Massachusetts customers who turned 30 before 1/1/97. To find the customers who live in Connecticut, you must enter this "OR" criterion on another part of the filter screen.
4. Click the **Or tab** for the Customer Form, click in the **Birth Date field**, type **<1/1/67**, click the **State field list arrow**, click **CT**, then click on the Filter/Sort toolbar
   This filter found four customers as shown in Figure G-13. Print the results of this filter to be able to use this information at a later time.
5. Click the **Print Preview button** on the Form View toolbar, then click the **Next page button**
   You view the four forms on the screen, and they look just fine.
6. Click the **Print button** to print the records
   Now, close the Print Preview window and remove the filter.
7. Click **Close** on the Print Preview toolbar to return to the Customer Form, then click the **Remove Filter button** on the Form View toolbar
   Now you can save then close the form.
8. Click the **Save button** on the toolbar, then click the **Customer Form Close button**

FIGURE G-12: Filter by Form

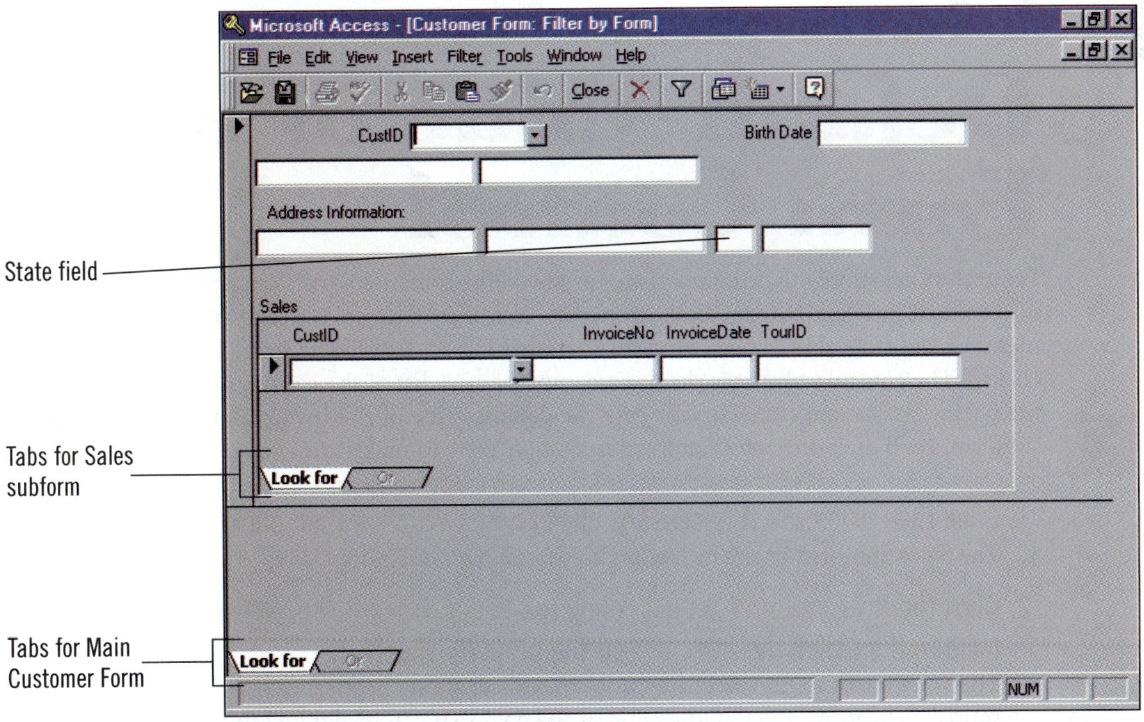

FIGURE G-13: Filtered Customer Form

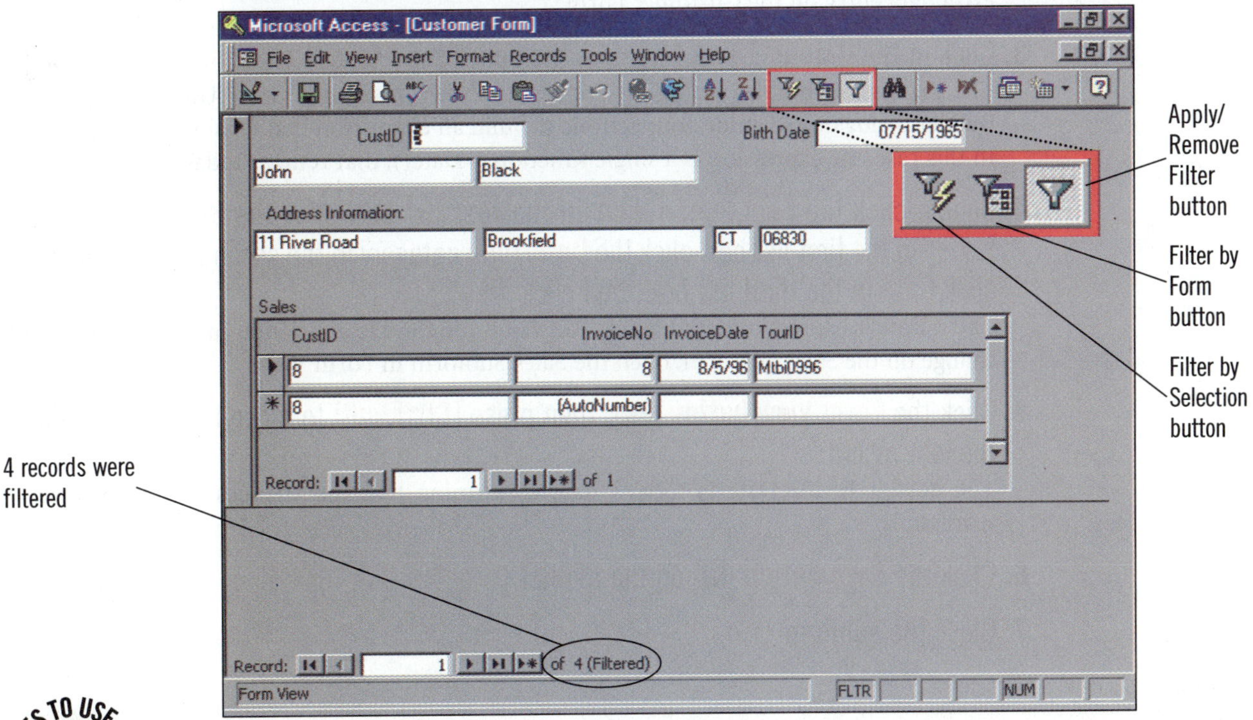

CLUES TO USE

Filtering with complex criteria expressions

When criteria are entered in more than one field of the Filter by Form window, both criteria must be true for the record to be displayed. These are called AND criteria. To enter OR criteria, in which only one or another set of criteria must be true for a record to be displayed, use the Or tab at the bottom of the Filter by Form window. You can use wildcard characters such as the asterisk * for multiple characters and the question mark ? for single characters with either AND or OR criteria. These criteria evaluation rules are exactly the same as those used to evaluate criteria in the Query design grid.

Access 97

Changing the Default Value of a Form Control

Properties are simply the characteristics of the controls on the Form. You change the properties of a control in Form Design View. Properties can be as basic as the control's color, text alignment, or default value, or as complex as branching to a different form when the control is clicked. The control's property sheet is a comprehensive list of the control's properties. Michael wants to make the current date the default value of the InvoiceDate field on the Sales subform. He'll open the Sales Subform in Design View to make this change.

Steps

1. Click the **Forms tab** if necessary, click **Sales Subform**, then click **Design**
   The Sales Subform opens in Design View as shown in Figure G-14.
2. Click the **InvoiceDate text box**, click the **Properties button** on the Form Design toolbar, then click the **Data tab** on the property sheet
   The Data tab of the InvoiceDate properties sheet shows properties that have to do with the source, validation, and default value of the data that can be entered in the InvoiceDate text box. Change the default value of this text box to display today's date. This will eliminate extra data entry on the Customer Form.
3. Click in the **Default Value text box**, then click the **Expression Builder button**
   The Expression Builder dialog box opens as shown in Figure G-15. Use the Expression Builder dialog box to guide your actions to build an expression that results in a single value. In this case, the expression is a single function, =Date(), that returns today's date.
4. Double-click the **Functions folder** in the first list box, click the **Built-In Functions folder** in the first list box, click the **Date/Time** category in the second list box, double-click **Date** in the third list box, then click **OK**
   The =Date() expression is added as the value for the Default Value property. To see the change on the Sales Subform, open the Sales Subform in Form View.
5. Click the **Form View button**, then press **[Ctrl][End]** to move to the last field of the last record
   The default InvoiceDate is today's date confirming that the changes to the form were successful.
6. Click the **Save button** on the toolbar
7. Close the subform

CLUES TO USE

Inherited properties

If you change a control's property setting on a form, the change doesn't affect the underlying query or table. Likewise, if you change the property setting for a field in a table or query after you've created a form that uses the field, the property setting for the control on the form isn't updated; you must do this manually. There are exceptions to the last rule, however. If you change the Default Value, Validation Rule, or Validation Text properties in a table's Design View, these changes will be enforced in any controls based on these fields later.

FIGURE G-14: Sales subform in Form Design View

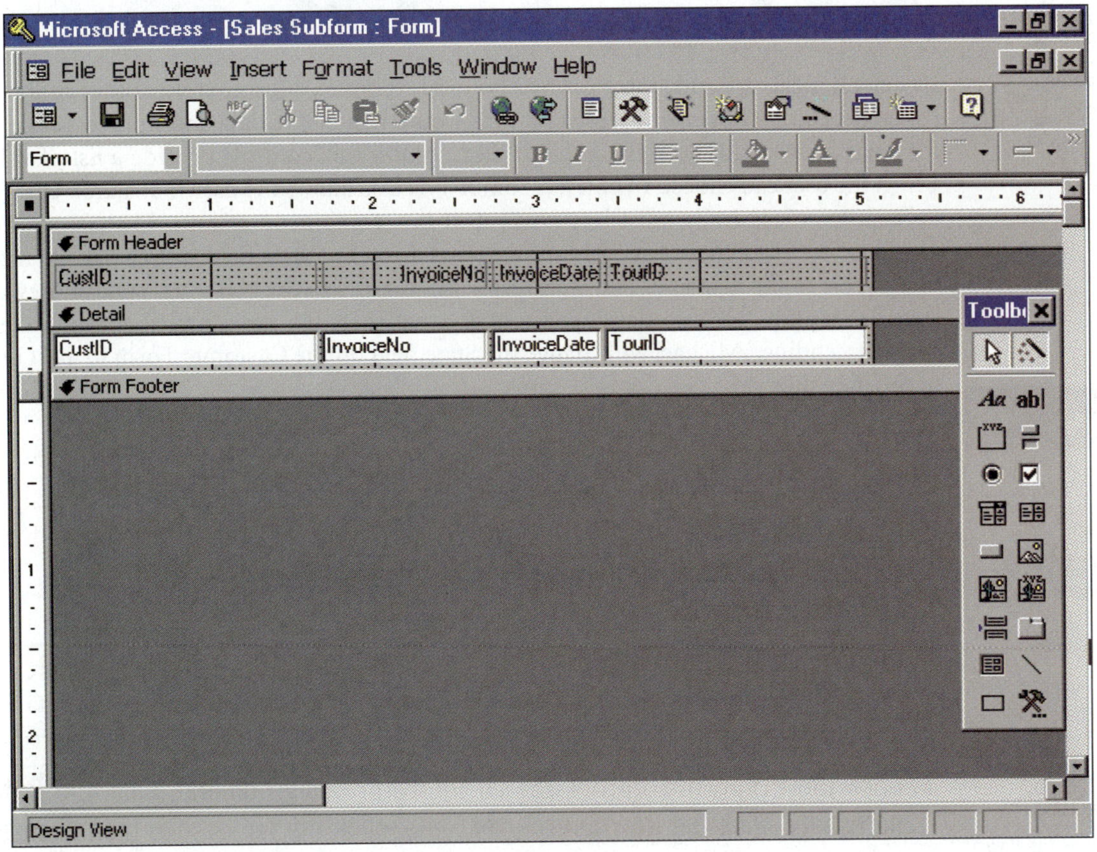

FIGURE G-15: Expression Builder dialog box

Expression text box

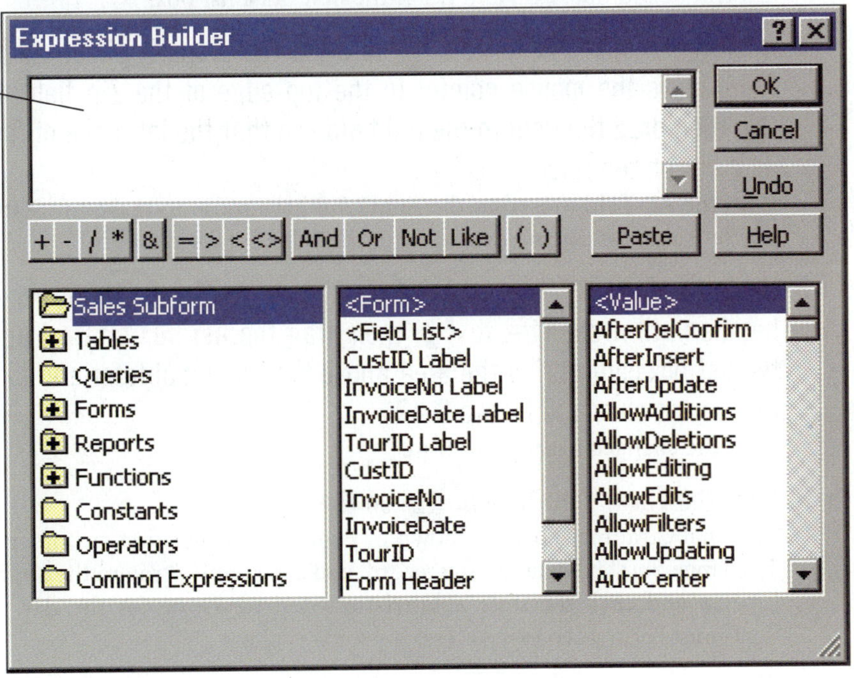

Access 97

Adding List Boxes

By default, fields are added to a form as bound text boxes, but sometimes other controls such as list boxes, combo boxes, or options buttons would handle the data entry process easier or faster for a particular field. Both the **list box** and **combo box** controls provide a list of values from which the user can choose an entry. A combo box also allows the user to make an entry from the keyboard, so it is really a list box plus a text box combined. Michael realizes that it would be easier to choose an appropriate entry from the State field from a list. He has added a States table to the database. The States table has two fields: the two-letter state abbreviation and state description. He also developed a query that sorts the states alphabetically called "States sorted ascending." Michael will change the State field on the Customer Form to a list box bound to the state query.

Steps

QuickTip

Double-click a control to access its property sheet.

Trouble?

Be sure to change the Row Source property instead of the Control Source property. The Control Source property controls what underlying field in a table or query is updated. The Row Source property controls what items are displayed in the list box.

Trouble?

If the text box is not wide enough, click the Design View button and resize the control.

1. Click the **Customer Form** on the Forms tab in the Database window, click **Design**, if necessary click the **Maximize button**, then if necessary click the **Properties button** on the Form Design toolbar to close the property sheet
   Change the State field from a text box to a list box.
2. Right-click the **State field text box**, point to **Change To**, then click **List Box**
   When you create a list box that looks up values, you need to decide where the data for the list will come from. Change the Row Source property for the list box to handle this requirement.
3. Click the **Properties button** on the Form Design toolbar, click the **Data tab** if necessary, click the **Row Source text box**, click the **list arrow**, then choose **States sorted ascending** as shown in Figure G-16
   List boxes need more width to display the information than text boxes. Therefore move the Zip text box to the right, and resize the new State list box.
4. Click the **Properties button** to close the property sheet, click the **Zip text box field**, move the mouse pointer to the top edge of the Zip field until it changes to, then drag the field to the right side so that the left edge of the field rests at the **4" mark** on the ruler
   With the Zip field moved to the right, you have room to make the State list box wider and shorter so that it doesn't overlap with the Sales Subform control.
5. Click the **State list box**, position the mouse pointer on the lower-right corner resize handle until it changes to ↘, then drag the **list box control** up and right so that the list box control fills the area above the Sales Subform and to the left of the Zip text box as shown in Figure G-17
   View the changed Customer Form.
6. Click the **Form View button** on the toolbar
   The final Customer Form is shown in Figure G-18. The first customer lives in Salem, MA. To change the state data for any record, you can simply scroll to the appropriate entry in the list box and click the state abbreviation desired. Done for the day, save then close the Customer Form, then exit Access.
7. Click the **Save button**, click the Customer Form **Close button**, then click the **Access Close button**

FIGURE G-16: Property sheet for State list box

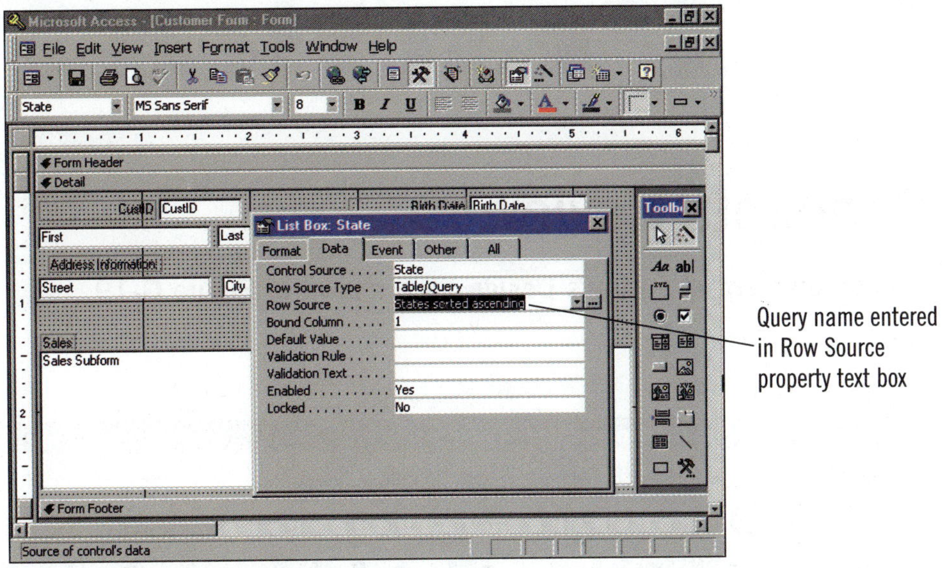

FIGURE G-17: Resized State list box

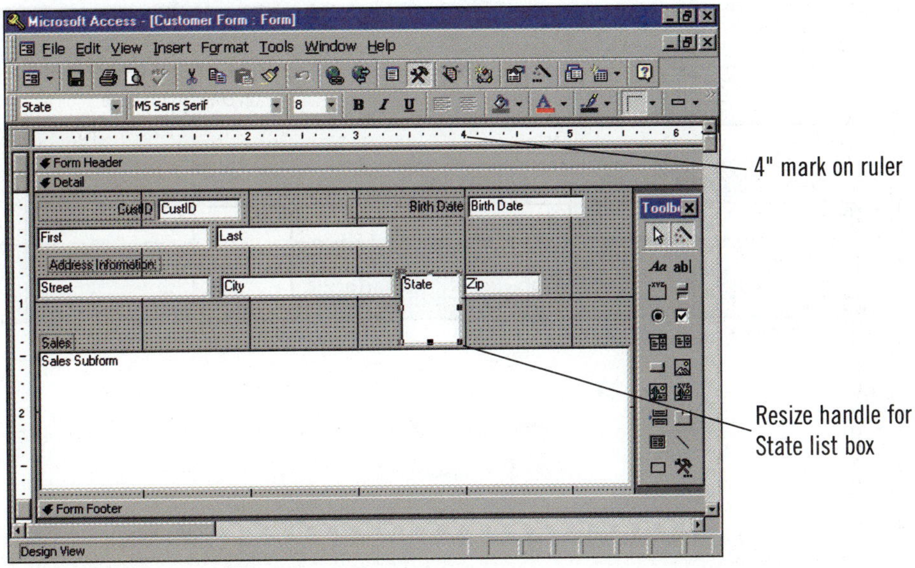

FIGURE G-18: Customer Form with State list box

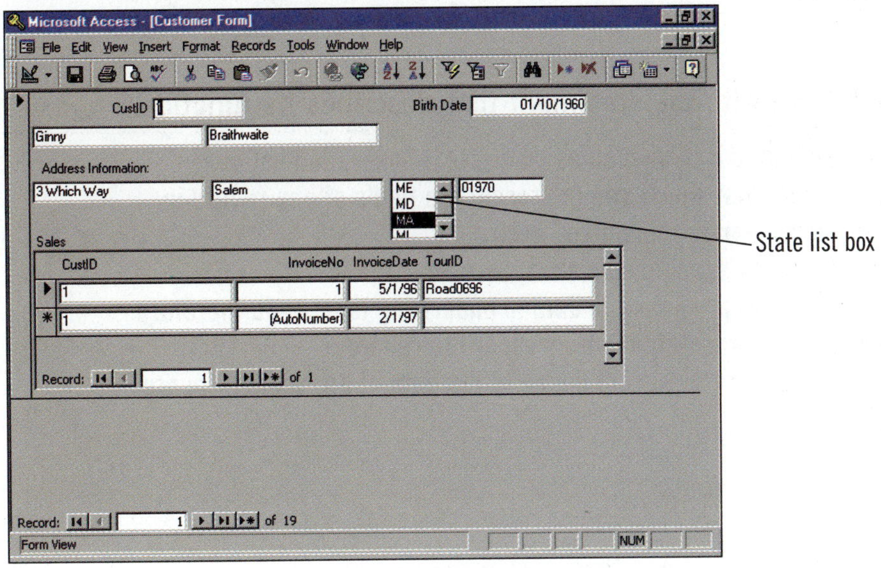

Practice

► Concepts Review

Identify each element of a form's Design View shown in Figure G-19.

FIGURE G-19

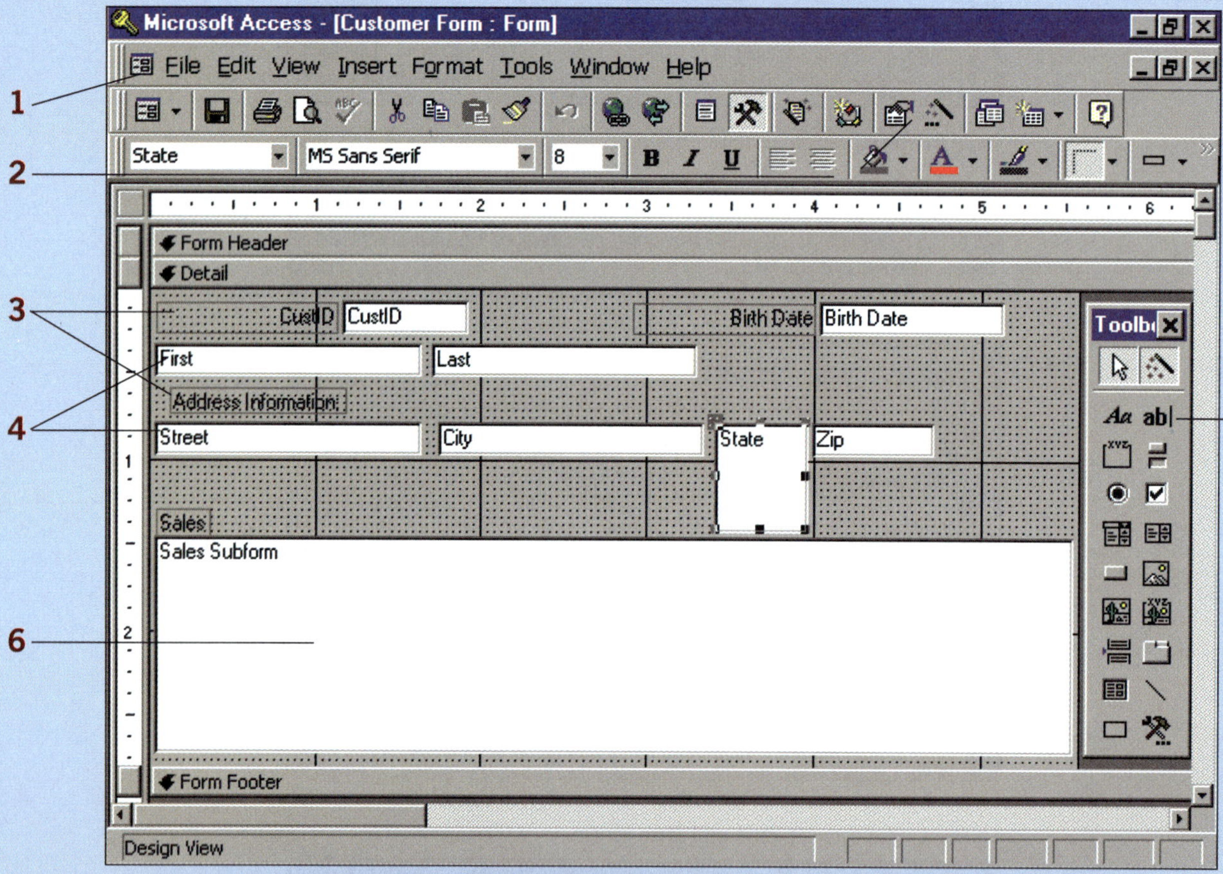

Match each term with the statement that describes its function.

7. Elements you add to a form such as labels, text boxes, and list boxes
8. An Access object that allows you to present the fields of one record in almost any screen arrangement you desire
9. The ability to locate specific subsets of records
10. Form elements that are linked to data in underlying tables and therefore change when the form switches from record to record
11. An element on a form that is not linked to the data of any table or query

- a. Bound control
- b. Controls
- c. Filter
- d. Form
- e. Unbound control

Select the best answer from the list of choices.

12. To select records based on criteria, you should use which feature?
- a. Filter
- b. Find
- c. Form Wizard
- d. Sort

13. Which of the following is the most common type of bound control?
- a. Option group
- b. List box
- c. Text box
- d. Label

14. Which of the following is the most common type of unbound control?
- a. Check box
- b. Field label
- c. List box
- d. Combo box

15. To quickly access a new blank record to enter new data, use which buttons?
- a. Toolbox
- b. Form Design View toolbar
- c. Record Navigation
- d. Formatting toolbar

16. To view multiple linked records of one table simultaneously with a single record of another table in a form use a:
- a. Subform
- b. List box
- c. Design template
- d. Link control

Skills Review

1. Create a form from multiple tables.

a. Start Access and open the database Addresses-G.

b. Create a new form using the Form Wizard.

c. Add all the fields from both the Names and the Zips tables. By choosing all of the fields from both tables, you'll be adding the linking Zip field from both tables. When the Form Wizard is complete, you'll notice the Zip field from the Zips table in the main form and the Zip field in the Names table in the subform.

d. View the data with the Form with subform option by Zips.

e. Choose a Tabular layout and a Colorful 1 style.

f. Title the Form "Names within Zips" and the subform "Names Subform".

g. View the form, then close the form.

2. Move and resize controls.

a. Open the Names Subform in Design View.

b. In the Detail section, select the first four field text boxes: First, Last, Street, and Zip and narrow them to about half of their current width. Repeat this process in the Form Header section for the first four labels: First, Last, Street, and Zip.

c. In the Detail section, individually move the Last, Street, Zip, and Birthday text boxes left. All of the five text box controls in the Detail section should fit between the 0" and 5" marks on the ruler. Repeat this process in the Form Header section for the labels.

d. Save and close the Names Subform.

e. Open the Names within Zips form to view the changes to the Names Subform within the main form. You should be able to see all five fields of the subform clearly.

3. Add labels and formatting controls.

a. Open the Names within Zips form in Design View.

b. Add a label in the upper-right corner of the form with the text, "This form is used to enter new zip codes and contact information."

c. Select all of the labels (Zip, City, and State) on the form, and right align the text within the control by changing the Text Align property to Right in the property sheet.

d. Close the property sheet.

e. View the form.

4. Sort records within a form.

a. Open the Names within Zips form in Form View.

b. Sort the records in ascending order by City. Print the first record using the Selected Records option on the Print dialog box. Click File on the menu bar, click Print to open the Print dialog box, click Selected Records, then click OK.

c. Sort the records in ascending order by State. Print the first record.

d. Using the Advanced Filter/Sort option from the Filter option of the Records menu, further refine the sort to first sort ascending by State and then ascending by Zip. Print the first two records.

5. **Find records within a form.**
   - a. Click the State text box then click the Find button on the toolbar.
   - b. Enter MO in the Find What text box, then click Find First to find the first record with the State equal to MO.
   - c. Print the record.
   - d. Close the Find dialog box.

6. **Filter records within a form.**
   - a. Use the Filter by Form button to filter for records where the Zip equals 50837. Apply the filter.
   - b. Print the record.
   - c. Use the Filter by Form button to filter for all contacts where the birth dates are before 1/1/55 (less than 1/1/55).
   - d. Print the first record.

7. **Change the default value of a form control.**
   - a. Open the Names within Zips form in Design View.
   - b. Open the property sheet for the State text box and change the Default Value property to IA.
   - c. Open the Names within Zips form in Form View, click the New Record button to move to a blank record at the end of the datasheet, enter 50846 in the Zip text box, then enter Fontanelle in the City text box.
   - d. Print the record. It should show the default IA entry in the State field even though you didn't directly enter this data on the form.

8. **Add list boxes.**
   - a. Open the Names within Zips form in Design View.
   - b. Right-click the State text box, then click Change to change the State text box to a list box.
   - c. Change the Row Source property of the State list box to the States table. (The States table was added to the Addresses-G database for this exercise.)
   - d. Widen and shorten the State list box so that you can clearly see the entries in Form View and so that the list box doesn't overlap the Names subform.
   - e. Save the changes to the form.
   - f. Print the first record.
   - g. Close the database and exit Access.

► Independent Challenges

1. As the president of a civic organization, you have developed a database that tracks donations of recyclable material called Cleanup-G. Now that several deposits have been made and recorded, you wish to develop a form to record the deposits.

To complete this independent challenge:

1. Start Access and open the database Cleanup-G.
2. Using the Form Wizard, create a form/subform based on the Deposits By Club query.
3. Use all four fields in the form, and view the form by Clubs.
4. Use a datasheet layout, and a Colorful2 style.
5. Name the form "Deposits By Clubs Form" and the subform "Deposits Subform".
6. Filter the form so that only those deposits of 50 pounds or greater are displayed.
7. Sort the resulting records in descending order on club name and print the first record.
8. Close the database and exit Access.

2. Now that you've developed a relational database that documents the books you've read called Readings-G, you'd like to develop a form to quickly enter new records.

To complete this independent challenge:

1. Start Access and open the database Readings-G.
2. Using the Form Wizard, create a form/subform using all the fields of both the Books and Authors tables.
3. View the data by Authors.
4. Use a datasheet layout, and an Evergreen style.
5. Name the form "Books within Authors" and the subform "Books Subform".
6. Open the Books Subform in Design View, then narrow the Category and Author Number text boxes in the Detail section and the Category and Author Number labels in the Form Header section to about half of their current size.
7. Move the text boxes in the Detail section and the labels in the Form Header section so that they all fit within the first five inches of the form.
8. Save and close the subform.
9. Return to the Books within Authors form and filter the form so that only Non-Fiction books are displayed.
10. Print the first record.
11. Close and save the form.
12. Close the database and exit Access.

3. You have recently helped the medical director of a large internal medical clinic put together and update a database called Doctors-G that tracks extra-curricular activities. You wish to develop a form to use as a data entry mechanism for the database.

To complete this independent challenge:

1. Start Access and open the database Doctors-G.
2. Using the Form Wizard, create a form/subform using all the fields from the Physicians and Activities tables, and only the Program Name field from the Programs table.
3. View the data by Physicians.
4. Use a datasheet layout, and a Stones style.
5. Name the form "Activities by Physician" and the subform "Activities Subform".
6. Open the Activities Subform in Design View, then delete the Physician Number and Program Number text boxes in the Detail section. Also, delete the Physician Number and Program Number labels in the Form Header section.
7. Move the Name label and Name text box next to the Hours label and text box so that all of the remaining controls in the Activities Subform fit within the first three inches of the form.
8. Save and close the subform.
9. Return to the Activities by Physician form and sort it in ascending order by First Name within Last Name.
10. Print the first record.
11. Close and save the form, then close the database and exit Access.

WEB WORK

4. Your dance club is making a trip to the famous Alberto's Nightclub, and has asked you to develop a small Access database to track the special events that Alberto's Nightclub offers. You've called the database Alberto-G. Now you'll go to the Alberto's Nightclub web site to find out what events are offered for this week and will add the information into the database using a form you've already developed. Then you will sort, filter, and query the information for various requests from dance club members.

To complete this independent challenge:

1. Log on to the Internet and use your browser to go to http://www.course.com. From there, click Student Online Companions, click the link for this text, then click the Access link for Unit G.
2. Use the Alberto's Nightclub site to find out what events are being offered for the week, and print the web page.
3. Start Access, then open the Alberto-G database.
4. Enter the week's event information into the Days of the Week form. The Days of the Week form is a form that contains a subform of events linked to the main form by the day of the week. The first event for Monday has already been entered. Leave this event in the database as an example of how to enter the event information and simply add the rest of the current week's events that you found on the web site.
5. Print the Monday record from the Days of the Week form.
6. Sort the records alphabetically on the Theme field and print the first record.
7. Filter the records so that only the Salsa themes are showing. Print the Salsa records.
8. Find the records who have a teacher named "DJ Polo." Print the DJ Polo records.
9. Create a query that sorts the Theme Name field in the Themes table in an ascending order and call it "Sorted Themes".
10. Delete the Theme text box in the Days of the Week form. Add the Theme field back to the form as a list box that uses the Sorted Themes query as the source of the information.
11. Resize the Theme list box so that it doesn't overlap with the Events Subform.
12. Close and save the form.
13. Close the database and exit Access.

▶ Visual Workshop

Open the VW-G database and create a new form/subform as shown in Figure G-20. Use all of the fields in both the Alumni and Donations tables. Notice that the labels in the main form have been right aligned.

FIGURE G-20

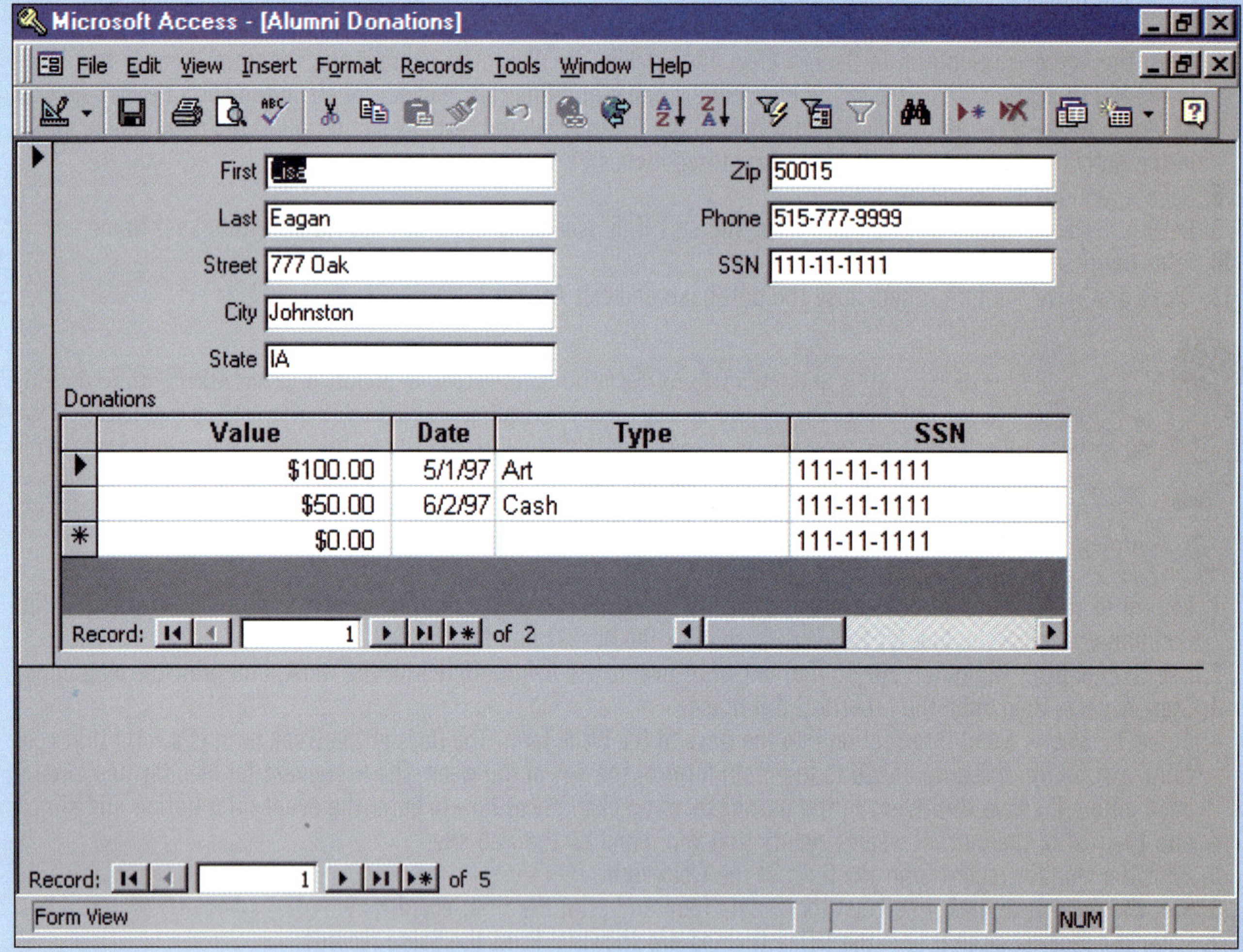

Creating Complex Reports

Objectives

- Create a report from a query
- Use report sections
- Use group headers
- Add calculations to group footers
- Modify control alignment
- Add graphics to reports
- Use color
- Add special effects

Although you can print data in forms and datasheets, **reports** give you more control over how data is displayed and greater flexibility in presenting summary information such as subtotals on groups of records. Reports are often used to distribute information in formal presentations or meetings. Since a report definition (the report object) can be saved, it can be developed once but used many times to produce a paper report. Printed reports always reflect the most up-to-date data in a consistent format each time they are printed. As with form designs, report designs allow you to add bound controls such as text boxes and unbound controls such as lines, graphics, or labels. Michael's datasheet and form printouts have been very valuable; however, he wants to create more professional documents that include subtotals on groups of records to share with potential investors. In addition, he wants the reports to contain clip art images, various colors, and advanced formatting enhancements.

Access 97

Creating a Report from a Query

The **Report Wizard** provides an interactive way to select fields from multiple tables or queries for a report. It also asks questions regarding how you want the records of the report to be grouped and formatted. **Grouping** provides a way to sort records so that summary statistics can be applied to a group of records that meet certain criteria. Grouping is not allowed within a form object. Another way to differentiate between a form and report object is to think about the primary purpose of the object. Forms are used for effective data entry. Reports provide effective printed output. A potential investor has asked for a report showing sales and profit information for each tour. Michael will use the Report Wizard to create the report.

Steps

1. Start Access and open the **Nomad-H** database, click the **Reports tab** in the Nomad-H : Database window, then click **New**
   The options in the New Report dialog box are very similar to those used to develop a form. Design View allows you to manually add controls to the report. AutoReport creates reports based on the chosen object with predefined settings.
2. Click **Report Wizard** in the New Report dialog box, then click **OK**
3. Click the **Tables/Queries: list arrow**, then click **Query: Profits**
   The Profits query has the four fields needed for this report as shown in Figure H-1.
4. Click the **Select all fields button** [>>], then click [Next >]
   The next wizard dialog box determines how the records are displayed.
5. Click **by Tours**, then click [Next >]
   Since the records are already grouped by individual tour, you don't need to establish further grouping levels.
6. Click [Next >]
   The next wizard dialog box determines how the records within the detail section of the report are sorted. Choose to sort the invoices in ascending order.
7. Click the **first list arrow**, click **InvoiceNo**, then click [Next >]
   Finally, choose the layout, orientation, style, and title for the report.
8. Click the **Block Layout option button**, verify that the **Portrait Orientation option button** is selected, click [Next >], click the **Corporate** style, click [Next >], type **Profit by Tour Report** as the report title, click [Finish], then **Maximize** the report window
   Print Preview of the Profit by Tour Report is shown in Figure H-2. Print Preview won't allow you to make any changes to the report, but does allow you to see exactly how your report will print. Refer to Table H-1 for more information on the buttons on the Print Preview toolbar.

QuickTip

If you can't see the entire report, scroll to see all the records and fields. Click on the report to reduce the printout to show an entire printed page on the screen. To magnify a portion of the report on the screen, click on the part of the report you wish to magnify.

FIGURE H-1: Report Wizard

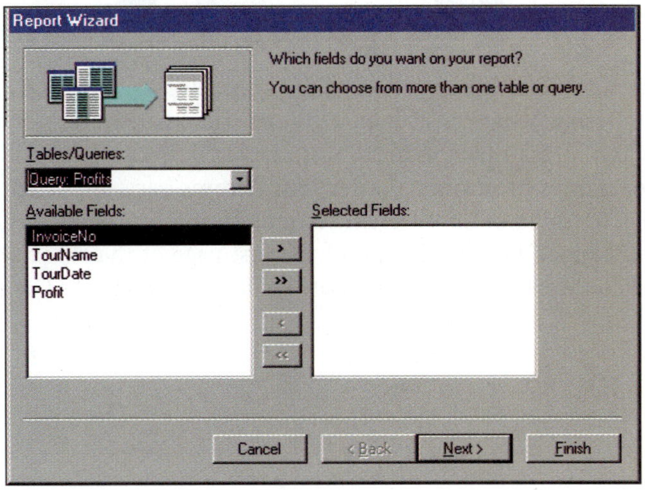

FIGURE H-2: Print Preview

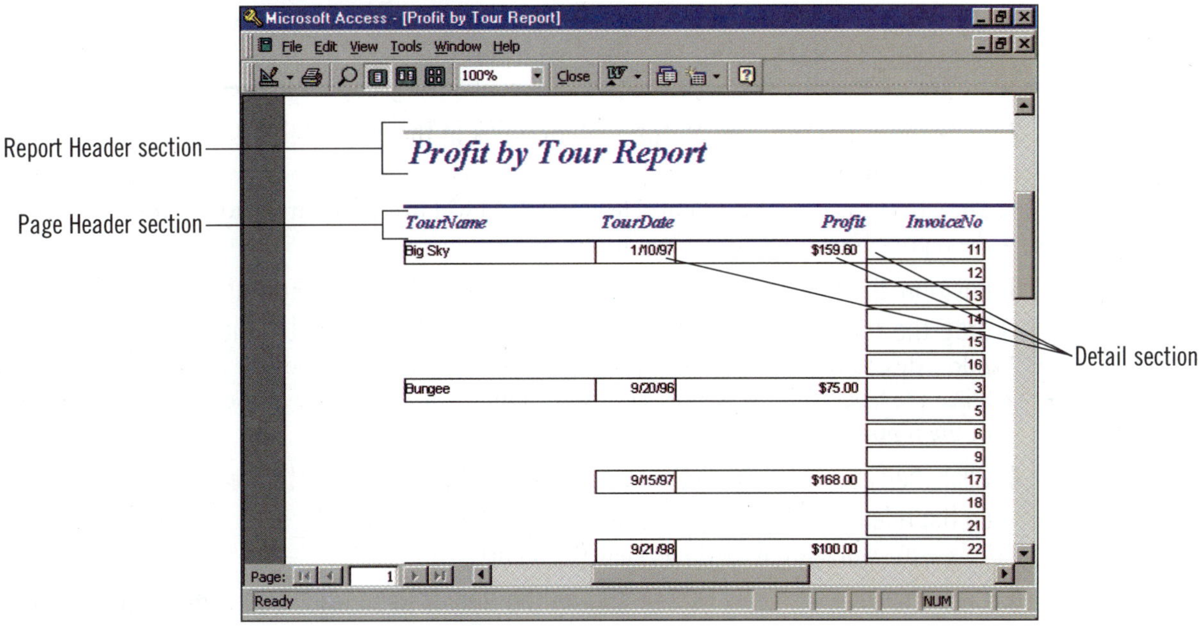

TABLE H-1: Buttons on the Print Preview toolbar

name	button	description
Print		Send a copy of the report to the default printer
Zoom		Toggles the print preview screen between 100% zoom and fit one page zoom
One page		Adjusts the zoom (magnification) level to fit one page of the report on the screen
Two pages		Adjusts the zoom level to fit two pages of the report on the screen
Multiple Pages		Displays multiple full pages in a matrix (2 rows by 3 columns, for example)
Zoom control	Fit	Adjusts the zoom level by clicking the list arrow and choosing the desired percentage
Close window	Close	Closes the print preview screen and displays the report's Design View
OfficeLinks		Sends the report to Word or Excel by clicking the list arrow and clicking Word or Excel
Database Window		Displays the database window which lists all objects in the database
New Object		Creates a new database object
Office Assistant		Provides Help topics or tips to help you complete a task

Access 97

Using Report Sections

Just as Form Design View is used to modify forms, Report Design View is used to modify reports. Report Design View consists of **sections** (designated areas of the report design) in which controls and formatting specifications are placed. Because reports allow more sophisticated analysis of groups of records, the sections become very important design elements. See Table H-2 for a description of the different sections of a report. Michael wants to add the company name, "Nomad Ltd," to the top of the first page of the report. He'll switch to Report Design View to add the label to the appropriate section of the report's Design View.

Steps

1. Click the **Design View button** on the Print Preview toolbar to close the Print Preview window
   The Profit by Tour Report Design View is shown in Figure H-3. Each report consists of several sections that determine how the final report will print. Because the underlying records are grouped by TourName, this report also contains a group header section.
2. Click the **Label tool** on the Toolbox, click in the **Report Header section** at the 4" mark on the ruler, then type **Nomad Ltd**
   The label you add to the Report Header section will print only at the top of the first page of the report. Next, expand the Report Footer section.
3. Position the mouse pointer at the **bottom of the Report Footer section bar**, then drag the **resize pointer** as shown in Figure H-4 down 1/2 inch
   Add a descriptive label to the Report Footer section that identifies the author of the report. Since the label is in the Report Footer section, it will print once at the end of the last page of the report.
4. Click the **Label tool** on the Toolbox, click in the **Report Footer section** at the 1" mark on the ruler, then type **Report Created by Michael Belmont**
   To see the work you have done, view the report.
5. Click the **Print Preview button** on the Report Design toolbar, scroll to observe the new labels, then click the **One Page button** on the Print Preview toolbar
   The entire page of the report is now in the Print Preview window as shown in Figure H-5. Close the Print Preview window.
6. Click to return to Design View
7. Click the **Save button** on the toolbar to save the report

Trouble?

If the Toolbox isn't displayed, click the Toolbox button to display it.

TABLE H-2: Report sections

section	description
Report header	Appears only at the top of the first page of the report and usually contains the report name or company logo
Page header	Appears at the top of every page (but below the report header on the first page) and usually contains field labels
Group header	Appears at the beginning of a group of records ("Group" is replaced by the field name)
Detail	Appears once for every record in the underlying datasheet and usually contains bound field text boxes
Group footer	Appears at the end of each group of records ("Group" is replaced by the field name)
Page footer	Appears at the bottom of each page and usually contains the current date and page number
Report footer	Appears at the end of the last page of the report, before the page footer

FIGURE H-3: Report Design View

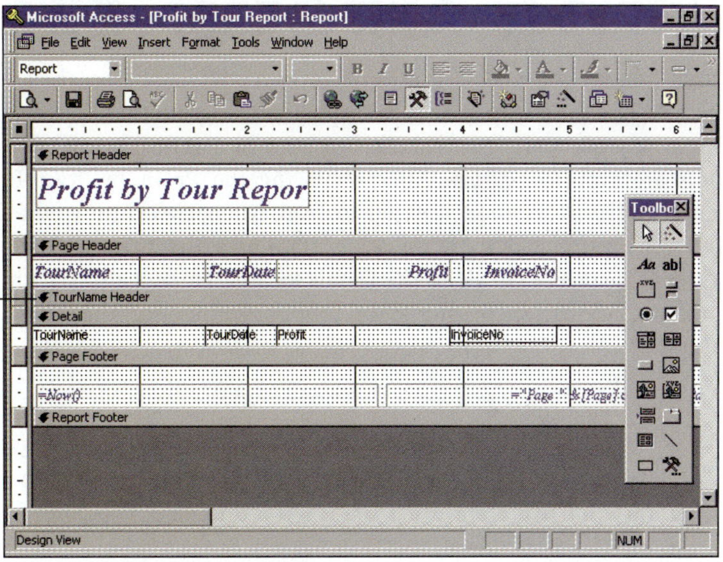

FIGURE H-4: Resizing report sections

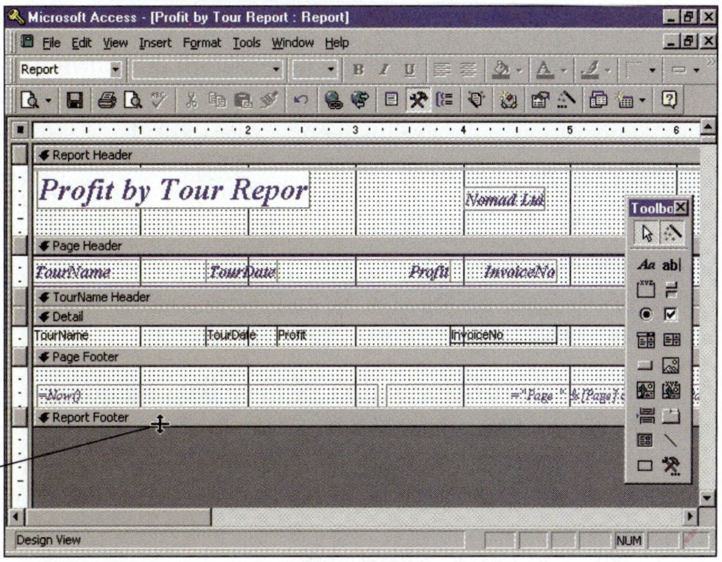

FIGURE H-5: Print Preview at One Page Magnification

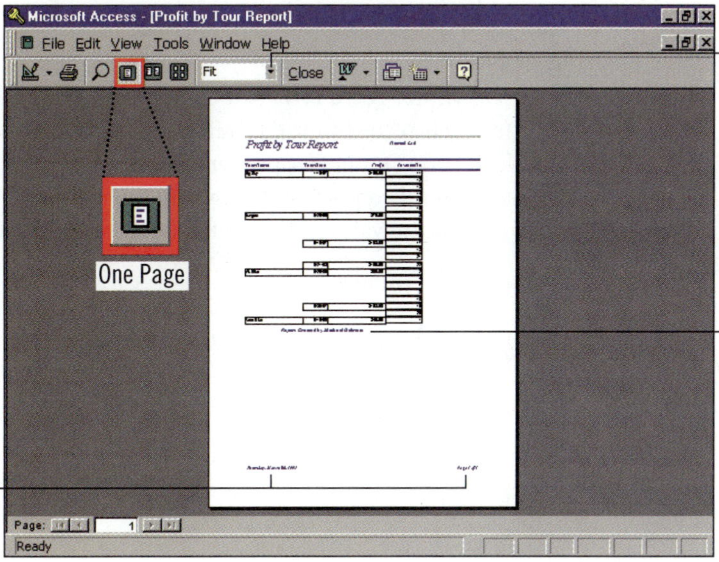

Access 97

Using Group Headers

A **group header** appears on its own line on a report just before the Detail section of a new group of records. Use the group header to display information that applies to the group of records. For example, you can include a field text box control that displays the name of the field by which the records are grouped. After reviewing the Profit by Tour Report, Michael decides to expand the report to make it easier to read. Michael will move the TourName text box to the TourName group header section rather than have this print on the same line as the TourDate, Profit, and InvoiceNo fields in the Detail section. He will also reformat the TourName text box control to make each new tour group more prominent on the report.

Steps

1. Position the mouse pointer on the **section divider bar** between the TourName Header section and the Detail section, then drag down to the top of the Page Footer section
   Now that the TourName Header section is opened, you can move the TourName control from the Detail section to the TourName Header section.
2. Click the **TourName text box** in the Detail section, position the mouse pointer at the top edge of the control when it changes to, then drag the **TourName text box** straight up into the TourName Header section as shown in Figure H-6
   With the TourName text box still selected, you will reformat the control to enhance the TourName section and make the report easier to read.
3. Click the **Line/Border Color list arrow** on the Formatting (Form/Report) toolbar, click **Transparent**, click the **Font Size list arrow** on the Formatting (Form/Report) toolbar, then click **10**
   In addition to removing the border and increasing the font size, change the text color and attributes.
4. Click the **Font/Fore Color button** on the Formatting (Form/Report) toolbar, click the **Bold button**, then click the **Italic button**
   View the report to verify that you have increased the visibility of the TourName field by formatting it as red, bold, italic text in the TourName header section.
5. Click the **Print Preview button**
   Adjust the view to see the report in the window at 100% view.
6. Click the **Zoom list arrow** on the Print Preview toolbar, click **100% View**, then scroll to observe the new labels
   The final report is shown in Figure H-7. Notice that the TourDate and Profit text box controls don't appear for each record in the Detail section even though the controls appear in the Detail section. The Hide Duplicates property has been set to "Yes" for the TourDate and Profit text box controls in this report, and therefore this field prints only once for the group of records that have duplicate values in these fields.
7. Click **Close** on the Print Preview toolbar
8. Click the **Save button** on the toolbar to save the report

FIGURE H-6: Moving report controls

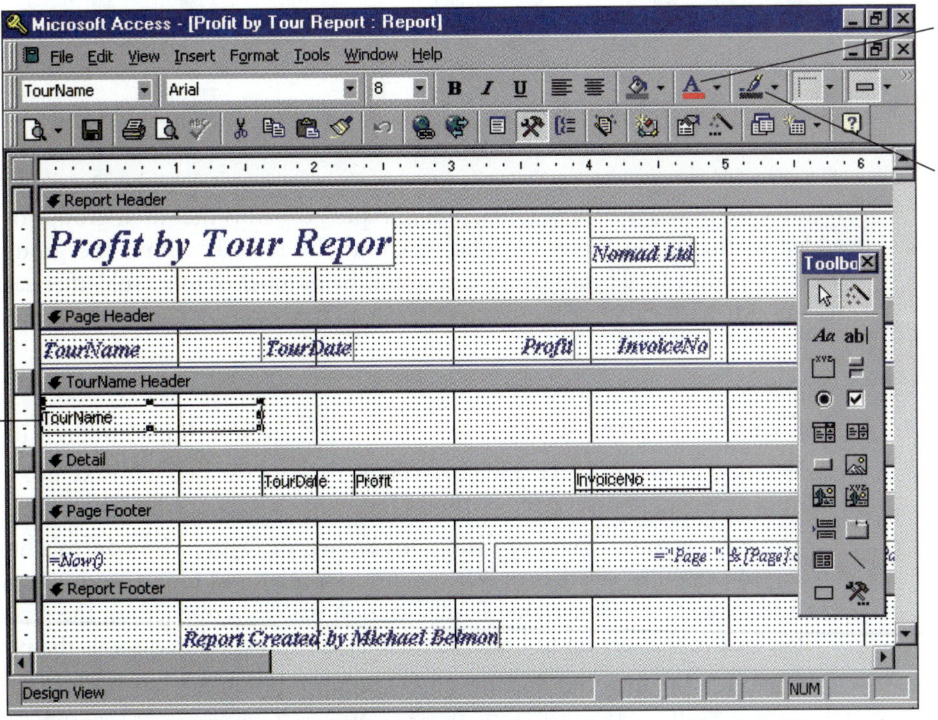

FIGURE H-7: Print Preview of a report with a group header section

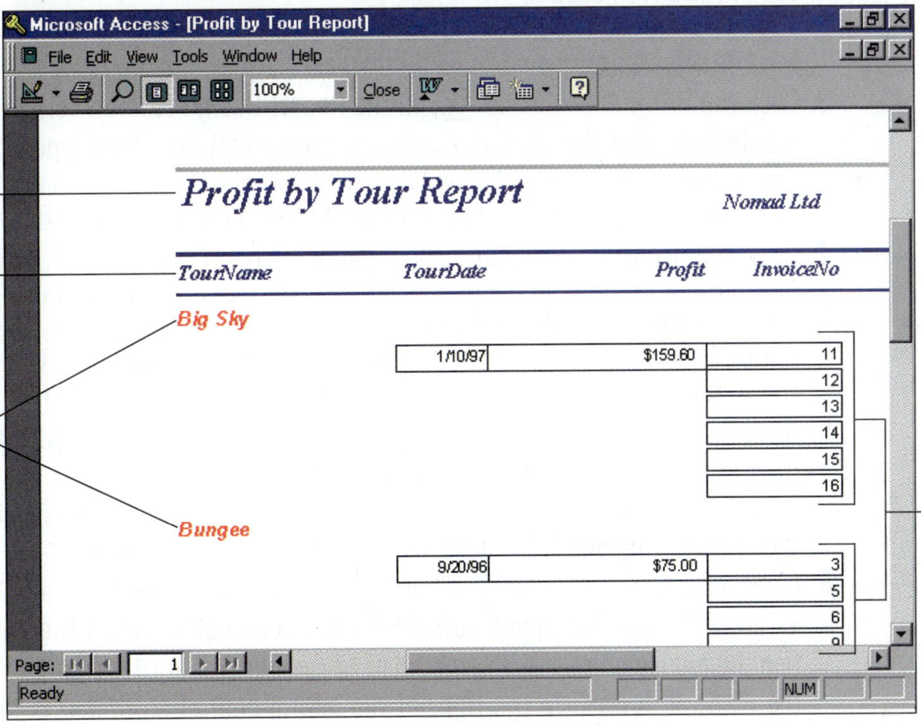

Access 97

CLUES TO USE

Hide Duplicates property

The Hide Duplicates property hides multiple occurrences of the same data for the fields in the Detail section of the report. To view or change the Hide Duplicates property, click the field in Report Design View, click the Properties button on the toolbar, then click the Format tab.

Access 97

Adding Calculations to Group Footers

A **group footer** appears on its own line on a report just below the Detail section of a group of records. **Calculated expressions**, bound report controls that total groups of records, are often added to the group footer to total or count the records within the group. Michael decides to add a total profit figure and count the number of tours sold after each unique group of records. Michael will place these two calculated expressions in the TourDate group footer.

Steps

1. Click the **Sorting and Grouping button** on the Report Design toolbar, verify that the **TourName field** is selected, click the **Group Footer text box**, click the **Group Footer property list arrow**, then click **Yes**
   The Sorting and Grouping dialog box shown in Figure H-8 controls how the records are sorted as well as whether or not the group header and footer sections appear for each sort field. Now that a TourName Footer section has been opened on the report, you will add a text box to the section to hold the calculated expression that totals the profits.
2. Click to close the Sorting and Grouping dialog box, click the **Text Box button** on the Toolbox, then click in the **TourName Footer** section just below the Profit text box in the Detail section
   With the unbound text box in place, access the Control Source property for the new text box and enter the appropriate expression that will calculate the total profit.
3. Click the **Properties button** on the Report Design toolbar, verify that the **Data tab** is selected, click the **Control Source property text box**, then type **=Sum([Profit])**
   The expression is shown in Figure H-9. Next, close the property sheet and delete the unnecessary label control that was automatically added to the left of the text box control.
4. Click to close the property sheet, click the new **label control**, then press **[Delete]**
   In addition to adding up the profits per tour, you can count the number of sales that contributed to that profit figure. Rather than type a new expression, copy the existing text box control in the TourName footer, paste it in the section, then edit the Control Source property so that it counts the InvoiceNo field rather than sums the Profit field.
5. Click the **=Sum([Profit]) text box**, right-click, click **Copy**, click at the 1" mark on the ruler in the TourName Footer, right-click, then click **Paste**
   Now that the text box with the calculated expression has been duplicated, edit the expression to count the number of invoices, and position the control under the InvoiceNo field.
6. Click and drag to select **=Sum([Profit])** inside the **new control**, then type **=Count([InvoiceNo])**, click outside the control, click to select the **new control**, position the mouse pointer at the **top edge of the control** until it changes to , then drag the **=Count control** to the right of the =Sum control so that it is directly below the InvoiceNo field
   View the report to see the changes you made.
7. Click the **Print Preview button**, then scroll to view the total profit and number of invoices
   The updated report is shown in Figure H-10. Close the Print Preview window.
8. Click **Close** on the Print Preview toolbar
   Now you can save the report.
9. Click the **Save button** on the toolbar to save the report

Trouble?
Be sure to click the Text Box button, NOT the Label button to insert a text box.

Trouble?
The label control on your screen may or may not be labeled Text 16. It won't affect your work if it is a different number.

QuickTip
Clicking inside a text box control and editing the expression accomplishes the same task as changing the expression in the Control Source property of the property sheet.

FIGURE H-8: Sorting and Grouping dialog box

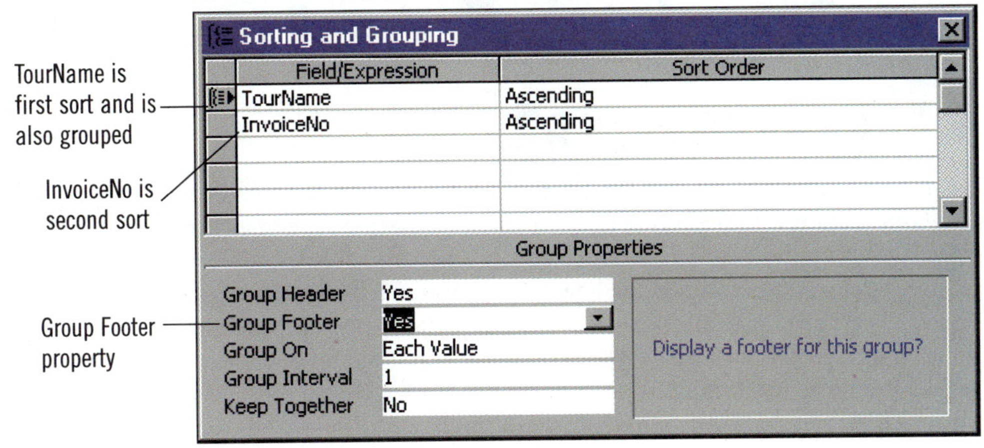

FIGURE H-9: Entering a calculated expression

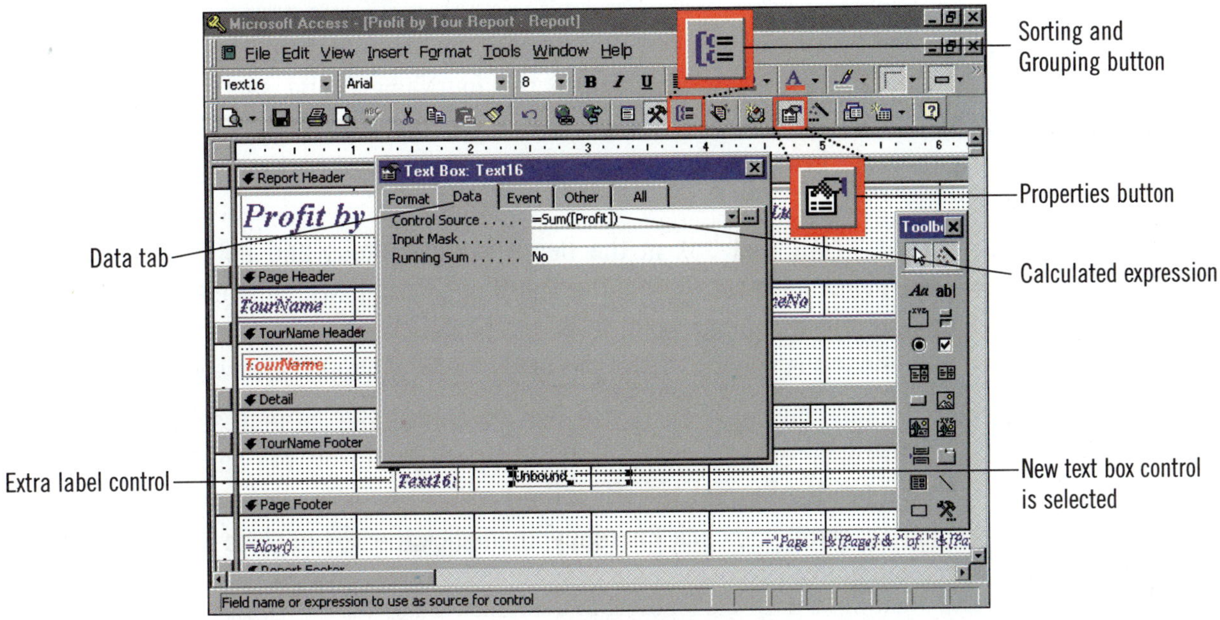

FIGURE H-10: Print Preview of a report with calculated expressions in the group footer

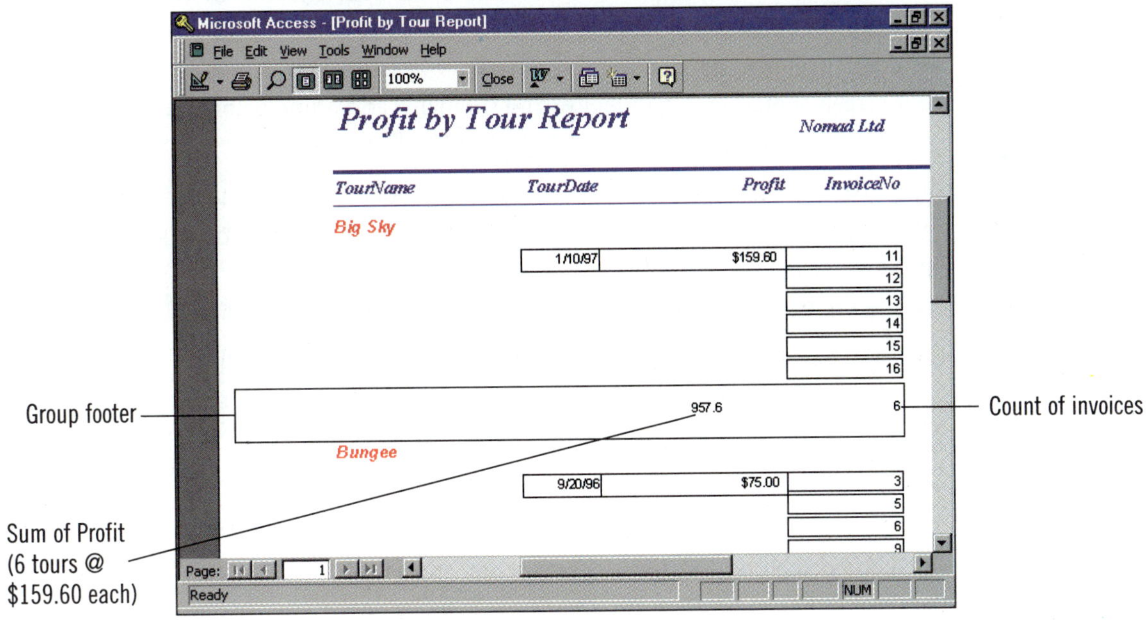

Access 97

Access 97

Modifying Control Alignment

By default, the information displayed within a single numeric or currency field is right aligned and the information within a text field is left aligned. Another type of alignment involves aligning the edges of multiple controls with respect to each other. For example, the text boxes in the TourName Footer section would look better if they were precisely aligned underneath the information they summarize in the Detail section. See Table H-3 for more information on aligning controls with respect to each other. Michael wants to format and align the new text boxes in the TourName Footer section to make the report clearer. He aligns the new expressions under their respective columns and also modifies the summarized Profit text box to appear with a currency format.

Steps

1. Click the **InvoiceNo text box** in the Detail section, press and hold **[Shift]**, click the **=Count([InvoiceNo]) expression** in the TourName Footer section, release **[Shift]**, click **Format** on the menu bar, point to **Align**, then click **Right**
   Now that the InvoiceNo fields are right aligned with respect to each other, align the Profit fields.
2. Click the **Profit text box** in the Detail section, press and hold **[Shift]**, click the **=Sum([Profit]) expression** in the TourName Footer section, release **[Shift]**, click **Format** on the menu bar, point to **Align**, then click **Right**
   In addition to aligning the controls, format the =Sum([Profit]) expression as currency.
3. Click in the TourName Footer section to cancel the current selection, click the **=Sum([Profit]) expression**, click the **Properties button** on the Report Design toolbar, click the **Format tab**, click the **Format text box**, click the **Format property list arrow**, scroll and click **Currency**, then click the to close the property sheet
   Add a descriptive label in the TourName Footer section so that the reader can clearly understand that this part of the report shows summary statistics.
4. Click the **Label tool** on the Toolbox, click near the top at the left edge in the **TourName Footer section**, type **Summarized profit and count statistics:**, then click outside the control
   Your screen should look like Figure H-11. Finally, add a line below the calculated expressions to further differentiate between the groups of records.
5. Click the **Line tool** in the Toolbox, click below the new label in the **TourName Footer section** at the left edge of the report, then drag + to the right to the 5" mark on the ruler
   Look at the report in Print Preview to see the work you have done.
6. Click the **Print Preview button** on the Report Design toolbar
   The horizontal lines add definition to the different sections of the report. They make it easier to understand which records are summarized in the TourName footer.
7. Click the **Print button** on the Print Preview toolbar
   The final report is shown in Figure H-12. Close the Print Preview window and save the report.
8. Click **Close** on the Print Preview toolbar, click the **Save button** on the Report Design toolbar, then click the **Profit by Tour Report Close button**

QuickTip

Press and hold [Shift] while creating a line to make it perfectly horizontal or vertical.

FIGURE H-11: Modifying controls in Report Design View

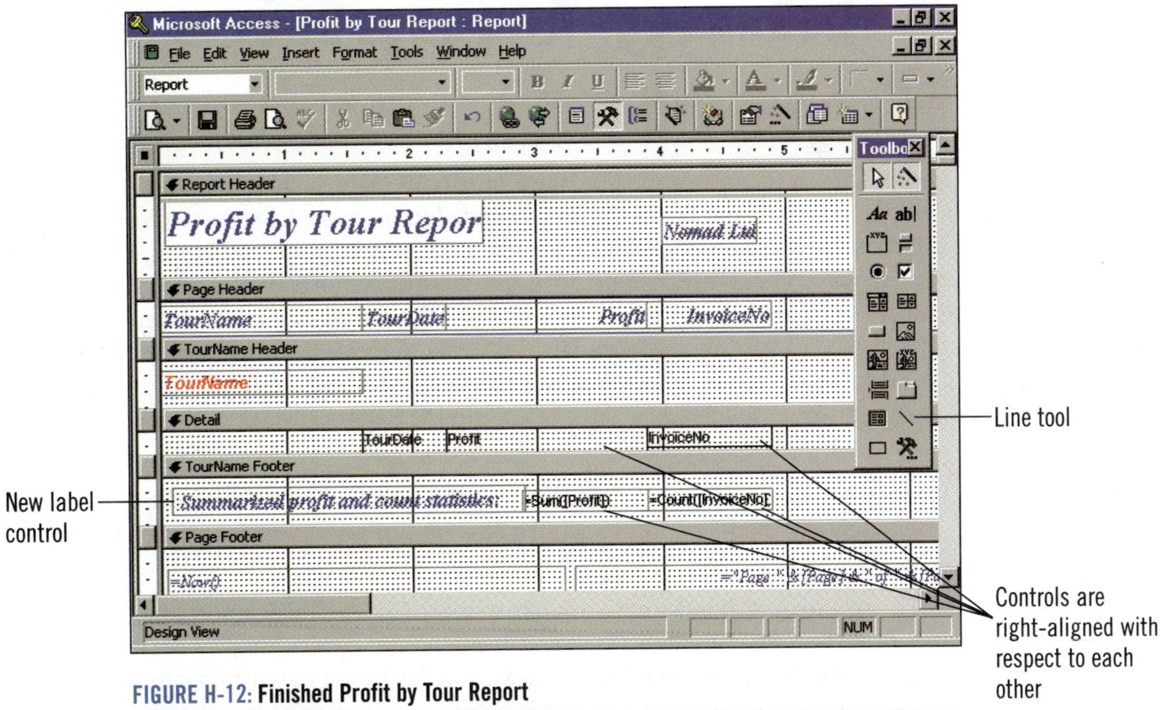

FIGURE H-12: Finished Profit by Tour Report

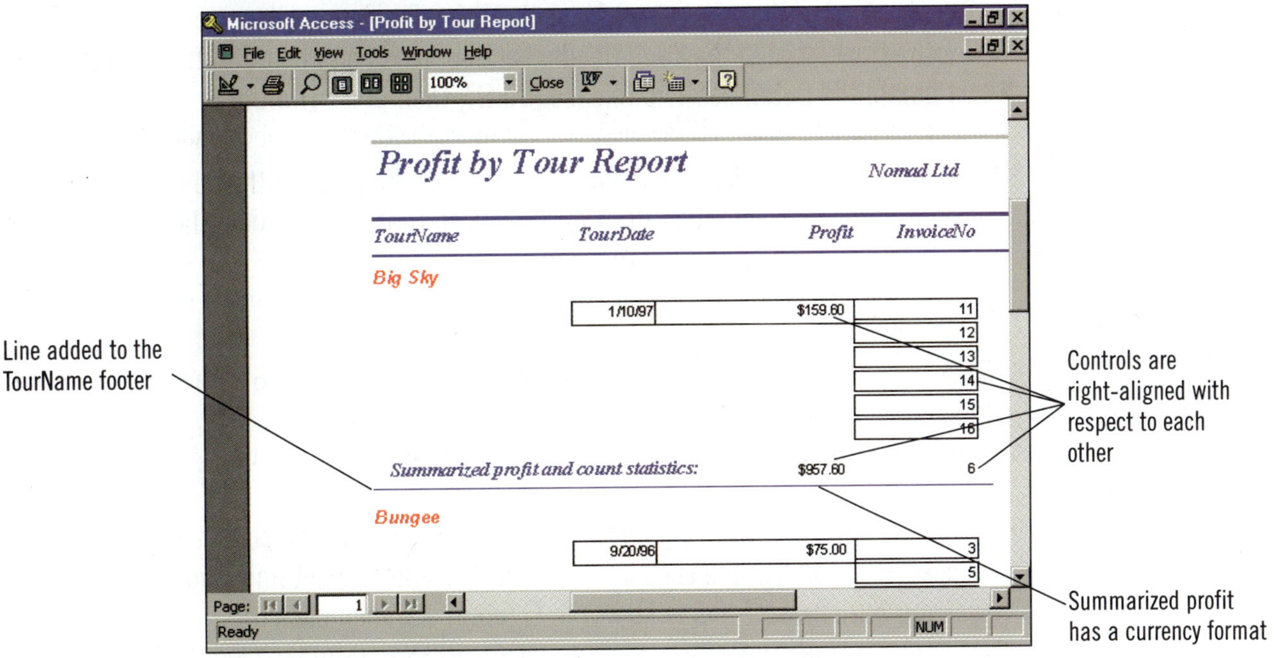

TABLE H-3: Aligning controls with respect to each other

menu option	description
Format|Align|Left	Aligns the left edges of the selected controls with the left edge of the leftmost control in the selection
Format|Align|Right	Aligns the right edges of the selected controls with the right edge of the rightmost control in the selection
Format|Align|Top	Aligns the top edges of the selected controls with the top edge of the topmost control in the selection
Format|Align|Bottom	Aligns the bottom edges of the selected controls with the bottom edge of the bottommost control in the selection
Format|Align|Grid	Aligns the upper-left corner of each selected control to the nearest point on the grid

Access 97

Adding Graphics to Reports

Graphics refers to any non-text or non-numeric element such as lines, clipart, or boxes placed in the report. Lines and boxes are usually added to increase the report's clarity and professionalism. Clipart is usually added to create visual interest in a report that might otherwise be dull with just numbers and text. When you use the AutoReports or Reports Wizard, Access automatically adds lines to certain sections of the Report Design View to differentiate the sections and make it easier to read. Michael wants to create an attractive Tours Report listing all of Nomad's past and present tours as a customer handout. Michael will use the AutoReport: Tabular option and then add a clipart image to the Report Header section.

Steps

1. Click the **Reports tab** if necessary, click **New**, click **AutoReport: Tabular**, click the **Choose the table or query where the object's data comes from list arrow**, click **Tours**, then click **OK**
   The **AutoReport: Tabular** option automatically creates a tabular report as shown in Figure H-13 with all the fields of the Tours table and opens in Print Preview mode. After scrolling through the report, you decide to delete the Cost field (you don't want the customer to see this field!)
2. Click the **Design View button** on the Print Preview toolbar, scroll to the right, click the **Cost label** in the Page Header section, press and hold **[Shift]**, click the **Cost text box** in the Detail section, release **[Shift]**, then press **[Delete]**
   With the Cost information eliminated, you can move the Handicap label to the left.
3. Click the **Handicap label** in the Page Header section, point to the edge so the mouse pointer changes to , then drag to the left so that the Handicap label is centered over the checkmark in the Detail section
   The realigned label is shown in Figure H-14. Now you can add a clipart image to enhance the Report Header section.
4. Click the **Image button** on the Toolbox, then click at the 6" mark in the **Report Header**
   The Insert Picture dialog box opens, allowing you to select the clipart image you wish to add to the report.
5. Click the **Preview button** on the Insert Picture dialog box toolbar, click the folders as needed to position the Look in: box to the drive letter containing your student disk, click the **Buttrfly.wmf** file as shown in Figure H-15, then click **OK**
   The butterfly clipart image was added to the report view; print the report.
6. Click the **Print Preview button** then click the **Print button** on the Print Preview toolbar
   The final report is shown in Figure H-16. The butterfly adds an interesting visual touch to an otherwise basic report. After looking over all your enhancements, close the Print Preview window.
7. Click **Close** on the Print Preview toolbar
   Save the report, naming it Tours Report.
8. Click the **Save button** on the Report Design toolbar, then type **Tours Report** in the Name text box, then click **OK**
   Now you can close the report.

Trouble?

If the Handicap field appears on the report as a textbox displaying "Yes" or "No" instead of a checkbox, change it to a checkbox in Design View. Delete the Handicap textbox in the report's Detail section, click , drag the Handicap field from the field list back to the same location. The new Handicap field appears as a checkbox. Delete the attached new "Handicap" label.

Time To

- Close the report

FIGURE H-13: AutoReport created from the Tours table

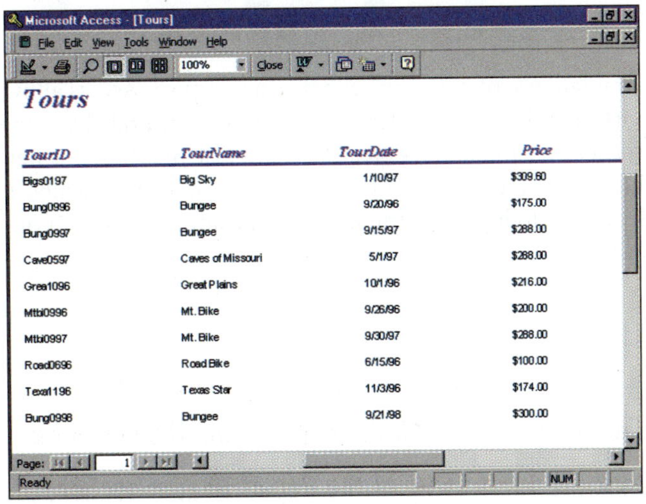

FIGURE H-14: Moving controls

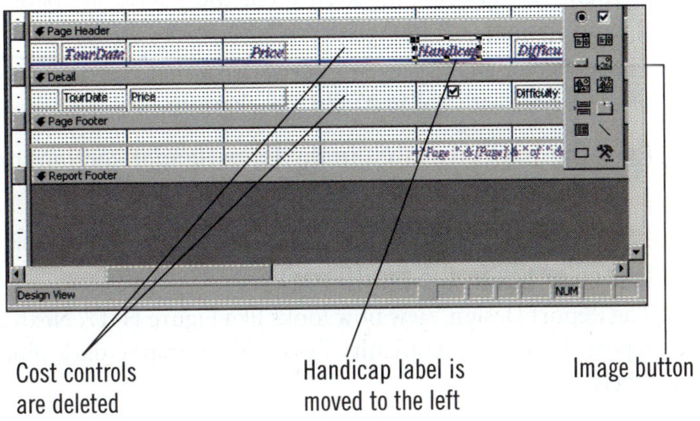

FIGURE H-15: Insert Picture dialog box

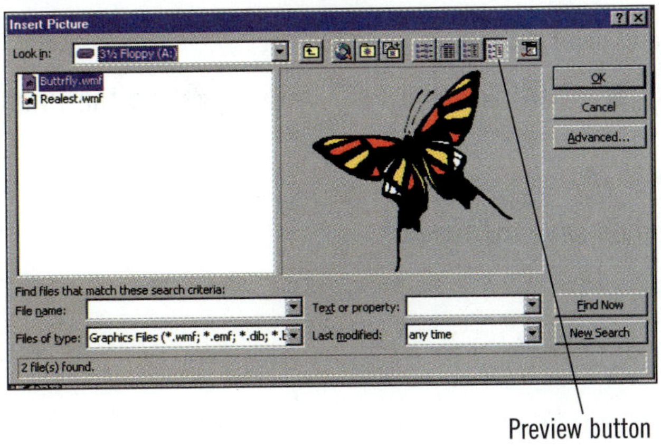

FIGURE H-16: Final report with clipart

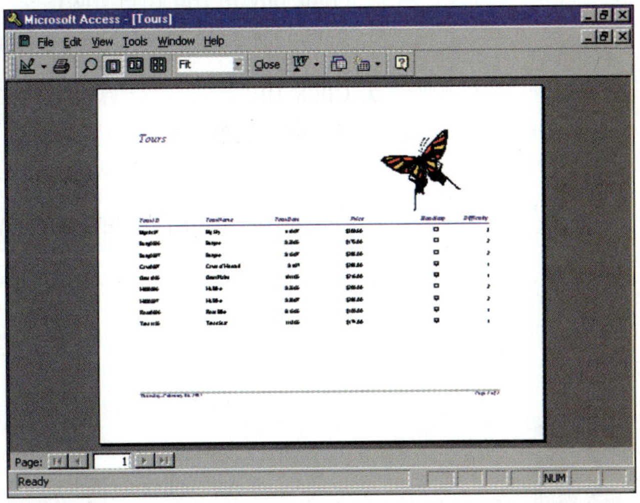

CLUES TO USE

Graphic image files supported by Access

You can insert many popular graphic file formats into a form or report. You don't need a separate graphic filter to insert the following graphic file formats: Enhanced Metafile (.emf), Windows Bitmap (.bmp, .rle, .dib), Windows Metafile (.wmf) and Icon (.ico) graphics. Metafiles scale better than bitmaps because they're made up of lines rather than patterns of individual dots.

Using Color

Discriminate use of color can enhance any report. Access allows you to change several colors of a report including the borders, text, and backgrounds by using the buttons on the Formatting (Form/Report) toolbar. Michael just purchased a new color laser printer for Nomad and has decided to add color to the Tours Report. Specifically, he'll change text, background, and border colors to highlight the most important information on the report.

Steps

1. Click **Tours Report** on the Reports tab, then click **Design**
2. Click the **Tours label** in the Report Header section, press and hold **[Shift]**, click the **TourName label** in the Page Header section, click the **TourName text box** in the Detail section, release **[Shift]**, then click the **Font/Fore Color button** on the Report Design toolbar
   The text color changes to bright red. Now that you have accented the most important words of the report with red text, add a background color to the TourDate information.
3. Click the **TourDate label** in the Page Header section, press and hold **[Shift]**, click the **TourDate text box** in the Detail section, release **[Shift]**, click the **Fill/Back Color list arrow** on the Report Design toolbar, then click the **light gray color box** (the last color box in the fourth row)
   The Report Design View now looks like Figure H-17. Next, add one more accent color to the report. Border the Difficulty field with the same dark blue color displayed in many of the labels.
4. Scroll and click the **Difficulty text box** in the Detail section, click the **Line/Border list arrow** on the Report Design toolbar, then click the **dark blue box** (the sixth color box in the first row)
   Review the changes, then preview and print the report.
5. Click the **Print Preview button**, then click the **Print button** on the Print Preview toolbar
   The final report is shown in Figure H-18.
6. Close the Print Preview window, then save the report

Clues to Use: How to create custom colors

If you change a control's property setting on a report, the change doesn't affect the underlying query or table. Likewise, if you change the property setting for a field in a table or query after you've created a report that uses the field, the property setting for the control on the report isn't updated; you must do this manually. There are exceptions to the last rule, however. If you change the Default Value, Validation Rule, or Validation Text properties in a table's Design View, these changes will be enforced in any controls based on these fields later.

FIGURE H-17: Changing control colors

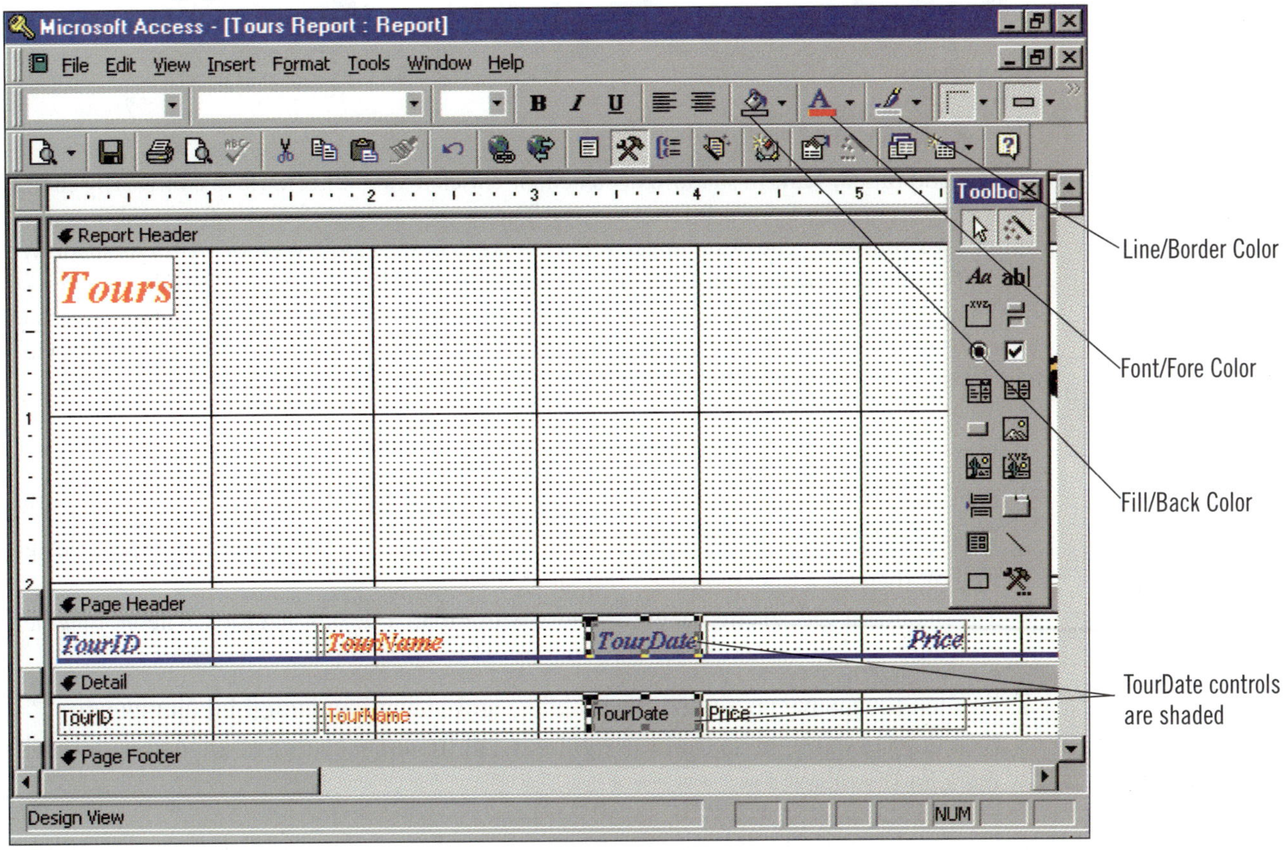

FIGURE H-18: Finished report with color accents

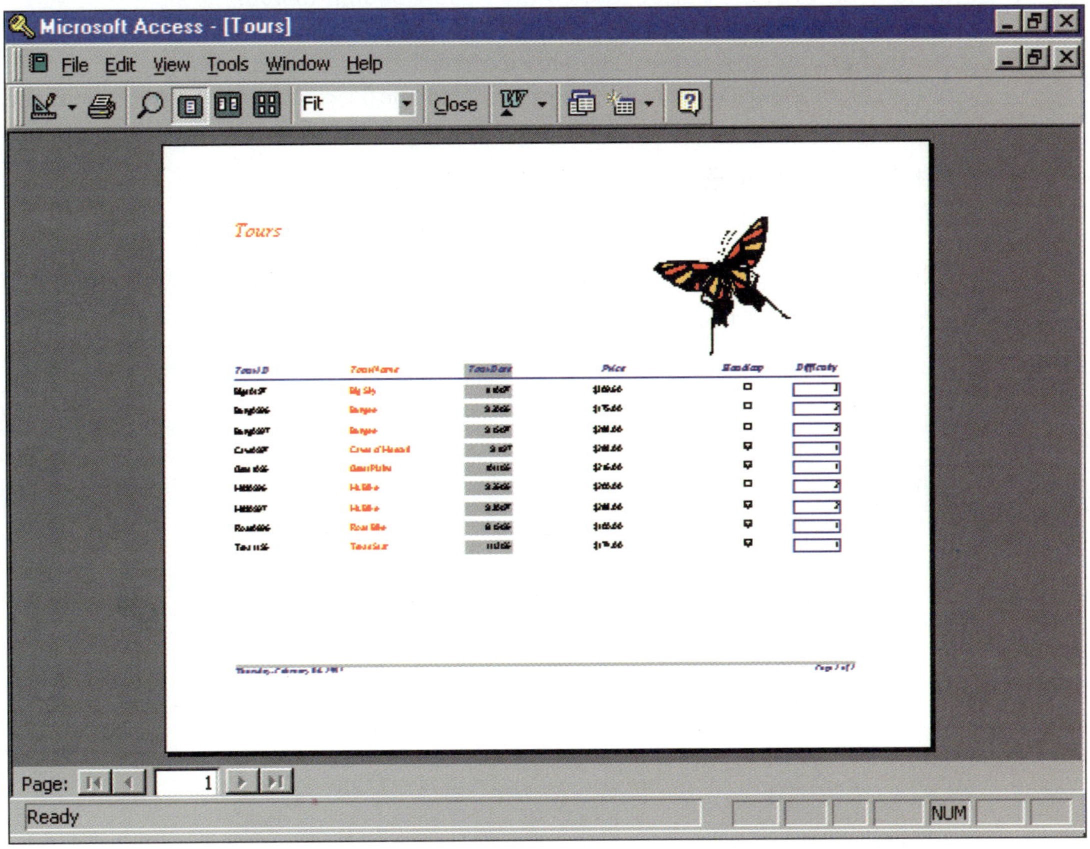

Adding Special Effects

You can add raised, sunken, shadowed, etched, or chiseled **special effects** to controls by changing the settings of the Special Effect property. The sunken special effect is often used to make a button look indented. The raised special effect makes a button look not indented. The shadowed effect is especially attractive for titles, and the etched and chiseled special effects create interesting borders. Refer to Table H-4 for an example of each of the special effects. Michael wants to add some special effects to the Tours report to continue to enhance its appearance. He'll add a shadowed effect to the title and a chiseled effect to the Price fields.

Steps 1 2 3 4

1. Click the **Design View button** to view the report's design, click the **Tours label** in the Report Header section, click the **Special Effect list arrow** on the Report Design toolbar, then click the **Special Effect: Shadowed button**
   The shadowed special effect requires more width than a default flat look. Therefore widen the Tours label to make sure it has enough room to look proper on the report.
2. Position the mouse pointer on the **middle**, **right sizing handle** until it changes to ↔, then drag to the right so that the right edge of the label control is aligned with the 1" mark on the ruler
   Now add a chiseled effect to the Price text box.
3. Click the **Price text box** in the Detail section, click the **Special Effect list arrow**, then click the **Special Effect: Chiseled button**
4. Click the **Print Preview button** on the Report Design toolbar
   The final report is shown in Figure H-19. The shadowed effect on the title really draws attention to that area of the report. The chiseled effect helps keep the information in the TourDate column aligned with the information in the Price column. Satisfied with the changes, print a hard copy of the report.
5. Click the **Print button** on the Print Preview toolbar
   Done for the day, save and close the report, then exit Access.
6. Click **Close** on the Print Preview toolbar to close the Print Preview window
7. Save the report, close the report, then exit Access

FIGURE H-19: Tours Report with special effects

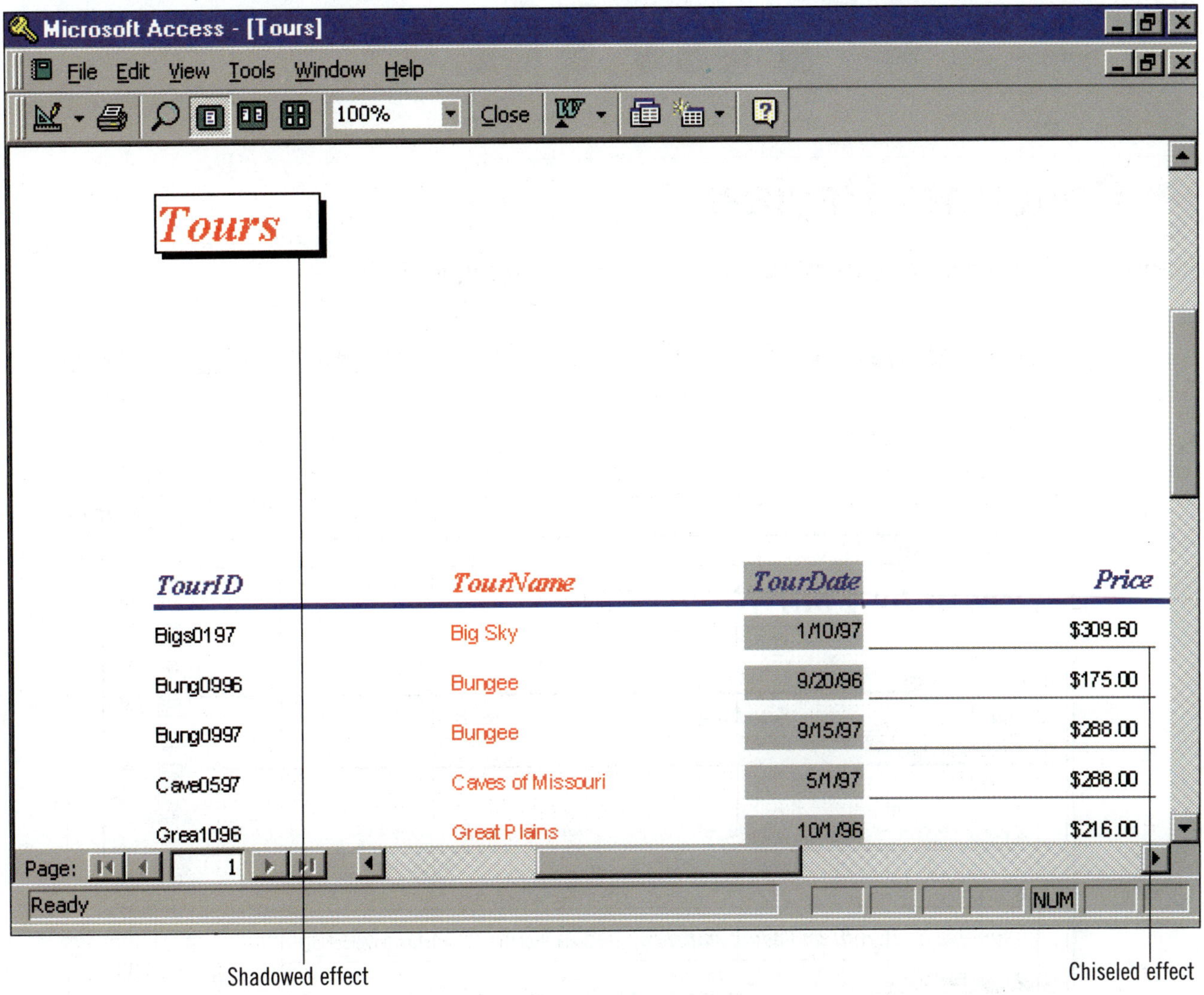

Access 97

TABLE H-4: Special effects

special effect	sample
Flat	Alaska
Raised	Alaska
Sunken	Alaska
Etched	Alaska
Shadowed	Alaska
Chiseled	Alaska

Practice

Concepts Review

Identify each element of a form's Design View shown in Figure H-20.

FIGURE H-20

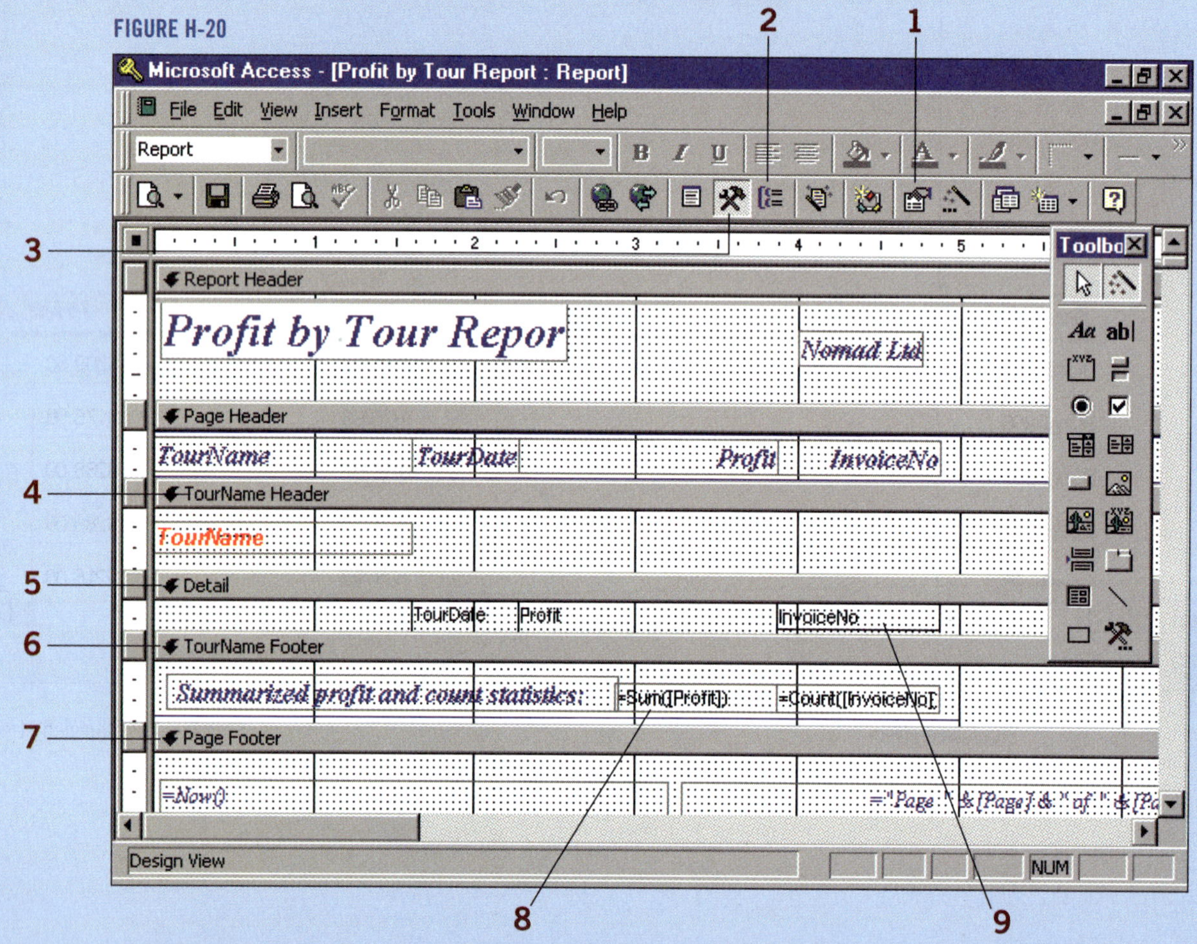

Match each term with the statement that describes its function.

10. An entry in an unbound text box that returns a value such as the sum or count of a field
11. Automatically creates a columnar or tabular report
12. The database objects most likely used to distribute information in formal presentations or meetings
13. Sorting records in a certain order, and distinguishing them with an identifying header and/or footer in the body of the report
14. Sunken, etched, or chiseled "looks" added to a report control
15. A report section that appears just before the Detail section
16. A report section that appears just after the Detail section
17. A report section that appears once for every record
18. An element such as a line or clipart placed on the report

a. Group header
b. Group footer
c. Calculated expressions
d. Reports
e. Grouping
f. Detail section
g. Special effects
h. Graphic
i. AutoReport

Select the best answer from the list of choices.

19. Which of the following is a benefit of reports over forms?
- **a.** Reports allow you to add calculations on groups of records.
- **b.** Reports allow you to add bound or unbound controls.
- **c.** Reports allow you to sort records.
- **d.** Reports allow you to add graphic images such as lines and clipart.

20. Which of the following is NOT a valid report section?
- **a.** Report Header
- **b.** Group Header
- **c.** Detail
- **d.** Summary

21. Which of the following report sections would you probably use to add group calculations?
- **a.** Page Header
- **b.** Detail
- **c.** Group Footer
- **d.** Summary

22. Which of the following calculated expressions displays the correct syntax to return the total of the values in the Cost field?
- **a.** =Total((Cost))
- **b.** =Sum(Cost)
- **c.** =Total([Cost])
- **d.** =Sum([Cost])

23. Which of the following is NOT a valid color property?
- **a.** Interior Color
- **b.** Fill/Back Color
- **c.** Font/Fore Color
- **d.** Line/Border Color

Skills Review

1. Create a report from a query.

- **a.** Start Access and open the database Addresses-H.
- **b.** Begin to create a Report using the Report Wizard based on the Basic Address List query.
- **c.** Add all the fields from the Basic Address List query.
- **d.** View the data within the report by Zips but do not include any additional grouping levels.
- **e.** Sort the records in ascending order by Last within the groups.
- **f.** Choose an Outline 1 layout, a Landscape orientation, and a Soft Gray Style.
- **g.** Title the Report "Address Report by City".
- **h.** Print the Address Report by City.

2. Use report sections.

- **a.** Open the Address Report by City report in Design View.
- **b.** Expand the Page Header section about one half inch.
- **c.** Add the descriptive label "Report is sorted by City, then by Last" to the left edge of the Page Header section.
- **d.** Save the report.

3. Use group headers.

- **a.** View the Address Report by City report in Design View.
- **b.** In the City Header section, move the State text box to the right of the City text box.
- **c.** Delete the State label.
- **d.** In the City Header section, move the City label, City text box, and State text box down so that the bottom edge of the three controls rests slightly above the Last, First, and Street labels.
- **e.** Save the report.

4. Add calculations to group footers.

- **a.** View the Address Report by City report in Design View.
- **b.** Use the Sorting and Grouping button to access the properties for the City group, and display the group footer for this section.
- **c.** In the City Footer section, use the label tool to add the label "Count of addresses in this city:" to the left edge of the section.
- **d.** In the City Footer section, use the text box tool to add an unbound text box at the 3" mark.
- **e.** Modify the Control Source property of the new text box to the following expression: =Count([Last]) to count the number of entries in the Detail section for each city.
- **f.** In the City Footer section, delete the extra label.
- **g.** Move and resize the controls as necessary.
- **h.** Save and print the report.

5. Modify control alignment.

- **a.** Open the Address Report by City report in Design View.
- **b.** Resize the City label in the City Header so that the right edge ends at the 0.75" mark on the ruler.
- **c.** In the City Header, move the City text box to the left by dragging the upper left corner of the control so that the left edge is even with the Last label beneath it.
- **d.** In the City Header, make sure that the City text box and the Last label are left aligned with respect to each other. Several horizontal lines surround the Last, First, and Street labels in the City Header section. Don't forget about the Undo button if your alignment commands go awry.
- **e.** In the City Header, resize the City text box so that the right edge is even with the Last label beneath it.
- **f.** In the City Header, move the State text box so that the left edge is even with the First label beneath it.
- **g.** In the City Header, make sure that the State text box and the First label are left aligned with respect to each other.
- **h.** Save the report and print it.

6. Add report graphics.

- **a.** View the Address Report by City report in Design View.
- **b.** In the Report Header section, add an appropriate image control to the 5" mark.
- **c.** Insert the Realest.wmf picture in the image control. It should be found on your student disk. If you can't find this image, insert another one of your choice.
- **d.** Save and print the report.

7. Use color.

- **a.** View the Address Report by City report in Design View.
- **b.** In the City Header section, select the City label, City text box, and State text box and apply a red text color to the controls.
- **c.** In the Detail section, select the Last, First, and Street text boxes and apply a bright blue border to the controls.
- **d.** In the Detail section, select the Last text box and apply a light gray fill color to the control.
- **e.** Save and print the report.

8. Add special effects.

- **a.** View the Address Report by City report in Design View.
- **b.** In the Report Header section, select the Address Report by City label and apply a raised special effect.
- **c.** In the City Header section, select the City label and apply an etched special effect.
- **d.** Save, print, and close the report.
- **e.** Close the database and exit Access.

Independent Challenges

1. As the president of a civic organization, you have developed a database that tracks donations of recyclable material called Cleanup-H. Now that several deposits have been made and recorded, you wish to create several reports.

To complete this independent challenge:

1. Start Access and open the Cleanup-H database.
2. Use the Report Wizard to develop a report from the Deposits by Club query.
3. Use all the fields in the query and view the information by Recycle Centers.
4. Do not add any additional grouping levels, sort the records in ascending order by Date, use an Outline 1 layout, use a portrait orientation, and specify a Casual style.
5. Name the report "Recycle Center Deposits".
6. Modify the Recycle Centers.Name label in the Recycle Centers.Name Header section so that the label only displays "Recycle Centers".
7. Using the Reports Wizard, develop another report on the Deposits by Club query with the same choices except for the following: view the information by Clubs and name the report "Club Deposits".
8. Modify the Clubs.Name label in the Clubs.Name Header section so that the label only displays "Clubs."
9. Print both reports and note the differences in the way the records are grouped.
10. Close the database and exit Access.

2. Now that you've developed a relational database that documents the books you've read called Readings-H, you'd like to develop a couple of reports to professionally display the information.

To complete this independent challenge:

1. Start Access and open the Readings-H database.
2. Use the Report Wizard to develop a report from the Books I've Read query.
3. Use all the fields in the query, view the data by Authors, don't add further grouping levels, sort the records by Title, use a Block layout, use a portrait orientation, and apply a Bold style.
4. Title the report "Books I've Read Report".
5. Change the text color of the label in the Report Header section to black.
6. Change the Line/Border color of all of the lines in the Report Header and Page Header section to red.
7. Apply bold formatting to the Last Name text box in the Detail section.
8. Apply a shadowed special effect to the label in the Report Header section. Be sure to widen the label to accommodate for the special effect.
9. Print and save the report.
10. Close the database and exit Access.

3. You have recently helped the medical director of a large internal medical clinic put together and update a database that tracks extra-curricular activities called Doctors-H. You wish to develop a report of activities in the database.

To complete this independent challenge:

1. Start Access and open the Doctors-H database.
2. Use the Report Wizard to develop a report from the Physician Activities query.
3. Use all the fields in the query, view the data by Physicians, do not add any more grouping levels, sort the fields by date, use a Stepped Layout, use a portrait orientation, and apply a Formal style.

4. Title the report "Physician Activities Report".
5. Open the First Name Footer section and add an unbound text box to the section.
6. Modify the Control Source property of the text box to be the expression =Sum([Hours]).
7. Modify the label in the First Name Footer section to read "Total Number of Hours Volunteered", and make sure it is positioned just to the left of the new expression text box.
8. Make sure the new label and text box in the First Name Footer section are top aligned with respect to each other.
9. Make sure the Hours label in the Page Header, the Hours text box in the Detail section, and the new expression text box in the First Name Footer are all right aligned as well as right aligned with respect to each other.
10. Add a line control at the bottom of the First Name Footer section that stretches from the 0" to the 6" mark on the ruler.
11. Save and print the report.
12. Close the database and exit Access.

WEB WORK

4. You are considering attending Keller Graduate School of Management to obtain an MBA after you finish your undergraduate degree. You'd like to analyze the courses Keller offers by discipline (information systems, marketing, management, and so on) to determine if they have the depth and breadth of electives you desire. You have started an Access database called MBA-H to record Keller's courses. Now you need to return to Keller's home page to find the current listing of information systems courses and add them to your database before you can build a report that analyzes the courses by discipline.

To complete this independent challenge:

1. Log on to the Internet and use your browser to go to http://www.course.com. From there, click Student Online Companions, click the link for this textbook, then click the Access link for Unit H.
2. Print the pages (about five) describing the MBA courses available from Keller Graduate School of Management.
3. Log off the Internet and open the MBA-H database.
4. Add the five elective Information Systems courses to the courses table.
5. Use the Report Wizard and create a report using all the fields from the Courses Sorted Alphabetically within Discipline query, group the records by Disciplines Name, sort ascending on Course Number, use a Stepped layout, use a portrait orientation, apply the Formal style, and name the report "KGSM Courses Report".
6. Add a Discipline Name group footer then add a control that counts the number of offerings within each discipline within the footer. Align the counting control under the Course Number column and make sure that a descriptive label clarifies the expression.
7. Add a horizontal line at the bottom of the Discipline Name Footer to help separate the groups of records.
8. Add a shadow effect to the label in the Report Header.
9. Preview the report and make sure that all labels print clearly. (*Hint:* You may have to adjust the labels in the various headers.)
10. Save and print the report.
11. Close the database and exit Access.

▶ Visual Workshop

Open the VW-H database and create a new report as shown in Figure H-21. The report is based on the Donations Query, viewed by Alumni, further sorted by Value, given a Stepped layout, a portrait orientation, and a Corporate style. Also, notice that the Value field is summarized for each donor and a horizontal line separates the donors.

FIGURE H-21

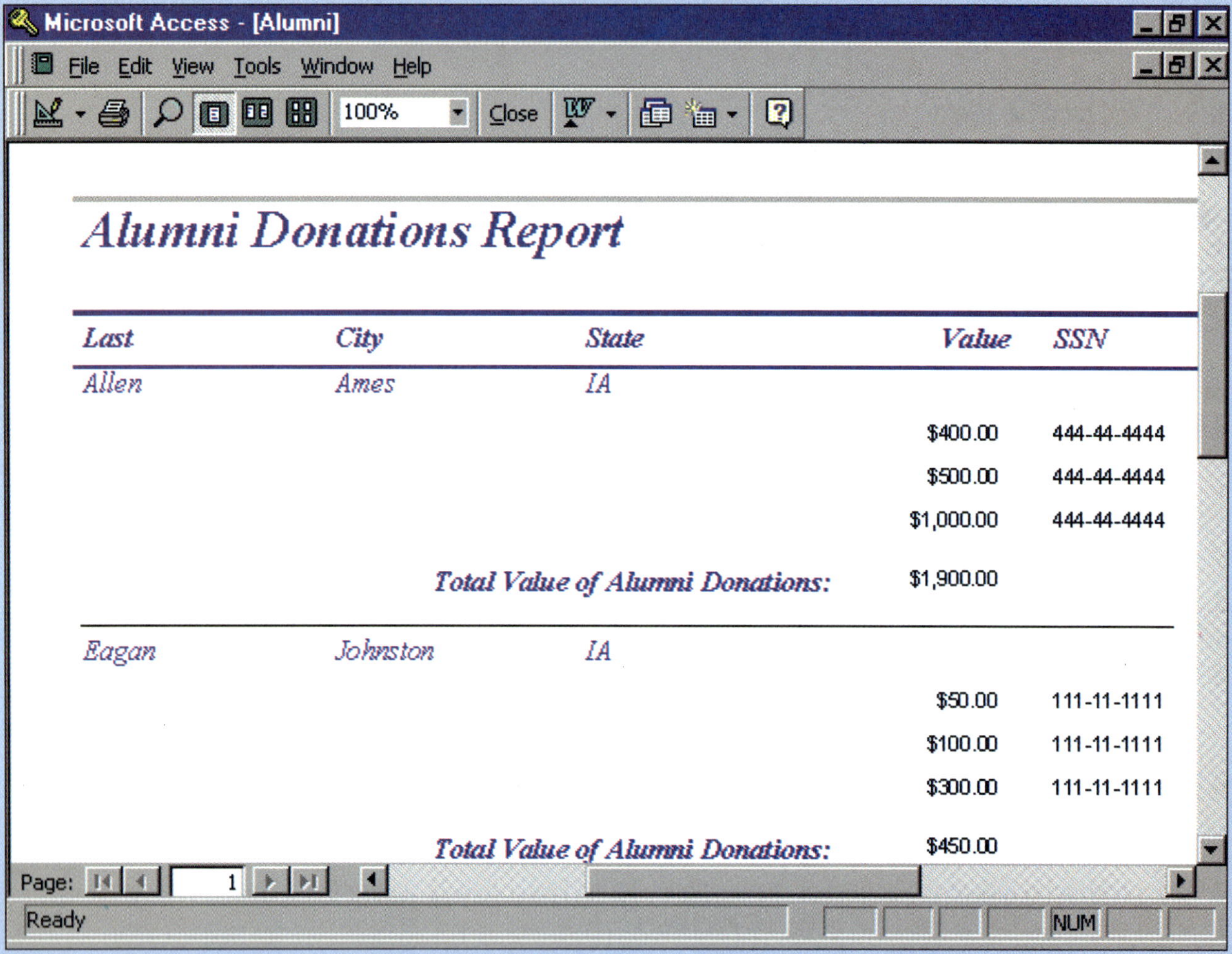

Access 97

Glossary

Aggregate functions Functions such as Sum, Avg, and Min that are used in the Query Design grid to calculate statistics across several records.

AND query A query in which more than one criteria must be satisfied for the record to be displayed in the resulting datasheet. AND criteria are placed in the same row of the Query Design grid.

Append query An update query used to add records to an existing table.

AutoForm Wizards Options in the New Form dialog box that allow quick creation of tabular, columnar, or datasheet AutoForms.

AutoReport A report created with the New Object button on the toolbar. Access displays all fields and records in the selected table or query with field names used as labels.

AutoReport Wizard Two options in the New Report dialog box that allow quick creation of tabular or columnar AutoReports.

Bitmap A clip art or image file format that is made up of patterns of individual dots. The file type for bitmap files is usually .BMP.

Bound control A control on a form or report that is linked to a field in an underlying table or query.

Bound object frame A control on a form or report that is linked to images stored in a table.

Calculated expressions Bound report controls that total groups of records and are most likely placed in the group footer section of the report.

Calculated field Created in the Query Design grid by entering a field name followed by a colon in the Field cell followed by an expression such as New Price:[Price]*1.1

Cell The intersection of a row and a column.

Check box A square box on a dialog box or form used to indicate whether an option is selected (checked) or cleared (unchecked). Also used to indicate yes/no choices.

Clipboard A temporary storage area for cut or copied text or graphics, You can paste the contents of the Clipboard into any Microsoft program file. The Clipboard holds the information until you cut or copy another piece of text or a graphic.

Column A vertical stack of cells, usually representing the values for a database field.

Combo box A list box with the additional capability of allowing the user to type an entry from the keyboard.

Control A graphical object used on a form or report that displays data or other information.

Criteria A set of conditions used in a filter or query that selects a particular group of records.

Crosstab query A query that presents information in a cross-tabular report, usually with one field counted or summarized by rows and columns within the body of the report.

Data The information stored in a database.

Data type A specification that controls what kind of data a field can contain.

Database An organized collection of data for a specific purpose.

Database management system A computer program that organizes and manages data.

Database window The window that opens when you start an Access database. It lists all the objects contained in the database.

Dataset A set of records retrieved by applying a filter or running a query.

Datasheet Data from a table, form, or query displayed as rows and columns.

Delete query An update query used to delete a chosen subset of records.

Design grid The grid that you use to design a query or filter.

Design view A window that shows the structure of a table, form, query, or report.

Detail section The section of the report that prints once for each record in the underlying record set.

Expression A combination of values and functions that evaluates to a single result.

Field The part of a table that contains a particular type of data. Also used to name the column of cells containing a particular type of data.

Field list A window available in Design view to display all the fields in a table or query being used.

Field properties The qualities of a field that affect how it appears or what type of data it receives.

Field selector The gray bar at the top of a field column that selects the entire column.

Filter Criteria used to retrieve a specific set of records.

Find A feature that allows you to search for a string of characters in one or many fields.

Form An object, resembling a paper form, used for entering and editing single records.

Form view A window that displays the contents of a database in a form.

Function A preprogrammed mathematical activity that returns a value.

Graphic Any nontext or nonumeric element such as lines, clip art, or boxes placed in the report.

Group footer A section of a form or report that appears on its own line on a report just after the Detail section of a new group of records. Group footer sections are often used to add summary statistics to groups of records.

Group header A section of a form or report that appears on its own line on a report just before the Detail section of a new group of records.

Grouping A report feature that provides a way to sort records so that summary statistics can be applied to a group of records that meet a certain criteria.

Handle A small black square used to move or resize controls in Design view.

Help An online collection of information about Access that you reach from the Help menu.

Hide Duplicates property Hides multiple occurrences of the same data for the fields in the Detail section of the report.

Icon A small graphical representation of an object.

Imported table A new Access table in your database created from information copied from an external file.

Key Field A field that contains unique information for each record.

Key field combination Using two or more fields together as the key field for a record.

Label A control that displays unbound text on a form or report.

Linked table A table created in Excel or other database product that is stored in a file outside of the open database.

List box A box that displays a list of choices.

Menu A list of related commands displayed by clicking a menu name.

Menu bar The row at the top of a window that contains menu names.

Metafile A clip art or image file format that is made up of lines. The file type for metafiles is often .WMF or .EMF.

Move handle The large black square in the upper-left corner of a selected control that you drag to reposition the control.

Navigation buttons The arrows in the lower-left corner of a datasheet or form that are used to move through records.

Object The principal component of an Access database. Tables, forms, queries, reports, macros and modules are all referred to as "objects" in Access.

One-to-many relationship The link between two tables in which the "one" side of the relationship is a key field and the "many" side of the relationship allows the data in that field to be entered many times in that table.

Operators Instructions added to criteria to create new criteria conditions. Mathematical operators such as + (add), and * (multiply) can be used to calculate new criteria. Logical operators such as AND and OR can be used to create more complex criteria expressions.

Option button A button, typically part of a group, that selects an option. Only one option can be selected at a time.

OR query A query in which only one of two or more criteria rows must be satisfied for the record to be displayed in the resulting datasheet. OR criteria are placed on different rows in the Query Design grid.

Page footer The text that appears at the bottom of each page in printed output.

Page header The text that appears at the top of each page in printed output.

Pointer Used to select items; repositioned by movement of the mouse.

Primary key A field whose value uniquely identifies each record.

Print Preview An on-screen view of how an item will appear on paper.

Property An attribute of a object that you can change to control the object's appearance or behavior.

Property sheet The window that displays all the properties for the chosen control on a form or report.

Query A set of instructions used to extract specific records from a database. A "question" asked to the database.

Record All the pieces of information (fields) about one item. A row composed of fields in a datasheet.

Record number box The small box that displays the current record number in the lower-left corner of a datasheet or form.

Referential integrity A set of rules to help maintain the accuracy of a database. For example, enforcing referential integrity will not allow entry of records with data on the "many" side of a one-to-many relationship before the data is first recorded for the "one" side.

Relational database A database such as Access, where information is stored in tables that can be related to one another.

Relationship The connection between two or more tables established by fields common to two or more tables.

Replace A feature that allows you to search for a string of characters and replace it with a different entry.

Report An Access object that presents data selected and formatted for printed output.

Report window The window that presents reports in Design view.

Row A horizontal grouping of a record's data fields in a datasheet.

Row selector A gray box at the left edge of a datasheet that is used to select an entire row.

Run A command or button used to run a query.

Section A designated area of a form or report in which controls can be placed. For example, a Page Header section displays/prints at the top of every page, but a Report Header section displays/prints only at the top of the entire report.

Select query A query that creates a record set without changing any of the affected records.

Shortcut key A key or key combination that lets you carry out a command without opening a menu or using a button.

Shortcut menu A floating menu that opens when the right mouse button is clicked. Menu contents vary, depending on the task in process.

Sizing handle A small black square at the edge of a selected control that you drag to resize the control.

Sorting Placing the records in a certain order (such as ascending order) according to the data in the Lastname field.

Sort order The order that records are displayed in either-Ascending (A-Z) or Descending (Z-A).

Special effects Raised, sunken, shadowed, etched, or chiseled effects added to controls on forms or reports.

Status bar The gray bar across the bottom of the screen that shows supplementary information about commands or actions.

Subform A form contained inside another form.

Text box The most common type of bound control on a form or report. When using a form, the text box allows the user to make an entry for a record by typing information at the keyboard. When reading a report, the text box displays the information in the field on the report.

Toolbar The row of buttons just below the menu bar that provides shortcuts for frequently used commands.

Toolbox The tools used to place controls on a form or report in Design view.

Unbound control A control that is stored entirely in the design for a form or report. There is no link to data in a table.

Unbound object frame A frame containing an image that is stored entirely in the design for a form or report. There is no link to an image stored in the database.

Update query A query that updates the information in the resulting datasheet.

Validation properties Properties of a field that help you eliminate unreasonable entries in a field at the point of data entry.

Value The contents of a field.

View A window that lets you work with Access objects in a specific way, including Form view, Design view, and Report view.

Wizard A tool that helps you create objects such as tables, queries, and forms.

Zoom box A dialog box that lets you view and edit the full contents of an entry that is too large to be viewed in a single cell.

Index

special characters

* wildcard character, AC F-9, AC G-13
< (less than sign), forcing lowercase with, AC E-12
> (greater than sign), forcing uppercase with, AC E-12
? wildcard character, AC F-9, AC G-13

A

Access 97
  basics, AC A-1-17
  closing, AC A-16-17
  Help, AC A-14-15
  starting, AC A-4-5
  startup window, AC A-6-7
Access 97 window
  elements of, AC A-6
  File menu, AC A-7
  viewing, AC A-6-7
Advanced Filter/Sort, AC B-12, AC G-8
aggregate functions, AC F-12-13
alignment
  of controls, AC H-10-11
  of fields in reports, AC D-6-7
  of form labels, AC G-6, AC G-7
All Fields button, AC C-2
AND criteria, AC G-13
  in complex queries, AC B-16, AC B-17
  AND queries, AC F-6-7
  Append queries, AC F-16
  Apply Filter button, AC B-12
  arithmetic operators in criteria, AC B-16
  for mathematical calculations in queries, AC F-10-11
ascending sort order, AC B-11-12
asterisk (*) wildcard, in Find command, AC B-9
AutoForm, AC G-2, AC C-3
AutoNumber data type, AC B-7
AutoNumber field, AC A-10
AutoReport, AC D-3
  lines added by, AC H-12
  Tabular, AC H-12-13
Avery labels, printing, AC D-16
Avg function, AC F-13

B

backups, for databases, AC B-3
Bold, Extra, AC C-10
bound controls, AC C-4
  adding expressions to, AC D-10
  defined, AC G-4
Build button, AC C-8
built-in functions, AC F-10, AC G-14

C

calculated controls, AC C-4
calculated expressions, adding to group footers, AC H-8-9
calculated fields, AC F-10-11
  functions in, AC F-10
  case, field properties, AC E-12
  Chart form layout, AC G-3
  chiseled special effect, AC H-16, AC H-17
  clipart, adding to reports, AC H-12-13
color
  custom, AC H-14
  in reports, AC H-14-15
Columnar form layout, AC C-2, AC G-3
columns, moving, AC A-10
combo boxes, on forms, AC G-16
common fields, AC E-2, AC E-4
comparison operators, for query criteria, AC F-7
complex criteria expressions, filtering with, AC G-13
complex queries, AC B-16-17
control headings, Page Header section, AC D-6-7
controls, AC G-1
  bound, AC C-4, AC G-4
  calculated, AC C-4
  changing default value for, AC G-14-15
  for database forms, AC A-2
  defined, AC C-4, AC G-4
  deleting, AC C-10
  formatting, AC C-10-11
  handles on, AC C-4
  modifying alignment of, AC H-10-11
  moving, AC G-4-5, AC H-12, AC H-13
  resizing, AC D-8-9, AC G-4-5
  unbound, AC C-4, AC G-4
Control Source property, AC G-16, AC H-8-9
Count function, AC F-13
criteria
  AND queries, AC B-16, AC B-17, AC F-6-7
  arithmetic operators in, AC B-16, AC F-10-11
  comparison operators, AC F-7
  field validation properties, AC E-16-17
  for filtering tables, AC B-12
  long expressions, AC F-8
  OR queries, AC B-16, AC B-17
  wildcard characters, AC F-9
crosstab queries, AC F-14-15
  defined, AC F-1
  sketch, AC F-15
Crosstab Query Wizard, AC F-14-15
Currency data type, AC B-7
currency format, controls, AC H-10
custom color, for reports, AC H-14
Custom Order list box, AC C-6

D

database objects
  object buttons for, AC A-8-9
  types of, AC A-8
databases, See also tables
  backups for, AC B-3
  building, AC B-1-17
  complex queries, AC B-16-17
  creating tables, AC B-4-5, AC E-6-7
date/time field properties, AC E-14-15
defined, AC A-2, AC E-2, AC E-3
deleting fields, AC E-10-11
  field properties, AC E-12-13
  field validation properties, AC E-16-17
  filtering tables, AC B-12-13
  finding records in, AC B-6-7
  input for, AC B-2
  modifying structure of, AC E-1-17
  modifying tables, AC B-4-5
  naming, AC B-2
  one-to-many relationships, AC E-8-9
  output of, AC B-2
  planning, AC B-2-3
  planning tables, AC E-4-5
  requirements, AC E-2-3
  simple queries, AC B-14-15
  sorting tables, AC B-10-11
  structure, AC A-3
  tables in, AC E-2
database software, AC A-2-3
Database toolbar, AC A-8
  commands, AC A-6
  Datasheet form layout, AC G-3
  datasheets defined, AC A-10
  entering data into, AC A-10-11
  keystrokes for navigating, AC B-8
  previewing, AC A-12-13
  printing, AC A-12-13
  using magnifier pointer with, AC A-12, AC A-13
Datasheet View, AC F-2
  calculated fields in, AC F-10
  sorting multiple field queries in, AC F-4-5
  viewing query results in, AC B-14, AC B-15, AC B-16
Data Type list arrow, AC B-6
data types, AC B-6
  description of, AC B-7
  of fields, AC B-2
Date built-in function, AC F-10
dates, 21st century, AC E-14

Index

Date/Time
- data type, AC B-6, AC B-7
- field properties, defining, AC E-14-15
- predefined formats, AC E-15

Decimal Places box, in Field Properties, AC B-6
defaults, for forms, changing, AC G-14-15
Default Value Field Property text box, AC E-12
Delete queries, AC F-16
deleting
- controls, AC C-10
- fields, AC E-10-11

descending sort order, AC B-11-12
Design View
- adding fields to forms in, AC C-12-13
- creating AND queries in, AC F-6-7
- creating tables in, AC E-6-7
- Detail section, AC C-4
- Form Footer section, AC C-4
- Form Header section, AC C-4
- modifying tables in, AC B-6-7
- viewing query grid in, AC B-14, AC B-16

Design View button, AC C-4
Detail section, AC C-4
- forms, AC G-6
- reports, AC H-14
- in reports, AC D-6
- Units control, AC D-8

duplicate information, hiding, in reports, AC H-6, AC H-7

E

Enforce Referential Integrity check box, AC E-8, AC E-9
Enhanced Metafile (.emf) files, AC H-13
etched special effect, AC H-17
exiting, Access, AC A-16-17
Expression Builder, AC C-8-9, AC G-14-15
expressions
- adding to reports, AC D-10-11
- in calculated fields, AC F-10-11
- defined, AC B-16, AC F-10
- in queries, AC B-16-17

Extra Bold, AC C-10

F

F1 key, accessing Office Assistant with, AC A-14
field descriptions
- adding to tables, AC B-6-7
- defined, AC B-6

field label, AC C-4
Field List button, AC C-12
field names, defining properties for, AC E-12-13
field properties, AC B-6, AC E-1
- Date/Time, defining, AC E-14-15
- defining, AC E-12-13

Field Properties section, AC B-6
fields, See also key fields
- adding to forms, AC C-12-13
- adding to reports, AC D-10
- aligning in reports, AC D-6-7
- calculated, AC F-10-11
- common, AC E-2, AC E-4
- data types, AC B-2
- defined, AC A-2
- defining in labels, AC D-17
- deleting, AC E-10-11
- grouping into subject-matter tables, AC E-4
- linking, AC E-2, AC E-4
- planning, AC E-4
- selecting, AC C-4

Field Size Field Property text box, AC E-12
field validation properties, AC E-16-17
field value text box, AC C-4
Filter by Form, AC G-12, AC G-13
Filter by Selection, AC G-12
filter grid, AC B-12, AC B-13
filtering
- advanced sorting with, AC G-8-9
- with complex criteria expressions, AC G-13
- criteria for, AC B-12
- defined, AC B-12
- determining when to use, AC B-12
- records within forms, AC G-12-13
- sorting vs., AC B-12
- tables, AC B-12-13
- vs. querying, AC F-3

Filter/Sort toolbar, AC G-12
filter window, AC B-12, AC B-13, AC G-8-9
Find dialog box, AC G-10-11
Find Duplicates Query Wizard, AC F-14
finding records
- in tables, AC B-8-9
- using wildcards, AC B-9
- within forms, AC G-10-11

Find Unmatched Query Wizard, AC F-14
First function, AC F-13
flat special effect, AC H-17
Font Weight, displaying, AC C-10
Format Field Property text box, AC E-12
formatting, controls, AC C-10-11
Formatting toolbar, for form labels, AC G-6
form controls. See controls
Form Design Toolbar, AC C-12
Form Design View
- changing form control defaults in, AC G-14-15
- editing forms in, AC G-4
- mouse pointer shapes in, AC G-5

Form Footer section, AC C-4, AC G-6
Form Header section, AC C-4
form layouts
- Chart, AC G-3
- Columnar, AC G-3
- Datasheet, AC G-3
- PivotTable, AC G-3
- Tabular, AC G-2, AC G-3

forms, AC G-1-17
- adding combo boxes to, AC G-16-17
- adding fields to, AC C-12-13
- adding graphic images to, AC C-14-15
- adding labels to, AC G-6-7
- adding list boxes to, AC G-16-17
- adding records with, AC C-16-17
- alignment, AC G-6, AC G-7
- AutoForm, AC G-2
- changing tab order, AC C-6-7
- Columnar layout, AC C-2
- controls, AC G-1, AC G-4-5
- creating with Form Wizard, AC C-2-3
- creating from multiple tables, AC G-2-3
- for databases, AC A-2, AC A-3
- defined, AC G-1
- Detail section, AC G-6
- Expression Builder, AC C-8-9

filtering records within, AC G-12-13
finding records within, AC G-10-11
formatting controls, AC C-10-11
Form Footer, AC G-6
Form Header, AC G-6
- modifying layout, AC C-4-5
- Page Footer, AC G-6
- Page Header, AC G-6
- reports vs., AC H-2
- saving as reports, AC D-14-15
- sections, AC G-6
- sorting records within, AC G-8-9

Form View
- adding graphic images to forms, AC C-14
- formatting controls, AC C-10-11
- forms displayed in, AC C-6, AC C-7

Form Wizard, AC C-2-3
- creating forms from multiple tables, AC G-2-3

functions
- aggregate, AC F-12-13
- built-in, AC F-10, AC G-14
- in calculated expressions, AC F-10
- defined, AC D-10

G

graphics
- adding to forms, AC C-14-15
- adding to reports, AC H-12-13
- common types, AC C-14
- defined, AC H-12
- image files supported by Access, AC H-13

group footers, adding calculations to, AC H-8-9
Group Footer section, reports, AC H-14
Group Header, AC D-6
group headers, defined, AC H-6
Group Header section, reports, AC H-6-7, AC H-14
grouping, records in reports, AC D-4-5, AC H-2
Grouping dialog box, AC D-3

H

handles, on controls, AC C-4
Hide Duplicates property, AC H-6, AC H-7

I

Icon (.ico) files, AC H-13
Image button, on Toolbox toolbar, AC C-14
image files, See also graphics
  supported by Access, AC H-13
imported tables, defined, AC E-7
indicators, in row selectors, AC B-6
inherited properties, AC G-14
input, for databases, AC B-2
Insert Picture dialog box, AC C-14-15, AC H-12

K

keyboard shortcuts, for tables, AC A-10, AC A-11
key field combinations, AC E-5
key fields, AC E-2
  identifying, AC E-4
keystrokes, for navigating datasheets, AC B-8

L

label controls, for calculated expressions, AC H-8-9
labels
  adding to forms, AC G-6-7
  creating, AC D-16-17
  defining fields in, AC D-17
Label tool, AC H-10
Label Wizard, AC D-16-17
Last function, AC F-13
lines, adding to reports, AC H-12
Line tool, AC H-10
linked tables, AC E-2
  defined, AC E-7
  one-to-many relationships, AC E-8-9
  planning, AC E-4-5
linking fields, AC E-2, AC E-4
list boxes, adding to forms, AC G-16-17
Lookup Wizard data type, AC B-7

M

Magnifier pointer
  using in datasheets, AC A-12, AC A-13
  using in reports, AC D-5
Max function, AC F-13
Maximize button, AC A-6
Memo data type, AC B-7
menu bar, sorting with, AC B-12
Microsoft Access dialog box, AC A-4
Min function, AC F-13
Modify the table design option button, AC B-4
mouse pointer shapes, AC C-5
  in Form Design View, AC G-5
  moving columns, AC A-10
  controls, AC H-12, AC H-13, AC G-4-5
multiple sort fields, AC F-4-5
multiple tables, creating forms from, AC G-2-3

N

navigation buttons, AC G-8
New Database button, on Database toolbar, AC B-4
New Form dialog box, AC C-2-3
New Object button, AC D-2, AC D-12
  creating simple forms with, AC C-3
New Record button, AC A-10, AC C-16
New Report dialog box, AC D-2, AC D-13, AC D-16,
  AC H-2
New Table dialog box, AC E-6
Number data type, AC B-6, AC B-7

O

object buttons, for Access database objects, AC A-8-9
Office Assistant, AC D-10
  changing appearance of, AC A-14
  Standard toolbar button, AC A-14
  using in Access, AC A-14-15
OLE object data type, AC B-7
one-to-many join lines, AC F-2
one-to-many relationships, AC E-2, AC E-3
  creating, AC E-8-9
  planning, AC E-4-5
Open Database dialog box, AC A-8
operators
  arithmetic, AC B-16, AC F-10-11
  comparison, AC F-7
OR, AC F-8
OR criteria, AC G-13
  in complex queries, AC B-16, AC B-17
OR operator, AC F-8
OR queries, AC F-8-9
output, of databases, AC B-2

P

Page Footer, AC D-6
Page Footer section, AC D-2
  forms, AC G-6
  reports, AC H-14
Page Header, AC D-6
Page Header section, AC D-2
  control headings, AC D-6-7
  forms, AC G-6
  reports, AC H-14
  Units control, AC D-8
Page Setup dialog box, AC A-13
PivotTable form layout, AC G-3
planning
  databases, AC B-2-3
  tables, AC E-4-5
pound sign (#) wildcard, in Find command, AC B-9
previewing, datasheets, AC A-12-13
primary key
  defined, AC A-2
  setting, AC B-4
Print dialog box, options, AC A-12, AC A-13
printing, datasheets, AC A-12-13
Print Preview
  color in reports, AC H-14
  controls, AC H-10
  forms, AC G-12
  graphics in reports, AC H-12
  group headers, AC H-6, AC H-7
  reports, AC H-2, AC H-3
  special effects, AC H-16
  Zoom, AC D-4
properties
  defined, AC G-14
  for forms, changing default values, AC G-14
  inherited, AC G-14
Properties Sheet
  Expression Builder, AC C-8-9
  formatting controls with, AC C-10-11

Q

queries
  AND, AC F-6-7
  Append, AC F-16
  complex, AC B-16-17
  creating reports from, AC D-12-13, AC H-2-3
  crosstab, AC F-1, AC F-14-15
  defined, AC A-2, AC F-1
  Delete, AC F-16
  expressions in, AC B-16-17
  filters vs., AC F-3
  multiple, AC F-1-17
  OR, AC F-8-9
  saving, AC B-14, AC B-15, AC B-16, AC B-17
  select, AC B-14-15, AC F-1, AC F-2-13
  simple, AC B-14-15
  sorting, AC F-2-3
  types of, AC F-1
  update, AC F-1, AC F-16-17
  uses of, AC F-1
  wildcard characters, AC F-9
Queries tab, AC F-2
Query Datasheet toolbar, AC F-4
Query design grid, AC F-2, AC F-3, AC F-4-5
  aggregate functions, AC F-12-13
  AND queries, AC F-6-7
  OR queries, AC F-8-9
Query Design toolbar, AC B-14-15
  update queries, AC F-16
Query Design View
  creating select queries in, AC F-2-3
  Crosstab queries, AC F-14-15
Query Wizards
  Crosstab, AC F-14-15
  Find Duplicates, AC F-14
  Find Unmatched, AC F-14
question mark (?) wildcard, in Find command, AC B-9

R

raised special effect, AC H-16, AC H-17
record navigation buttons, AC G-8
records
  adding calculations on groups of, AC F-12-13
  adding with forms, AC C-16-17
  adding to tables, AC B-8

Index

editing, AC A-10-11
entering, AC A-10-11
filtering within forms, AC G-12-13
finding, AC B-8-9
finding within forms, AC G-10-11
grouping, AC D-4-5, AC H-2
key fields for, AC E-2
sorting within forms, AC G-8-9
referential integrity, AC E-8, AC E-9
relational databases, AC E-1-17, See also databases; tables
defined, AC A-2, AC E-2, AC E-3
relationships, one-to-many, AC E-2, AC E-3, AC E-4-5, AC E-8-9
Relationships dialog box, AC E-8
Remove Filter button, AC B-12
Remove Single Field button, AC C-2
Replace feature, forms, AC G-10
report definitions, reusing, AC H-1
Report Design View
modifying controls in, AC H-10-11
sections, AC H-4-5
Report Detail section, AC D-2
Report Footer section, AC D-2, AC D-6, AC H-14
reports, AC H-14
Report Header section, AC D-2, AC D-6, AC H-14
reports, AC D-1-17, AC H-1-17
adding expressions to, AC D-10-11
adding fields to, AC D-10
aligning fields, AC D-6-7
calculations in group footers, AC H-8-9
color in, AC H-14-15
control alignment, modifying, AC H-10-11
creating, AC D-1-2
creating from queries, AC D-12-13, AC H-2-3
creating labels, AC D-16-17
database, AC A-2
defined, AC H-1
forms vs., AC H-2
graphics in, AC H-12-13
group headers, AC H-6-7, AC H-14
grouping records in, AC D-4-5
resizing controls, AC D-8-9
resizing sections, AC H-4, AC H-5
saving forms as, AC D-14-15
scrolling, AC H-2
sections, AC H-4-5, AC H-14
special effects in, AC H-16-17
tabular, AC H-12-13
value of, AC D-1
Report Wizard, AC D-2, AC H-2-3, AC H-5
dialog box, AC D-2, AC D-12, AC D-13
lines added by, AC H-12
resizing
controls, AC G-4-5
report sections, AC H-4, AC H-5
row selectors, indicators in, AC B-6
Row Source property, AC G-16
Run button, Query Design toolbar, AC F-16

S

Save As dialog box, for queries, AC B-14, AC B-15
Save As/Export dialog box, for queries, AC B-16, AC B-17
Save As Report command, AC D-14-15
saving
forms as reports, AC D-14-15
queries, AC B-14, AC B-15, AC B-16, AC B-17
searching, records in forms, AC G-10-11
section divider bar, moving report sections with, AC H-6
sections
in forms, AC G-6
in reports, AC H-4-5
select queries, AC B-14-15
creating, AC F-2-3
defined, AC F-1
Select Query window, AC B-14-15
shadowed special effect, AC H-16, AC H-17
Show Table dialog box, AC E-8, AC F-2
simple queries, AC B-14-15
Single Field button, AC B-4
sizing, controls, AC D-8-9
sorting
Advanced Filter/Sort option, AC G-8
defined, AC B-11, AC F-4
filtering vs., AC B-12
queries, AC F-2-3
queries on multiple fields, AC F-4-5
records within forms, AC G-8-9
tables, AC B-10-11
using menu bar, AC B-12
Sorting and Grouping dialog box, AC H-8-9
sort order
ascending, AC B-11-12
descending, AC B-11-12
selecting, AC D-4, AC D-5
Sort Order button, AC D-4
special effects, AC H-16-17
Start button, starting Access 97 with, AC A-4
StDev function, AC F-13
subforms, defined, AC G-2
Sum function, AC F-13
Summary Options dialog box, AC D-5
sunken special effect, AC H-16, AC H-17

T

Table Design toolbar, AC E-6
tables, See also databases; relational databases
adding new records to, AC B-8
complex queries of, AC B-16-17
creating, AC B-4-5, AC E-6-7
creating manually, AC B-5
creating with Table Wizard, AC B-4-5
criteria for filtering, AC B-12
data types in, AC B-6, AC B-7
defined, AC A-2, AC A-8
entering and editing records in, AC A-10-11
filtering, AC B-12-13
finding records in, AC B-8-9
imported, AC E-7
keyboard shortcuts, AC A-10, AC A-11
linked, AC E-2, AC E-3, AC E-4-5, AC E-7, AC E-8-9
modifying, AC B-6-7
moving columns in, AC A-10
multiple, creating forms from, AC G-2-3
multiple queries, AC F-1-17
one-to-many relationships between, AC E-8-9
opening, AC A-8-9, AC B-8
planning, AC E-4-5
in relational databases, AC E-2-3
simple queries of, AC B-14-15
sorting, AC B-10-11
Table Wizard, AC B-4
tab order, on forms
changing, AC C-6-7
defined, AC C-6
Tab Order dialog box, AC C-6, AC C-7
Tabular form layout, AC G-2
tabular reports, AC H-12-13
Text box button, AC D-10
Text data type, AC B-6, AC B-7
toolbox buttons, locking, AC C-14
Toolbox toolbar, AC C-4
ToolTips, in Access 97, AC A-6

U

unbound controls, AC C-4
adding expressions to, AC D-10
defined, AC G-4
Units control
Detail section, AC D-8
Page Header section, AC D-8
update queries, AC F-16-17
defined, AC F-1

V

Validation Rule field property, AC E-16-17
expressions, AC E-17
Validation Text field property, AC E-16-17
Var function, AC F-13

W

wildcards
in complex criteria expressions, AC G-13
in Find command, AC B-9
in query criteria, AC F-9
Windows Bitmap (.bmp, .rle, .dib) files, AC H-13
Windows Metafile (.wmf) files, AC H-13

Y

Yes/No data type, AC B-7

Z

Zoom, Print Preview, AC D-4